Study Guide
for the
Discovering Psychology Telecourse

Richard O. Straub
University of Michigan-Dearborn

Study Guide
for the Discovering Psychology Telecourse

for use with

DAVID G. MYERS *PSYCHOLOGY*

Fifth Edition

WORTH PUBLISHERS

Study Guide for the Discovering Psychology Telecourse
by Richard O. Straub

Copyright © 1998 by Worth Publishers

All rights reserved.

Printed in the United States of America.

This *Study Guide* is part of a full college course, which also includes 26 half-hour television programs; **Psychology**, Fifth Edition, by David G. Myers (Worth Publishers); and a *Faculty Guide*. For information about licensing the course, or purchasing videocassettes and audiocassettes call 1-800-LEARNER or write Annenberg/CPB Collection, P.O. Box 2345, South Burlington, VT 05407. Visit the Annenberg/CPB Project's Web site at http://www.learner.org. Print components are available from Worth Publishers (1-800-446-8923).

Funding for *Discovering Psychology* is provided by the Annenberg/CPB Project.

ISBN: 1-57259-546-9

Printing: 2 3 4 5   Year: 01 00 99

Worth Publishers
33 Irving Place
New York, New York 10003

CONTENTS

Preface		vii
Discovering Psychology Study Guide		ix
	Features of This Study Guide	ix
	How to Manage Your Time Efficiently and Study More Effectively	x
PROGRAM 1	**Past, Present, and Promise**	1
	Textbook Assignment: **Introduction, 1–9**	
PROGRAM 2	**Understanding Research**	15
	Textbook Assignment: **Chapter 1: Introduction: Thinking Critically With Psychology, pp. 10–39**	
PROGRAMS 3 and 4	**The Behaving Brain** / **The Responsive Brain**	36
	Textbook Assignment: **Chapter 2: Neuroscience, Genetics, and Behavior, pp. 41–64; Chapter 3: The Developing Person, pp. 83–84**	
PROGRAM 5	**The Developing Child**	72
	Textbook Assignment: **Chapter 3: The Developing Person, pp. 77–83 and 85–113**	
PROGRAM 6	**Language Development**	98
	Textbook Assignment: **Chapter 10: Thinking and Language, pp. 319–331**	
PROGRAM 7	**Sensation and Perception**	113
	Textbook Assignment: **Chapters 5 and 6: Sensation and Perception, pp. 147–163 and 183–200**	
PROGRAM 8	**Learning**	138
	Textbook Assignment: **Chapter 8: Learning, pp. 243–267**	
PROGRAM 9	**Remembering and Forgetting**	162
	Textbook Assignment: **Chapter 9: Memory, pp. 269–303**	
PROGRAMS 10 and 11	**Cognitive Processes** / **Judgment and Decision Making**	186
	Textbook Assignment: **Chapter 10: Thinking and Language, pp. 305–319**	
PROGRAM 12	**Motivation and Emotion**	210
	Textbook Assignment: **Chapter 12: Motivation, pp. 363–366, 368–384; Chapter 10: Emotion, pp. 393–417**	

PROGRAM 13	**The Mind Awake and Asleep**	238
	Textbook Assignment: **Chapter 7: States of Consciousness,** pp. 207–221	
PROGRAM 14	**The Mind Hidden and Divided**	256
	Textbook Assignment: **Chapter 7: States of Consciousness,** pp. 221–241	
PROGRAM 15	**The Self**	276
	Textbook Assignment: **Chapter 14: Personality,** pp. 419–430 and 436–451	
PROGRAM 16	**Testing and Intelligence**	300
	Textbook Assignment: **Chapter 11: Intelligence,** pp. 333–361	
PROGRAM 17	**Sex and Gender**	321
	Textbook Assignment: **None**	
PROGRAM 18	**Maturing and Aging**	330
	Textbook Assignment: **Chapter 4: Adolescence and Adulthood,** pp. 127–145	
PROGRAMS 19 and 20	**The Power of the Situation** **Constructing Social Reality**	347
	Textbook Assignment: **Chapter 18: Social Psychology,** pp. 549–564, 571–578, 580–587	
PROGRAM 21	**Psychopathology**	372
	Textbook Assignment: **Chapter 15: Psychological Disorders,** pp. 453–485	
PROGRAM 22	**Psychotherapy**	393
	Textbook Assignment: **Chapter 16: Therapy,** pp. 487–513	
PROGRAM 23	**Health, Mind, and Behavior**	415
	Textbook Assignment: **Chapter 17: Stress and Health,** pp. 515–547	
PROGRAM 24	**In Space, Toward Peace**	435
	Textbook Assignment: **Chapter 18: Social Psychology,** pp. 564–571, 578–580, 587–589	
PROGRAMS 25 and 26	**A Union of Opposites** **New Directions**	449
	Textbook Assignment: **None**	

PREFACE

Discovering Psychology is an introductory telecourse in psychology—the scientific study of why people think, feel, and act as they do. The series explores the work of leading researchers and relatively recent developments in our understanding of human nature, from the ways in which the brain directs behavior to the role of psychology in space travel and the prevention of international conflicts. The telecourse consists of twenty-six half-hour public television programs, the Study Guide, and *Psychology*, 5/e, by David G. Myers.

The series host is Philip G. Zimbardo, professor of psychology at Stanford University. Professor Zimbardo, who has been teaching introductory psychology for more than 30 years, is the recipient of distinguished teaching awards from Stanford University, New York University, and the American Psychological Association. A prolific scientist, he has published more than a dozen books and more than 100 journal articles covering a wide range of topics, including shyness, aggression, and the effects of social situations on individual behavior.

This Study Guide is designed to help you evaluate and enhance your understanding of the telecourse material. It also provides information on how to use the Study Guide for maximum benefit ("How to Manage Your Time Efficiently and Study More Effectively," p. x). This section offers additional study suggestions for time management, effective note-taking, evaluation of exam performance, and ways to improve your reading comprehension.

I am grateful to everyone who has contributed to this project. Special thanks go to Betty Probert of The Special Projects Group. Betty's vast knowledge of psychology and superb writing skills are evident on every page of this Study Guide.

I hope your journey through the telecourse experience will be an enjoyable one and will provide you with information that enhances your insight into your own nature and that of others.

Richard O. Straub, Ph.D.
Professor of Psychology
University of Michigan–Dearborn

The Discovering Psychology Study Guide

This study guide has many features that will help you study more effectively. Part I of this introduction describes these features. Part II provides suggestions that can help you to use your study time more effectively.

Part I FEATURES OF THIS STUDY GUIDE

THE PROGRAMS

Each Study Guide chapter consists of four major sections designed to help direct your study activities. After a while, you will discover which sections are the most helpful for you, and you can concentrate on them.

Orientation This section provides an overview of the program, highlighting important themes, placing facts in context, and integrating the program with the textbook. It also introduces issues presented in each video program and helps you relate its content to important ideas covered in other programs.

Goals These goals—typically four or five for each chapter—identify the major themes of each chapter. They are drawn from both the textbook and the video program.

Guided Study

Textbook Assignment This section contains several specific objectives drawn from important facts and concepts presented in the textbook assignment. Once you have finished reading the assignment, try to answer the objectives in your own words. Completing the objectives will help you to identify those points you may need to review.

Program Assignment This section contains several specific objectives drawn from the important facts and concepts covered in the video program. Once you have finished watching the program, try to answer the objectives in your own words. Completing this section will help you to identify concepts you may need to review by replaying portions of the program.

Progress Test This section consists of multiple-choice questions drawn from both the video program and textbook assignments. Questions related to the video program and the textbook are randomly ordered to enhance learning and reduce rote memorization. They should be answered only after you have watched the program, read the textbook assignment, and completed the Guided Study. Correct answers, along with explanations and textbook page references (as appropriate), are provided at the end of the chapter. If you miss a question, read the explanation and, if you need to, review the appropriate text pages or portion of the video program.

Answers

Guided Study Organized into separate sections for the video program and the textbook, this section will help you to evaluate your answers to questions in the Guided Study section of the Study Guide. Taken together, the items provide a summary of the main points covered in the chapter.

Progress Test This section can be used to evaluate your performance on the questions in the "Progress Test" section of the Study Guide. For each question, the correct answer is given, along with the question's source—whether material in the video program, the text, or both. For questions based on the text, page references are given where the answer can be found.

KEEPING TRACK

The following grid will help you keep track of your progress through the *Discovering Psychology* telecourse. Your actual assignments, of course, will depend on your instructor. For example, your instructor may not give a quiz on each program but may instead test you on several programs at one time.

Program(s)	Quiz Score
1	_____
2	_____
3/4	_____
5	_____
6	_____
7	_____
8	_____
9	_____
10/11	_____
12	_____
13	_____
14	_____
15	_____
16	_____
17	_____
18	_____
19/20	_____
21	_____
22	_____
23	_____
24	_____
25/26	_____
Total	_____
Average	_____
Quiz average	_____
Mid-term exam	_____
Final exam	_____
Overall Average	_____
Final Grade	_____

Part II HOW TO MANAGE YOUR TIME EFFICIENTLY AND STUDY MORE EFFECTIVELY

Students who are new to college life or who are returning after a long absence may be unsure of their study skills. Suggestions for making the best use of your time and improving your skills may be found in the following section of the Study Guide. These suggestions will help you not only with *Discovering Psychology* but also with many of your other college courses.

How effectively do you study? Good study habits make the job of being a college student much easier. Many students, who could succeed in college, fail or drop out because they have never learned to manage their time efficiently. Even the best students can usually benefit from an in-depth evaluation of their current study habits.

There are many ways to achieve academic success, of course, but your approach may not be the most effective or efficient. Are you sacrificing your social life or your physical or mental health in order to get A's on your exams? Good study habits result in better grades *and* more time for other activities.

EVALUATE YOUR CURRENT STUDY HABITS

To improve your study habits, you must first have an accurate picture of how you currently spend your time. Begin by putting together a profile of your present living and studying habits. Answer the following questions by writing "yes" or "no" on each line.

_____ 1. Do you usually set up a schedule to budget your time for studying, recreation, and other activities?

_____ 2. Do you often put off studying until time pressures force you to cram?

_____ 3. Do other students seem to study less than you do, but get better grades?

_____ 4. Do you usually spend hours at a time studying one subject, rather than dividing that time between several subjects?

_____ 5. Do you often have trouble remembering what you have just read in a textbook?

_____ 6. Before reading a chapter in a textbook, do you skim it and read the section headings?

_____ 7. Do you try to predict exam questions from your lecture notes and reading?

_____ 8. Do you usually attempt to paraphrase or summarize what you have just finished reading?

_____ 9. Do you find it difficult to concentrate very long when you study?

_____ 10. Do you often feel that you studied the wrong material for an exam?

Thousands of college students have participated in similar surveys. Students who are fully realizing their academic potential usually respond as follows: (1) yes, (2) no, (3) no, (4) no, (5) no, (6) yes, (7) yes, (8) yes, (9) no, (10) no.

Compare your responses with those of successful students. The greater the discrepancy, the more you could benefit from a program to improve your study habits. The questions are designed to identify areas of weakness. Once you have identified your weaknesses, you will be able to set specific goals for improvement and implement a program for reaching them.

MANAGE YOUR TIME

Do you often feel frustrated because there isn't enough time to do all the things you must and want to do? Take heart. Even the most productive and successful people feel this way at times. But they establish priorities for their activities and they learn to budget time for each of them. There's much in the saying, "If you want something done, ask a busy person to do it." A busy person knows how to get things done.

If you don't now have a system for budgeting your time, develop one. Not only will your academic accomplishments increase, but you will actually find more time in your schedule for other activities. And you won't have to feel guilty about "taking time off," because all your obligations will be covered.

Establish a Baseline

As a first step in preparing to budget your time, keep a diary for a few days to establish a summary, or baseline, of the time you spend in studying, socializing, working, and so on. If you are like many students, much of your "study" time is nonproductive; you may sit at your desk and leaf through a book, but the time is actually wasted. Or you may procrastinate. You are always getting ready to study, but you rarely do.

Besides revealing where you waste time, your diary will give you a realistic picture of how much time you need to allot for meals, commuting, and other fixed activities. In addition, careful records should indicate the times of the day when you are consistently most productive. A sample time-management diary is shown in Table 1.

Plan the Term

Having established and evaluated your baseline, you are ready to devise a more efficient schedule. Buy a calendar that covers the entire school term and has ample space for each day. Using the course outlines provided by your instructors, enter the dates of all exams, term paper deadlines, and other important academic obligations. If you have any long-range personal plans (concerts, weekend trips, etc.), enter the dates on the calendar as well. Keep your calendar up to date and refer to it often. I recommend carrying it with you at all times.

Develop a Weekly Calendar

Now that you have a general picture of the school term, develop a weekly schedule that includes all of your activities. Aim for a schedule that you can live with for the entire school term. A sample weekly schedule, incorporating the following guidelines, is shown in Table 2.

1. Enter your class times, work hours, and any other fixed obligations first. *Be thorough.* Using information from your time-management diary, allow plenty of time for such things as commuting, meals, laundry, and the like.

2. Set up a study schedule for each of your courses. The study habits survey

Table 1 Sample Time-Management Diary

	Monday	
Behavior	Time Completed	Duration Hours: Minutes
Sleep	7:00	7:30
Dressing	7:25	:25
Breakfast	7:45	:20
Commute	8:20	:35
Coffee	9:00	:40
French	10:00	1:00
Socialize	10:15	:15
Video game	10:35	:20
Coffee	11:00	:25
Psychology	12:00	1:00
Lunch	12:25	:25
Study Lab	1:00	:35
Psych. Lab	4:00	3:00
Work	5:30	1:30
Commute	6:10	:40
Dinner	6:45	:35
TV	7:30	:45
Study Psych.	10:00	2:30
Socialize	11:30	1:30
Sleep		

Prepare a similar chart for each day of the week. When you finish an activity, note it on the chart and write down the time it was completed. Then determine its duration by subtracting the time the previous activity was finished from the newly entered time.

and your time-management diary will direct you. The following guidelines should also be useful.

   a. Establish regular study times for each course. The 4 hours needed to study one subject, for example, are most profitable when divided into shorter periods spaced over several days. If you cram your studying into one 4-hour block, what you attempt to learn in the third or fourth hour will interfere with what you studied in the first 2 hours. Newly acquired knowledge is like wet cement. It needs some time to "harden" to become fixed in your memory.

   b. Alternate subjects. The type of interference just mentioned is greatest between similar topics. Set up a schedule in which you spend time on several *different* courses during each study session. Besides reducing the potential for interference, alternating subjects will help to prevent mental fatigue with one topic.

   c. Set weekly goals to determine the amount of study time you need to do well in each course. This will depend on, among other things, the difficulty of your courses and the effectiveness of your methods. Many professors recommend studying at least 1 to 2 hours for each hour in class. If your time-management diary indicates that you presently spend less time studying than that, do not plan to jump immediately to a much higher level. Increase study time from your baseline by setting weekly goals [see (4)] that will gradually bring you up to the desired level. As an initial schedule, for example, you might set aside an amount of study time for each course that matches class time.

   d. Schedule for maximum effectiveness. Tailor your schedule to meet the demands of each course. For the course that emphasizes lecture notes, schedule time for a daily review soon after the class. This will give you a chance to revise your notes and clean up any hard-to-decipher shorthand while the material is still fresh in your mind. If you are evaluated for class participation (for example, in a language course), allow time for a review just *before* the class meets. Schedule study time for your most difficult (or least motivating) courses during hours when you are the most alert and distractions are fewest.

   e. Schedule open study time. Emergencies, additional obligations, and the like could throw off your schedule. And you may simply need extra time periodically for a project or for review in one of your courses. Schedule several hours a week for such purposes.

3. After you have budgeted time for studying, fill in slots for recreation,

Table 2 Sample Weekly Schedule

Time	Mon.	Tues.	Wed.	Thurs.	Fri.	Sat.
7–8	Dress Eat	Dress Eat	Dress Eat	Dress Eat	Dress Eat	
8–9	Psych.	Study Psych.	Psych.	Study Psych.	Psych.	Dress Eat
9–10	Eng.	Study Eng.	Eng.	Study Eng.	Eng.	Study Eng.
10–11	Study French	Free	Study French	Open Study	Study French	Study Stats.
11–12	French	Study Psych. Lab	French	Open Study	French	Study Stats.
12–1	Lunch	Lunch	Lunch	Lunch	Lunch	Lunch
1–2	Stats.	Psych. Lab	Stats.	Study or Free	Stats.	Free
2–3	Bio.	Psych. Lab	Bio.	Free	Bio.	Free
3–4	Free	Psych.	Free	Free	Free	Free
4–5	Job	Job	Job	Job	Job	Free
5–6	Job	Job	Job	Job	Job	Free
6–7	Dinner	Dinner	Dinner	Dinner	Dinner	Dinner
7–8	Study Bio.	Study Bio.	Study Bio.	Study Bio.	Free	Free
8–9	Study Eng.	Study Stats.	Study Psych.	Open Study	Open Study	Free
9–10	Open Study	Open Study	Open Study	Open Study	Free	Free

This is a sample schedule for a student with a 16-credit load and a 10-hour-per-week part-time job. Using this chart as an illustration, make up a weekly schedule, following the guidelines outlined here.

hobbies, relaxation, household errands, and the like.

4. Set specific goals. Before each study session, make a list of specific goals. The simple note "7–8 PM.: study psychology" is too broad to ensure the most effective use of the time. Formulate your daily goals according to what you know you must accomplish during the term. If you have course outlines with advance assignments, set systematic daily goals that will allow you, for example, to cover fifteen chapters before the exam. And be realistic: Can you actually expect to cover a 78-page chapter in one session? Divide large tasks into smaller units; stop at the most logical resting points. When you complete a specific goal, take a 5- or 10-minute break before tackling the next goal.

5. Evaluate how successful or unsuccessful your studying has been on a daily or weekly basis. Did you reach most of your goals? If so, reward yourself immediately. You might even make a list of five to ten rewards to choose from. If you have trouble studying regularly, you may be able to motivate yourself by making such rewards contingent on completing specific goals.

6. Finally, until you have lived with your schedule for several weeks, don't hesitate to revise it. You may need to allow more time for chemistry, for example, and less for some other course. If you are trying to study regularly for the first time and are feeling burned-out, you probably have set your initial goals too high. Don't let failure cause you to despair and abandon the program. Accept your limitations and revise your schedule so that you are studying only 15 to 20 minutes more each evening than you are used to. The

point is to *identify a regular schedule with which you can achieve some success*. Time management, like any skill, must be practiced to become effective.

TECHNIQUES FOR EFFECTIVE STUDY

Knowing how to put study time to best use is, of course, as important as finding a place for it in your schedule. Here are some suggestions that should enable you to increase your reading comprehension and improve your note-taking. A few study tips are included as well.

Using PRTR to Increase Reading Comprehension

How do you study from a textbook? If you are like many students, you simply read and reread in a passive manner. Studies have shown, however, that most students who simply read a textbook cannot remember more than half the material ten minutes after they have finished. Often, what is retained is the unessential material rather than the important points upon which exam questions will be based.

This Study Guide employs a program known as PRTR (Preview, Read, Think actively and critically, Review) to facilitate, and allow you to assess, your comprehension of the important facts and concepts in the *Discovering Psychology* telecourse. It will help you to integrate material from the video and television programs with that in David Myers's text, *Psychology, 5/e*.

Research has shown that students using PRTR achieve significantly greater comprehension of textbooks than students reading in the more traditional passive manner. Once you have learned this program, you can improve your comprehension of any textbook.

Another suggestion is to read the textbook assignment prior to watching the video, if that is possible. Research indicates that this sequence enhances learning.

Preview Before reading a textbook assignment, for each section, read the preview (in bold face) and "Summing Up." Next, read the assigned textbook sections fairly quickly, paying special attention to the major headings and subheadings. This preview will give you an idea of the assignment's content and organization. You will then be able to divide the material into logical sections in order to formulate specific goals for a more careful reading.

Although you will want to review the "Orientation" and "Goals" in the Study Guide prior to watching the video, you may find them useful reading now. The "Orientation" summarizes the major topics of both the textbook assignment and the video program; the "Goals" identify the major themes.

You will retain material longer when you have a use for it. If you look up a word's definition in order to solve a crossword puzzle, for example, you will remember it longer than if you merely fill in the letters as a result of putting other words in. Previewing the textbook assignment will allow you to generate important questions that the text will proceed to answer. These questions correspond to "mental files" into which knowledge will be sorted for easy access.

As you preview, jot down several questions for each textbook section. One simple technique is to generate questions by rephrasing a section heading. For example, the "Preoperational Thought" head could be turned into "What is preoperational thought?" Good questions will allow you to focus on the important points in the text. Examples of good questions are those that begin as follows: "List two examples of" "What is the function of?" "What is the significance of?" Such questions give a purpose to your reading. The video program and textbook assignment objectives in the "Guided Study" in this Study Guide can be used for this purpose. Or you can formulate your own questions based on the chapter outline.

Read When you have established "files" for each section of the text assignment, review your first question or objective, begin reading, and continue until you have discovered its answer. If you come to material that seems to answer an important question you don't have a file for, stop and write down the question.

Be sure to read everything. Don't skip photo or art captions, graphs, or marginal notes. In some cases, what may seem vague in reading will be made clear by a simple graph. Keep in mind that test questions are sometimes drawn from illustrations and charts.

Think critically and actively When you have found the answer to a question, close your eyes and mentally recite the question and its answer. Then *write* the answer next to the question. It is important that you recite an answer in your own words rather than the author's. Don't rely on your short-term memory to repeat the author's words verbatim.

In responding to the questions, pay close attention to what is called for. If you are asked to identify or list, do just that. If asked to compare, contrast, or do both, you should focus on the similarities (compare) and differences (contrast) between the concepts or theories. Answering the questions carefully will not only help you to focus your attention on the important concepts of the video program and the text, but it will also provide excellent practice for essay exams.

Recitation is an extremely effective study technique, recommended by many learning experts. In addition to increasing reading comprehension, it is useful for review. Trying to explain something in your own words clarifies your knowledge, often by revealing aspects of your answer that are vague or incomplete. If you repeatedly rely upon "I know" in recitation, you really *may not know*.

Recitation has the additional advantage of simulating an exam, especially an essay exam; the same skills are required in both cases. Too often students study without ever putting the book and notes aside, which makes it easy for them to develop false confidence in their knowledge. When the material is in front of you, you may be able to *recognize* an answer, but will you be able to *recall* it later, when you take an exam that does not provide these retrieval cues?

After you have recited and written your answer, continue with your next question. Read, recite, and so on.

Review When you have answered the last question on the material you have designated as a study goal, go back and review. Read over each question and your written answer to it. Your review might also include a brief written summary that integrates all of your questions and answers. This review need not take longer than a few minutes, but it is important. It will help you retain the material longer and will greatly facilitate a final review of each chapter before the exam.

An excellent way to review your understanding of the chapters of *Psychology, 5/e*, is to reread the preview at the beginning of each relevant section. Then go through the "Guided Study" section of this Study Guide. You may be surprised to discover that you didn't know the material as well as you thought you did!

Also provided to facilitate your review are multiple-choice questions in the "Progress Test" section of the Study Guide. These questions cover both video program and textbook content and should *not* be answered until you have listened to the program, read the textbook assignment, and completed the "Guided Study" in the Study Guide. Correct answers, along with explanations of why each alternative is incorrect, are provided at the end of the chapter. The relevant text page numbers for each question are also given. If you miss a question, read these explanations and, if you need to, review the text pages to further understand why. The questions do not test every aspect of a concept, so you should treat an incorrect answer as an indication that you need to review the concept.

One final suggestion: Incorporate PRTR into your time-management calendar. Set specific goals for completing PRTR with each assigned chapter. Keep a record of chapters completed, and reward yourself for being conscientious. Initially, it takes more time and effort to "read" using PRTR, but with practice, the steps will become automatic. More important, you will comprehend significantly more material and retain what you have learned longer than passive readers do.

Watching the Video Programs

Using television programs for learning requires much more active attention to their content than when these media are used simply for entertainment.

In following the steps outlined in each Study Guide program, you will gain the most from each program by applying the PRTR method to your program viewing. You will find it helpful to read the program "Orientation," "Goals," and "Guided Study" objectives before watching the program. You may choose to watch the entire program first and then answer the objectives; if you have the opportunity, you may want to watch the video a second time. If you are able to watch the videotapes on your own, you may find it works better for you to answer the questions as you go along, stopping the tape as necessary. Soon after watching the program, you should compare your answers with material in the "Guided Study" in the Study Guide. Make sure that you have a good grasp of the answer to each video objective before you continue with the program.

Evaluating Your Exam Performance

How often have you received a grade on an exam that did not do justice to the effort you spent preparing for the exam? This is a common experience that can leave one feeling bewildered and abused. "What do I have to do to get an A?" "The test was unfair!" "I studied the wrong material!"

The chances of this happening are greatly reduced if you have an effective time-management schedule and use the study techniques described here. But it can happen, even to the best-prepared student. It is most likely to occur on your first exam in a new course.

Remember that there are two main reasons for studying. One is to learn for your own general academic development. Many people believe that such knowledge is all that really matters. Of course it is possible, though unlikely, to be an expert on a topic without achieving commensurate grades, just as one can, occasionally, earn an excellent grade without truly mastering the course material. During a job interview or in the workplace, however, your A in Java won't mean much if you can't actually program a computer.

In order to keep career options open after you graduate, you must both know the material *and* maintain competitive grades. In the short run, this means performing well on exams, which is the second main objective in studying.

Probably the single best piece of advice to keep in mind when studying for exams is to *try to predict exam questions*. This means ignoring the trivia and focusing on the important questions and their answers (with your instructor's emphasis in mind).

A second point is obvious. How well you do on exams is determined by your mastery of *both* lecture (or, in this case, videotape) and textbook material. Many students (partly because of poor time management) concentrate too much on one at the expense of the other.

To evaluate how well you are learning the videotape and textbook material, analyze the questions you missed on the first exam. Divide the questions into two categories, those drawn primarily from the video tapes and those drawn primarily from the textbook. Determine the percentage of questions you missed in each category. If your errors are evenly distributed and you are satisfied with your grade, you have no problem. If you are weaker in one area, you will need to set goals for increasing and/or improving your study of that area.

Similarly, note the percentage of test questions drawn from each category. While your instructor may not be entirely consistent in making up future exams, you may be able to tailor your studying by placing *additional* emphasis on the appropriate area.

Exam evaluation will also point out the types of questions your instructor prefers.

Does the exam consist primarily of multiple-choice or essay questions? You may also discover that an instructor is fond of wording questions in certain ways. For example, an instructor may rely heavily on questions that require you to draw an analogy between a theory or concept and a real-world example. Evaluate both your instructor's style and how well you do with each format. Use this information to guide your future exam preparation.

Important aids, not only in studying for exams but also in determining how well prepared you are, are the "Progress Test" sections of the Study Guide. If these tests don't include all of the types of questions your instructor typically writes, make up your own practice exam questions. Spend extra time testing yourself with question formats that are most difficult for you. There is no better way to evaluate your preparation for an upcoming exam than by testing yourself under the conditions most likely to be in effect during the actual test.

A FEW PRACTICAL TIPS

Even the best intentions for studying sometimes fail. Some of these failures occur because students attempt to work under conditions that are simply not conducive to concentrated study. To help ensure the success of your time-management program, here are a few suggestions that should assist you in reducing the possibility of procrastination or distraction.

1. If you have set up a schedule for studying, make your roommate, family, and friends aware of this commitment, and ask them to honor your quiet study time. Close your door and post a "Do Not Disturb" sign.

2. Set up a place to study that minimizes potential distractions. Use a desk or table, not your bed or an extremely comfortable chair. Keep your desk and the walls around it free from clutter. If you need a place other than your room, find one that meets as many of the above requirements as possible—for example, in the library stacks.

3. Do nothing but study in this place. It should become associated with studying so that it "triggers" this activity, just as a mouth-watering aroma elicits an appetite.

4. Never study with the television on or with other distracting noises present. If you must have music in the background in order to mask outside noise, for example, play soft instrumental music. Don't pick vocal selections; your mind will be drawn to the lyrics.

5. Study by yourself. Other students can be distracting or can break the pace at which *your* learning is most efficient. In addition, there is always the possibility that group studying will become a social gathering. Reserve that for its own place in your schedule.

If you continue to have difficulty concentrating for very long, try the following suggestions.

6. Study your most difficult or most challenging subjects first, when you are most alert.

7. Start with relatively short periods of concentrated study, with breaks in between. If your attention starts to wander, get up immediately and take a break. It is better to study effectively for 15 minutes and then take a break than to fritter away 45 minutes out of an hour. Gradually increase the length of study periods, using your attention span as an indicator of successful pacing.

SOME CLOSING THOUGHTS

I hope that these suggestions help make you more successful academically and that they enhance the quality of your college life in general. Having the necessary skills makes any job a lot easier and more pleasant. Let me repeat my warning not to attempt to make too drastic a change in your lifestyle immediately. Good habits require time and self-discipline to develop. Once established, they can last a lifetime.

PROGRAM 1

Past, Present, and Promise

TEXTBOOK ASSIGNMENT: Introduction, pp. 1–9

ORIENTATION

Program 1 of *Discovering Psychology* introduces psychology as the science of behavior and mental processes. The reading assignment and program explore the historical development of psychology and the range of behaviors and mental processes being investigated by psychologists in each of the major specialty areas. The program introduces Professor Philip Zimbardo, the host for the series, who differentiates three levels at which psychologists conduct their investigations. Several prominent psychologists describe their own research, illustrating these levels and the diversity of research interests among contemporary psychologists.

The reading assignment identifies the major issues that cut across psychology, including the stability of our traits, the rationality of our thoughts and actions, and the relative contribution of biology and experience to intelligence, personality, and behavior. It also describes the major subfields and theoretical perspectives within which psychologists conduct research and provide professional services. No matter which perspective guides their work, all psychologists share a scientific attitude and aim to approach the study of psychology objectively, with a healthy dose of open-minded skepticism.

NOTE: Answer guidelines for all Program 1 questions begin on page 9.

GOALS

After you have read the text and viewed the program, you should be prepared to:

1. Define *psychology* and trace its historical development.

2. Describe the different perspectives from which psychologists work and identify the major subfields and goals of psychology.

3. Identify three major issues that cut across psychology.

4. Explain the differences among the micro, molecular, and macro levels of analysis and describe how psychology as a behavioral science is similar to other sciences.

GUIDED STUDY

Textbook Assignment

The text chapter should be studied one section at a time. Before you read, preview each section by skimming it, noting headings and boldface items. Then

read the appropriate section objectives from the following outline. Keep these objectives in mind and, as you read the chapter section, search for the information that will enable you to meet each objective. Once you have finished a section, write out answers for its objectives.

Psychology's Roots (pp. 2–4)

1. Define psychology and briefly trace its historical development.

Psychology's Perspectives (pp. 4–5)

2. Describe the different perspectives from which psychologists examine behavior and mental processes.

Psychology's Big Issues (p. 6)

3. Identify and briefly explain three major issues that cut across psychology.

4. Describe the historical roots of the nature-nurture issue in psychology.

Psychology's Subfields (pp. 7–8)

5. Identify the major subfields of psychology.

Studying Psychology (pp. 8–9)

   6. Explain the PRTR method of study.

Program Assignment

Read the following objectives before you watch Program 1: "Past, Present, and Promise." As you watch, be alert for information that will help you answer each objective. Taking notes during the program will help you to formulate your answers later. After the program, write answers to the objectives. If you have access to the program on videotape, you may replay portions of the program if you need to refresh your memory.

   1. What are some of the questions that psychology in general, and this series in particular, seek to answer?

   2. What is the best known application of psychology? How is this application illustrated in the program?

   3. What do the "Candid Camera" film clips illustrate about the field of psychology? In your answer, be sure to explain the difference between dispositional and situational factors.

   4. Explain the differences among the micro, the molecular, and the macro levels of analysis and describe how each was illustrated in the program.

Discovering Psychology

5. Explain what psychology has in common with the other sciences and state the contributions of Wilhelm Wundt, G. Stanley Hall, and William James to psychology.

PROGRESS TEST

Circle your answers to the following questions and check them with the answers on page 11. If your answer is incorrect, read the explanation for why it is incorrect and then review the program video or consult the appropriate pages of the text (in parentheses following the correct answer).

1. In its earliest days, psychology was defined as the:
   a. science of mental life.
   b. study of conscious and unconscious activity.
   c. science of observable behavior.
   d. science of behavior and mental processes.

2. Who would be most likely to agree with the statement, "Psychology should investigate only behaviors that can be observed"?
   a. Wilhelm Wundt
   b. Sigmund Freud
   c. John Watson
   d. William James

3. Today, psychology is defined as the:
   a. study of mental phenomena.
   b. study of conscious and unconscious activity.
   c. study of behavior.
   d. scientific study of behavior and mental processes.

4. In the program, a woman is interviewed twice. During the first interview she seems to be a little child. During the second, she seems to be a tough adolescent. This woman has been diagnosed as suffering from:
   a. chronic stress syndrome.
   b. schizophrenia.
   c. multiple personality disorder.
   d. depression.

5. Which psychological perspective emphasizes the interaction of the brain and body in behavior?
   a. neuroscience
   b. cognitive
   c. behavioral
   d. behavior genetics

6. Which of the following is *not* a major issue in psychology?
   a. stability versus change
   b. rationality versus irrationality
   c. top-down versus bottom-up processing
   d. nature versus nurture

7. The seventeenth-century philosopher who believed that the mind is blank at birth and that most knowledge comes through sensory experience is:
   a. Plato.
   b. Aristotle.
   c. Descartes.
   d. Locke.

8. Professor Donchin's research involving the P-300 wave demonstrated:
   a. that brain wave tests can be used to screen people for mental illness.
   b. that environmental events trigger specific brain wave patterns.
   c. that men, but not women, display the P-300 wave.
   d. all the above.

9. Two historical roots of psychology are the disciplines of:
   a. philosophy and chemistry.
   b. physiology and chemistry.
   c. philosophy and physiology.
   d. philosophy and physics.

10. Which of the following individuals is also a physician?
    a. clinical psychologist
    b. personality psychologist
    c. psychiatrist
    d. biological psychologist

11. The Greek philosopher who believed that intelligence was inherited was:
    a. Aristotle.
    b. Plato.
    c. Descartes.
    d. Simonides.

12. The way the mind processes, stores, and retrieves information is the primary concern of the _____ perspective.
    a. neuroscience
    b. social-cultural
    c. behavioral
    d. cognitive

13. The first experimental psychology laboratory in the United States was established by:
    a. William James.
    b. Wilhelm Wundt.
    c. G. Stanley Hall.
    d. Robert Rosenthal.

14. The first psychology laboratory was established by _____ in the year _____ .
    a. Wundt; 1879
    b. James; 1890
    c. Freud; 1899
    d. Watson; 1913

15. The main goal of psychological research is to:
    a. understand, predict, and in some cases control behavior and mental processes.
    b. treat those individuals suffering from mental illness.
    c. explain the impact of social situations, culture, and other "molar" influences on behavior.
    d. understand the workings of the brain at the micro level of analysis.

16. Robert Rosenthal has found that the best way to tell whether people are lying is to:
    a. watch their body language.
    b. listen to their tone of voice.
    c. observe their body language if they are female, and listen to their tone of voice if they are male.
    d. determine whether or not they will look into your eyes when talking.

17. Dr. Jones's research centers on the relationship between changes in our thinking and moral reasoning over the life span. Dr. Jones is most likely a:
    a. clinical psychologist.
    b. personality psychologist.
    c. biological psychologist.
    d. developmental psychologist.

18. Which subfield is most directly concerned with studying human behavior in the workplace?
    a. clinical psychology
    b. personality psychology
    c. industrial/organizational psychology
    d. psychiatry

19. In defining psychology, the text notes that psychology is most accurately described as a:
    a. way of asking and answering questions.
    b. field engaged in solving applied problems.
    c. set of findings related to behavior and mental processes.
    d. nonscientific approach to the study of mental disorders.

20. Robert Rosenthal's research is a good example of research being conducted at the:
    a. micro level.
    b. molecular level.
    c. molar level.
    d. hypothetical level.

21. At the sorority party, Chantay is very lively and outgoing. What is the most likely cause of her gregariousness?
    a. dispositional factors
    b. situational factors
    c. both dispositional and situational factors
    d. It is impossible to say.

22. Which perspective emphasizes the learning of observable responses?
    a. behavioral
    b. evolutionary
    c. social-cultural
    d. behavior genetics

23. A psychologist who studies how worker productivity might be increased by changing office layout is engaged in _____ research.
    a. applied
    b. basic
    c. clinical
    d. developmental

24. A major principle underlying the PRTR study method is that:
    a. people learn and remember material best when they actively process it.
    b. many students overestimate their mastery of text and lecture material.
    c. study time should be spaced over time, not crammed into one session.
    d. overlearning disrupts efficient retention.

25. William James is best known for:
    a. introducing Sigmund Freud to the American public.
    b. opening the first experimental psychology laboratory in the United States.
    c. writing an important psychology textbook in 1890.
    d. insisting that psychology be patterned after the model of the physical sciences.

26. Psychologist Christine Hall has found that cultural background is an important factor in how people act in social situations. This is an example of research being conducted at the:
    a. micro level.
    b. molecular level.
    c. molar level.
    d. hypothetical level.

27. According to William James, psychology should focus on the study of:
    a. consciousness.
    b. self.
    c. emotions.
    d. all of the above.

28. To say that "psychology is a science" means that:
    a. psychologists study only observable behaviors.
    b. psychologists derive their conclusions from direct observations and rigorous analysis.
    c. psychological research should be free of value judgments.
    d. all of the above are true.

29. In defining psychology, "behavior" includes:
    a. anything a person says, does, or feels.
    b. any action we can observe and record.
    c. any action, whether observable or not.
    d. anything we can infer from a person's actions.

30. Dr. Waung investigates how a person's interpretation of a situation affects his or her reaction. Evidently, Dr. Waung is working within the _____ perspective.
    a. evolutionary
    b. behavioral
    c. cognitive
    d. social-cultural

31. A psychologist who conducts experiments solely intended to build psychology's knowledge base is engaged in:
    a. basic research.
    b. applied research.
    c. industrial/organizational research.
    d. clinical research.

32. Concerning the major psychological perspectives on behavior, the author of the text suggests that:
    a. researchers should work within the framework of only one perspective.
    b. only those perspectives that emphasize objective measurement of behavior are useful.
    c. the different perspectives often complement one another; together, they provide a fuller understanding of behavior than that provided by any single perspective.
    d. psychologists should avoid all of these traditional perspectives.

33. G. Stanley Hall, and other psychologists who followed in the tradition of _____, _____.
    a. William James; broadened the scope of psychology to include the study of consciousness, self, and religion
    b. Sigmund Freud; readily accepted William James's ideas
    c. Wilhelm Wundt; broadened the scope of psychology to include the study of consciousness, self, and religion
    d. Wilhelm Wundt; rejected William James's ideas as unscientific

34. Most psychological research is conducted at the _____ level of analysis.
    a. micro
    b. molecular
    c. molar
    d. macro

35. The electroencephalograph (EEG) is a device that measures:
    a. brain activity.
    b. blood pressure.
    c. hormonal activity.
    d. whether a person is lying or telling the truth.

KEY TERMS

Using your own words, write a brief definition or explanation of each of the following.

Textbook Terms

1. psychology

2. nature-nurture issue

3. basic research

4. applied research

5. clinical psychology

6. psychiatry

Program Terms

7. dispositional factor

8. situational factor

9. event-related potential

10. micro level

11. molecular level

12. molar level

ANSWERS

Guided Study

The following guidelines provide the main points that your answers should have touched upon.

Textbook Assignment

1. Psychology, the science of behavior and mental processes, is a young science with roots in many disciplines, primarily biology and philosophy. The Greek philosopher Aristotle theorized about many contemporary psychological phenomena, including learning, memory, motivation, emotion, perception, and personality. In the 1830s, naturalist Charles Darwin introduced the ideas of natural selection and evolution—ideas that remain important organizing principles for psychology. Wilhelm Wundt, who founded the first psychology laboratory in 1879, was a philosopher and a physiologist. In its early years psychological research focused on inner sensations, feelings, and thoughts. From the 1920s into the 1960s, psychology in the United States was most influenced by John Watson and others who redefined it as the "science of observable behavior." In the 1960s, psychology began to recapture its interest in mental processes so that today psychology encompasses the scientific study of both overt behavior and covert thoughts and feelings.

2. Psychologists who work from a neuroscience perspective study how the body and brain create behavior and mental processes. Psychologists who work from an evolutionary perspective study how natural selection favors traits that promote the perpetuation of one's genes. Behavior geneticists study how genes and environment contribute to individual differences. The behavioral perspective emphasizes how observable behaviors are learned. The cognitive perspective explores how people process, store, and retrieve information. The social-cultural perspective calls attention to the importance of each person's social and cultural environment in shaping his or her thoughts, emotions, and behaviors. The important point is that these perspectives need not contradict one another. In fact, they usually complement one another.

3. The first issue, "stability versus change," has to do with whether the individual's traits persist or change throughout life. The second issue, "rationality versus irrationality," concerns the extent to which our thoughts and actions are logical and efficient and the extent to which they are prone to inaccuracy. The nature-nurture issue is concerned with the relative contributions of genes (nature) and experience (nurture).

4. The nature-nurture debate has its roots in ancient Greek philosophy. Plato believed that much of human character and intelligence was inherited, whereas Aristotle believed that experience accounts for the contents of the mind. In the 1600s, John Locke and René Descartes revived the controversy, with Locke arguing that knowledge depends on experience and Descartes maintaining that some knowledge is inborn.

5. Some psychologists conduct basic research that builds psychology's knowledge base. Biological psychologists explore the links between brain and mind, developmental psychologists study our changing abilities, and personality psychologists investigate our inner traits. Others conduct applied research to solve practical problems. Industrial/organizational psychologists, for example, study and advise on behavior in the workplace. Still others provide professional services. Clinical psychologists study, assess, and treat

troubled people. Psychiatrists are physicians who treat the physical causes of psychological disorders.

6. The PRTR study method incorporates the idea that mastery of a subject requires active processing of it. PRTR stands for the four steps of the method: Preview, Read, Think actively and critically, and Review. The text and this study guide are organized to facilitate use of the PRTR method.

Program Assignment

1. The program opens with several questions that will serve as the central theme for the entire *Discovering Psychology* series: "What can psychology tell us about the relationships among the mind, brain, and behavior? What makes us similar to other people, yet so uniquely different? Why do we think, feel, and behave as we do? Are we molded more by heredity or shaped by experience? How can the same brain that gives us the capacity for creativity, rationality, and love also become the crucible for mental illness?"

2. The best known application of psychology is the treatment and prevention of behavioral and mental disorders. This application is highlighted in two interviews with a woman with *multiple personality disorder*, a bizarre disorder in which two or more distinct personalities inhabit the same human body.

3. While some psychologists treat mental disorders, others conduct scientific research that aims to objectively understand, predict, and sometimes control behavior. Two clips from the television program "Candid Camera" illustrate how psychologists attempt to explain behavior (in this case, the reactions of adolescent students to a young, attractive teacher of the opposite sex) by relating it to *dispositional factors* within the individual, such as genetic makeup and personality, and to external *situational factors*, such as the reactions of other people, rewards, and the context in which behavior is occurring.

4. Psychologists analyze behavior and mental processes at three different levels. Researchers such as Dr. Emanual Donchin, who describes how environmental events trigger specific changes in the electrical activity of the brain (event-related potentials), are working at the *micro level*, the smallest unit of analysis in psychology.

    Most psychologists study larger units of observable behavior and therefore are working at the *molecular level*. Psychologist Robert Rosenthal, for instance, has found that our body language can reveal much of what we are thinking and feeling on the molecular level, just as brain waves do on the micro level.

    At the *molar level* of analysis researchers investigate large units of behavior of the whole person in complex situations, factoring in the individual's cultural background and social experiences. Psychologists working at this level might study violent behavior, sexual attraction, worker morale, or the nature of prejudice. For example, Christine Hall studies the impact of culture and perceived differences in social power on the behavior of minority group members.

5. Like other sciences, psychology employs the methodology, principles, practices, and procedures that yield conclusions based on data, on research-generated evidence.

    Modern psychology began in 1879 when Wilhelm Wundt founded the first experimental psychology laboratory in Germany. Early studies focused on attention, word associations, and measuring reactions to experimental tasks, such as reaction times to sensory stimuli.

The first American psychology lab was founded in 1883 by G. Stanley Hall at Johns Hopkins University. Hall, who later became the first president of the American Psychological Association, also introduced Sigmund Freud to the American public.

In 1890 William James published *Principles of Psychology*, which is considered by many to be the most important psychology text of all time. A professor at Harvard, James was interested in all the ways in which people interact with and adapt to their environment. Although James found a place in psychology for the study of human consciousness, emotions, the self, personal values, and even religion, Wundtian psychologists such as G. Stanley Hall rejected his ideas as unscientific. They argued that psychology should be patterned after the physical sciences, and focused their work on topics such as on sensation, perception, and the measurement of mental reactions to physical stimuli.

Progress Test

1. **a.** is the answer. (p. 4)

    b. Psychology has never been defined in terms of conscious and unconscious activity.

    c. From about 1920 to 1960, under the influence of John Watson, psychology was defined as the science of observable behavior.

    d. Psychology today is defined as the science of behavior and mental processes. In its earliest days, however, psychology focused exclusively on mental phenomena.

2. **c.** is the answer. (p. 4)

    a. Wilhelm Wundt, the founder of the first psychology laboratory, used the method of introspection to study mental phenomena.

    b. Sigmund Freud developed an influential theory of personality that focused on unconscious processes.

    d. William James, the author of an important psychology textbook published in 1890, was a philosopher and therefore more interested in mental phenomena than observable behavior.

3. **d.** is the answer. (video; p. 4)

    a. In its earliest days, psychology was defined as the science of mental life.

    b. Psychology has never been defined in terms of conscious and unconscious activity.

    c. Following the Wundtian tradition of patterning psychology after the physical sciences, psychology was once defined as the science of behavior. Contemporary psychology, however, has abandoned this narrow definition.

4. **c.** is the answer. (video)

    a., b., & d. These disorders were not discussed in the program.

5. **a.** is the answer. (pp. 4–5)

    b. The cognitive perspective is concerned with how we process, store, and retrieve information.

    c. The behavioral perspective studies the mechanisms by which observable responses are acquired and changed.

    d. The behavior genetics perspective emphasizes the relative influence of genes and environment on behavior.

6. **c.** is the answer. (p. 6)

7. **d.** is the answer. For Locke, the mind at birth was a blank slate. (p. 2)

   a. Plato assumed that much of intelligence is inherited and therefore present at birth. Moreover, he was a philosopher of ancient Greece.

   b. Aristotle held essentially the same viewpoint as Locke, but he lived in the fourth century B.C.

   c. Descartes believed that knowledge does not depend on experience.

8. **b.** is the answer. (video)

9. **c.** is the answer. (video; p. 2)

10. **c.** is the answer. After earning their M.D. degrees, psychiatrists specialize in the diagnosis and treatment of mental-health disorders. (p. 7)

    a., b., & d. These psychologists generally earn a Ph.D. rather than an M.D.

11. **b.** is the answer. (pp. 2, 6)

    a. Aristotle believed that all knowledge originates with sensory experience.

    c. Descartes was a philosopher of the seventeenth century.

    d. Simonides was a well-known Greek orator.

12. **d.** is the answer. (pp. 4–5)

    a. The neuroscience perspective studies the biological bases for a range of psychological phenomena.

    b. The social-cultural perspective focuses on similarities and differences in thinking and behavior as the products of different social and cultural environments.

    c. The behavioral perspective studies the mechanisms by which observable responses are acquired and modified in particular environments.

13. **c.** is the answer. (video; p. 3)

    a. William James was the author of an important psychology textbook published in 1890.

    b. Wilhelm Wundt, a German psychologist, established the first psychology laboratory.

    d. Robert Rosenthal is a contemporary psychologist who studies body language.

14. **a.** is the answer. (video; p. 2)

15. **a.** is the answer. (video)

    b., c., & d. These are valid goals of *some*, but certainly not all, psychologists.

16. **b.** is the answer. (video)

    a. Because people have greater control over their body language than over their tone of voice, body language often is deceiving.

    c. Rosenthal's research did not address sex differences in lying.

    d. Eye gaze is a form of body language.

17. **d.** is the answer. The emphasis on change during the life span indicates that Dr. Jones is most likely a developmental psychologist. (p. 7)

    a. Clinical psychologists study, assess, and treat people who are psychologically troubled.

    b. Personality psychologists study our inner traits.

    c. Biological psychologists explore the links between brain and mind.

18. **c.** is the answer. (p. 7)

a. Clinical psychologists study, assess, and treat people with psychological disorders.

b. & d. Personality psychologists and psychiatrists do not usually study people in work situations.

19. **a.** is the answer. (p. 4)

    b. Psychology is equally involved in basic research.

    c. Psychology's knowledge base is constantly expanding.

    d. Psychology is the *science* of behavior and mental processes.

20. **b.** is the answer. (video)

    a. Research at the micro level focuses on the smallest units of behavior, such as brain waves or biochemical changes.

    c. Research at the molar level analyzes larger units of behavior of the whole person, taking into account cultural background, social experiences, and other such factors.

    d. This is not a level at which psychologists analyze behavior or mental processes.

21. **c.** is the answer. (video)

22. **a.** is the answer. (pp. 4–5)

    b. The evolutionary perspective emphasizes the influence of natural selection on behavior tendencies.

    c. The social-cultural perspective compares behaviors across different situations and cultures.

    d. The behavior genetics perspective emphasizes the relative influence of genes and environment on behavior.

23. **a.** is the answer. The research is addressing a practical issue. (p. 7)

    b. Basic research is aimed at contributing to the base of knowledge in a given field, not at resolving particular practical problems.

    c. & d. Clinical and developmental research would focus on issues relating to psychological disorders and life-span changes, respectively.

24. **a.** is the answer. (p. 9)

    b. & c. Although each of these is true, PRTR is based on the more general principle of active learning.

    d. In fact, just the opposite is true.

25. **c.** is the answer. (video; p. 2)

    a. & b. Both of these are credited to G. Stanley Hall.

    d. In fact, James *resisted* the Wundtian tradition of patterning psychology after the physical sciences.

26. **c.** is the answer. This research is at the molar level because it focuses on the influence of culture on complex social behavior, rather than the analysis of biological processes (a) or discrete observable behaviors (b). (video)

    d. This is not a level at which psychologists analyze behavior and mental processes.

27. **d.** is the answer. (video)

28. **b.** is the answer. (p. 4)

    a. Psychologists study both overt (observable) behaviors and covert thoughts and feelings.

    c. Psychologists' values definitely do influence their research.

29. **a.** is the answer. (p. 4)
30. **d.** is the answer. (pp. 4–5)
31. **a.** is the answer. (p. 7)
32. **c.** is the answer. (p. 5)

    a. The text suggests just the opposite: By studying behavior from several perspectives, psychologists gain a fuller understanding.

    b. & d. Each perspective is useful in that it calls researchers' attention to different aspects of behavior. This is equally true of those perspectives that do not emphasize objective measurement.

33. **d.** is the answer. (video)

    a. & b. James and Freud were contemporaries of Hall. Moreover, James and Hall had very different views of the proper subject matter of psychology.

    c. James, rather than Wundt, attempted to broaden the scope of psychology to include the study of consciousness, self, and religion.

34. **b.** is the answer. (video)
35. **a.** is the answer. (video; see also photograph on p. 53)

Key Terms

Textbook Terms

1. **Psychology** is the science of behavior and mental processes. (p. 4)
2. The **nature-nurture issue** is the controversy over the relative contributions of genes (nature) and experience (nurture) to the development of psychological traits and behaviors. (p. 6)
3. **Basic research** aims to increase psychology's knowledge base, rather than to solve practical problems. (p. 7)
4. **Applied research** aims to solve specific practical problems. (p. 7)
5. **Clinical psychology** is the branch of psychology concerned with the study, assessment, and treatment of people with psychological disorders. (p. 7)
6. **Psychiatry** is the branch of medicine concerned with the physical diagnosis and treatment of psychological disorders. (p. 7)

Program Terms

7. **Dispositional factors**, such as an individual's genetic makeup and personality traits, are internal characteristics that interact with situational factors to influence behavior.
8. **Situational factors**, such as rewards and the actions of other people, are external factors that influence behavior.
9. **Event-related potentials** are brain-wave reactions to sensory stimuli that are recorded by the electroencephalograph (EEG).
10. Research at the **micro level** focuses on the smallest units of behavior and mental processes, such as brain waves and biochemical changes.
11. Research at the **molecular level** analyzes discrete units of observable behaviors such as reaction time or body language.
12. Research at the **molar level** analyzes larger units of behavior of the whole person in complex situations.

PROGRAM 2

Understanding Research

TEXTBOOK ASSIGNMENT: Chapter 1: Thinking Critically With Psychological Science, pp. 10–39

ORIENTATION

Program 2 of *Discovering Psychology* demonstrates how psychologists use the scientific method, with its emphasis on systematic observation and data collection, to answer questions about behavior and mental processes. Chapter 1 of the text explains how psychologists employ the research strategies of description, correlation, and experimentation in order to objectively observe, predict, and explain behavior and mental processes. It also discusses several questions people often ask about psychology, including why animal research is relevant, whether laboratory experiments are ethical, whether psychological theories aren't simply based on common sense, and whether psychology's principles don't have the potential for misuse.

The video describes the various ways in which scientists try to eliminate faulty reasoning from their research. These include testing hypotheses under controlled conditions, ruling out alternative explanations, resisting the tendency to conclude that things that merely occur together are causally related, and making sure that the subjects in an experiment are representative of the population from which they are selected. The program concludes with a "recipe" for critical thinking that will help the viewer become a more sophisticated consumer of information.

NOTE: Answer guidelines for all Program 2 questions begin on page 27.

GOALS

After completing your study of the program and reading assignment, you should be prepared to:

1. Identify the characteristics of the scientific method and explain how researchers use theories and hypotheses in their work.

2. Describe the major research methods of psychology and discuss the nature and advantages of experimentation.

3. Identify several common pitfalls in reasoning and explain how researchers guard against them.

4. Discuss several commonly asked questions about psychology, including the ethics of experimentation, the relevance of animal research, and whether psychology is potentially dangerous.

GUIDED STUDY

Textbook Assignment

The textbook chapter should be studied one section at a time. Before you read, preview each section by skimming it, noting headings and boldface items. Then read the appropriate section objectives from the following outline. Keep these objectives in mind and, as you read the chapter section, search for the information that will enable you to meet each objective. Once you have finished a section, write out answers for its objectives.

The Scientific Attitude (pp. 12–13)

1. Discuss the attitudes that characterize scientific inquiry and explain the nature of critical thinking.

The Limits of Intuition and Common Sense (pp. 13–16)

2. Identify two pitfalls in thinking that make intuition and common sense untrustworthy.

Research Strategies: How Psychologists Ask and Answer Questions (pp. 16–30)

3. Describe the various descriptive research strategies.

4. Discuss the meaning of correlation, both positive and negative, and explain why correlation enables prediction but not explanation.

5. Describe the nature and advantages of experimentation.

6. Discuss the importance of operational definitions and control techniques in research.

Commonly Asked Questions About Psychology (pp. 31–37)

7. Discuss questions regarding the artificiality of experimentation and whether psychological principles are culture-free.

8. Explain why psychologists study animals and discuss the ethics of experimentation.

9. Describe how psychologists' values influence their work and discuss whether psychology is potentially dangerous.

Program Assignment

Read the following objectives before you watch Program 2. As you watch, be alert for information that will help you answer each objective. Taking notes during the program will help you to formulate your answers later. After the program, write answers to the objectives. If you have access to the program on videotape, you may replay portions if you need to refresh your memory.

1. Describe the scientific method.

2. Explain how psychologists use hypotheses and theories to guide their research and why research is often conducted in laboratories.

3. Discuss the possible dangers of forming beliefs without thinking critically about the issues involved.

4. Identify the common features of psychological healing, explaining how such healing may produce a placebo effect.

5. Explain why the placebo effect complicates the job of researchers and how researchers attempt to prevent its occurrence.

6. State two things that researchers must rule out before concluding that a particular treatment caused the results of an experiment.

7. Describe the flaws in the "mind reading" demonstration and in laughter therapy.

8. Discuss the importance of sample size in analyzing data, using the "Hite Report" as an example.

9. Explain how a polygraph works and why it is not an accurate lie detector.

10. State several guidelines for thinking critically about psychological phenomena.

PROGRESS TEST

Circle your answers to the following questions and check them with the answers on page 30. If your answer is incorrect, read the explanation for why it is incorrect and then consult the appropriate pages of the text (in parentheses following the correct answer).

1. After detailed study of a gunshot wound victim, a psychologist concludes that the brain region destroyed is likely to be important for memory functions. Which research did the psychologist use to deduce this?
    a. case study
    b. survey
    c. correlational
    d. experimental

2. The scientific method is best described as:
    a. a set of general procedures for gathering and interpreting data.
    b. the use of controlled laboratory experiments to study psychological phenomena.
    c. the observation of behavior in its natural environment.
    d. the skeptical attitude shared by all researchers.

3. Hypotheses are:
    a. integrated sets of principles that help organize observations.
    b. testable predictions, often derived from theories.
    c. hunches about mental processes.
    d. measures of relationships between two factors.

4. In an experiment to determine the effects of exercise on motivation, exercise is the:
   a. control condition.
   b. intervening variable.
   c. independent variable.
   d. dependent variable.

5. A psychologist studies the play behavior of third-grade children by watching groups during recess at school. Which research strategy is being used?
   a. correlation
   b. case study
   c. experiment
   d. naturalistic observation

6. Which of the following is not a basic research strategy used by psychologists?
   a. description
   b. replication
   c. experimentation
   d. correlation

7. Psychologists' personal values:
   a. have little influence on how their experiments are conducted.
   b. do not influence the interpretation of experimental results because of the use of statistical techniques that guard against subjective bias.
   c. can bias both scientific observation and interpretation of data.
   d. have little influence on the methods of investigation but a significant effect on interpretation.

8. If shoe size and IQ are negatively correlated, which of the following is true?
   a. People with large feet tend to have high IQs.
   b. People with small feet tend to have high IQs.
   c. People with small feet tend to have low IQs.
   d. IQ is unpredictable based on a person's shoe size.

9. Which of the following research strategies would be best to use to determine whether alcohol impairs memory?
   a. case study
   b. naturalistic observation
   c. survey
   d. experiment

10. The group that receives the treatment of interest in an experiment is the:
    a. test group.
    b. random sample.
    c. experimental group.
    d. control group.

11. In order to determine the effects of a new drug on memory, one group of subjects is given a pill that contains the drug. A second group is given a sugar pill that does not contain the drug. This second group constitutes the:
    a. random sample.
    b. experimental group.
    c. control group.
    d. test group.

12. According to psychiatrist Jerome Frank, all forms of psychological healing:
    a. trigger emotional arousal.
    b. are based in part on a placebo effect.
    c. increase the patient's sense of mastery over his or her world.
    d. are characterized by all of the above.

13. Which of the following statements about the ethics of experimentation with people and animals is *false*?
    a. Only a small percentage of animal experiments use shock.
    b. Allegations that psychologists routinely subject animals to pain, starvation, and other inhumane conditions have not been found to be true.
    c. The American Psychological Association has set strict guidelines for the care and treatment of human and animal subjects.
    d. Animals are used as subjects in almost 25 percent of all psychology experiments.

14. In an experiment to determine the effects of attention on memory, memory is the:
    a. control condition.
    b. intervening variable.
    c. independent variable.
    d. dependent variable.

15. Which of the following best describes the hindsight bias?
    a. Events seem more predictable before they have occurred.
    b. Events seem more predictable after they have occurred.
    c. A person's intuition is usually correct.
    d. A person's intuition is usually not correct.

16. Which of the following procedures is an example of the use of a placebo?
    a. In a test of the effects of a drug on memory, a subject is led to believe that a harmless pill actually contains an active drug.
    b. A subject in an experiment is led to believe that a pill, which actually contains an active drug, is harmless.
    c. Subjects in an experiment are not told which treatment condition is in effect.
    d. Neither the subjects nor the experimenter knows which treatment condition is in effect.

17. The procedure designed to ensure that the experimental and control groups do not differ in any way that might affect the experiment's results is called:
    a. variable controlling.
    b. random assignment.
    c. representative sampling.
    d. stratification.

18. Which type of research strategy would allow you to determine whether students' college grades accurately predict later income?
    a. case study
    b. naturalistic observation
    c. experiment
    d. correlation

19. In a test of the effects of air pollution, groups of students performed a reaction-time task in either a polluted or unpolluted room. To what condition were students in the unpolluted room exposed?
    a. experimental
    b. control
    c. randomly assigned
    d. dependent

20. In order to study the effects of lighting on mood, Dr. Cooper had students fill out questionnaires in brightly lit or dimly lit rooms. In this study, the independent variable consisted of:
    a. the number of subjects assigned to each group.
    b. the students' responses to the questionnaire.
    c. the room lighting.
    d. the subject matter of the questions asked.

21. The purpose of the double-blind procedure is to:
    a. replicate the findings of another researcher.
    b. eliminate bias due to subject and experimenter expectancy.
    c. test the effects of more than one treatment on behavior.
    d. create a testable prediction regarding two events.

22. The "mind reading" demonstration in the program was flawed because:
    a. procedural controls were absent.
    b. chance was not ruled out as a factor in the results.
    c. the illusionist could easily have "rigged" the results.
    d. of all the above reasons.

23. Scientists would not attribute Norman Cousins's recovery from spinal arthritis to laughter therapy because:
    a. single-subject research is unacceptable in the scientific method.
    b. the effects of this particular treatment cannot be separated from other possible causes of the cure.
    c. Cousins's actual condition was not professionally diagnosed at the start of the "experiment."
    d. of all the above reasons.

24. Your roommate is conducting a survey to learn how many hours the typical college student studies each day. She plans to pass out her questionnaire to the members of her sorority. You point out that her findings will be flawed because:
    a. she has not specified an independent variable.
    b. she has not specified a dependent variable.
    c. the sample will probably not be representative of the population of interest.
    d. of all the above reasons.

25. The concept of control is important in psychological research because:
    a. without control over independent and dependent variables, researchers cannot describe, predict, or explain behavior.
    b. experimental control allows researchers to study the influence of one or two independent variables on a dependent variable while holding other potential influences constant.
    c. without experimental control, results cannot be generalized from a sample to a population.
    d. of all the above reasons.

26. Martina believes that high doses of caffeine slow a person's reaction time. In order to test this belief, she has five friends each drink three 8-ounce cups of coffee and then measures their reaction time on a learning task. What is wrong with Martina's research strategy?
    a. No independent variable is specified.
    b. No dependent variable is specified.
    c. There is no control condition.
    d. There is no provision for replication of the findings.

27. If eating saturated fat and the likelihood of contracting cancer are positively correlated, which of the following is true?
    a. Saturated fat causes cancer.
    b. People who are prone to develop cancer prefer foods containing saturated fat.
    c. A separate factor links the consumption of saturated fat to cancer.
    d. None of the above is necessarily true.

28. Psychologists use experimental research in order to reveal or to understand:
    a. correlational relationships.
    b. hypotheses.
    c. theories.
    d. cause-and-effect relationships.

29. Your best friend criticizes psychological research for being artificial and having no relevance to behavior in real life. In defense of psychology's use of laboratory experiments you point out that:
    a. psychologists make every attempt to avoid artificiality by setting up experiments that closely simulate real-world environments.
    b. psychologists who conduct basic research are not concerned with the applicability of their findings to the real world.
    c. most psychological research is not conducted in a laboratory environment.
    d. psychologists intentionally study behavior in simplified environments in order to gain greater control over variables and to test general principles that help explain many behaviors.

30. Experimentation, which seeks to explain events, involves _____ factors, whereas correlation, which serves only to predict events, involves _____ factors.
    a. determining relationships between; direct manipulation of
    b. direct manipulation of; determining relationships between
    c. direct observation of; random selection of
    d. random selection of; direct observation of

31. A major flaw in the "Hite Report" is that:
    a. there was no control group in the experiment.
    b. the double-blind procedure was not used.
    c. the sample was very small, and unrepresentative of the population from which it was drawn.
    d. all the above occurred.

32. A friend majoring in anthropology is critical of psychological research because it often ignores the influence of culture on thoughts and actions. You point out that:

a. there is very little evidence that cultural diversity has a significant effect on specific behaviors and attitudes.
b. most researchers assign subjects to experimental and control conditions in such a way as to fairly represent the cultural diversity of the population under study.
c. it is impossible for psychologists to control for every possible variable that might influence the thoughts and actions of research participants.
d. even when specific thoughts and actions vary across cultures, as they often do, the underlying processes are much the same.

33. Rashad, who is participating in a psychology experiment on the effects of alcohol on perception, is truthfully told by the experimenter that he has been assigned to the "high-dose condition." What is wrong with this experiment?
    a. There is no control condition.
    b. Rashad's expectations concerning the effects of "high doses" of alcohol on perception may influence his performance.
    c. Knowing that Rashad is in the "high-dose" condition may influence the experimenter's interpretations of Rashad's results.
    d. Both b. and c. are correct.

34. Well-done surveys measure attitudes in a representative subset, or _____ , of an entire group, or _____ .
    a. population; random sample
    b. control group; experimental group
    c. experimental group; control group
    d. random sample; population

35. Psychologist Leonard Saxe is opposed to the use of lie detectors because:
    a. they represent an invasion of privacy and could easily be used for unethical purposes.
    b. there often are serious discrepancies among the various indicators of arousal such as perspiration and heart rate.
    c. the polygraph cannot distinguish the various possible causes of arousal.
    d. most people find taking a lie detector test so traumatic that emotional side effects often last for days afterward.

KEY TERMS

Using your own words, write a brief definition or explanation of each of the following.

Textbook Terms

1. critical thinking

2. hindsight bias

3. theory

4. hypothesis

5. replication

6. case study

7. survey

8. false consensus effect

9. population

10. random sample

11. naturalistic observation

12. correlation

13. illusory correlation

14. experiment

15. experimental condition

16. control condition

17. random assignment

18. independent variable

19. dependent variable

20. operational definition

21. placebo

22. double-blind procedure

23. culture

Program Terms

24. field study

25. subjective reality

26. polygraph

ANSWERS

Guided Study

The following guidelines provide the main points that your answers should have touched upon.

Textbook Assignment

1. As scientists, psychologists attempt to study thoughts and actions with an attitude of open-minded, curious skepticism. Scientists must also possess an attitude of humility because they may have to reject their ideas in the light of new evidence. Whether applied to reading news reports or listening to a lecture, critical thinking examines assumptions, discerns hidden values, evaluates evidence, and assesses conclusions.

2. Two reliable phenomena—hindsight bias and judgmental overconfidence—make intuition and common sense untrustworthy. Hindsight bias is the tendency to perceive an outcome that has already occurred as being obvious and predictable. Overconfidence is the tendency to think we know more about an issue than we actually do, and to overestimate the accuracy of that knowledge.

3. The simplest research design is description; examples include case studies, surveys, and naturalistic observation. In the case study one or more individuals are studied in great depth in the hope of revealing general principles underlying the behavior of all people. Surveys measure the self-reported attitudes or behaviors of a randomly selected representative sample of an entire group, or population. Naturalistic observation seeks to observe and record the behavior of organisms (including humans) in their natural environments.

4. A correlation is a statistical measure of relationship, revealing how accurately one event predicts another. A positive correlation indicates a *direct* relationship in which two things increase or decrease together. A negative correlation indicates an *inverse* relationship in which one thing increases as the other decreases. A zero correlations means no relationship exists. A correlation between two events or behaviors means only that one event can be predicted from the other. Because two events may both be caused by some other event, a correlation between the two events does not mean that one caused the other. Correlation thus does not enable explanation.

5. Conducting experiments allows psychologists to explain behaviors in terms of cause-and-effect relationships. This is because experiments allow researchers to manipulate one or more experimental factors (the independent variables) while holding all other potential independent variables constant. If a subject's behavior (the dependent variable) changes, the change can be attributed to the influence of the independent variable under study. In the typical experiment, subjects are randomly assigned to either a control condition, in which the experimental treatment is absent, or an experimental condition, in which the treatment of interest is present.

6. Operational definitions specify the procedures that manipulate the independent variable or measure the dependent variable. Such definitions prevent ambiguity by providing an exactness of meaning that allows others to replicate the study. Two control techniques involve use of a placebo and the double-blind procedure. These help ensure that any changes in the dependent variable that occur are due to the independent variable rather than to researchers' or subjects' expectations.

7. Psychologists intentionally conduct experiments on simplified behaviors in an artificial laboratory environment in order to gain control over the numerous independent and dependent variables present in more complex behaviors and the "real world." By studying simplified behaviors under controlled circumstances psychologists are able to test general principles of behavior that also operate in the real world.

    For similar reasons, psychologists often apply their findings from psychological studies of people from one culture to people in general. Although attitudes and behaviors vary greatly from culture to culture, the underlying principles are much the same. Furthermore, although males and females are different in many ways, psychologically and biologically they are also overwhelmingly alike.

8. Some psychologists study animals simply to understand animal behavior. For the same reasons that psychologists investigate human behavior in simplified laboratory environments before attempting to understand more complex everyday behaviors, other psychologists attempt to learn more about human behavior by studying simpler, yet similar, behaviors in animals.

    Although animals in psychological research rarely experience pain, opposition to animal experimentation raises two important issues: (1) whether it is morally right to place the well-being of humans above that of animals, and (2) what safeguards should protect the well-being of animals.

    Ethical standards developed by the American Psychological Association and the British Psychological Society provide strict guidelines regarding the treatment of people and animals in psychology experiments.

9. No science, including psychology, is value-free. Psychologists' values influence their choice of research topics, their observations, and their interpretations of research findings. Psychological knowledge is a power that, like all powers, can be used for good or evil. Many psychologists conduct research aimed at solving some of the world's most serious problems, including war, prejudice, overpopulation, and crime.

Program Assignment

1. The scientific method is a set of general procedures for gathering and interpreting data. To be accurate, data must be collected from carefully controlled observations and measurements. And other researchers working independently must be able to obtain the same results using the same methods.

2. Although some research is carried out in the field where naturally occurring behavior can be observed, laboratories allow psychologists to carefully control conditions and measure behavior. In such research psychologists test theories about behavior and mental phenomena by formulating hypotheses—predictions about how two or more factors are likely to be related. To test a specific hypothesis, researchers randomly assign some subjects to an experimental group which receives the treatment. Other subjects are assigned to a control group which does not receive the treatment. The results are then compared.

3. Many of our beliefs, which may come from our culture or from our individual experiences, are accepted without question. These beliefs form a subjective reality that can influence how we see the world. If we don't learn to think critically, we may believe in the unproven or unexplained—psychic predictions, mystical forces, miracle cures, and cosmic signs, for example. Even worse, if we don't learn to think for ourselves, we may become recruits in social, religious, or political cults.

4. Psychiatrist Jerome Frank has found that all forms of psychological healing share certain common features, including a relationship with a healer in an accepted setting and the tendency to increase the patient's sense of mastery over his or her world, to trigger emotional arousal, and to encourage belief in the healing process. In addition, they all may produce a placebo effect, which occurs when belief in the power of a treatment, rather than the treatment itself, results in a cure. In medicine, a placebo is a substance, such as a sugar pill, that has no direct pharmacological effect but can have a therapeutic effect for people who believe it will work. Placebos can be so powerful that virtually any credible, socially sanctioned treatment administered in an accepted setting can be effective.

5. The placebo effect complicates the job of researchers by making it impossible to differentiate the actual effects of a treatment from the therapeutic effects of the patient's belief in the treatment. To prevent this effect, researchers use the double-blind technique, in which neither the researcher nor the subjects are aware of which subjects have received the treatment of interest, and which have received the placebo. Thus, any improvement can be attributed to the treatment itself, rather than to the subject's mere belief in its efficacy.

6. Before concluding that a particular treatment has influenced the behavior in an experiment, psychologists must first rule out the possibility that chance alone could have explained the results. Second, a psychologist must be able to rule out hypotheses other than the specific one being tested as possible explanations of the experimental results.

7. In the "mind reading" demonstration, by chance alone the subject could have picked the correct card one time out of six. Moreover, the absence of procedural controls that allowed the illusionist to "rig" the demonstration is a valid alternative explanation of the subject's apparent ability to read the illusionist's mind.

    Norman Cousins's recovery from spinal arthritis, which some have attributed to laughter therapy, might also have been caused by Cousins's optimistic personality, his taking control of his treatment, or his taking of massive amounts of vitamin C. The scientific method requires that the effects of a particular treatment (in this case the regimen of laughter) be separated from all the other possible causes of the cure.

8. A potential problem in analyzing data comes from using small samples to draw significant conclusions. To reduce the possibility of errors, researchers start out with a random sample of subjects that is representative of the larger population from which the subjects were drawn.

    Shere Hite's controversial report on married women's attitudes about sex and marriage illustrates the importance of representative sampling. Hite's conclusions were based on a biased sample that consisted of only 4 percent of those surveyed. When the same questions were posed to a larger, random (and therefore more representative) sample of women, quite different results were obtained.

9. The polygraph, or lie detector, measures bodily changes in autonomic arousal, such as heart rate, breathing, and sweating. The tester asks a number of control questions on which the subject is assumed to tell the truth. The subject's arousal to these questions is compared to that in response to questions on which he or she may be lying. There is, however, no unequivocal connection between lying and physical arousal. Liars may not always become aroused, and those telling the truth may become aroused simply from test nervousness. Recent studies demonstrate that a crucial element in the test is the extent to which subjects believe that lie detectors actually

work. Subjects who believe the test cannot actually detect lying are often able to deceive it. On the other hand, liars who believe in the test are more likely to become nervous and thus be caught.

10. For any study, find out who the subjects were, including how many participated and how they were selected. Avoid the assumption that two things that go together are cause and effect. Question any data that aren't collected using the rigorous procedures of the scientific method. Remember that any conclusion about human behavior is only as good as the data on which it is based. Keep in mind the power of placebos and refrain from making judgments about scientific breakthroughs until the results have been replicated by other researchers. Remember that scientific conclusions are always tentative and open to change should better data come along.

Progress Test

1. **a.** is the answer. In a case study one subject is studied in depth. (p. 18)

   b. In survey research many people are interviewed.

   c. In correlational research an experimenter attempts to determine whether two factors are related.

   d. In experimental research an investigator manipulates one variable to observe its effect on another.

2. **a.** is the answer. (video; p. 17)

   b. The scientific method is not limited to laboratory research.

   c. This describes field studies.

   d. Although skepticism is an important aspect of critical thinking, the scientific method consists of explicit procedures for gathering and analyzing data.

3. **b.** is the answer. (video; p. 17)

   a. This describes theories.

   c. Hypotheses are formal statements rather than mere hunches.

   d. This describes correlation.

4. **c.** is the answer. Exercise is the variable being manipulated by the experiment. (p. 28)

   a. A control condition for this experiment would be a group of people not permitted to exercise.

   b. An intervening variable is a variable other than those being manipulated that may influence behavior.

   d. The dependent variable is the behavior measured by the experimenter, in this case, the effects of exercise.

5. **d.** is the answer. In this case the children are being observed in their normal environment, rather than in a laboratory. (p. 20)

   a. Correlation is a measure of the relationship between two factors. The psychologist may later want to determine whether there are correlations between the variables studied under natural conditions.

   b. In a case study one subject is studied in depth.

    c. This is not an experiment because the psychologist is not directly controlling the variables being studied.

6. **b.** is the answer. Replication is the repetition of an experiment in order to determine whether its findings are reliable. It is not a research strategy. (p. 17)

7. **c.** is the answer. (p. 36)

    a. & b. Psychologists' personal values can influence both how experiments are conducted and how experimental findings are interpreted.

    d. The issue of values is no less important in psychology than in other scientific fields.

8. **b.** is the answer. (p. 21)

    a. & c. These answers would have been correct had the question stated that there is a positive correlation between shoe size and IQ.

    d. Actually, there probably is no correlation at all, but that is not the question here.

9. **d.** is the answer. In an experiment it would be possible to manipulate alcohol consumption and observe the effects, if any, on memory. (pp. 26–28)

    a., b., & c. These answers are incorrect because only by directly controlling the variables of interest can a researcher uncover cause-and-effect relationships.

10. **c.** is the answer. (video; p. 27)

    a. Both the experimental and control groups are test groups.

    b. A random sample is a representative sample of the population under study. If one were to use a random sample in an experiment, one would use it for both the control and the experimental groups.

    d. The control condition is the condition in which the treatment is absent.

11. **c.** is the answer. (video; p. 27)

12. **d.** is the answer. (video)

13. **d.** is the answer. Only about 7 percent of all psychological experiments involve animals. (p. 34)

14. **d.** is the answer. (p. 28)

    a. The control condition is the comparison group, in which the experimental treatment is absent.

    b. Memory is a directly observed and measured dependent variable in this experiment.

    c. Attention is the independent variable, which is being manipulated.

15. **b.** is the answer. (p. 14)

    a. The phenomenon is related to hindsight rather than foresight.

    c. & d. The phenomenon doesn't involve the correctness or incorrectness of intuitions but rather people's attitude that they had the correct intuition.

16. **a.** is the answer. (video; p. 30)

    b. Use of a placebo tests whether the behavior of an experimental subject, who mistakenly believes that a treatment (such as a drug) is in effect, is the same as it would be if the treatment were actually present.

c. & d. These are examples of blind and double-blind control procedures.

17. **b.** is the answer. If enough subjects are used in an experiment and they are randomly assigned to the two groups, any differences that emerge between the groups should stem from the experiment itself. (p. 27)

a., c., & d. None of these terms describes precautions taken in setting up groups for experiments.

18. **d.** is the answer. Correlations show how well one factor can be predicted from another. (p. 21)

a. Since a case study focuses in great detail on the behavior of an individual, it's unlikely to be useful in showing whether predictions are possible.

b. Naturalistic observation is a method of describing, rather than predicting, behavior.

c. In experimental research the effects of manipulated independent variables on dependent variables are measured. It is not clear how an experiment could help determine whether IQ tests predict academic success.

19. **b.** is the answer. The control condition is the one in which the treatment—in this case, pollution—is absent. (p. 27)

a. Students in the polluted room would be in the experimental condition.

c. Presumably, all students in both the experimental and control conditions were randomly assigned to their groups. Random assignment is a method for establishing groups, rather than a condition.

d. The word dependent refers to a kind of variable in experiments; conditions are either experimental or control.

20. **c.** is the answer. The lighting is the factor being manipulated. (p. 28)

a. & d. These answers are incorrect because they involve aspects of the experiment other than the variables.

b. This answer is the dependent, not the independent, variable.

21. **b.** is the answer. (video; p. 30)

22. **d.** is the answer. (video)

23. **b.** is the answer. (video)

a. Although large random samples are necessary before the results of an experiment can be generalized to the population from which the sample is drawn, this case study explains the improvement of only one subject.

c. Cousins *was* professionally diagnosed at the start of his "experiment."

24. **c.** is the answer. The members of one sorority are likely to share more interests, traits, and attitudes than will the members of a random sample of college students. (p. 19)

a. & b. Unlike experiments, surveys do not specify or directly manipulate independent and dependent variables. In a sense, however, the questions of a survey are independent variables, and the answers, dependent variables.

25. **b.** is the answer. (p. 25)

a. Although case studies, surveys, naturalistic observation, and correlational research do not involve control of variables, they nevertheless enable researchers to describe and predict behavior.

c. Whether or not a sample is representative of a population, rather than control over variables, determines whether results can be generalized from a sample to a population.

26. **c.** is the answer. In order to determine the effects of caffeine on reaction time, Martina needs to measure reaction time in a control, or comparison, group that does not receive caffeine. (p. 27)

   a. Caffeine is the independent variable.

   b. Reaction time is the dependent variable.

   d. Whether or not Martina's experiment can be replicated is determined by the precision with which she reports her procedures, which is not an aspect of research strategy.

27. **d.** is the answer. (video; p. 21)

   a. Correlation does not imply causality.

   b. A positive correlation simply means that the two factors tend to increase or decrease together; further relationships are not implied.

   c. A separate factor may or may not be involved. That the two factors are correlated does not imply a separate factor, however. There may, for example, be a direct causal relationship between the two factors themselves.

28. **d.** is the answer. (video; p. 26)

   a. Correlational relationships can be revealed by statistical analyses of data; experimentation is not necessary.

   b. & c. Hypotheses and theories give direction to experimental research.

29. **d.** is the answer. (p. 32)

30. **b.** is the answer. (pp. 21, 26)

   a. Correlational research does not involve direct manipulation of factors.

   c. & d. Both experimentation and correlational research involve hypotheses, which are testable predictions of relationships between specific, rather than random, factors.

31. **c.** is the answer. (video; pp. 19–20)

   a. & b. Control groups and double-blind procedures pertain to experiments; the "Hite Report" is an example of survey research.

32. **d.** is the answer. (p. 32)

   a. In fact, just the opposite is true.

   b. In fact, psychological experiments tend to use the most readily available subjects, often white North American college students.

   c. Although this may be true, psychological experiments remain important because they help explain underlying processes of human behavior everywhere. Therefore, d. is a much better response than c.

33. **d.** is the answer. (video; pp. 27, 30)

   a. The low-dose comparison group *is* the control group.

34. **d.** is the answer. (video; p. 19)

   a. A sample is a subset of a population.

   b. & c. Control and experimental groups are used in experimentation, not in survey research.

35. **c.** is the answer. (video)

Key Terms

Textbook Terms

1. **Critical thinking** is careful reasoning that examines assumptions, discerns hidden values, evaluates evidence and conclusions, and does not blindly accept arguments and conclusions. (p. 13)

2. **Hindsight bias** refers to the tendency to exaggerate the obviousness of an outcome—including a psychological research finding—after one has heard about it. (p. 14)

3. A **theory** is an explanation using an integrated set of principles that organizes a set of observations and makes testable predictions. (p. 17)

4. A **hypothesis** is a testable prediction derived from a theory; testing the hypothesis helps scientists to test the theory. (p. 17)

    Example: In order to test his theory of why people conform, Solomon Asch formulated the testable **hypothesis** that an individual would be more likely to go along with the majority opinion of a large group than with that of a smaller group.

5. **Replication** is the process of repeating an experiment, often with different subjects and in different situations, to see whether the basic finding generalizes to other subjects and circumstances. (p. 17)

6. The **case study** is a descriptive research strategy in which one person is studied in great depth, often with the intention of revealing universal principles. (p. 18)

7. The **survey** is a descriptive research strategy in which a representative, random sample of people are questioned about their attitudes or behavior. (p. 19)

8. The **false consensus effect** is the tendency to overestimate the extent to which others share our beliefs and behaviors. (p. 19)

9. A **population** consists of all the members of a group being studied. (p. 19)

10. A **random sample** is one that is representative because every member of the population has an equal chance of being included. (p. 19)

11. **Naturalistic observation** involves observing and recording behavior in naturally occurring situations without trying to manipulate or control the situation. (p. 20)

12. **Correlation** is a statistical measure that indicates the extent to which two factors vary together and thus how well one factor can be predicted from the other; correlations can be positive or negative. (p. 21)

    Example: If there is a **positive correlation** between air temperature and ice cream sales, the warmer (higher) it is, the more ice cream is sold. If there is a **negative correlation** between air temperature and sales of cocoa, the cooler (lower) it is, the more cocoa is sold.

13. **Illusory correlation** is the false perception of a relationship between two events when none exists. (p. 22)

14. An **experiment** is a research strategy in which a researcher directly manipulates one or more factors (independent variables) in order to observe their effect on some behavior or mental process (the dependent variable); experiments therefore make it possible to establish cause-and-effect relationships. (p. 26)

15. The **experimental condition** of an experiment is one in which subjects are exposed to the independent variable being studied. (p. 27)

    Example: In the study of the effects of a new drug on reaction time, subjects in the **experimental condition** would actually receive the drug being tested.

16. The **control condition** of an experiment is one in which the treatment of interest, or independent variable, is withheld so that comparison to the experimental condition can be made. (p. 27)

    Example: The **control condition** for an experiment testing the effects of a new drug on reaction time would be a group of subjects given a placebo (inactive drug or sugar pill) instead of the drug being tested.

17. **Random assignment** is the procedure of assigning subjects to the experimental and control conditions by chance in order to minimize preexisting differences between the groups. (pp. 27–28)

18. The **independent variable** of an experiment is the factor being manipulated and tested by the investigator. (p. 28)

    Example: In the study of the effects of a new drug on reaction time, the drug is the **independent variable**.

19. The **dependent variable** of an experiment is the factor being measured by the investigator. (p. 28)

    Example: In the study of the effects of a new drug on reaction time, the subjects' reaction time is the **dependent variable.**

20. **Operational definitions** are precise statements of the procedures (operations) used to define independent and dependent variables. (p. 28)

21. A **placebo** is an inert substance or condition that is administered as a test of whether an experimental subject, who mistakenly thinks a treatment is in effect, behaves the same as he or she would if the treatment were actually present. (p. 30)

22. A **double-blind procedure** is a control procedure in which neither the experimenter nor the research subjects are aware of which condition is in effect. It is used to prevent experimenters' and subjects' expectations from influencing the results of an experiment. (p. 30)

23. **Culture** is the enduring behaviors, ideas, attitudes, and traditions shared by a large group of people and transmitted from one generation to the next. (p. 32)

Program Terms

24. **Field studies**, like naturalistic observation, involve observing and recording behavior in naturally occurring situations, without trying to influence the situation.

25. Each person's beliefs, acquired from his or her cultural background and experiences, form a **subjective reality** that influences how the world is perceived.

26. The **polygraph**, or lie detector, is a device that measures physical arousal of the autonomic nervous system.

PROGRAMS 3 & 4

The Behaving Brain
The Responsive Brain

TEXTBOOK ASSIGNMENT: Chapter 2: Neuroscience, Genetics, and Behavior, pp. 41–64
Chapter 3: The Developing Child, pp. 83–84

ORIENTATION

Because the text and program material for Programs 3 and 4 overlap considerably, these programs should be studied together. Program 3 focuses on the basic structures and functions of the nervous system, including the brain. Under the direction of the brain, the nervous system, along with the endocrine system, coordinates a variety of voluntary and involuntary behaviors and serves as the body's mechanism for communication with the external environment. Knowledge of the workings of the nervous system has increased with recent advances in the new field of neuroscience. These advances are discussed, as are several new areas of research aimed at improving memory in those who have suffered brain damage and the cognitive deficits that accompany Alzheimer's and Parkinson's diseases.

The reading assignment also describes the structures of the brain, but continues with an explanation of the brain's role in language and other complex information-processing tasks.

Because the brain is designed to be modified by the behaviors it has caused, and by environmental stimulation, the brain is constantly open to change in its structure and function. This capacity for internal modification is the theme of Program 4, which showcases the research of several prominent neuroscientists. This research demonstrates various ways in which early experiences may cause permanent alterations in the structure and functioning of the brain.

Because the two programs plus the reading assignment together cover quite a bit of information, you may want to break your study into two parts: the nervous system in general, then the brain and its interaction with the environment.

NOTE: Answer guidelines for all Programs 3 and 4 questions begin on page 56.

GOALS

After completing your study of the program and reading assignment, you should be prepared to:

1. Describe a neuron and explain how nerve cells communicate.
2. Identify the major parts of the nervous system and describe their functions.
3. Explain the methods used in studying the brain.
4. Describe the functions of lower-level brain structures.
5. Describe the structure and functions of the cerebral cortex.

6. Discuss how damage to several different cortical areas can impair language functioning and outline the process by which the brain directs reading aloud.

7. Explain how environmental experiences can alter the structure and functioning of the brain.

GUIDED STUDY

Textbook Assignment

The textbook chapter should be studied one section at a time. Before you read, preview each section by skimming it, noting headings and boldface items. Then read the appropriate section objectives from the following outline. Keep these objectives in mind and, as you read the chapter section, search for the information that will enable you to meet each objective. Once you have finished a section, write out answers for its objectives.

The Nervous System (pp. 42–52)

1. Explain why psychologists are concerned with human biology.

2. Describe the structure of a neuron and the process by which an action potential is triggered.

3. Describe how nerve cells communicate and discuss the importance of neurotransmitters for human behavior.

4. Discuss the significance of endorphins and explain how drugs influence neurotransmitters.

5. Identify the major divisions of the nervous system and their primary functions, noting how information is carried throughout the system.

6. Describe the operation of reflexes in the spinal cord and neural networks in the brain.

7. Discuss the functioning of the endocrine system.

The Brain (pp. 52–72)

8. Identify and explain the methods used in studying the brain.

9. Describe the functions of structures within the brainstem, as well as those of the thalamus and cerebellum.

10. Describe the functions of the structures in the limbic system.

Programs 3 & 4: The Behaving Brain and The Responsive Brain

11. Describe the structure and functions of the cerebral cortex.

12. Discuss how damage to several different cortical areas can impair language functioning and outline the process by which the brain directs reading aloud.

Program Assignment

Read the following objectives before you watch Programs 3 and 4 on the nervous system and the brain. As you watch, be alert for information that will help you answer each objective. Taking notes during the programs will help you to formulate your answers later. After the programs, write answers to the objectives. If you have access to the programs on videotape, you may replay portions of them if you need to refresh your memory.

Program 3

1. Identify the major functions of nerve cells and differentiate between excitatory and inhibitory mechanisms in neural transmission.

2. State the major assumption guiding the new field of neuroscience.

3. Explain the science of neurometrics and state several of its recent discoveries.

4. Discuss recent research findings concerning the impact of brain chemicals and drugs on learning and memory.

5. Discuss the findings of recent studies involving brain tissue transplants and state their possible significance for humans.

Program 4

Philip Zimbardo's description of brain structures is covered in the textbook assignment (questions 9–11 of the guided study).

6. Contrast the dispositions of people who are comfortable with touching others with those of people who are not.

7. State the results of Dr. Tiffany Field's studies of touch stimulation with premature infants.

8. Discuss the detrimental effects on children of being deprived of normal emotional stimulation.

9. Describe the findings of Dr. Saul Schanberg's studies of touch deprivation on laboratory animals.

Programs 3 & 4: The Behaving Brain and The Responsive Brain

10. Discuss the impact on rats' brains of being raised in an enriched, stimulating environment.

11. Describe the effects of stress on the brain as demonstrated in laboratory studies with animals and explain Michael Meaney's hypothesis regarding the relationship between an individual's ability to cope with stress and intellectual functioning during later life.

12. Explain the meaning of "survival of the fittest" and give an example of this principle.

13. Describe the impact of social success on the brain and body of the African cichlid fish.

14. Discuss Robert Sapolsky's research findings regarding the impact of social rank on baboon health.

PROGRESS TEST

Circle your answers to the following questions and check them with the answers on page 60. If your answer is incorrect, read the explanation for why it is incorrect and then consult the appropriate pages of the text (in parentheses following the correct answer).

The Nervous System

1. In a resting state, the axon:
   a. is depolarized, with mostly negatively charged ions outside and positively charged ions inside.
   b. is depolarized, with mostly positively charged ions outside and negatively charged ions inside.
   c. is polarized, with mostly negatively charged ions outside and positively charged ions inside.
   d. is polarized, with mostly positively charged ions outside and negatively charged ions inside.

2. Heartbeat, digestion, glandular activity, and other self-regulating bodily functions are governed by the:
   a. voluntary nervous system.
   b. autonomic nervous system.
   c. sympathetic division of the autonomic nervous system.
   d. skeletal nervous system.

3. The part of the neuron that generally carries messages away from the soma is the:
   a. dendrite.
   b. myelin sheath.
   c. synapse.
   d. axon.

4. Which is the correct sequence in the transmission of a neural impulse?
   a. axon → dendrite → cell body → synapse
   b. dendrite → axon → cell body → synapse
   c. dendrite → cell body → axon → synapse
   d. axon → synapse → cell body → dendrite

5. A strong stimulus can increase the:
   a. speed of the impulse the neuron fires.
   b. intensity of the impulse the neuron fires.
   c. number of times the neuron fires.
   d. threshold that must be reached before the neuron fires.

6. The pain of heroin withdrawal may be attributable to the fact that:
   a. under the influence of heroin, the brain ceases production of endorphins.
   b. under the influence of heroin, the brain ceases production of all neurotransmitters.
   c. during withdrawal, the brain's production of all neurotransmitters is greatly increased.
   d. heroin destroys endorphin receptors in the brain.

7. Which is the correct sequence in the transmission of a simple reflex?
   a. motor neuron → interneuron → sensory neuron
   b. interneuron → motor neuron → sensory neuron
   c. sensory neuron → interneuron → motor neuron
   d. interneuron → sensory neuron → motor neuron

8. Dr. Hernandez is studying neurotransmitter abnormalities in depressed patients. She would most likely describe herself as a:
   a. psychiatrist.
   b. clinical psychologist.
   c. psychoanalyst.
   d. biological psychologist.

9. Melissa is so elated after running a marathon that she feels little fatigue or discomfort. Her lack of pain is probably the result of the release of:
   a. acetylcholine.
   b. endorphins.
   c. dopamine.
   d. norepinephrine.

10. Voluntary movements, such as writing with a pencil, are directed by:
    a. the sympathetic nervous system.
    b. the skeletal nervous system.
    c. the parasympathetic nervous system.
    d. the autonomic nervous system.

11. A neuron will generate action potentials more often when it:
    a. remains below its threshold.
    b. receives an excitatory input.
    c. receives more excitatory than inhibitory inputs.
    d. is stimulated by a neurotransmitter.

12. When Sandy scalded her toe in a tub of hot water, the pain message was carried to her spinal cord by the _____ nervous system.
    a. skeletal
    b. sympathetic
    c. parasympathetic
    d. central

13. The myelin sheath that is present on some neurons:
    a. increases the speed of neural transmission.
    b. slows neural transmission.
    c. regulates the release of neurotransmitters.
    d. does a. and c.
    e. does b. and c.

14. The neurotransmitter acetylcholine (ACh) is most likely to be found:
    a. at the junction between sensory neurons and muscle fibers.
    b. at the junction between motor neurons and muscle fibers.
    c. at junctions between interneurons.
    d. in all of the above locations.

15. The junction at which neural impulses communicate is called a:
    a. synapse.
    b. dendrite.
    c. myelin sheath.
    d. neurotransmitter.

16. A neuroscientist would be more likely to study:
    a. how you learn to express emotions.
    b. how to help people overcome emotional disorders.
    c. life-span changes in the expression of emotion.
    d. the chemical changes that accompany emotions.

17. Parkinson's disease and Alzheimer's disease involve:
    a. a degeneration of brain tissue that produces vital neurotransmitters.
    b. impaired function in the right hemisphere only.
    c. impaired function in the left hemisphere only.
    d. excess production of the neurotransmitters dopamine and acetylcholine.

18. Epinephrine and norepinephrine are _____ that are released by the _____ gland.
    a. neurotransmitters; pituitary
    b. hormones; pituitary
    c. neurotransmitters; adrenal
    d. hormones; adrenal

19. Which of the following is *not* one of the ways that drugs influence neural transmission?
    a. Drugs may cause the brain to stop producing certain neurotransmitters.
    b. Drugs may mimic a particular neurotransmitter.
    c. Drugs may block a particular neurotransmitter.
    d. Drugs may disrupt a neuron's all-or-none firing pattern.

20. You are able to pull your hand quickly away from hot water before a sensation of pain is felt because:
    a. movement of the hand is a reflex that involves intervention of the spinal cord only.
    b. movement of the hand does not require intervention by the central nervous system.
    c. the brain reacts quickly to prevent severe injury.
    d. the autonomic nervous system intervenes to speed contraction of the muscles of the hand.

21. In research conducted by neuroscientist Joseph Martinez, what effect did the drug scopolamine have on brain functioning?
    a. It enabled the rats to learn the task more quickly.
    b. It disrupted the rats' memory of a recently learned task.
    c. It produced physical tremors similar to those that accompany Parkinson's disease.
    d. It had no effect.

22. I am a relatively slow-acting (but long-lasting) chemical messenger carried throughout the body by the bloodstream. What am I?
    a. a hormone
    b. a neurotransmitter
    c. acetylcholine
    d. dopamine

23. The effect of a drug that is an agonist is to:
    a. cause the brain to stop producing certain neurotransmitters.
    b. mimic a particular neurotransmitter.
    c. block a particular neurotransmitter.
    d. disrupt a neuron's all-or-none firing pattern.

The Brain

1. Which of the following was a major problem with phrenology?
    a. It was "ahead of its time" and no one believed it could be true.
    b. The brain is not neatly organized into structures that correspond to our categories of behavior.
    c. The brains of humans and animals are much less similar than the theory implied.
    d. All of the above were problems with phrenology.

2. In the brain, learning occurs as experience strengthens certain connections in cell work groups called:
    a. action potentials.
    b. neural networks.
    c. synaptic gaps.
    d. dendrites.

3. The new science of neurometrics:
   a. measures patterns of electrical activity in different parts of the brain.
   b. has described the abnormal electrical patterns of brain activity that occur in schizophrenia, depression, and alcoholism.
   c. has found that even "normal" brains sometimes temporarily enter abnormal electrical states.
   d. has discovered all of the above.

4. Neuroscientist Fred Gage has improved the ability of aged laboratory rats to learn and remember simple tasks by:
   a. using the drug physostigmine to block the activity of the neurotransmitter acetylcholine.
   b. grafting healthy young nerve cells onto damaged areas of the aged rats' brains.
   c. increasing the level of endorphins in the rats' brains.
   d. having them housed with younger rats.

5. Which of the following is the *newest* method of probing the inner structure and function of the brain?
   a. the EEG
   b. brain imaging
   c. electrical and chemical stimulation
   d. lesioning

6. The brain research technique that involves monitoring the brain's usage of glucose is called the:
   a. PET scan.
   b. CT scan.
   c. EEG.
   d. MRI.

7. Cortical areas that are not primarily concerned with sensory, motor, or language functions are:
   a. called projection areas.
   b. called association areas.
   c. located mostly in the parietal lobe.
   d. located mostly in the temporal lobe.

8. Professor Zimbardo states that the relationship between the brain and behavior is reciprocal. By this he means that:
   a. our behavior selects the experiences that shape the brain.
   b. the brain controls behavior, but behavior also feeds back information to influence the brain.
   c. the brain and behavior are both in a constant state of flux.
   d. all of the above are true.

9. In one study both men and women were gently touched by a nurse just before an operation. The effect of the nurse's touch was to:
   a. lower blood pressure and anxiety in men but not women.
   b. lower blood pressure and anxiety in women but not men.
   c. lower blood pressure and anxiety in both women and men.
   d. raise blood pressure and anxiety in both women and men.

10. Damage to _____ will usually cause a person to lose the ability to comprehend language.
    a. the angular gyrus
    b. Broca's area
    c. Wernicke's area
    d. frontal lobe association areas

11. As the brain evolved, the increasing complexity of animals' behavior was accompanied by a(n):
    a. increase in the size of the brainstem.
    b. decrease in the ratio of brain to body weight.
    c. increase in the size of the frontal lobes.
    d. increase in the amount of association area.

12. Regardless of gender, people who are comfortable touching others tend to be:
    a. more cheerful.
    b. less conforming.
    c. less suspicious of others' motives.
    d. all of the above.

13. In a study conducted by Tiffany Field, premature infants who received daily massage:
    a. cried more than infants who were not massaged.
    b. were less active than infants who were not massaged.
    c. at 8 months showed better cognitive and motor development than infants who were not massaged.
    d. did all of the above.

14. In his work with laboratory rats, Saul Schanberg found that:
    a. infant rats who were isolated from their mothers had lower levels of an enzyme important for growth and development.
    b. touch is less important for rats during infancy than it is for human infants.
    c. rats raised in deprived social environments developed thinner cortexes than those raised in normal environments.
    d. a rat's social rank is strongly correlated with its physical health.

15. The visual cortex is located in the:
    a. occipital lobe.
    b. temporal lobe.
    c. frontal lobe.
    d. parietal lobe.

16. Psychosocial dwarfism has been attributed to a failure on the part of the:
    a. amygdala.
    b. cortex.
    c. hypothalamus.
    d. adrenal gland.

17. Beginning at the front of the brain and working backward then down and around, which of the following is the correct order of cortical regions?
    a. occipital lobe, temporal lobe, parietal lobe, frontal lobe
    b. temporal lobe, frontal lobe, parietal lobe, occipital lobe
    c. frontal lobe, occipital lobe, temporal lobe, parietal lobe
    d. frontal lobe, parietal lobe, occipital lobe, temporal lobe

18. Following a gunshot wound to his head, Jack became more uninhibited, irritable, and profane. It is likely that his personality change was the result of injury to his:
    a. parietal lobe.
    b. temporal lobe.
    c. occipital lobe.
    d. frontal lobe.

19. In order to pinpoint the location of a tumor, a neurosurgeon electrically stimulated parts of the patient's sensory cortex. If the patient was conscious during the procedure, which of the following was probably experienced?

a. "hearing" faint sounds
   b. "seeing" random visual patterns
   c. movement of the arms or legs
   d. a sense of having the skin touched

20. Institutionalized infants who are deprived of a normal, loving environment:
    a. often suffer from psychosocial dwarfism.
    b. often are smaller in stature than nondeprived infants.
    c. begin to grow at a faster rate when placed in loving families.
    d. do all of the above.

21. Rats raised in deprived, uninteresting environments:
    a. are superior learners as adults.
    b. develop thicker cortexes, especially in the occipital area.
    c. have more spines on their dendrites.
    d. have none of the above.

22. In response to stress, the brain's production of _____ is increased, the effect of which is to _____ .
    a. glucocorticoids; mobilize the body's resources to meet the demands of the stressor
    b. glucocorticoids; decrease the body's resistance to illness
    c. endorphins; mobilize the body's resources to meet the demands of a stressor
    d. endorphins; decrease the body's resistance to illness

23. Extensive exposure to glucocorticoids has been shown to:
    a. destroy certain neurons in the hippocampus of the brain.
    b. increase an animal's resistance to disease.
    c. enhance an animal's social status in the wild.
    d. block transmission of neurotransmitters.

24. In Michael Meaney's research, rats who were not handled at an early age:
    a. had greater deficits in learning and memory skills in later life.
    b. had a lower glucocorticoid response to stress than rats who were handled.
    c. had less loss of neurons in the hippocampus.
    d. had a greater ability to cope with stress than those who were handled.

25. A stroke leaves a patient paralyzed on the left side of the body. Which region of the brain has been damaged?
    a. the reticular formation
    b. the limbic system
    c. the left hemisphere
    d. the right hemisphere

26. Raccoons have much more precise control of their paws than dogs. You would expect that raccoons have more cortical space dedicated to "paw control" in the _____ of their brains.
    a. frontal lobes
    b. parietal lobes
    c. temporal lobes
    d. occipital lobes

27. Dr. Meaney speculates that individual differences in intellectual functioning among elderly people may be directly related to:
    a. individual differences in their abilities to cope with stress.

b. the network of social support they are able to bring to bear in response to a stressor.
c. their overall physical health.
d. their social status.

28. Following Jayshree's near-fatal car accident, her physician noticed that the pupillary reflex of her eyes was abnormal. This may indicate that Jayshree's _____ was (were) damaged in the accident.
   a. skeletal nervous system
   b. autonomic nervous system
   c. interneurons
   d. endocrine system

29. Although there is no single "control center" for emotions, their regulation is primarily attributed to the brain region known as the:
   a. limbic system.
   b. reticular formation.
   c. brainstem.
   d. cerebral cortex.

30. Your brother has been taking prescription medicine and experiencing a number of unpleasant side effects, including unusually rapid heartbeat and excessive perspiration. It is likely that the medication is exaggerating activity in the:
   a. skeletal nervous system.
   b. sympathetic nervous system.
   c. parasympathetic nervous system.
   d. pituitary gland.

31. A bodybuilder friend of yours suddenly seems to have grown several inches in height. You suspect that your friend has been using drugs that affect the:
   a. pituitary gland.
   b. sympathetic nervous system.
   c. adrenal glands.
   d. parasympathetic nervous system.

32. In Charles Darwin's theory of evolution, survival of the fittest refers to
   a. survival of the individual.
   b. survival of the group or species.
   c. the fact that the strongest animals survive.
   d. the fact that animals who are able to maintain the largest territories have the most offspring.

33. In his studies of African fish, Russell Fernald found that territorial males who are socially dominant:
   a. grow larger testes filled with mature sperm.
   b. remain socially dominant for life.
   c. have smaller brain nuclei in a specific brain region near the hypothalamus.
   d. lose the distinctive coloration of subordinate males.

34. In order of increasing evolutionary complexity, the three brain structures are:
   a. cerebrum, brainstem, limbic system.
   b. brainstem, limbic system, cerebrum.
   c. limbic system, brainstem, cerebrum.
   d. limbic system, cerebrum, brainstem.

35. Jessica experiences difficulty keeping her balance after receiving a blow to the back of her head. It is likely that she injured her:

a. medulla.
b. thalamus.
c. hypothalamus.
d. cerebellum.

36. A scientist from another planet wishes to study the simplest brain mechanisms underlying emotion and memory. You recommend that the scientist study the:
   a. brainstem.
   b. limbic system.
   c. cerebrum.
   d. cortex.

37. Researcher Robert Sapolsky has found that baboons who have high ranks in the troop's social hierarchy:
   a. have high rank because they are physically healthier than others in the troop.
   b. become healthier, particularly if their dominance is achieved in part through cooperation and affiliation with others in the troop.
   c. have the most stressful lives of any in the troop.
   d. are more likely to develop stress-related illnesses.

38. "Top management" in the hierarchy of all the brain's activities takes place in the:
   a. hippocampus.
   b. amygdala.
   c. cerebrum.
   d. cerebral cortex.

In the diagrams to the right, the numbers refer to brain locations that have been damaged. Match each location with its probable effect on behavior.

Location   Behavioral Effect

_____ 1.   a. vision disorder
_____ 2.   b. insensitivity to touch
                 c. motor paralysis
_____ 3.   d. hearing problem
_____ 4.   e. lack of coordination
                 f. abnormal hunger
_____ 5.   g. sleep/arousal
_____ 6.   disorder
                 h. loss of smell
_____ 7.   i. loss of taste
_____ 8.   j. altered personality

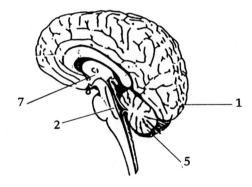

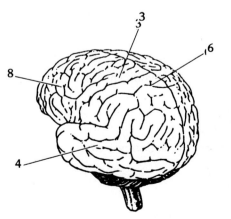

MATCHING ITEMS

Match each structure with its corresponding function or description.

Structures   *Functions or Descriptions*

_____ 1. hypothalamus
_____ 2. frontal lobe
_____ 3. parietal lobe
_____ 4. temporal lobe
_____ 5. reticular formation
_____ 6. occipital lobe
_____ 7. thalamus
_____ 8. corpus callosum
_____ 9. cerebellum
_____ 10. amygdala
_____ 11. medulla

a. includes auditory areas
b. includes visual areas
c. serves as sensory switchboard
d. contains pleasure centers
e. includes sensory cortex
f. includes motor cortex
g. controls arousal
h. links cerebral hemispheres
i. elicits rage and fear
j. regulates breathing and heartbeat
k. enables coordinated movement

KEY TERMS

Using your own words, write a brief definition or explanation of each of the following.

The Nervous System

Textbook Terms

1. biological psychology

2. neuron

3. dendrites

4. axon

5. myelin sheath

6. action potential

7. threshold

8. synapse

9. neurotransmitter

10. acetylcholine (ACh)

11. endorphins

12. nervous system

13. central nervous system

14. peripheral nervous system

15. nerves

16. sensory neurons

17. interneurons

18. motor neurons

19. skeletal nervous system

20. autonomic nervous system

21. sympathetic nervous system

22. parasympathetic nervous system

23. reflex

24. neural network

25. endocrine system

26. hormones

27. adrenal glands

28. pituitary gland

Program Terms
29. glial cells

30. cell body (soma)

31. terminal buttons

32. Parkinson's disease

The Brain

Textbook Terms

1. lesion

2. electroencephalogram (EEG)

3. CT (computed tomograph) scan

4. PET (positron emission tomograph) scan

5. MRI (magnetic resonance imaging)

6. brainstem

7. medulla

8. reticular formation

9. thalamus

10. cerebellum

11. limbic system

12. amygdala

13. hypothalamus

14. cerebral cortex

15. frontal lobes

16. parietal lobes

17. occipital lobes

18. temporal lobes

19. motor cortex

20. sensory cortex

21. association areas

22. aphasia

23. Broca's area

24. Wernicke's area

Program Terms
25. neuroscientist

26. brain imaging

27. neurometrics

28. neuronal implantation

29. glucocorticoids

30. psychosocial dwarfism

31. neuroethologist

ANSWERS

Guided Study

The following guidelines provide the main points that your answers should have touched upon.

Textbook Assignment

The Nervous System

1. Biological processes underlie every aspect of our behavior and mental processes. By studying the links between biology and psychology, *biological psychologists* achieve a greater understanding of such basic behaviors as sleep, hunger, and sex, and gain new insights into how best to treat stress, disease, depression, and other human conditions.

2. Each neuron consists of a cell body, branching fibers called dendrites that receive information from other neurons, and an extension fiber called an axon through which the neuron passes information to other neurons or to muscles or glands. Some axons are insulated with a myelin sheath, which helps speed neural impulses.

    A neural impulse, or action potential, occurs if the excitatory signals minus the inhibitory signals received by the neuron on its dendrites or cell body exceeds the neuron's threshold. Then, the gates in the axon open, allowing positively charged ions to rush inside. This depolarizes that part of the axon, which causes the axon's next channel to open and leads to the electrical chain reaction by which an electrical charge travels down the axon into junctions with other neurons and with the muscles and glands of the body.

3. When an action potential reaches the end of the axon, chemical messengers called neurotransmitters are released into the synaptic gap between the sending and receiving neuron. This junction is called a synapse. Neurotransmitter molecules bind to receptor sites on the receiving neuron and have either an excitatory or inhibitory influence on that neuron's tendency to generate its own action potential. If the receiving neuron receives more excitatory than inhibitory inputs, more neural impulses are generated.

    A particular neural pathway may use only one or two neurotransmitters, each of which may have a specific effect on behavior. Acetylcholine, for example, is the neurotransmitter at every synapse between a motor neuron and a muscle.

4. Endorphins are morphinelike neurotransmitters found in the brain that are released in response to pain and vigorous exercise. The existence of endorphins may help explain good feelings such as the "runner's high," the painkilling effects of acupuncture, and the indifference to pain in some injured people.

    Drugs have a number of different effects on neurotransmitters. Some drugs (agonists) mimic a particular neurotransmitter; some (antagonists) block a neurotransmitter. Others interfere with the breakdown or reabsorption of the neurotransmitter. Opiate drugs, for example, may cause the brain to stop producing endorphins.

5. The central nervous system includes all the neurons in the brain and spinal cord. The peripheral nervous system, which links the central nervous system with the body's sense receptors, muscles, and glands, has two divisions: skeletal and autonomic. The skeletal nervous system controls the voluntary movements of the skeletal muscles.

The autonomic nervous system, which influences the glands and muscles of our internal organs, also is a dual system. The sympathetic nervous system arouses the body during emergencies by accelerating heartbeat, slowing digestion, raising blood sugar, dilating arteries, and creating perspiration. When the emergency has passed, the parasympathetic nervous system relaxes the body by producing the opposite effects.

Sensory neurons relay information from the body's tissues and sensory organs to the brain and spinal cord. Interneurons of the brain and spinal cord (the central nervous system) are involved in processing this information from the sensory neurons. The central nervous system then sends instructions to the body's tissues by means of the motor neurons.

6. Reflexes, which are automatic responses to stimuli, are governed by the simplest neural connections. In response to a painful stimulus to the fingertips, for example, a sensory neuron conveys the message to an interneuron in the spinal cord. The interneuron triggers an action potential in motor neurons that cause muscles of your arm to jerk your hand away.

   To enable complex operations, the neurons in the brain cluster into work groups called neural networks. Each cell in a given layer of the network connects with various cells in the next layer.

7. The endocrine system is a relatively slow-acting chemical communication system of glands that secrete hormones influencing growth, reproduction, metabolism, mood, and reactions to stress. For example, the adrenal glands release epinephrine (adrenaline) and norepinephrine (noradrenaline) during emergencies. These hormones provide a source of energy by increasing heart rate, blood pressure, and blood sugar. The pituitary gland, located in the base of the brain, releases hormones that influence growth and the release of hormones by other glands. It forms an elaborate feedback system with the brain in its influence on behavior.

The Brain

8. The oldest method of studying the brain is by observing the effects of brain disease and injuries. More recently, electrical, chemical, or magnetic stimulation in humans and surgical lesions of brain tissue in animals have been used to study the brain. Another technique, the electroencephalogram (EEG), is a recording of the brain's electrical activity from electrodes placed on its surface. Scientists also examine the brain with CT (computed tomograph) scans, PET (positron emission tomograph) scans, and magnetic resonance imaging (MRI). Although the text discusses the use of scanning and imaging on the brain only, these techniques are also used to diagnose problems elsewhere in the body.

9. The brainstem is the oldest and innermost region of the brain. It begins where the spinal cord enters the skull and contains the medulla and reticular formation. The medulla controls breathing and heartbeat and is the point where nerves to and from each side of the brain cross over to connect with the opposite side of the body. The reticular formation helps control arousal. The thalamus serves as the brain's sensory switchboard, routing information from sensory neurons to higher brain regions dealing with seeing, hearing, tasting, and touching. The cerebellum influences learning and memory; its most obvious function is coordinating voluntary movement.

10. In the limbic system, the hippocampus processes memory. The amygdala influences aggression and fear. When this region is surgically lesioned, aggressive behavior in animals is diminished. When one region of the amygdala is electrically stimulated, a normally placid domestic animal will

behave aggressively; when another area is stimulated, the animal will display signs of fear.

The hypothalamus contains neurons that regulate hunger, thirst, body temperature, and sexual behavior; it also contains the so-called "pleasure centers." The hypothalamus also secretes hormones that control the pituitary gland, which influences hormone release by other glands, which the hypothalamus monitors.

11. The cerebral cortex is a thin sheet of nerve cells covering the left and right cerebral hemispheres. Each hemisphere is divided into four regions called lobes: frontal, parietal, temporal, and occipital. The frontal lobes control movement through the motor cortex and contain association areas that are involved in making plans and judgments. When specific parts of the motor cortex in the left and right hemispheres are electrically stimulated, movement is triggered in specific body parts on the opposite side of the body.

    The parietal lobes house the sensory cortex which, when electrically stimulated, triggers a sense of a particular body part having been touched. The more sensitive a body region, the greater the area of sensory cortex that is devoted to it.

    The temporal lobes receive auditory information primarily from the opposite ear, and the occipital lobes similarly receive input from the eyes.

    Approximately three-fourths of the cortex consists of uncommitted association areas that communicate with one another and with neurons of the sensory and motor areas. Association areas influence personality, recognition of faces, and many other "higher" mental abilities.

12. Damage to any one of several areas of the cortex can cause aphasia, an impaired use of language. Damage to Broca's area in the left frontal lobe disrupts speaking. Damage to Wernicke's area in the left temporal lobe disrupts language comprehension and leaves people able to speak words but in a meaningless way. Damage to the angular gyrus will disrupt the ability to read aloud.

    When you read aloud, words are registered in the visual area of the cortex and then relayed to the angular gyrus, which transforms the words into an auditory code. This code is comprehended by Wernicke's area and then sent to Broca's area, which directs the motor cortex to produce speech.

Program Assignment

Program 3

1. There are about 10 trillion cells in the brain. These cells, called neurons and glial cells, are designed to do three things: receive information from other cells, process it, and then transmit it to the rest of the body. The constant flow of nerve impulses and transmitter chemicals throughout the body gives human behavior its incredible complexity. These impulses regulate our metabolism, temperature, and respiration, *and* enable us to learn, remember, and make decisions.

2. Neuroscientists—who have been drawn from many fields, including psychology—are guided by the assumption that everything the brain does is explainable by biological and chemical events taking place within it. For these researchers, understanding behavior means knowing its biological foundations.

3. Neurometrics, as described by E. Roy John, uses computers to quantitatively describe normal electrical activity in the brain. An individual's brain electrical activity is then statistically compared with these normative data to reveal abnormal electrical transactions between different regions of the

brain. Brain activity within a particular anatomical region is color-coded to indicate normal, excessive, or deficient electrical activity. Neurometrics has identified abnormal electrical patterns that accompany many major psychiatric disorders, including depression, dementia, schizophrenia, and alcoholism.

4. By manipulating brain neurotransmitters, researchers have been able to coax the brain to either forget or remember an experience. Recently formed memories are not permanent. Therefore, before experiences are converted into long-term memory, injecting a drug such as scopolamine will disrupt the memory by blocking the receptor sites for the neurotransmitter acetylcholine. In contrast, the drug physostigmine blocks an enzyme that breaks down acetylcholine, effectively increasing the availability of this neurotransmitter at the synapse. The impact of this treatment is to enhance the memory. Because acetylcholine is significantly reduced in people with Alzheimer's disease, there is hope that by understanding this chemical system, drugs that can help such patients will be developed.

5. Researchers are investigating whether damaged, diseased, and senile brains can be rejuvenated. Neuroscientist Fred Gage has found that grafting healthy brain tissue onto damaged brain areas of aged laboratory rats can dramatically improve their ability to learn and remember simple tasks. Another example concerns Parkinson's disease, a degenerative disorder caused by a loss of dopamine-producing brain cells. Animals in which this condition has been created have shown improvement after researchers transplanted healthy dopamine-producing cells into the damaged areas. Experimentation with human tissue transplants is currently underway.

Program 4

6. Regardless of gender, those who are comfortable with touching others are more cheerful, less conforming, and less suspicious of others' motives. Those who are uncomfortable tend to have lower self-esteem and are generally more socially withdrawn.

7. Premature infants who received daily 45-minute massages for 10 days prior to discharge gained 47 percent more weight, were more active, and more alert than babies who were not massaged. At 8 months, the massaged babies still showed a weight advantage. In addition, their cognitive and motor skills were more advanced.

8. John Bowlby and Renée Spitz found that the rate of growth of institutionalized children was significantly below the normal range for their age groups. Because physical growth is affected by psychological experience, this phenomenon is called psychosocial dwarfism. The mechanism seems to be the failure of the brain's hypothalamus, which normally stimulates the pituitary gland to secrete growth hormones. When children are placed with a loving family, they begin to return to normal size, sometimes growing at a rate as great as 8 inches per year.

9. Working with laboratory rats, Saul Schanberg has shown that a mother's touch is essential to maintain normal growth and development. When rat babies were removed from the mother even for short periods of time, the amount of enzyme ODC, which is crucial for growth, declined precipitously. The effects of deprivation were reversed only by touch, either from the mother or a technician stroking the rat pups with a brush.

10. Researcher Mark Rosenzweig found that rats raised in enriched environments grew larger brains, especially in the area of the occipital cortex where vision is processed. These rats also had a greater number of certain

neurotransmitters, and more and larger spines on the dendrites—the branch fibers of neurons that receive signals from other neurons.

11. Developmental psychologist Michael Meaney has found that stress causes an increase in hormones called glucocorticoids. The short-term effect of these hormones is to increase heart rate and blood pressure and better enable the animal to cope with the stressor. Extensive exposure to glucocorticoids, however, may actually destroy brain cells, specifically those in the hippocampus, a structure critical for learning and memory. Meaney has found that aged animals with degeneration in this area often have deficits in learning and memory. During later life, animals who were handled regularly during infancy were more immune to the degeneration of neurons, perhaps because they were better able to "turn off" the maladaptive hormonal response to stress.

   Meaney speculates that individual differences in intellectual functioning among elderly people may be related to differences in their ability to cope with stress. Those who show intellectual impairments at 55 to 60 years of age may be less capable of dealing with stressors, and therefore more likely to show stress-related glucocorticoid exposure, loss of hippocampal cells, and the cognitive impairments that derive from this damage.

12. The best example of the brain altering its structure and functioning in response to social situations can be seen when the brain works together with evolution to ensure the survival of the species. In his theory of evolution, Charles Darwin pointed out that animals who are the best able to adapt to the challenges of their environment pass on their genes to their offspring. Within any species it is not survival of the individual that matters, but survival of the group. For example, birds that sound alarm calls when enemies are near threaten their own lives but increase the survival chances of their relatives.

13. Neuroethologist Russell Fernald has studied the African cichlid fish as an example of how the brain is altered when behavior changes. The social system among these fish is based upon territoriality, with visual cues serving an important communicative function. When males acquire territory, changes in their brains trigger the fish's testes to grow rapidly and become full of sperm. At the same time, the body changes color and the underlying brain regions grow. These physical changes quickly disappear when a male loses his territory.

14. Sapolsky has found that baboons become much healthier after they have attained high social rank. More generally, he has found that animals' cholesterol level, immune functioning, and hormonal response to stress all vary with their social rank. Sapolsky has further found that an animal's style in attaining social dominance has a lot to do with its health. Those who attain their status by cooperating with other animals and forging alliances fare better than those who are dominant, but socially isolated.

Progress Test

The Nervous System

1. **d.** is the answer. (p. 43)

2. **b.** is the answer. The autonomic nervous system controls internal functioning, including heartbeat, digestion, and glandular activity. (p. 48)

   a. The functions mentioned are all automatic, not voluntary, so this answer cannot be correct.

c. This answer is incorrect because most organs are affected by both divisions of the autonomic nervous system.

d. The skeletal nervous system transmits sensory input to the central nervous system and directs the movements of skeletal muscles.

3. **d.** is the answer. (video; p. 42)

   a. The dendrite is the part of the neuron that receives information from other neurons.

   b. The myelin sheath insulates some axons and helps speed neural impulses, but it is the axon itself that carries neural messages.

   c. A synapse is a junction between two neurons, not part of either neuron's structure.

4. **c.** is the answer. A neuron receives incoming stimuli on its dendrites and cell body. These electrochemical signals are combined in the cell body, generating an impulse that travels down the axon, causing the release of neurotransmitter substances into the synaptic cleft or gap. (video; p. 43)

5. **c.** is the answer. Stimulus strength can affect only the number of times a neuron fires or the number of neurons that fire. (p. 44)

   a., b., & d. These answers are incorrect because firing is an all-or-none response, so intensity remains the same regardless of stimulus strength. Nor can stimulus strength change the neuronal threshold or the impulse speed.

6. **a.** is the answer. Endorphins are neurotransmitters that function as natural painkillers. When the body has a supply of artificial painkillers like heroin, endorphin production stops. (p. 46)

   b. The production of neurotransmitters other than endorphins does not cease.

   c. Neurotransmitter production does not increase during withdrawal.

   d. Heroin makes use of the same receptor sites as endorphins.

7. **c.** is the answer. In a simple reflex, a sensory neuron carries the message that a sensory receptor has been stimulated to an interneuron in the spinal cord. The interneuron responds by activating motor neurons that will enable the appropriate response. (p. 49)

8. **d.** is the answer. Biological psychologists study the links between biology (in this case, neurotransmitters) and psychology (depression, in this example). (p. 42)

   a., b., & c. These mental health professionals are more involved in the *treatment* of troubled behavior than in research.

9. **b.** is the answer. Endorphins are neurotransmitters that function as natural painkillers and are evidently involved in the "runner's high" and other situations in which discomfort or fatigue are expected but not experienced. (video; p. 46)

   a. Acetylcholine (ACh) is a neurotransmitter involved in muscular control.

   c. Dopamine is a neurotransmitter involved in, among other things, motor control.

   d. Norepinephrine is an adrenal hormone released to help us respond in moments of danger.

10. **b.** is the answer. (p. 48)

   a., c., & d. The autonomic nervous system, which is divided into the sympathetic and parasympathetic divisions, is concerned with regulating basic bodily maintenance functions.

11. **c.** is the answer. (p. 44)

   a. An action potential will occur only when the neuron's threshold is *exceeded*.

   b. An excitatory input that does not reach the neuron's threshold will not trigger an action potential.

   d. This answer is incorrect because some neurotransmitters inhibit a neuron's readiness to fire.

12. **a.** is the answer. Sensory neurons in the skeletal nervous system relay such messages. (p. 48)

   b. & c. These divisions of the autonomic nervous system are concerned with the regulation of bodily maintenance functions such as heartbeat, digestion, and glandular activity.

   d. The spinal cord itself is part of the central nervous system, but the message is carried to the spinal cord by the skeletal division of the peripheral nervous system.

13. **a.** is the answer. (p. 42)

   b. The myelin sheath speeds rather than slows neural transmission.

   c., d., & e. Myelin sheaths are not involved in regulating the release of neurotransmitters.

14. **b.** is the answer. ACh is a neurotransmitter that causes the contraction of muscle fibers when stimulated by motor neurons. This function explains its location. (p. 45)

   a. & c. Sensory neurons and interneurons do not directly stimulate muscle fibers.

15. **a.** is the answer. (video; p. 44)

   b. Dendrites are the neuron extensions that receive incoming signals from other neurons.

   c. The myelin sheath is a layer of fatty cells covering many axons that speeds neural impulses.

   d. Neurotransmitters are chemical messengers that cross the synaptic gap between neurons.

16. **d.** is the answer. Neuroscientists study the links between biology (chemical changes in this example) and behavior (emotions in this example). (video)

   a., b., & c. Developmental, experimental, and clinical psychologists would be more concerned with life-span changes in emotions, learning of emotional expressions, and the treatment of emotional disorders, respectively.

17. **a.** is the answer. Parkinson's and Alzheimer's cause degeneration of brain tissue that produces dopamine and acetylcholine, respectively. (video)

   b. & c. These diseases affect both hemispheres of the cortex.

   d. These diseases cause insufficient production of the neurotransmitters.

18. **d.** is the answer. Also known as adrenaline and noradrenaline, epinephrine and norepinephrine are hormones released by the adrenal glands. (p. 51)

19. **d.** is the answer, by elimination. (p. 47)

a., b., & c. Various drugs have each of these influences on neural transmission. For example, heroin causes the brain to stop producing endorphins.

20. **a.** is the answer. Because this reflex is an automatic response and involves only the spinal cord, the hand is jerked away before the brain has even received the information that causes the sensation of pain. (p. 49)

b. The spinal cord, which organizes simple reflexes such as this one, is part of the central nervous system.

c. The brain is not involved in directing spinal reflexes.

d. The autonomic nervous system controls the glands and the muscles of the internal organs; it does not influence the skeletal muscles controlling the hand.

21. **b.** is the answer. (video)

22. **a.** is the answer. (p. 50)

b., c., & d. Acetylcholine and dopamine are fast-acting neurotransmitters released at synapses, not in the bloodstream.

23. **b.** is the answer. (p. 46)

a. Abuse of certain drugs, such as heroin, may have this effect.

c. This describes the effect of an antagonist.

d. Drugs do not have this effect on neurons.

The Brain

1. **b.** is the answer. (p. 42)

a. "Ahead of its time" implies that the theory had merit, which later research clearly showed it did not. Moreover, phrenology was accepted as an accurate theory of brain organization by many scientists.

c. Phrenology said nothing about the similarities of human and animal brains.

2. **b.** is the answer. (p. 50)

a. Action potentials are neural impulses that occur in all forms of communication in the nervous system.

c. Synaptic gaps are the spaces between neurons.

d. Dendrites are the branching extensions of neurons that receive messages from other nerve cells.

3. **d.** is the answer. (video)

4. **b.** is the answer. (video)

5. **b.** is the answer. (video)

6. **a.** is the answer. The PET scan measures glucose consumption in different areas of the brain to determine their levels of activity. (p. 53)

b. The CT scan is a series of x-rays taken from different positions and then analyzed by a computer to create an image representing a slice through the brain.

c. The EEG is a measure of electrical activity in the brain.

d. MRI uses magnetic fields and radio signals to produce computer-generated images of soft tissues of the body.

7. **b.** is the answer. Association areas interpret, integrate, and act on information from other areas of the cortex. (p. 62)

8. **b.** is the answer. (video)

9. **c.** is the answer. (video)

10. **c.** is the answer. Wernicke's area is involved in comprehension, and aphasics with damage to Wernicke's are unable to understand what is said to them. (p. 63)

    a. The angular gyrus translates printed words into speech sounds; damage would result in the inability to read.

    b. Broca's area is involved in the physical production of speech; damage would result in the inability to speak fluently.

    d. The association areas of the cortex are involved, among other things, in processing language; damage to these areas wouldn't specifically affect comprehension.

11. **d.** is the answer. As animals increase in complexity, there is an increase in the amount of association areas. (p. 62)

12. **d.** is the answer. (video)

13. **c.** is the answer. (video)

14. **a.** is the answer. (video)

    b. Touch is no less important for brain development in rats than it is for humans.

    c. This describes the results of Mark Rosenzweig's research.

    d. This describes the results of Robert Sapolsky's research with African baboons.

15. **a.** is the answer. The visual cortex is located at the very back of the brain. (p. 61)

16. **c.** is the answer. (video)

17. **d.** is the answer. The frontal lobe is in the front of the brain. Just behind is the parietal lobe. The occipital lobe is located at the very back of the head and just below the parietal lobe. Next to the occipital lobe and toward the front of the head is the temporal lobe. (p. 59)

18. **d.** is the answer. As demonstrated in the case of Phineas Gage, injury to the frontal lobe may produce such changes in personality. (p. 62)

    a. Damage to the parietal lobe might disrupt functions involving the sensory cortex.

    b. Damage to the temporal lobe might impair hearing.

    c. Occipital damage might impair vision.

19. **d.** is the answer. Stimulation of the sensory cortex elicits a sense of touch, as Penfield's experiments demonstrated. (p. 61)

    a., b., & c. Hearing, seeing, or movement might be expected if the temporal, occipital, or motor regions of the cortex, respectively, were stimulated.

20. **d.** is the answer. (video)

    a. & b. Answer b. is the definition of psychosocial dwarfism.

    c. Such children may grow as much as 8 inches per year.

21. **d.** is the answer. (video)

    a., b., & c. These are the effects of being raised in an *enriched*, stimulating environment.

22. **a.** is the answer. (video)

c. & d. Endorphins are neurotransmitters that mediate the body's response to painful stimuli.

23. **a.** is the answer. (video)

24. **a.** is the answer. (video)

   b., c., & d. Nonhandled rats had a *higher* glucocorticoid response to stress, a *greater* loss of hippocampal neurons, and a *reduced* ability to cope with stress.

25. **d.** is the answer. The motor cortex in each hemisphere controls movement on the opposite side of the body. If the left side is paralyzed, the damage occurred in the right hemisphere. (p. 60)

   a. The reticular formation is involved in arousal, not the control of movement.

   b. The limbic system regulates emotional states; it does not control movement.

   c. A stroke in the left hemisphere would result in paralysis on the right side of the body.

26. **a.** is the answer. The motor cortex, which determines the precision with which various parts of the body can be moved, is located in the frontal lobes. (p. 60)

   b. The parietal lobes contain the sensory cortex, which controls sensitivity to touch.

   c. The temporal lobes contain the primary projection areas for hearing and, on the left side, are also involved in language use.

   d. The occipital lobes contain the primary projection areas for vision.

27. **a.** is the answer. (video)

   b., c., & d. Although these are factors in a person's ability to cope with stress, they are not the focus of Dr. Meaney's hypothesis.

28. **b.** is the answer. Simple reflexes, such as this one, are governed by activity in the autonomic nervous system. (p. 48)

   a. The skeletal nervous system controls voluntary movements; it plays no role in the reflexive response of the pupils to light.

   c. Interneurons link sensory and motor neurons.

   d. The endocrine system consists of glands that secrete hormones into the bloodstream.

29. **a.** is the answer. (p. 56)

   b. The reticular formation is linked to arousal.

   c. The brainstem governs the mechanisms of basic survival—heartbeat and breathing—and has many other roles.

   d. The cerebral cortex governs the "higher" functions of the brain.

30. **b.** is the answer. Arousal of the sympathetic nervous system produces a number of effects, including accelerated heartbeat and excessive perspiration. (p. 48)

   a. The skeletal nervous system controls voluntary movements.

   c. Arousal of the parasympathetic nervous system would have effects opposite those stated.

   d. If the medication were affecting his pituitary gland, your brother might experience changes in his body's growth rate.

31. **a.** is the answer. Hormones of the pituitary gland regulate body growth. (p. 51)

    b. & d. These divisions of the autonomic nervous system are not involved in regulating body growth.

    c. The adrenal glands produce hormones that provide energy during emergencies; they are not involved in regulating body growth.

32. **b.** is the answer. (video)

    a. As illustrated in the alarm-calling example, animals often place their own welfare in jeopardy in order to ensure group survival.

    c. & d. Both of these emphasize survival of the individual rather than the species.

33. **a.** is the answer. (video)

    b. Fernald's research indicates that an animal's position in the dominance order frequently changes.

    c. Such animals have *larger* hypothalamic nuclei.

    d. The distinctive coloration of the African cichlid is characteristic of *dominant* males.

34. **b.** is the answer. The oldest region, the brainstem, is present even in lower vertebrates; the limbic system is found in all mammals; and the most recently evolved structure, the cortex, is found only in higher mammals. (pp. 54–55)

35. **d.** is the answer. The cerebellum is involved in the coordination of muscular movements. (video; p. 56)

    a. The medulla regulates breathing and heartbeat.

    b. The thalamus relays sensory inputs to the appropriate higher centers of the brain.

    c. The hypothalamus is concerned with the regulation of basic drives and emotions.

36. **b.** is the answer. The amygdala in the limbic system regulates fear and rage; the hippocampus plays an important role in memory. (video; p. 56)

    a. The brainstem controls vital functions such as breathing and heartbeat; it is not directly involved in either emotion or memory.

    c. & d. These answers are incorrect because the limbic system is an older brain structure than the cerebrum. Its involvement in emotion and memory is therefore more basic.

37. **b.** is the answer. (video)

    a. Sapolsky's research indicates that social success precedes, rather than follows, improved physical health.

    c. & d. Sapolsky's research did not find these to be true.

38. **d.** is the answer. (video; p. 58)

    a. & b. These limbic structures are involved in memory and emotion.

    c. "Cerebrum" simply refers to the two hemispheres of the brain. The outer covering of the cerebrum, the cortex, manages the activities of all lower regions of the brain.

Brain Damage Diagram (pp. 55–64)

1. a
2. h
3. c
4. d
5. e
6. b
7. f
8. j

Programs 3 & 4: The Behaving Brain and The Responsive Brain

Matching Items

1. d (p. 66)
2. f (p. 55)
3. e (p. 53)
4. a (p. 63)
5. g (p. 53)
6. b (p. 63)
7. c (p. 63)
8. h (p. 56)
9. k (p. 62)
10. i (p. 64)
11. j (p. 63)

Key Terms

The Nervous System

Textbook Terms

1. **Biological psychology** is the study of the links between biology and behavior. (p. 42)

2. The **neuron**, or nerve cell, is the basic building block of the nervous system. (p. 42)

3. The **dendrites** of a neuron are the bushy extensions that receive messages from other nerve cells and conduct impulses toward the cell body. (p. 42)

4. The **axon** of a neuron is the extension that sends impulses to other nerve cells. (p. 42)

5. The **myelin sheath** is a layer of fatty cells that covers many axons and helps speed neural impulses. (p. 42)

6. An **action potential** is a neural impulse generated by the movement of positively charged atoms in and out of channels in the axon's membrane. (p. 43)

7. A neuron's **threshold** is the level of stimulation that must be exceeded in order for the neuron to fire, or generate an electrical impulse. (p. 44)

8. A **synapse** is the junction between the axon tip of the sending neuron and the dendrite or cell body of the receiving neuron. The tiny gap at this junction is called the synaptic cleft or gap. (p. 44)

9. **Neurotransmitters** are chemicals that are released into synaptic gaps and so *transmit neural messages* from neuron to neuron. (p. 44)

10. **Acetylcholine (ACh)** is a neurotransmitter that triggers muscle contractions. (p. 45)

11. **Endorphins** are natural, opiatelike neurotransmitters linked to pain control and pleasure. (p. 46)

    Memory aid: <u>End</u>orphins *end* pain.

12. The **nervous system** is the speedy, electrochemical communication system, consisting of all the nerve cells in the peripheral and central nervous systems. (p. 47)

13. The **central nervous system** consists of the brain and spinal cord; it is located at the *center*, or internal core, of the body. (p. 47)

14. The **peripheral nervous system** connects the central nervous system to the body's sense receptors, muscles, and glands; it is at the *periphery* of the body relative to the brain and spinal cord. (p. 47)

15. **Nerves** are bundles of neural axons that connect the central nervous system with muscles, glands, and sense organs. (p. 47)

16. **Sensory neurons** carry information about internal and external stimuli to the central nervous system for processing. (p. 48)

17. **Interneurons** are the neurons of the central nervous system that link the sensory and motor neurons in the transmission of sensory input and motor output. (p. 48)

18. **Motor neurons** carry information and instructions for action from the central nervous system to muscles and glands. (p. 48)

19. The **skeletal nervous system** is the division of the peripheral nervous system that controls voluntary movements of the skeletal muscles. (p. 48)

20. The **autonomic nervous system** is the division of the peripheral nervous system that controls the glands and the muscles of internal organs and thereby controls internal functioning; it regulates the *automatic* behaviors necessary for survival. (p. 48)

21. The **sympathetic nervous system** is the division of the autonomic nervous system that arouses the body, mobilizing its energy in stressful situations. (p. 48)

22. The **parasympathetic nervous system** is the division of the autonomic nervous system that calms the body, conserving its energy. (pp. 48–49)

23. A **reflex** is a simple, automatic, inborn response to a sensory stimulus; it is governed by a very simple neural pathway. (p. 49)

24. **Neural networks** are interconnected neural cells, the specific connections of which are strengthened as learning occurs. (p. 50)

25. The **endocrine system**, the body's "slower" chemical communication system, consists of glands that secrete hormones into the bloodstream. (p. 50)

26. **Hormones** are chemical messengers, mostly those manufactured by the endocrine system, that are produced in one tissue and circulate through the bloodstream to their target tissues, on which they have specific effects. (p. 50)

27. The **adrenal glands** produce epinephrine and norepinephrine, hormones that prepare the body to deal with emergencies or stress. (p. 51)

28. The **pituitary gland**, under the influence of the hypothalamus, regulates growth and controls other endocrine glands; sometimes called the "master gland." (p. 51)

Program Terms

29. **Glial cells**, together with neurons, make up the 10 trillion cells in the brain.

30. The **cell body**, or **soma**, of a neuron receives incoming messages from the

nerve cell's dendrites. This information is then sent on as an electrical discharge down the length of the neuron's axon.

31. **Terminal buttons** are extensions of nerve cell axons that release neurotransmitters into synapses, sending chemical messages to adjacent nerve cells.

32. **Parkinson's disease** is a disease in which dopamine-producing neurons die, resulting in the muscular tremors characteristic of this disease.

The Brain

Textbook Terms

1. A **lesion** is destruction of tissue; studying the consequences of lesions—both surgically produced in animals and naturally occurring—in different regions of the brain helps researchers to determine the normal functions of these regions. (p. 53)

2. An **electroencephalogram (EEG)** is an amplified recording of the waves of electrical activity of the brain. *Encephalo* comes from a Greek word meaning "related to the brain." (p. 53)

3. The **CT (computed tomograph) scan** is a series of x-ray photographs of the brain taken from different positions and analyzed by computer, creating an image that represents a slice through the brain. (p. 53)

4. The **PET (positron emission tomograph) scan** measures the levels of activity of different areas of the brain by tracing their consumption of a radioactive form of glucose, the brain's fuel. (p. 53)

5. **MRI (magnetic resonance imaging)** uses magnetic fields and radio signals to produce computer-generated images that show brain structures more clearly. (p. 53)

6. The **brainstem**, the oldest and innermost region of the brain, is an extension of the spinal cord and is the central core of the brain; its structures direct automatic survival functions. (p. 55)

7. Located in the brainstem, the **medulla** controls breathing and heartbeat. (p. 55)

8. Also part of the brainstem, the **reticular formation** is a nerve network that plays an important role in controlling arousal. (p. 55)

9. Located atop the brainstem, the **thalamus** routes incoming messages to the appropriate cortical centers and transmits replies to the medulla and cerebellum. (p. 55)

10. The **cerebellum** assists in balance and the coordination of voluntary movement. (p. 56)

11. A doughnut-shaped neural system, the **limbic system** plays an important role in the regulation of emotions and basic physiological drives. (p. 56)

    Memory aid: Its name comes from the Latin word *limbus*, meaning "border"; the **limbic system** is at the border of the brainstem and cerebral hemispheres.

12. The **amygdala** is part of the limbic system and is involved in regulation of the emotions of fear and rage. (p. 56)

13. Also part of the limbic system, the **hypothalamus** regulates hunger, thirst, and body temperature and contains the so-called pleasure centers of the brain. It also helps govern the endocrine system through the pituitary gland. (p. 57)

14. The **cerebral cortex** is the thin outer covering of the cerebral hemispheres. The seat of information processing, the cortex is responsible for those complex functions that make us distinctively human. (p. 58)

    Memory aid: Cortex in Latin means "bark." As bark covers a tree, the **cerebral cortex** is the "bark of the brain."

15. Located at the front of the brain, just behind the forehead, the **frontal lobes** are involved in speaking and muscle movements and in making plans and judgments. (p. 59)

16. Situated between the frontal and occipital lobes, the **parietal lobes** contain the sensory cortex. (p. 59)

17. Located at the back and base of the brain, the **occipital lobes** contain the visual cortex, which receives information from the eyes. (p. 59)

18. Located on the sides of the brain, the **temporal lobes** contain the auditory areas, which receive information from the ears. (p. 59)

    Memory aid: The **temporal lobes** are located near the *temples*.

19. Located at the back of the frontal lobe, the **motor cortex** controls voluntary movement. (p. 60)

20. The **sensory cortex** is located at the front of the parietal lobes, just behind the motor cortex. It registers and processes body sensations. (p. 61)

21. Located throughout the cortex, **association areas** of the brain are involved in higher mental functions, such as learning, remembering, and abstract thinking. (p. 62)

    Memory aid: Among their other functions, **association areas** of the cortex are involved in integrating, or *associating*, information from different areas of the brain.

22. **Aphasia** is an impairment of language as a result of damage to any of several cortical areas, including Broca's area and Wernicke's area. (p. 63)

23. **Broca's area**, located in the left frontal lobe, is involved in controlling the motor ability to produce speech. (p. 63)

24. **Wernicke's area**, located in the left temporal lobe, is involved in language comprehension. (p. 63)

Program Terms

25. **Neuroscientists** study behavior and mental processes by attempting to uncover their biological foundations in the events taking place within the brain.

26. **Brain imaging** measures the brain's structure and function by providing actual pictures of the brain's inner workings. An example is a CAT scan.

27. **Neurometrics** is a new science that examines patterns of electrophysiological activity in different regions of the brain.

28. **Neuronal implantation** is an experimental technique in which healthy brain cells are grafted onto damaged brain areas in the hope that they will assume the functions of the damaged cells.

29. **Glucocorticoids** are hormones produced by the adrenal glands that help mobilize the individual's resources in coping with stress.

30. **Psychosocial dwarfism** refers to the decreased physical stature of institutionalized children who are deprived of a normal, loving family environment.

31. A **neuroethologist** is a scientist who uses the methodologies of brain science to study the behaviors of animals in their natural habitats.

PROGRAM 5

The Developing Child

TEXTBOOK ASSIGNMENT: Chapter 3: The Developing Child, pp. 77–83, 85–113

ORIENTATION

Developmental psychologists study the life cycle, from conception to death, examining how we change physically, cognitively, and socially. The reading assignment for Program 5 (Chapter 3 of the textbook) covers prenatal, infant, and childhood development and examines three major issues in developmental psychology: (1) the relative impact of genes and experience on behavior, (2) whether development is best described as gradual and continuous or as a discontinuous sequence of stages, and (3) whether the individual's personality remains stable or changes over the life span.

Program 5 focuses on how advances in research technology have corrected early views of the infant as totally helpless at birth. Developmental psychologists have discovered that newborns enter the world well-prepared to accomplish the three basic tasks of infancy: getting the sustenance they need, defending against harmful stimulation, and making social contact.

Research and theoretical issues introduced in this first lesson on development provide a base for further study in Program 6. Pay particular attention to the research of Harlow and others on attachment and social deprivation, to Piaget's theory of cognitive development, to the studies of twins and adopted children, and to the controversy surrounding the developmental issues.

NOTE: Answer guidelines for all Program 5 questions begin on page 86.

GOALS

After completing your study of the program and reading assignment, you should be prepared to:

1. Describe the normal patterns of development from the prenatal period through childhood.
2. Discuss Piaget's contributions to developmental psychology.
3. Discuss the major theoretical issues that pervade developmental psychology.

GUIDED STUDY

Textbook Assignment

The text chapter should be studied one section at a time. Before you read, preview each section by skimming it, noting headings and boldface items. Then read the appropriate section objectives from the following outline. Keep these objectives in mind and, as you read the chapter section, search for the information that will enable you to meet each objective. Once you have finished a section, write out answers for its objectives.

Developmental Issues (pp. 77–78)

1. Identify and briefly describe three major issues that pervade developmental psychology.

Prenatal Development and the Newborn (pp. 78–82)

2. Describe conception and explain how sex is determined.

3. Outline the course of prenatal development.

4. Discuss the possible effects of teratogens on the developing embryo and fetus.

5. Describe the capacities of the newborn.

Infancy and Childhood (pp. 82–107)

6. Describe the brain development that occurs from infancy through childhood, including its impact on memory.

7. Discuss brain plasticity and what it reveals about brain reorganization.

8. Describe the roles of nature and nurture in motor development through infancy and childhood.

9. Discuss Piaget's view of how the mind develops and describe his cognitive stages.

10. Discuss current views of Piaget's theory of cognitive development.

11. Discuss the origins and effects of early attachment, and the roles of temperament and parenting in attachment throughout life.

12. Discuss how caregiving, infant day care, and divorce influence attachment.

13. Explain how children's behavior provides evidence of an emerging self-concept and discuss the possible effects of different parenting styles and cultures on children.

14. Differentiate between gender and gender identity and explain two theories of gender-typing.

Reflections on the Nature-Nurture Issue (pp. 108–113)

15. Explain the rationale for twin and adoption studies and discuss criticisms of them.

16. Summarize the results and implications of research on the nature-nurture issue.

Program Assignment

Read the following objectives before you watch Program 5. As you watch, be alert for information that will help you answer each objective. Taking notes during the program will help you to formulate your answers later. After the program, write answers to the objectives. If you have access to the program on videotape, you may replay portions if you need to refresh your memory.

1. Explain the nature-nurture debate and cite its history in science.

2. What is the significance of "the wild boy of Avignon" in the history of the nature-nurture debate?

3. State the views of William James, John Watson, and many other psychologists regarding the newborn infant's capabilities.

4. State the contemporary view regarding the competencies of newborns and briefly describe them.

5. Describe the visual abilities of the newborn.

6. Explain how developmental psychologists study infant abilities.

7. Describe Piaget's conservation-of-volume experiment and discuss his contributions to developmental psychology.

8. Describe recent findings regarding the age at which children acquire object permanence and the ability to use symbols.

9. Describe the visual cliff experiment and what it reveals regarding the emergence of depth perception in children.

10. Identify several traits that are influenced by heredity and discuss how heredity and environment interact in determining their development.

PROGRESS TEST

Circle your answers to the following questions and check them with the answers on page 91. If your answer is incorrect, read the explanation for why it is incorrect and then consult the appropriate pages of the text (in parentheses following the correct answer).

1. Piaget's theory is primarily concerned with:
   a. motor development.
   b. social development.
   c. biological development.
   d. cognitive development.

2. Which parenting style usually produces children with the greatest confidence and self-esteem?
   a. permissive
   b. authoritarian
   c. authoritative
   d. rejecting-neglecting

3. The nature-nurture controversy considers the degree to which traits and behaviors are determined by:
   a. genes or heredity.
   b. genes or experience.
   c. continuity or stages.
   d. life-span stability or change.

4. The rooting reflex occurs when a:
   a. newborn's foot is tickled.
   b. newborn's cheek is touched.
   c. newborn hears a loud noise.
   d. newborn makes eye contact with his or her caregiver.

5. Harlow's studies of attachment in monkeys showed that:
   a. provision of nourishment was the single most important factor motivating attachment.
   b. a cloth mother produced the greatest attachment response.
   c. whether a cloth or wire mother was present mattered less than the presence or absence of other infants.
   d. attachment in monkeys is based on imprinting.

6. Nature is to nurture as the views of _____ are to those of _____.
   a. Locke; Rousseau
   b. Rousseau; Locke
   c. James; Watson
   d. Watson; James

7. The case of the "wild boy of Avignon" convinced many scientists that:
   a. nature is a more potent influence on development than nurture.
   b. nurture has a stronger impact on development than nature.
   c. nature and nurture interact in determining most behaviors.
   d. newborns enter the world almost completely helpless.

8. The phenomenon in which young birds follow the first moving object they observe is:
   a. imprinting.
   b. bonding.
   c. assimilation.
   d. accommodation.

9. The developmental theorist who suggests that securely attached children develop an attitude of basic trust is:
   a. Piaget.
   b. Erikson.
   c. Harlow.
   d. Freud.

10. According to which theory does gender become a lens through which children view their experiences?
    a. social learning theory
    b. Vygotsky's sociocultural theory
    c. Piaget's theory
    d. gender schema theory

11. The fertilized egg will develop into a boy if, at conception:
    a. an X chromosome is contributed by the father's sperm.
    b. a Y chromosome is contributed by the father's sperm.
    c. an X chromosome is contributed by the mother's egg.
    d. a Y chromosome is contributed by the mother's egg.

12. Stranger anxiety develops at the same time as:
    a. the concept of conservation.
    b. egocentrism.
    c. a theory of mind.
    d. the concept of object permanence.

13. The primary social achievement of infancy is the development of:
    a. self-concept.
    b. gender identity.
    c. attachment.
    d. initiative.

14. The concept of habituation refers to:
    a. the tendency to adapt to almost any environment.
    b. a decrease in response to a repeated stimulus.
    c. a tendency to prefer novel stimuli.
    d. a shift in interest from a repeated stimulus to a novel stimulus.

15. Robert Fantz's studies of infant preferences revealed that infants prefer:
    a. complex stimuli to simple ones.
    b. whole faces over jumbled parts of faces.
    c. contours to straight lines.
    d. all of the above.

16. Within a few hours of birth a newborn can:
    a. turn its eyes in the direction of a voice.
    b. turn its head to follow a moving face.
    c. show pleasure in response to certain tastes and smells.
    d. do all of the above.

17. Newborns' hearing is:
    a. extremely deficient at birth.
    b. best for low-pitched sounds.
    c. functioning even before birth.
    d. all of the above.

18. Which is the correct sequence of stages in Piaget's theory of cognitive development?
    a. sensorimotor, preoperational, concrete operational, formal operational
    b. sensorimotor, preoperational, formal operational, concrete operational
    c. preoperational, sensorimotor, concrete operational, formal operational
    d. preoperational, sensorimotor, formal operational, concrete operational

19. Which is the correct order of stages of prenatal development?
    a. zygote, fetus, embryo
    b. zygote, embryo, fetus
    c. embryo, zygote, fetus
    d. embryo, fetus, zygote

20. The term *critical period* refers to:
    a. prenatal development.
    b. the initial 2 hours after a child's birth.
    c. the preoperational stage.
    d. a restricted time for learning.

21. At birth, a newborn's vision is _____ its hearing.
    a. better developed than
    b. less well developed than
    c. about the same as
    d. less predictable

22. By about _____ months of age, infants can bring distant objects into focus almost as well as an adult.
    a. 1
    b. 2
    c. 3
    d. 4

23. Insecurely attached infants who are left by their mothers in an unfamiliar setting often will:
    a. hold fast to their mothers on their return.
    b. explore the new surroundings confidently.
    c. be indifferent or even hostile toward their mothers on their return.
    d. display little emotion under any circumstances.

24. Compared to those raised in Western societies, children raised in communal societies such as Japan or China:
    a. grow up with a stronger integration of the sense of family into their self-concepts.
    b. exhibit greater shyness toward strangers.
    c. exhibit greater concern for loyalty and social harmony.
    d. have all of the above characteristics.
    e. have none of the above characteristics.

25. Research regarding the effects of day care on development in preschoolers suggests that children placed in day care:
    a. receive far less quality time from adults.
    b. are slower to develop clear self-concepts than children raised at home.
    c. are no less attached to their parents than children raised at home.
    d. show less social competence than children raised at home.

26. "Infantile amnesia" is most likely caused by:
    a. prenatal exposure to teratogens.
    b. premature birth.
    c. the immature nervous system.
    d. prenatal malnutrition.

27. As a child observes, liquid is transferred from a tall, thin tube into a short, wide jar. The child is asked if there is now the same amount of or less liquid in order to determine if she has mastered:
    a. the processes of accommodation and assimilation.
    b. the concept of object permanence.
    c. the concept of conservation.
    d. the ability to reason abstractly.

28. Before Piaget, people were more likely to believe that:
    a. the child's mind is a miniature model of the adult's.
    b. children think about the world in radically different ways than adults.
    c. the child's mind develops through a series of stages.
    d. children interpret their experiences in terms of their current understandings.

29. Chad, who grew up in the United States, is more likely to encourage _____ in his children than Asian-born Hidiyaki, who is more likely to encourage _____ in his children.
    a. obedience; independence
    b. independence; emotional closeness
    c. emotional closeness; obedience
    d. loyalty; emotional closeness

30. If a toddler's father points out the lion at the zoo and calls it "kittie," he is trying to help his son to _____ , that is, to modify his schema for cat in order to incorporate the new experience.
    a. accommodate
    b. assimilate
    c. use cognition
    d. conserve

31. Two-year-old Naveed, who has a simple schema for "mom" and calls each new woman with a child he encounters "mom," is demonstrating Piaget's process of:
    a. accommodation.
    b. assimilation.
    c. cognition.
    d. conservation.

32. Researchers today believe that Piaget:
    a. underestimated what children can do at a certain age.
    b. overestimated what most children can do at a certain age.
    c. focused too much on large group studies of children, thus losing sight of the importance of individual differences in ability.
    d. emphasized motor development and neglected cognitive development.

33. Although Piaget claimed that children do not attain object permanence until _____ months, researcher Renée Baillargeon has found that infants as young as _____ month(s) demonstrate a rudimentary understanding of this principle.
    a. 5; 1
    b. 6; 2
    c. 8 or 9; 3 1/2
    d. 12; 6

34. In terms of object permanence, Renée Baillargeon's results differed from Piaget's because:
    a. she used a simpler task.
    b. she measured the infant's eye gaze rather than the more mature physical responses on which Piaget based his conclusions.
    c. of both a. and b.
    d. she used a larger, more representative sample of children.

35. I am 3 years old, can use language, and have trouble taking another person's perspective. I am in Piaget's _____ stage of cognitive development.
    a. sensorimotor
    b. preoperational
    c. concrete operational
    d. formal operational

36. Developmental researcher Judy DeLoache has found that:
    a. most children are incapable of symbolic reasoning until they start first grade.
    b. female toddlers outperform males on tests of symbolic reasoning.
    c. male toddlers outperform females on tests of symbolic reasoning.
    d. children's ability to use symbols develops much earlier than Piaget supposed.

37. Studies of the visual cliff have provided evidence that depth perception is closely linked to the development of:
    a. conservation.
    b. crawling.
    c. visual acuity.
    d. motor reflexes.

38. The term that refers to the rudiments of an individual's personality, especially emotional excitability, is:
    a. ego.
    b. self-concept.
    c. temperament.
    d. autonomy.

39. In Piaget's theory, conservation is to egocentrism as the _____ stage is to the _____ stage.
    a. sensorimotor; formal operational
    b. formal operational; sensorimotor
    c. preoperational; sensorimotor
    d. concrete operational; preoperational

40. One of the best ways to distinguish how much genetic and environmental factors affect behavior is to compare children who have:
    a. the same genes and environments.
    b. different genes and environments.
    c. similar genes and environments.
    d. similar genes and similar families.
    e. the same genes but different environments.

41. Psychologist Jerome Kagan believes that:
    a. 10 to 15 percent of children are born with a slight "push" from nature to be either outgoing or more timid.
    b. genetic shyness cannot be modified by the child's upbringing.
    c. a. and b. are true.
    d. personality is entirely the product of environmental factors.

42. Working with monkeys, researcher Steven Suomi has found that genetically shy monkeys become much more outgoing when they are:
    a. raised by extremely nurturant foster mothers.
    b. isolated from their shy biological parents.
    c. raised in very large groups.
    d. reinforced for bold behaviors in the laboratory.

43. Despite growing up in the same home environment, Karen and her brother John have personalities as different from one another as two people selected randomly from the population. Why is this so?
    a. Personality is inherited. Since Karen and John are not identical twins, it is not surprising that they have very different personalities.
    b. Gender is the most important factor in personality formation. If Karen had a sister, the two of them would probably be much more alike.
    c. The interaction of their individual genes and nonshared experiences accounts for the common finding that children in the same family are usually very different.
    d. Their case is unusual; children in the same family usually have similar personalities.

KEY TERMS

Using your own words, write a brief definition or explanation of each of the following terms.

Textbook Terms

1. developmental psychology

2. X chromosome

3. Y chromosome

4. testosterone

5. gender

6. zygote

7. embryo

8. fetus

9. teratogens

10. fetal alcohol syndrome (FAS)

11. rooting reflex

12. maturation

13. plasticity

14. cognition

15. schema

16. assimilation

17. accommodation

18. sensorimotor stage

19. object permanence

20. habituation

21. preoperational stage

22. conservation

23. egocentrism

24. concrete operational stage

25. formal operational stage

26. stranger anxiety

27. attachment

28. critical period

29. imprinting

30. temperament

31. basic trust

32. self-concept

33. gender identity

34. gender-typing

35. social learning theory

36. gender schema theory

Program Terms

37. habituation

38. dishabituation

ANSWERS

Guided Study

The following guidelines provide the main points that your answers should have touched upon.

Textbook Assignment

1. The nature/nurture issue is concerned with how much our development is influenced by heredity and how much by our experience. The continuity or stages issue concerns whether development is a gradual, continuous process or a sequence of separate stages. The stability or change issue asks whether individual traits persist over the life span or people become different persons as they age.

2. A woman's ovary releases a mature egg. The few sperm from the man that reach the egg release digestive enzymes that eat away the egg's protective covering. As soon as one sperm penetrates the egg, the egg's surface blocks out all other sperm. The egg and sperm nuclei fuse and become one.

    Sex is determined by the twenty-third pair of chromosomes, the sex chromosomes, one of which comes from each parent. The mother always contributes an X chromosome. The father's sperm contributes an X or a Y chromosome; with an X chromosome, the developing person becomes a girl; with a Y chromosome, a boy develops. The presence of a Y chromosome triggers development of the testes and the production of the principal male hormone, testosterone.

3. Prenatal development is divided into three stages: zygote (from conception to 2 weeks); embryo (2 weeks through 8 weeks); and fetus (9 weeks to birth).

    During the period of the zygote, cell division is the primary task. Within two weeks of conception the increasingly numerous cells begin to differentiate—to specialize in structure and function. At this time the zygote's outer part attaches to the mother's uterine wall, becoming the placenta. During the period of the embryo, body organs begin to form and function. By the end of the sixth month the fetus's internal organs have become sufficiently functional to allow a premature fetus a chance of survival.

4. Teratogens are damaging agents such as drugs and viruses that pass from the mother's bloodstream through the placenta into that of the embryo or fetus. Teratogens may result in a variety of physical and cognitive abnormalities in the developing child. For example, mothers who are heavy smokers often give birth to underweight infants. Mothers addicted to drugs such as heroin give birth to addicted newborns. If a mother is a heavy alcohol drinker, her infant may suffer from fetal alcohol syndrome, which involves small, misproportioned heads and brain abnormalities, which lead to mental retardation.

5. Newborns are born with a variety of reflexes that help ensure their survival. When touched on its cheek, for example, a baby will open its mouth and search for food (rooting reflex).

    The newborn's sensory capabilities facilitate social responsiveness. Newborns prefer human voices and drawings of human faces to artificial sounds and nonhuman visual patterns. Within days of birth, babies can distinguish their mother's odor and voice.

6. All the brain cells a person will ever have are present at birth. However, the neural connections that enable walking, talking, and memory are only

beginning to form. This neural immaturity may explain why we have no memories of events before 3 years of age. While lasting memories may not be formed before then, infants are capable of learning simple responses.

7. When a particular area of the brain is damaged, such as occurs following a stroke, other areas may in time reorganize and assume its functions (plasticity). Neurons near damaged ones compensate for the damage by making new neural connections that replace the damaged ones. The brains of young children, in which functions are not yet regionally fixed, exhibit the greatest plasticity. Throughout life, however, new neural connections are formed and are the brain's way of compensating for the gradual loss of neurons with age.

8. While nurture may play a role in motor development—Ugandan babies walk before age 10 months, as compared to babies with no experience—nature plays a major role. Before biological maturation creates a readiness to develop a particular skill, experience has a limited effect.

   Although the age at which infants sit, stand, walk, and control bowel and bladder varies from child to child, the sequence in which babies develop these abilities is universal. After the rapid pace of the first 2 years, physical growth occurs at a steady 2 to 3 inches per year during childhood.

9. Piaget believed that children actively construct their understanding of the world in radically different ways than adults. He further believed that children's minds develop through a series of stages in which they form increasingly complex schemas that organize their past experiences and provide a framework for understanding future experiences. New experiences that conform to existing schemas are assimilated. When new experiences do not fit existing schemas, children accommodate their schemas to incorporate the new experiences.

   In the sensorimotor stage, from birth to about 2 years, children experience their world through their senses and actions. During this stage object permanence (and stranger anxiety) develop.

   In the preoperational stage, from about 2 to 6 or 7 years, children are able to use language but lack logical reasoning. During this stage egocentrism develops.

   In the concrete operational stage, from about 6 or 7 to 11 years, children are able to think logically about concrete events and perform mathematical operations. Conservation also develops during this stage.

   The formal operational stage, from age 12 through adulthood, is characterized by abstract and systematic reasoning, as well as by the potential for mature moral reasoning.

10. Today's researchers see development as more continuous than did Piaget. For example, object permanence, conservation, and the abilities to take another's perspective and perform mental operations unfold gradually and are not utterly absent in one stage and then suddenly present. In fact, preschoolers acquire a "theory of mind" and come to realize that others may hold false beliefs.

    Researchers also believe that Piaget underestimated young children's competence. They have found rudiments of various cognitive abilities at an earlier age than Piaget supposed.

    In many ways, however, Piaget's theory continues to receive support. Despite variations in the rate at which children develop, cross-cultural research reveals that human cognition everywhere unfolds in the basic sequence he proposed.

11. Harlow's research with monkeys reveals that attachment usually grows from body contact with parents, rather than by association with feeding. In

many animals, attachment is also based on familiarity and forms during a critical period shortly after hatching or birth (a process called imprinting). Although human infants prefer faces and objects with which they are familiar, they do not have a critical period for becoming attached.

Attachment also depends on an infant's temperament, which includes inborn rudiments of personality, especially emotional excitability. The most emotionally reactive newborns tend also to be the most reactive, inhibited, and fearful 2-year-olds, shy 8-year-olds, and intense young adults. With age, these characteristics relax somewhat.

Responsive parenting is also a factor. Sensitive, responsive mothers tend to have infants who become securely attached. Insensitive, unresponsive mothers often have insecurely attached infants. Securely attached infants are less anxious and more socially competent, and these differences persist through early childhood.

12. Erik Erikson believed that infants with sensitive, loving caregivers form a lifelong attitude of basic trust—a sense that the world is predictable and reliable. Children who suffer parental neglect or abuse may form lasting scars—nightmares, depression, a troubled adolescence, and a greater tendency to later abuse their own children.

The impact of day care on children remains controversial. Some developmental psychologists believe that day-care children are at heightened risk of insecure attachment and of being disobedient and aggressive at older ages. Others believe that quality day care does not hinder secure attachment. In fact, research has shown that children who had experienced quality day care during their first six months were more outgoing, popular, and academically successful than those who hadn't.

The possible impact of divorce on children appears more clear-cut. Even when researchers rule out other factors that may affect child development, such as parental education, race, and income, children of divorced or never-married parents are about twice as likely to experience a variety of social, psychological, or academic problems.

13. Self-awareness emerges gradually over the first year, with the first sign being a child's self-recognition when staring into a mirror. By 15 to 18 months, children will wipe at a dab of rouge seen on their faces in a mirror's reflection. By school age, children begin to describe themselves in terms of gender, group memberships, and psychological traits.

Four parenting styles have been identified. Authoritarian parents impose rules and expect their children to be obedient. Authoritative parents are demanding, yet more responsive to their children. They set and enforce rules, but also are willing to explain and discuss the reasoning behind rules. Permissive parents make few demands of their children and submit to their wishes. Rejecting-neglecting parents expect little and invest little in their children's development. Children with the highest self-esteem, self-reliance, and social competence usually have authoritative parents, perhaps because their parents provide them with the greatest sense of self-control.

Social values vary from one culture to another. Most parents in Western societies value greater independence in their children than do parents in Asian and African cultures, who focus more on cultivating emotional closeness. Cross-cultural studies also reveal that people in Japanese and Chinese cultures exhibit greater shyness toward strangers and concern for social harmony and loyalty than do Westerners.

Researchers have found that although ethnic groups within a culture may differ in their behavior, they may be influenced by the same underlying processes. The behavior differences can result from differing inputs to the same process.

14. Gender, as noted earlier in the chapter, refers to the social definition of male or female; gender identity is our personal sense of being male or female. Gender-typing, which refers to the acquisition of a gender identity and role, has been alternatively explained by social learning theory and by gender schema theory. According to social learning theory, children acquire gender-linked behaviors by observing and imitating others and by being rewarded or punished. Gender schema theory assumes that the child's culture transmits a concept of what it means to be male or female. The child then adjusts his or her behavior to fit the concept.

15. Since identical twins are genetically identical, the findings that they are more similar in a trait than fraternal twins or other siblings suggest that there is a substantial genetic influence on that trait. In this way, twin studies provide psychologists with a greater understanding of the role of genes in development.

    Adoption studies enable psychologists to determine the relative influence of nature and nurture on development by asking whether adopted children are more like their biological parents, who contribute their genes, or their adoptive parents, who contribute a home environment.

    Critics of twin studies contend that twin similarities may merely be coincidental rather than a reflection of heredity. Moreover, because adoption agencies tend to place separated twins in similar homes, critics argue, similarities in traits may reflect the impact of similar experiences rather than heredity alone.

16. Twin and adoption studies reveal that genetic influences account for nearly 50 percent of the variation in traits such as outgoingness and emotional instability. The remaining variation has been attributed to each person's unique experiences in interacting with parents plus other peer and cultural influences.

    Because genes and experience interact in influencing development, it is *in*correct to say that a certain trait is x percent due to genes and y percent due to experience. That genes direct experience can be seen in how people select environments that suit their natures, and how genetically influenced traits may evoke certain responses.

Program Assignment

1. Two hundred years ago, the new science of mental medicine initiated the debate as scientists argued about the true essence of human nature. On one side was the French philosopher Jean-Jacques Rousseau, who believed that people are born with all the skills and qualities that make them who they are. For Rousseau, it was nature—that which we bring into the world at birth—that most affects our development. On the other side, English philosopher John Locke maintained that a baby is a blank tablet, devoid of any knowledge or skills. It is only experience, and the training of those who nurture us, that determines who we become. In time the debate became known as nature versus nurture.

2. In 1800, the nature-nurture debate was sharpened by the discovery of a wild 12-year-old who had apparently lived alone in the forests of France. Although attempts by Dr. Itard to socialize and educate the boy at first appeared to be successful, Itard gave up all hope after five years. The "wild boy" died at 40, still unable to speak and behave like a normal man. For many, this proved that nature more than nurture is the most important factor in development.

3. To William James at the turn of the century, an infant was a totally confused and helpless organism. In his words, "one great blooming, buzzing

confusion assailed the newborn as it entered the world." In the 1920s, John Watson, the founder of behaviorism, described the infant as a "lively, squirming bit of flesh capable of making a few simple responses." As recently as 1964, a medical text proclaimed that newborns cannot focus their eyes or respond to sound. Many doctors still believe that babies cannot feel pain.

4. Human infants are much less helpless than they once were believed to be. Over the past 20 years research has revealed that babies come into the world ready to perform all sorts of feats in order to accomplish the three basic tasks of infancy: getting the sustenance they need, defending against harmful stimulation, and making social contact. For example, a few minutes after birth newborns can turn their eyes in the direction of a voice, searching for sounds they prefer; they can reach out a hand to make contact and turn their head to follow a moving face. As early as 12 hours of age they show pleasure at certain tastes and smells and recoil from others. Furthermore, because their hearing is functioning even before birth, newborns are prepared to respond to certain sounds as soon as they enter the world. They prefer female voices, can immediately recognize their mother's speech, and are lulled to sleep by the sound of a heartbeat.

5. Vision is less well developed than hearing at birth. With 20/500 vision, newborns are legally blind. This deficit is caused by a deficiency of functioning retinal cells and by immature neural connections in the visual cortex. Both develop rapidly, however. A 1-month-old can detect the contours of a human head at close distances. A 7-week-old smiles at his or her mother's face. A 2-month-old can distinguish colors. A 3-month-old can bring distant objects into focus almost as well as an adult and can also perceive visual contrast well enough to detect differences in facial expressions.

6. Developmental researchers use simple behaviors, such as gazing at objects, touching, and sucking, to infer the infant's abilities and psychological states. Because babies prefer novel stimuli, they respond less to repeated events. This decreased responding is called *habituation* (see also text p. 90). When a baby then responds to another stimulus in a way that shows he or she perceives it to be different, dishabituation has occurred. Researchers use habituation and *dishabituation* as measures of attention, preferences, and perceptual ability. Changes in the rate of sucking, smiling, crying, and so forth can also be used to measure a response to different events.

7. In this experiment, two same-sized glasses are filled with equal amounts of colored liquid. The contents of one glass are then poured into a taller container. Piaget discovered that children's understanding of the problem varies with their age. Six-year-olds believe that the tall container now has more liquid. Seven-year-olds are uncertain. By eight years of age, however, children become aware that despite appearances, the volume of the liquid is conserved, no matter what container it is in.

    More recent research studies have revealed that Piaget confused children's physical abilities with their mental ones and thus underestimated what children can do at any given age.

8. Object permanence is the awareness that objects continue to exist when hidden. Although Piaget claimed that children do not master this principle until 8 or 9 months, researcher Renée Baillargeon (University of Illinois) has found that infants as young as 3 1/2 months demonstrate a rudimentary understanding of object permanence when the task is simplified.

    Similarly, researcher Judy DeLoache (also at Illinois) has found that children as young as 3 years of age are able to extrapolate from scale models to life-size rooms when searching for hidden objects. This demonstrates that the ability to use symbols develops much earlier than Piaget supposed.

9. The visual cliff was developed in 1960 by Eleanor Gibson and Richard Walk. One side of a plexiglass sheet is painted and the other side is transparent, with a painted pattern beneath it that creates the illusion of a drop-off. Babies who have just begun to crawl will cross the "drop-off" when coaxed by a parent or caregiver. From about 8 1/2 months on, however, children who are more accomplished at crawling and have a perception of depth will not cross the apparent drop-off.

10. Regardless of their culture, some babies are excitable and active while others are calm and passive. Such temperaments, which are exhibited at birth, are biologically based tendencies that can influence the developing child's personality. Harvard psychologist Jerome Kagan believes that 10 to 15 percent of children are born with a slight "push" from nature to be either outgoing or more timid. Kagan is quick to point out, however, that being shy at birth does not necessarily mean these tendencies cannot be modified by the child's upbringing. Later experiences can allow some to overcome their shyness, while creating shyness in others.

   In addition to shyness, the personality trait that shows the strongest genetic influence is activity level. Though biologically based, this trait can be modified by learning, training, and experience.

   Working with monkeys, researcher Steven Suomi has found that genetically shy monkeys become much more outgoing when they are raised by extremely nurturant foster mothers.

   Genetic influences are also significant for some cognitive abilities, such as verbal skills, and for some kinds of psychopathology.

Progress Test

1. **d.** is the answer. Piaget's theory is concerned with the qualitatively different stages of thinking, or cognition, that occur in children. (pp. 87–88).

2. **c.** is the answer. Children of authoritative parents tend to develop self-reliance and a positive self-image. (p. 104)

   a., b., & d. Children seem to fare best when they have been raised by parents who are not permissive, authoritarian, or rejecting-neglecting, but who are authoritative—exerting control without depriving their children of a sense of control over their own lives.

3. **b.** is the answer. Nature = genes; nurture = experience. (video; pp. 77–78)

   a. Genes and heredity both refer to the nature side of the nature-nurture controversy.

   c. & d. Whether development is continuous or occurs in stages and whether it is characterized by stability or change over the life span are two other developmental issues.

4. **b.** is the answer. The infant turns its head and begins sucking when its cheek is stroked. (p. 81)

   a., c., & d. These stimuli produce other reflexes in the newborn.

5. **b.** is the answer. (p. 95)

   a. When given the choice between a wire mother with a bottle and a cloth mother without, the monkeys preferred the cloth mother.

   c. The presence of other infants made no difference.

   d. Imprinting plays no role in the attachment of higher primates.

6. **b.** is the answer. Rousseau believed that nature rather than nurture was the primary factor in development. Locke took the opposite position. (video)

   c. & d. Both James and Watson emphasized the importance of nurture in development.

7. **a.** is the answer. This is so because, despite Dr. Itard's efforts, the boy never learned to speak and behave as a normal human would. (video)

8. **a.** is the answer. (p. 96)

   b. Bonding refers to the more general process, seen in a number of species, of immediate mutual attachment between infant and parent, formed on the basis of physical contact.

   c. & d. Assimilation and accommodation refer to Piagetian processes by which cognitive schemas develop.

9. **b.** is the answer. Erikson proposed that development occurs in a series of stages, in the first of which the child develops an attitude of either basic trust or mistrust. (p. 98)

   a. Piaget's theory is concerned with cognitive development.

   c. Harlow conducted research on attachment and deprivation.

   d. Freud's theory is concerned with personality development.

10. **d.** is the answer. The child's schema, or gender concept, becomes the lens through which experiences are viewed. (p. 106)

    a. Social learning theory assumes that children acquire their gender identity through observation, imitation, rewards, and punishment.

    b. & c. These theories are not specifically concerned with the development of gender identity.

11. **b.** is the answer. (p. 79)

    a. If the father's sperm contributes an X chromosome, a female will be produced.

    c. The mother's egg always contributes an X chromosome.

    d. This statement is factually incorrect. The mother's egg always contributes an X chromosome; a Y chromosome can be contributed only by the sperm.

12. **d.** is the answer. With object permanence, a child develops schemas for familiar objects, including faces, and may become upset by a stranger who does not fit any of these schemas. (p. 94)

    a. The concept of conservation develops during the concrete operational stage, whereas stranger anxiety develops during the earlier sensorimotor stage.

    b. & c. Egocentrism and a theory of mind both develop during the preoperational stage. This follows the sensorimotor stage, during which stranger anxiety develops.

13. **c.** is the answer. Attachment has profound repercussions for the individual's subsequent psychosocial growth. (p. 95)

    a. & b. Self-concept and gender identity, which is part of self-concept, emerge during the preschool years.

    d. In Erikson's theory, the emergence of initiative is associated with the preschool years.

14. **b.** is the answer. (video; p. 90)

    a. Habituation refers to a response to a specific stimulus.

c. Although this is true, it does not define habituation.

d. This is dishabituation.

15. **d.** is the answer. (video; p. 81)

16. **d.** is the answer. (video)

17. **c.** is the answer. (video)

18. **a.** is the answer. (p. 88)

19. **b.** is the answer. (pp. 79–80)

20. **d.** is the answer. A critical period is a restricted time during which an organism must be exposed to certain influences or experiences for a particular kind of learning to occur. (p. 96)

    a. Critical periods refer to developmental periods after birth.

    b. Critical periods vary from behavior to behavior, but they are not confined to the hours following birth.

    c. Critical periods are not specifically associated with the preoperational period.

21. **b.** is the answer. With 20/500 vision, newborns are legally blind. (video)

22. **c.** is the answer. (video)

23. **c.** is the answer. (p. 96)

    a. Insecurely attached infants often cling to their mothers when placed in a new situation; yet, when the mother returns after an absence, the infant's reaction tends to be one of indifference.

    b. These behaviors are characteristic of securely attached infants.

    d. Insecurely attached infants in unfamiliar surroundings will often exhibit a range of emotional behaviors.

24. **d.** is the answer. (p. 105)

25. **c.** is the answer. Children's attachments to their parents do not seem to be disrupted by day care, which, like parenting, can be of high or low quality. (pp. 100–101)

    a. Studies indicate that preschoolers, whether or not their parents work, tend to receive relatively little quality time from their parents; hence, it's unlikely that children in day care receive far less quality time from adults.

    b. Studies have not shown that day care disrupts development of the self-concept.

    d. There is no evidence that day care lessens social competence.

26. **c.** is the answer. (p. 83)

    a., b., & d. "Infantile amnesia" is a normal developmental phenomenon unrelated to teratogens, premature birth, or prenatal malnutrition.

27. **c.** is the answer. This test is designed to determine if the child understands that the quantity of liquid is conserved, despite the shift to a container that is different in shape. (video; p. 91)

    a. These are general processes related to concept building.

    b. Object permanence is the concept that an object continues to exist even when not perceived; in this case, the water is perceived throughout the experiment.

d. This experiment does not require abstract reasoning, only the ability to reason logically about the concrete.

28. **a.** is the answer. (video; p. 87)

    b., c., & d. Each of these is an understanding developed by Piaget.

29. **b.** is the answer. Although parental values differ from one time and place to another, studies reveal that Western parents today want their children to think for themselves, while Asian and African parents place greater value on emotional closeness. (pp. 105–106)

    d. Both of these values are more typical of Asian than Western cultures.

30. **a.** is the answer. (pp. 87–88)

    b. Assimilation is the process by which new experiences are incorporated into existing schemas.

    c. Cognition is a general term, referring to all mental activities associated with thinking, knowing, communicating, and remembering.

    d. Conservation is the ability to recognize that objects do not change whenever their appearances change.

31. **b.** is the answer. Naveed is assimilating each encounter with a new mother into his existing schema. (p. 87)

    a. Naveed is not accommodating because he does not have to adjust his schema to fit his new experiences.

    c. Cognition refers to all mental activities associated with thinking, knowing, communicating, and remembering.

    d. Conservation is the ability to recognize that objects do not change whenever their appearances change.

32. **a.** is the answer. (video; p. 93)

    c. Piaget typically studied the behavior of one or two children at a time.

    d. To the contrary, Piaget emphasized cognitive skills much more than motor skills—and some criticize him for not taking physical abilities into account.

33. **c.** is the answer. (video)

34. **c.** is the answer. (video)

35. **b.** is the answer. This child's age, ability to use language, and egocentrism clearly place him or her within Piaget's preoperational stage. (pp. 91–92)

36. **d.** is the answer. (video)

37. **b.** is the answer. (video)

38. **c.** is the answer. (video; p. 96)

    a. Ego is a Freudian term that has come to refer to an individual's sense of self.

    b. Self-concept refers to how individuals perceive themselves, rather than to their personality.

    d. Autonomy is only one factor of personality—specifically, that relating to an individual's independence, or self-determination.

39. **d.** is the answer. Conservation is a hallmark of the concrete operational stage; egocentrism is a hallmark of the preoperational stage. (pp. 91–93)

40. **e.** is the answer. To separate the influences of heredity and experience on behavior, one of the two must be held constant. (pp. 108–110)

a., b., c., & d. These situations would not allow one to separate the contributions of heredity and environment.

41. **a.** is the answer. (video)

    b. & c. Kagan believes that biology is not destiny.

42. **a.** is the answer. (video)

43. **c.** is the answer. (video)

    a. Although heredity does influence certain traits, such as outgoingness, it is the interaction of heredity and experience that ultimately molds personality.

    b. There is no single "most important factor" in personality. Moreover, for the same reason two sisters or brothers often have dissimilar personalities, a sister and brother may be very much alike.

    d. Karen and John's case is not at all unusual.

Key Terms

Textbook Terms

1. **Developmental psychology** is the branch of psychology concerned with physical, cognitive, and social change throughout the life span. (p. 79)

2. An **X chromosome** is found in both males and females. At conception, the egg always contributes an X sex chromosome; if the sperm also contributes an X chromosome, the child will be a girl. (p. 79)

3. A **Y chromosome** is found only in males. If, in addition to the X chromosome contributed by the egg, the sperm contributes a Y sex chromosome, the child will be a boy. (p. 79)

4. **Testosterone,** the most important male sex hormone, stimulates growth of the male sex organs in the fetus and development of the male sex characteristics during puberty. (p. 79)

    *Memory aid: Test*osterone is produced by the male's *test*es.

5. **Gender** is the biological and social definition of male and female. (p. 79)

6. The **zygote** (a term derived from the Greek word for "joint") is the fertilized egg, that is, the cluster of cells formed during conception by the union of sperm and egg. (p. 79)

7. The **embryo** is the developing prenatal organism from about 2 weeks through 2 months after conception. (p. 80)

8. The **fetus** is the developing prenatal human from 9 weeks after conception to birth. (p. 80)

9. **Teratogens** (literally, poisons) are any medications, drugs, viruses, or other substances that cross the mother's placenta and can harm the developing embryo or fetus. (p. 80)

10. The **fetal alcohol syndrome (FAS)** refers to the physical and cognitive abnormalities that heavy drinking by a pregnant woman may cause in the developing child. (p. 80)

11. The **rooting reflex** is the newborn's tendency, when his or her cheek is stroked, to orient toward the stimulus and begin sucking. (p. 81)

12. **Maturation** refers to the biological growth processes that enable orderly changes in behavior and are relatively uninfluenced by experience or other environmental factors. (p. 82)

Example: The ability to walk depends on a certain level of neural and muscular **maturation**. For this reason, until the toddler's body is physically ready to walk, practice "walking" has little effect.

13. **Plasticity** is the brain's capacity for modification, as evidenced by brain reorganization following damage (especially in children). (p. 85)

14. **Cognition** refers to the mental processes associated with thinking, knowing, remembering, and communicating. (p. 87)

15. In Piaget's theory of cognitive development, **schemas** are mental concepts that help organize and interpret information. (p. 87)

16. **Assimilation** refers to the interpretation of new information in light of existing cognitive schemas. (p. 87)

17. **Accommodation** refers to the modification of existing schemas in order to incorporate new information. (p. 87)

18. In Piaget's theory of cognitive stages, the **sensorimotor stage** lasts from birth to about age 2. During this stage, infants gain knowledge of the world through their senses and their motor activities. (p. 88)

19. **Object permanence,** which develops during the sensorimotor stage, is the awareness that things do not cease to exist when not perceived. (p. 88)

20. **Habituation** is a simple form of learning in which infants become less attentive to repeatedly presented stimuli. (p. 90)

21. In Piaget's theory, the **preoperational stage** lasts from about 2 to 6 or 7 years of age. During this stage language development is rapid, but the child is unable to understand the mental operations of concrete logic. (p. 91)

22. **Conservation** is the principle that properties such as number, volume, and mass remain constant despite changes in the forms of objects; it is acquired during the concrete operational stage. (p. 91)

23. In Piaget's theory, **egocentrism** refers to the difficulty that preoperational children have in considering another's viewpoint. "Ego" means "self," and "centrism" indicates "in the center"; the preoperational child is "self-centered." (p. 91)

24. During the **concrete operational stage,** lasting from about ages 6 or 7 to 11, children can think logically about events and objects. (p. 93)

25. In Piaget's theory, the **formal operational stage** normally begins about age 12. During this stage people begin to think logically about abstract concepts. (p. 93)

Memory aid: To help differentiate Piaget's stages, remember that "operations" are mental transformations. *Pre*operational children, who lack the ability to perform transformations, are "before" this developmental milestone. Concrete operational children can operate on real, or concrete objects. Formal operational children can perform logical transformations on abstract concepts.

26. **Stranger anxiety** is the fear of strangers that infants begin to display at about 8 months of age. (p. 94)

27. **Attachment** is an emotional tie with another person; shown in young children by their seeking closeness to a caregiver and showing distress on separation. (p. 95)

28. A **critical period** is a limited time shortly after birth during which an organ-

ism must be exposed to certain experiences or influences if it is to develop properly. (p. 96)

29. **Imprinting** is the process by which certain animals form attachments early in life, usually during a limited critical period. (p. 96)

30. **Temperament** refers to the rudiments of personality and a child's characteristic emotional reactivity and intensity. Temperament is a trait that is strongly linked to heredity. (p. 96)

31. According to Erikson, **basic trust** is a sense that the world is predictable and trustworthy—a concept that infants form if their needs are met by responsive caregiving. (p. 98)

32. **Self-concept** is a sense of one's own identity and personal worth. (p. 103)

33. **Gender identity** is each person's sense of being male or female. (p. 106)

34. **Gender-typing** refers to the acquisition of a male or female gender identity and role. (p. 106)

35. The **social learning theory** assumes that gender-typing (and other social behaviors) are learned through imitation of others and the receipt of rewards and punishments. (p. 106)

36. According to **gender schema theory**, children acquire a concept of what it means to be male or female in their particular culture and adjust their behavior accordingly. (p. 106)

Program Terms

37. **Habituation** refers to a decrease in response to a repeated stimulus—heart rate, eye gaze, and such in an infant. (also text p. 90)

38. Following habituation to a repeated stimulus, **dishabituation** occurs when an infant responds to another stimulus in a way that shows that he or she perceives it to be different.

PROGRAM 6

Language Development

TEXTBOOK ASSIGNMENT: Chapter 10: Thinking and Language, pp. 319–331

ORIENTATION

During the first years of life, cognitive development proceeds at a phenomenal pace as the infant is transformed from a baby who can know its world only through a limited set of reflexes into a toddler capable of imitating others, anticipating and remembering events, and pretending. Most significant among these advances is the development of language.

Program 6 of *Discovering Psychology* is concerned with language development during childhood. The reading assignment describes the structure of language, summarizes the stages of its development in children, and discusses the relationship of language to thinking. Two theories of language acquisition are evaluated: Skinner's theory that language acquisition is based entirely on learning, and Chomsky's theory that humans have a biological predisposition to acquire language.

Program 6 emphasizes that the *path* of language development is the same throughout the world. These paths are illustrated by actual examples, accompanied by the description of linguistic landmarks such as crying, cooing, babbling, and the emergence of the child's first words and sentences. In all cases, parents exhibit similar behaviors and speech patterns.

The similar developmental course of children the world over points to the importance of biological forces in language development. The grammatical errors, abbreviations, and overextensions of rules seen in children's speech suggest that humans have a natural propensity to acquire language and that children master its complicated rules by actively experimenting with them, rather than merely by imitating the speech that they hear.

NOTE: Answer guidelines for all Program 6 questions begin on page 106.

GOALS

After completing your study of the program and reading assignment, you should be prepared to:

1. Outline the main accomplishments and limitations of language development in children.

2. Explain the major theories of language acquisition.

3. Discuss the relationship between language and thinking.

GUIDED STUDY

Textbook Assignment

The text chapter should be studied one section at a time. Before you read, preview each section by skimming it, noting headings and boldface items. Then

Program 6: Language Development 99

read the appropriate section objectives from the following outline. Keep these objectives in mind and, as you read the chapter section, search for the information that will enable you to meet each objective. Once you have finished a section, write out answers for its objectives.

Language (pp. 319–328)

1. Describe the structure of language.

2. Trace the course of language acquisition and discuss alternative theories of language development.

3. Describe the research on animal communication and discuss the controversy over whether animals have language.

Thinking and Language (pp. 328–331)

4. Discuss the relationship between thought and language.

Program Assignment

Read the following objectives before you watch Program 6. As you watch, be alert for information that will help you answer each objective. Taking notes during the program will help you to formulate your answers later. After the program, write answers to the objectives. If you have access to the program on videotape, you may replay portions if you need to refresh your memory.

1. Explain the concept of an innate language acquisition device.

2. Describe "motherese" (or "parentese") and explain how this form of speech helps infants learn to communicate.

3. Discuss the universal features of preverbal communication between infants and their caregivers.

4. Discuss the importance of biological maturation in language development.

5. Describe how children first use single words.

6. Discuss how children master grammatical rules in their speech.

7. Identify the common features of speech dialogues and discuss how children learn to carry on dialogues.

PROGRESS TEST

Circle your answers to the following questions and check them with the answers on page 108. If your answer is incorrect, read the explanation for why it is incorrect and then consult the appropriate pages of the text (in parentheses following the correct answer).

1. The rules most directly involved in permitting a person to derive meaning from words and sentences are rules of:
   a. syntax.
   b. grammar.
   c. phonemic structure.
   d. semantics.

2. Which of the following is *not* true of babbling?
   a. It is imitation of adult speech.
   b. It is the same in all cultures.
   c. It typically occurs from about age 4 months to 1 year.
   d. Babbling increasingly comes to resemble a particular language.

3. Which of the following has been argued by critics of ape language research?
   a. Ape language is merely imitation of the trainer's behavior.
   b. There is little evidence that apes can equal even a 3-year-old's ability to order words with proper syntax.
   c. By seeing what they wish to see, trainers attribute greater linguistic ability to apes than actually exists.
   d. All of the above have been argued.

4. Phonemes are the basic units of _____ in language.
   a. sound
   b. meaning
   c. grammar
   d. semantics
   e. syntax

5. Whorf's linguistic relativity hypothesis states that:
   a. language is primarily a learned ability.
   b. language is partially an innate ability.
   c. the size of a person's vocabulary reflects his or her intelligence.
   d. our language shapes our thinking.

6. Which of the following *best* describes Chomsky's view of language development?
   a. Language is an entirely learned ability.
   b. Language is an innate ability.
   c. Humans have a biological predisposition to acquire language.
   d. There are no cultural influences on the development of language.

7. Biologist Karl von Frisch won the Nobel prize for his discovery that honeybees communicate with each other by:
   a. varying the acoustic pitch of their buzzing noises.
   b. secreting chemical odors called pheromones.
   c. performing an intricate dance.
   d. leading other worker bees on lengthy flights to find nectar.

8. Even very young babies:
   a. prefer human voices to other sounds.
   b. become distressed when the sound of a caregiver's voice is paired with a stranger's face.
   c. are sensitive to the intonation patterns of the speech that they hear.
   d. all of the above.

9. When parents speak to their children, they tend to:
   a. use short, simple sentences.
   b. speak too quickly for the child to follow the speech.
   c. violate grammatical rules.
   d. do all of the above.

10. The linguistic relativity hypothesis is challenged by the finding that:
    a. chimps can learn to communicate with one another spontaneously by using sign language.
    b. people with no word for a certain color can still perceive that color accurately.
    c. the Eskimo language contains a number of words for snow, whereas English has only one.
    d. infants' babbling contains many phonemes that do not occur in their own language and that they therefore cannot have heard.

11. Several studies have indicated that the generic pronoun *he*:
    a. tends for children and adults alike to trigger images of both males and females.
    b. tends for adults to trigger images of both males and females, but for children to trigger images of males.
    c. tends for both children and adults to trigger images of males but not females.
    d. for both children and adults triggers images of females about one-fourth of the time it is used.

12. Syntax refers to:
    a. the sounds in a word.
    b. the rules by which words are grouped into sentences.
    c. the rules by which meaning is derived from sentences.
    d. the overall rules of a language.

13. According to researcher Anne Fernald, the melody and pitch of a caregiver's speech:
    a. convey meaning that babies learn to understand.
    b. convey a unique meaning in every language.
    c. vary with the age of the child being spoken to.
    d. vary with the gender of the child being spoken to.

14. The typical word order in English is:
    a. actor, action, object.
    b. action, object, actor.
    c. object, action, actor.
    d. actor, object, action.

15. The rise-fall pattern in "motherese" (or "parentese") signifies:
    a. frustration.
    b. impending danger.
    c. praise.
    d. fear.
    e. anger.

16. Skinner and other behaviorists have argued that language development is the result of:
    a. imitation.
    b. reinforcement.
    c. association.
    d. all of the above.

17. Many psychologists are skeptical of claims that chimpanzees can acquire language because the chimps have not shown the ability to:
    a. use symbols meaningfully.
    b. acquire speech.
    c. acquire even a limited vocabulary.
    d. use syntax in communicating.

18. Before children can effectively use words as symbols they must:
    a. master the rules of grammar for their language.
    b. have reached the two- or three-word stage of language development.
    c. be able to store mental images of events and objects.
    d. have mastered the principle of universal adaptability.
    e. be able to understand the intent conveyed by a speaker.

19. According to the text, language acquisition is best described as:
    a. the result of conditioning and reinforcement.
    b. a biological process of maturation.
    c. an interaction between biology and experience.
    d. a mystery of which researchers have no real understanding.

20. Complete the following: -ed is to sh as _____ is to _____ .
    a. phoneme; morpheme
    b. morpheme; phoneme
    c. grammar; syntax
    d. syntax; grammar

21. The study in which people who immigrated to the United States at various ages were compared in terms of their ability to understand English grammar found that:
    a. age of arrival had no effect on mastery of grammar.
    b. those who immigrated as children understood grammar as well as native speakers.
    c. those who immigrated as adults understood grammar as well as native speakers.
    d. whether or not English was spoken in the home was the most important factor in mastering the rules of grammar.

22. Which of the following was *not* mentioned in the program as evidence that language acquisition cannot be explained by learning alone?
    a. Children master the complicated rules of grammar with relative ease.
    b. Children create sentences they have never heard.
    c. Children make the kinds of mistakes that suggest they are attempting to apply rules of grammar.
    d. Children raised in isolation from language spontaneously begin speaking words.

23. Researchers taught the chimpanzee Washoe and the gorilla Koko to communicate by using:
    a. various sounds.
    b. plastic symbols of various shapes and colors.
    c. sign language.
    d. all of the above.

24. Which of the following is true regarding the relationship between thinking and language?
    a. Real thinking requires the use of language.
    b. People sometimes think in images rather than in words.
    c. A thought that cannot be expressed in a particular language cannot occur to speakers of that language.
    d. All of the above are true.

25. One reason an English-speaking adult may have difficulty pronouncing Russian words is that:
    a. the vocal tracts of English- and Russian-speaking people develop differently in response to the demands of the two languages.
    b. although English and Russian have very similar morphemes, their phonemic inventories are very different.
    c. although English and Russian have very similar phonemes, the morphemic inventories are very different.
    d. after the babbling stage, a child who hears only English stops producing other phonemes.

26. Telegraphic speech is typical of the _____ stage.
    a. babbling
    b. one-word
    c. two-word
    d. three-word

27. A listener hearing a recording of Japanese, Spanish, and North American children babbling would:
    a. not be able to tell them apart.
    b. be able to tell them apart if they were older than 6 months.
    c. be able to tell them apart if they were older than 8 to 10 months.
    d. be able to tell them apart at any age.

28. The child who says "Milk gone" is engaging in _____ . This type of utterance demonstrates that children are actively experimenting with the rules of _____ .
    a. babbling; syntax
    b. telegraphic speech; syntax
    c. babbling; semantics
    d. telegraphic speech; semantics

29. The word *predates* contains _____ phonemes and _____ morphemes.
    a. 7; 3
    b. 3; 7
    c. 7; 2
    d. 3; 2

30. Which of the following utterances is an example of overgeneralization of a grammatical rule?
    a. We goed to the store.
    b. Ball pretty.
    c. The sky is crying.
    d. We eat paghetti.

31. The sentence "Blue jeans wear false smiles" has correct _____ but incorrect _____ .
    a. morphemes; phonemes
    b. phonemes; morphemes
    c. semantics; syntax
    d. syntax; semantics

32. Regarding the relationship between thinking and language, which of the following most accurately reflects the position taken in the text?
    a. Language determines everything about our thinking.
    b. Language determines the way we think.
    c. Thinking without language is not possible.
    d. Thinking affects our language, which then affects our thought.

33. Children first demonstrate a rudimentary understanding of syntax during the _____ stage.
    a. babbling
    b. one-word
    c. two-word
    d. three-word

34. The deep structure of language corresponds to its:
    a. rules of syntax.
    b. rules of grammar.
    c. physical characteristics.
    d. underlying meaning.

35. Conversational dialogues have all but which of the following essential features?
    a. a means of signaling the willingness to converse
    b. the participants' understanding of the rules for taking turns
    c. using appropriate forms of address
    d. a basis for closing conversations by mutual consent

KEY TERMS

Using your own words, write a brief definition or explanation of each of the following terms.

Textbook Terms

1. language

2. phonemes

3. morphemes

4. grammar

5. semantics

6. syntax

7. babbling stage

8. one-word stage

9. two-word stage

10. telegraphic speech

11. linguistic relativity

Program Terms

12. deep structure

13. universal adaptability

14. "motherese" (or "parentese")

ANSWERS

Guided Study

The following guidelines provide the main points that your answers should have touched upon.

Textbook Assignment

1. Phonemes are the basic units of sound in a language. Morphemes are the smallest units of speech that convey meaning. Most morphemes are combinations of two or more phonemes. Each language has a system of rules, or grammar, that enables people to use and understand it. Semantics refers to the grammatical rules used to derive meaning from the elements of language. Syntax specifies the rules for combining words into sentences.

2. At 3 to 4 months of age, babies enter a babbling stage in which they spontaneously utter phonemes of all languages. By 1 year children enter the one-word stage. In this stage, single-syllable words are used to name things and may even be inflected to convey the meaning of an entire sentence. By age 2 most children enter the two-word stage. At this time their speech consists of telegraphic utterances containing mostly nouns and verbs, yet placed in a sensible syntactic order. Children then quickly begin uttering longer and more complex phrases and sentences.

   According to B. F. Skinner, language development can be explained according to the learning principles of association, imitation, and reinforcement. In contrast, Noam Chomsky believes that children are biologically prepared to learn language as they interact with their caregivers. Most theorists today believe that language development is the product of both hereditary and environmental influences.

3. Numerous studies demonstrate that animals communicate effectively amongst themselves. Karl von Frisch, for example, discovered that explorer bees convey to other bees the direction and distance of a food source by means of an intricate dance.

   Several attempts have been made to teach sign language and other symbolic languages to chimpanzees. Although apes have a capacity to learn a relatively large vocabulary of sign words, critics contend that much of their signing is nothing more than imitation of their trainer's signs and shows little evidence of syntax.

4. According to Whorf's linguistic relativity hypothesis, language determines the way we think. Critics of this idea claim that our language *reflects* rather than creates the way we think. Studies of the ability of vocabulary enrichment to enhance thinking reveal that it is more accurate to say that language *influences*, rather than determines, thought. Some thoughts, such as the imagery involved in art, music, and athletics, do not depend on language.

Program Assignment

1. It was once assumed that nurture fully explained language acquisition. According to this view, language is a skill that children learn by imitating others. In 1957 Noam Chomsky revolutionized the field by questioning this assumption. Chomsky argued that children come into the world with a *language acquisition device (LAD)*, an actual neurological structure in the brain that makes it possible for children to learn any language. The language acquisition device makes it possible for children to understand the *deep structure*, or meaning, of any language, because the principles are innate.

2. Children's first conversations are wordless. They interact with others by coordinating sounds and intonations. According to Jean Berko Gleason, social interaction activates the LAD; when adults speak to, not around, children, the children learn intent and are able to associate actions with words. In turn, adults use melodic intonations usually reserved for soothing and arousing the baby. Caregivers who use this special speech, which is called "motherese" or "parentese," help their babies acquire language by speaking slowly in a high-pitched voice, enunciating clearly, and using short, simple sentences with lots of repetition.

3. Fernald hypothesizes that the musical contours of parents' speech conveys meaning long before actual words and sentences are used. Babies infer intention and emotion through the melody and pitch contours of others' speech. To praise a baby, for instance, speakers of English, Italian, German, Japanese and other languages use a rise-fall pattern of melodic speech. To warn a child of impending dangers, speakers of these same languages use a short, sharp pattern of speech that is much lower in pitch. The fact that the "melodies" of parents' speech are similar suggests that they, not the actual words, are carrying the meaning to the child.

4. Research has shown that every child in every culture goes through some of the same stages in language development. As in walking or eating, what a child can do with language depends on a developmental timetable that regulates brain development and the maturation of muscles in the mouth and throat that are needed for communication. During the babbling stage, for example, babies practice the making, grouping, and intonation of sounds. At this point an infant can distinguish and reproduce sounds of any language. This ability is called *universal adaptability*. By the time a child is 1

year old, he or she has lost this ability and becomes a specialist in his or her native language, distinguishing and reproducing only sounds common to that language.

5. Toward the end of the first year children enter the one-word stage. The first words are usually part of a behavioral ritual, such as saying "hi" or "bye." The next set of single words expresses relationships, first between objects and actions (such as saying "ball" to mean "throw it"), then between objects (such as saying "fishy" when pointing to an empty fish tank where fish once swam). Finally come words that are meant to influence events, such as saying "again" when a child wants an action repeated.

   Using words effectively as symbols can occur only when a number of mental abilities have matured sufficiently, in particular, when the child's memory is capable of storing images of events or objects and retrieving the appropriate words that symbolize them.

6. The use of grammar first becomes apparent during the *telegraphic* stage when children begin to form simple two-word sentences. These sentences, consisting mostly of nouns and verbs, lack plurals, articles, and tenses. They do maintain grammatical word order with actor first, action second, and object last.

   Psycholinguist Dan Slobin has studied how children around the world acquire a system of grammatical rules on their own without imitating the people around them. Common childhood utterances, such as "I breaked the glass" or "I falled down," indicate that children are actively experimenting with the rules of grammar rather than merely repeating speech they have heard.

7. Most dialogues are highly structured forms of social communication that include three essential features that must be understood and shared by both parties. The first is some mechanism for opening conversations in ways that signal a willingness to converse. The second is that both parties must understand the unwritten rules for taking turns. The third is some means of ending conversations by mutual agreement. When these simple acts are not carried out properly, the result is confusion and even distress.

   Parents teach children the rules of dialogue by engaging them in conversation, asking them questions, and teaching them what to say in response to another's utterance. This instruction helps children learn to use language and prepares them for more advanced social interactions.

Progress Test

1. **d.** is the answer. Semantic rules are directly concerned with the derivation of meaning from morphemes, words, and sentences. (p. 320)

   a. Syntax is the set of rules for a language that permits the combination of words into sentences.

   b. Grammar is the overall system of rules for using a language and, as such, includes syntax as well as semantics.

   c. Phonemic structure concerns the basic sounds, or phonemes, of a language.

2. **a.** is the answer. Babbling is not the imitation of adult speech since babbling infants produce phonemes from languages they have not heard and could not be imitating. (p. 321)

3. **d.** is the answer. (p. 326)

4. **a.** is the answer. (p. 319)

b. Morphemes are the basic units of meaning.

   c., d., & e. The text does not refer to basic units of grammar, semantics, or syntax.

5. **d.** is the answer. (p. 328)

   a. This is Skinner's position regarding language development.

   b. This is Chomsky's position regarding language development.

   c. The linguistic relativity hypothesis is concerned with the content of thought, not intelligence.

6. **c.** is the answer. (p. 323)

   a. This is Skinner's position.

   b. According to Chomsky, although the *ability* to acquire language is innate, the child can only acquire language in association with others.

   d. Cultural influences are an important example of the influence of learning on language development, an influence Chomsky fully accepts.

7. **c.** is the answer. The dance's direction and duration inform worker bees of the direction and distance of a food source. (p. 325)

8. **d.** is the answer. (video)

9. **a.** is the answer. (video)

   b. & c. Parents tend to speak more slowly, yet grammatically, to their babies.

10. **b.** is the answer. The evidence that absence of a term for a color does not affect ability to perceive the color challenges the idea that language always shapes thought. (p. 330)

    a. & d. These findings are not relevant to the linguistic relativity hypothesis, which addresses the relationship between language and thought.

    c. This finding is in keeping with the linguistic relativity hypothesis.

11. **c.** is the answer. The generic pronoun *he* evidently tends, for both adults and children, to conjure up images of males. (p. 329)

12. **b.** is the answer. (p. 320)

    a. Phonemes are the sounds in a word.

    c. Such rules are known as semantics.

    d. Such rules are the language's grammar, which would include its syntax as well as its semantics.

13. **a.** is the answer. (video)

    b. In fact, Fernald found that many languages use similar intonation patterns to convey a particular meaning.

    c. & d. Fernald's research did not address these issues.

14. **a.** is the answer. (video)

15. **c.** is the answer. (video)

16. **d.** is the answer. These are all basic principles of learning and explain language development. (p. 322)

17. **d.** is the answer. Syntax is one of the fundamental aspects of language, and chimps seem unable, for example, to use word order to convey differences in meaning. (p. 326)

a. & c. Chimps' use of sign language demonstrates both the use of symbols and the acquisition of fairly sizable vocabularies.

b. No psychologist would require the use of speech as evidence of language; significantly, all the research and arguments focus on what chimps are and are not able to do in acquiring other facets of language.

18. **c.** is the answer. (video)

    a. & b. The ability to use words as symbols begins to emerge well before these stages are reached.

    d. Universal adaptability refers to the fact that babies throughout the world are capable of reproducing sounds from any language.

    e. Children understand intent long before they use language.

19. **c.** is the answer. Children are biologically prepared to learn language as they and their caregivers interact. (video; text p. 325)

    a. This is Skinner's position.

    b. No psychologist, including Chomsky, believes that language is entirely a product of biological maturation.

    d. Although language acquisition is not completely understood, research has shed sufficient light on it to render it less than a complete mystery.

20. **b.** is the answer. The morpheme *-ed* changes the meaning of a regular verb to form its past tense; the phoneme *sh* is a unique sound in the English language. (pp. 319–320)

    c. & d. Syntax, which specifies rules for combining words into sentences, is one aspect of the grammar of a language.

21. **b.** is the answer. (p. 324)

22. **d.** is the answer. Researchers believe that the inborn capacity for language acquisition must be activated by exposure to language. And, in fact, children raised in isolation will not begin to speak spontaneously. (video; text pp. 322–325)

23. **c.** is the answer. (p. 326)

24. **b.** is the answer. (p. 330)

    a. Researchers do not make a distinction between real and other thinking, nor do they consider nonlinguistic thinking less valid than linguistic thinking.

    c. As indicated by several studies cited in the textbook, this is not true.

25. **d.** is the answer. Following the babbling stage, the child's ability to produce all phonemes becomes in a sense shaped and limited to the ability to produce those phonemes he or she hears. (p. 321)

    a. The vocal tract of *Homo sapiens* does not develop in specialized ways for different languages.

    b. & c. English and Russian differ significantly in both their phonemes and their morphemes. Nor is there any reason why differences in morphemes would in and of themselves cause pronunciation difficulties.

26. **c.** is the answer. (video; text pp. 321–322)

27. **a.** is the answer. (video; text p. 321)

28. **b.** is the answer. Such utterances, characteristic of a child of about 2 years, are like telegrams in that they consist mainly of nouns and verbs and show the use of syntax. (video; text p. 322)

a. & c. Babbling consists of phonemes, not words.

d. Semantics refers to the rules by which meaning is derived from sentences; this speech example indicates nothing in particular about the child's understanding of semantics.

29. **a.** is the answer. Each sound of the word is a phoneme (note that the second letter *e* does not itself represent a sound); the morphemes are *pre*, which means "before," *date*, and *s*, which indicates the plural. (pp. 319–320)

30. **a.** is the answer. Adding *-ed* to the irregular verb go results in the ungrammatical "goed"—an overgeneralization of the rule by which the past tense of regular verbs is formed. (p. 322)

    b. This is an example of telegraphic speech.

    c. This is a grammatical statement.

    d. *Paghetti* is simply an immature pronunciation of spaghetti; young children often have difficulty with consonant clusters like *sp*.

31. **d.** is the answer. This sentence, although semantically meaningless, nevertheless follows the grammatical rules of English syntax for combining words into sentences. (p. 320)

    a. & b. The phonemes (smallest units of sound) and morphemes (smallest units of meaning) of this sentence are equally correct.

32. **d.** is the answer. (p. 330)

33. **c.** is the answer. Although the child's utterances are only two words long, the words are placed in a sensible order. In English, for example, adjectives are placed before nouns. (video; text pp. 321–322)

    a. & b. These answers are incorrect because syntax specifies rules for *combining* two or more units in speech.

    d. There is no three-word stage.

34. **d.** is the answer. (video)

35. **c.** is the answer. (video)

Key Terms

Textbook Terms

1. **Language** refers to spoken, written, or gestured words and how we combine them to communicate meaning. (p. 319)

2. **Phonemes** are the smallest units of sound in a language that are distinctive for speakers of the language. (p. 319)

3. **Morphemes** are the smallest units of language that convey meaning. (p. 320)

   Example: The word *dogs*, which contains four phonemes, contains only two **morphemes**—*dog* and *-s*. Although most morphemes are combinations of two or more phonemes, the plural *-s* conveys a distinctive meaning of "more than one."

4. **Grammar** is a system of rules that enables us to communicate with and understand others. (p. 320)

5. **Semantics** is the aspect of grammar that specifies the rules used to derive meaning from morphemes, words, and sentences. (p. 320)

   Example: One **semantic** rule of English is that adding *-ed* to a verb gives the verb a past-tense meaning.

6. **Syntax** is the aspect of grammar specifying the rules for combining words into grammatical sentences. (p. 320)

   Example: One **syntactic** rule of English is that adjectives are positioned before nouns.

7. The **babbling stage** of speech development, which begins at 3 to 4 months, is characterized by the spontaneous utterance of speech sounds. During the babbling stage, children the world over sound alike. (pp. 320–321)

8. Between 1 and 2 years of age children speak mostly in single words; they are therefore in the **one-word stage** of linguistic development. (p. 321)

9. Beginning about age 2, children are in the **two-word stage** and speak mostly in two-word sentences. (pp. 321–322)

10. **Telegraphic speech** is the economical, telegramlike speech of children in the two-word stage. Utterances consist mostly of nouns and verbs; however, words occur in the correct order, showing that the child has learned some of the language's syntactic rules. (p. 322)

11. **Linguistic relativity** is Benjamin Whorf's hypothesis that language determines the way we think. (p. 328)

Program Terms

12. In Noam Chomsky's theory of language development, **deep structure** refers to the underlying meaning of an utterance in a particular language. Chomsky believes that children are biologically predisposed to acquire language because they have an innate understanding of the deep structure of language.

13. **Universal adaptability** refers to the fact that, during the babbling stage, infants can distinguish and reproduce the sounds of any language. By 1 year the child has lost this ability and becomes a specialist in his or her native language, distinguishing and reproducing only sounds common to that language.

14. **"Motherese" (or "parentese")** is the special speech that parents and caregivers use with babies to help them acquire language. Adults using motherese speak slowly in a high-pitched voice, enunciate clearly, and use short, simple sentences with lots of repetition.

PROGRAM 7

Sensation and Perception

TEXTBOOK ASSIGNMENT: Chapter 5: Sensation, pp. 147–163 and
Chapter 6: Perception, pp. 183–200

ORIENTATION

Program 7 is concerned with the processes by which our sense receptors and nervous system represent our experiences (sensation) and then organize and interpret them as meaningful events (perception). The reading assignment traces the path of light through the eye and describes the various stages in which visual images are processed in the brain. It explores the basic processes by which sensation becomes perception, and why it sometimes goes awry. In presenting research findings from studies of sensory restriction and subliminal stimulation, the text addresses the issue of the relative importance of experience and heredity in perception.

Program 7 focuses on the processes we use to create meaning out of the myriad images to which our eyes are exposed. A number of intriguing perceptual illusions and paradoxes are also demonstrated. Psychologists have learned a great deal about how perception works from studying these phenomena.

In this program, there are many terms to learn and several theories you must understand. Many of the terms are related to the structure of the eye and the neural pathways that enable visual perception. The theories discussed include several pertaining to color vision and the Gestalt theory of perception. As you study these theories, concentrate on understanding the strengths and weaknesses (if any) of each.

NOTE: Answer guidelines for all Program 7 questions begin on page 126.

GOALS

After completing your study of the program and reading assignment, you should be prepared to:

1. Describe the sequence of steps through which visual images are processed.

2. Discuss the effects of past experience, expectations, and contexts on perception.

3. Discuss the sensory and perceptual processes involved in perceiving form, color, and depth.

4. Explain the effects of sensory restriction on human perception.

GUIDED STUDY

Textbook Assignment

The text chapter should be studied one section at a time. Before you read, preview each section by skimming it, noting headings and boldface items. Then read the appropriate section objectives from the following outline. Keep these objectives in mind and, as you read the chapter section, search for the information that will enable you to meet each objective. Once you have finished a section, write out answers for its objectives.

1. Contrast the processes of sensation and perception.

Sensing the World: Some Basic Principles (pp. 148–153)

2. Distinguish between absolute and difference thresholds and discuss research findings on signal detection.

3. Discuss whether subliminal stimuli are sensed and whether they are persuasive.

4. Describe the phenomenon of sensory adaptation and show how it focuses our attention on changing stimulation.

Vision (pp. 153–163)

5. Explain the visual process, including the stimulus input, the structure of the eye, and the transduction of light energy.

6. Explain the cause of two common problems involving acuity.

7. Discuss how visual information is processed in parallel (through the eye's retina and the brain) and at increasingly abstract levels.

8. Discuss how both the Young-Helmholtz and the opponent-process theories contribute to our understanding of color vision and how context affects color vision.

Perceptual Illusions (pp. 183–184)

9. Explain how illusions help us to understand perception.

Perceptual Organization (pp. 184–194)

10. Describe Gestalt psychology's contribution to our understanding of perception, including the figure-ground relationship and principles of perceptual grouping in form perception.

11. Discuss research on depth perception involving the use of the visual cliff.

12. Explain how 3-D movies are made and describe the binocular and monocular cues in depth perception.

13. Describe the perceptual constancies and show how they operate in visual illusions.

Interpretation (pp. 194–200)

14. Explain the nature-nurture debate on the origins of perception, particularly as related to research findings on sensory restriction and restored vision.

15. Discuss the effects of assumptions, expectations, schemas, and contexts on our perceptions.

Program Assignment

Read the following objectives before you watch Program 7. As you watch, be alert for information that will help you answer each objective. Taking notes during the program will help you to formulate your answers later. After the program, write answers to the objectives. If you have access to the program on videotape, you may replay portions if you need to refresh your memory.

1. Differentiate *distal stimulus* from *proximal stimulus*.

2. Explain what the use of distorting goggles indicates regarding the adaptability of perception.

3. Define and contrast bottom-up and top-down processing in perception (see also text page 191).

4. Explain what the "young-old woman" and "rat-man" examples reveal about visual processing.

PROGRESS TEST

Circle your answers to the following questions and check them with the answers on page 130. If your answer is incorrect, read the explanation for why it is incorrect and then consult the appropriate pages of the text (in parentheses following the correct answer).

1. A decrease in sensory responsiveness accompanying an unchanging stimulus is called:
   a. sensory fatigue.
   b. accommodation.
   c. sensory restriction.
   d. sensory adaptation.

2. The size of the pupil is controlled by the:
   a. lens.
   b. retina.
   c. cornea.
   d. iris.

3. The process by which the lens changes its curvature is:
   a. accommodation.
   b. sensory adaptation.
   c. focusing.
   d. transduction.

4. Given normal sensory ability, a person standing atop a mountain can see a candle flame atop another mountain 30 miles away. This is a description of vision's:
   a. difference threshold.
   b. jnd.
   c. absolute threshold.
   d. signal detection.

5. Sensation is to _____ as perception is to _____ .
   a. recognizing a stimulus; interpreting a stimulus
   b. detecting a stimulus; recognizing a stimulus
   c. interpreting a stimulus; detecting a stimulus
   d. seeing; hearing

6. The transduction of light energy into neural impulses takes place in the:
   a. iris.
   b. retina.
   c. lens.
   d. optic nerve.

7. The brain breaks vision into subdimensions such as color, depth, movement, and form, and works on each aspect simultaneously. This is called:
   a. feature detection.
   b. parallel processing.
   c. accommodation.
   d. opponent processing.

8. _____ processing refers to how the physical characteristics of stimuli influence their interpretation.
   a. top-down
   b. bottom-up
   c. parapsychological
   d. human factors

9. One light may appear reddish and another greenish because they differ in:
   a. wavelength.
   b. amplitude.
   c. opponent processes.
   d. brightness.

10. After staring at a very intense red stimulus for a few minutes, Carrie shifted her gaze to a beige wall and "saw" the color _____ . Carrie's experience provides support for the _____ theory.
    a. green; trichromatic
    b. blue; opponent-process
    c. green; opponent-process
    d. blue; trichromatic

11. Which of the following is the correct order of the structures through which light passes after entering the eye?
    a. lens, pupil, cornea, retina
    b. pupil, cornea, lens, retina
    c. cornea, pupil, lens, retina
    d. cornea, retina, pupil, lens

12. Assuming that the visual systems of humans and other mammals function similarly, you would expect that the retina of a nocturnal animal (one active only at night) would contain:
    a. mostly cones.
    b. mostly rods.
    c. an equal number of rods and cones.
    d. more bipolar cells than an animal active only during the day.

13. Experiments with distorted visual environments demonstrate that:
    a. adaptation rarely takes place.
    b. animals adapt readily, but humans do not.
    c. humans adapt readily, while lower animals typically do not.
    d. adaptation is possible during a critical period in infancy but not thereafter.

14. Hubel and Wiesel discovered feature detectors in the _____ of a monkey's visual system.
    a. fovea
    b. optic nerve
    c. iris
    d. cortex

15. Concerning the evidence for subliminal stimulation, which of the following is the best answer?
    a. The brain processes some information without our awareness.
    b. Stimuli too weak to cross our thresholds for awareness may trigger a response in our sense receptors.
    c. Because the absolute threshold is a statistical average, we are able to detect weaker stimuli some of the time.
    d. All of the above are true.

16. Which of the following is the most accurate description of how we process color?
    a. Throughout the visual system, color processing is divided into separate red, green, and blue systems.
    b. Throughout the visual system, red-green, blue-yellow, and black-white opponent processes operate.
    c. Color processing occurs in two stages: (1) a three-color system in the retina and (2) opponent-process cells en route to the visual cortex.

d. Color processing occurs in two stages: (1) an opponent-process system in the retina and (2) a three-color system en route to the visual cortex.

17. The visual cortex is located:
    a. at the front of the brain.
    b. on the sides of the brain.
    c. in the occipital lobe of the brain.
    d. in the parietal lobe of the brain.

18. In the program, subjects were shown an ambiguous drawing that can be interpreted as a man or a rat. Subjects were more likely to identify the drawing as a rat if they:
    a. perceived the drawing analytically rather than holistically.
    b. perceived the drawing holistically rather than analytically.
    c. had just seen pictures of animals.
    d. were persuaded to use top-down processing.

19. One reason that your ability to detect fine visual details is greatest when scenes are focused on the fovea of your retina is that:
    a. there are more feature detectors in the fovea than in the peripheral regions of the retina.
    b. cones in the fovea are nearer to the optic nerve than those in peripheral regions of the retina.
    c. many rods, which are clustered in the fovea, have individual bipolar cells to relay their information to the cortex.
    d. many cones, which are clustered in the fovea, have individual bipolar cells to relay their information to the cortex.

20. In shopping for a new stereo, you discover that you cannot differentiate between the sounds of models *X* and *Y*. The difference between *X* and *Y* is below your:
    a. absolute threshold.
    b. signal detection.
    c. receptor threshold.
    d. difference threshold.

21. In comparing the human eye to a camera, the film would be analogous to the eye's:
    a. pupil.
    b. lens.
    c. cornea.
    d. retina.

22. To facilitate the rapid processing of an object's shape, our perceptual system relies especially on information regarding the object's:
    a. brightness.
    b. color.
    c. distance.
    d. edges.

23. Receptors are designed to:
    a. detect specific forms of physical energy.
    b. relay sensory information from one part of the brain to another.
    c. store memories of previous sensory experiences.
    d. do all of the above.

24. *Distal stimulus* refers to:
    a. an object's stimulation of a sensory receptor.
    b. the brain's identification of a sensory impression as an actual object.
    c. a cell in the visual cortex that responds to straight lines and contours.
    d. a visual paradox.

25. As the football game continued into the night, LeVar noticed that he was having difficulty distinguishing the colors of the players' uniforms. This is because the _____ , which enable color vision, have a _____ absolute threshold for brightness than the available light intensity.
    a. rods; higher
    b. cones; higher
    c. rods; lower
    d. cones; lower

26. Nearsightedness is a condition in which the:
    a. lens has become inflexible.
    b. lens is too thin.
    c. eyeball is longer than normal.
    d. eyeball is shorter than normal.

27. The historical movement associated with the statement "The whole is different from the sum of its parts" is:
    a. parapsychology.
    b. behavioral psychology.
    c. functional psychology.
    d. Gestalt psychology.

28. The figure-ground relationship has demonstrated that:
    a. perception is largely innate.
    b. perception is simply a point-for-point representation of sensation.
    c. the same stimulus can trigger more than one perception.
    d. different people see different things when viewing a scene.

29. When we stare at an object, each of our eyes receives a slightly different image, providing a depth cue known as:
    a. convergence.
    b. linear perspective.
    c. relative motion.
    d. retinal disparity.

30. In _____ perception, an object is broken down into its component parts.
    a. analytic
    b. holistic
    c. bottom-up
    d. top-down

31. As we move, viewed objects cast changing shapes on our retinas, although we do not perceive the objects as changing. This is the phenomenon of:
    a. perceptual constancy.
    b. relative motion.
    c. linear perspective.
    d. continuity.

32. Kittens reared seeing only horizontal lines:
    a. later had difficulty perceiving both horizontal and vertical lines.
    b. later had difficulty perceiving vertical lines but eventually regained normal sensitivity.
    c. later had difficulty perceiving vertical lines and never regained normal sensitivity.
    d. showed no impairment in perception, indicating that neural feature detectors develop even in the absence of normal sensory experiences.

33. Adults who were born blind but later have their vision restored:
    a. are almost immediately able to recognize familiar objects.
    b. typically fail to recognize familiar objects.
    c. are unable to follow moving objects with their eyes.
    d. have excellent eye-hand coordination.

34. The moon illusion occurs in part because distance cues at the horizon make the moon seem:
    a. farther away and therefore larger.
    b. closer and therefore larger.
    c. farther away and therefore smaller.
    d. closer and therefore smaller.

35. _____ processing refers to how our knowledge and expectations influence perception.
    a. Top-down
    b. Bottom-up
    c. Parapsychological
    d. Human factors

36. *Proximal stimulus* refers to:
    a. an object's stimulation of a sensory receptor.
    b. the brain's identification of a sensory impression as an actual object.
    c. a cell in the visual cortex that responds to straight lines and contours.
    d. a visual paradox.

37. Figure is to ground as _____ is to _____ .
    a. night; day
    b. top; bottom
    c. cloud; sky
    d. sensation; perception

38. The phenomenon that refers to the ways in which an individual's expectations influence perception is called:
    a. perceptual set.
    b. retinal disparity.
    c. convergence.
    d. visual capture.

39. All of the following are laws of perceptual organization except:
    a. proximity.
    b. closure.
    c. continuity.
    d. simplicity.

40. Which explanation of the Müller-Lyer illusion is offered by the text?
    a. The corners in our carpentered world teach us to interpret outward- or inward-pointing arrowheads at the end of a line as a cue to the line's distance from us and so to its length.
    b. The drawing's violation of linear perspective makes one line seem longer.
    c. Top-down processing of the illusion is prevented because of the ambiguity of the stimuli.
    d. All of the above were offered as explanations.

41. Visual paradoxes are difficult to interpret because:
    a. there is no proximal stimulus.
    b. the visual context is usually unfamiliar to us.
    c. there are conflicting visual cues in the proximal stimulus.
    d. there is no distal stimulus.

KEY TERMS

Using your own words, write a brief definition or explanation of each of the following terms.

Textbook Terms

1. sensation

2. perception

3. bottom-up processing

4. top-down processing

5. psychophysics

6. absolute threshold

7. signal detection theory

8. subliminal

9. difference threshold (jnd)

10. Weber's law

11. sensory adaptation

12. transduction

13. wavelength and hue

14. intensity

15. pupil

16. iris

17. lens

18. accommodation

19. retina

20. acuity

21. nearsightedness

22. farsightedness

23. rods and cones

24. optic nerve

25. blind spot

26. fovea

27. feature detectors

28. parallel processing

29. Young-Helmholtz trichromatic (three-color) theory

30. opponent-process theory

31. color constancy

32. visual capture

33. gestalt

34. figure-ground

35. grouping

36. depth perception

37. visual cliff

38. binocular cues

39. monocular cues

40. retinal disparity

41. convergence

42. phi phenomenon

43. perceptual constancy

44. perceptual adaptation

45. perceptual set

Program Terms

46. proximal stimulus

47. distal stimulus

ANSWERS

Guided Study

The following guidelines provide the main points that your answers should have touched upon.

Textbook Assignment

1. Sensation refers to how we detect physical energy from the environment and encode it as neural signals. Perception refers to how we select, organize, and interpret sensory information. Sensory analysis, which works at the entry level, is called "bottom-up" processing. Perception, which draws on our experience and expectations, is called "top-down" processing.

2. An absolute threshold is the minimum stimulation necessary to detect a particular environmental stimulus 50 percent of the time. A difference threshold, or just noticeable difference (jnd), is the minimum difference a person can detect between any two stimuli 50 percent of the time. Weber's law states that the difference threshold is a constant proportion of the stimulus.

   Signal detection studies indicate that thresholds depend not only on the strength of stimuli, but also on experience, expectations, motivation, and level of fatigue. Thus, thresholds are not constant.

3. Stimuli at or above the "absolute" threshold are detected half the time; subliminal stimuli, which are below the absolute threshold, are therefore detected less than half the time. Experiments show that under certain conditions, a weak stimulus may reach a part of the brain where it evokes a feeling but not conscious awareness. Claims that subliminal stimulation may lead to thought persuasion have not been supported, however. While subliminal messages may have a fleeting effect on thinking, they do not have an enduring effect on behavior.

4. Sensory adaptation refers to our diminishing sensitivity to an unchanging stimulus. By allowing us to focus our attention on informative changes in the environment, it keeps us from being distracted by the uninformative, constant stimulation of unchanging stimuli.

5. Visible light is a small portion of the larger spectrum of electromagnetic radiation. Light can be described by two physical characteristics, wavelength and intensity.

    Vision begins when light enters the eye through the opening in the iris called the pupil. Light passes through the lens, which changes its curvature (accommodation) in order to focus light on the retina. Within the retina are the rods and cones, which are responsible for the transduction of light energy into neural impulses. The optic nerve carries neural impulses from the retina to visual processing centers in the brain.

6. Acuity, or sharpness of vision, is affected by distortions in the shape of the eye. In nearsightedness, the eyeball is longer than normal, causing light rays to converge in front of the retina. In farsightedness the eyeball is shorter than normal, causing light rays to reach the retina *before* they have converged to produce a sharp image.

7. The lowest level of visual information processing—the encoding and analyzing of sensory information—is at the retina. As we view a scene, the rods and cones of the retina transduce the reflected light into neural impulses that are relayed to bipolar and ganglion cells and then sent to the brain via the optic nerve. The brain—the source of most information processing—processes these visual stimuli relatively quickly by breaking them down into various subdimensions and working on each simultaneously (parallel processing). Thus, feature detectors break the image into bars, edges, gradients of light, and other elementary features. Higher-level brain cells in the parietal and temporal lobes respond to specific visual scenes and then reassemble the features and compare the resulting image with previously stored images until a match, and therefore recognition, occurs.

8. The Young-Helmholtz trichromatic (three-color) theory states that the retina has three types of color receptors, each sensitive to one of three colors: red, green, or blue. To "see" other hues, such as yellow, there must be a unique combination of activity in two or three of these color receptors (red and green, in this case). This theory explains color processing at the level of the retina.

    According to the opponent-process theory, some cells in the retina and in the thalamus of the brain analyze visual information in terms of the opponent colors red and green, blue and yellow, and black and white. This theory explains why we see afterimages following intense stimulation with a particular color.

9. Understanding illusions requires an understanding of how we transform sensations into meaningful perceptions. Thus, for example, psychologists have learned a great deal about the interplay of size and distance from the Müller-Lyer illusion, about the principle of relative height from the horizontal-vertical illusion, and about principles of grouping and depth perception from the study of other illusions.

10 The Gestalt psychologists demonstrated that perception involves the organization of sensations into meaningful wholes, or gestalts, that may exceed the sum of their individual parts and be regrouped into more than one perception. They also showed that to recognize an object, we must first perceive it as a figure distinct from its surrounding stimuli, or ground. The

Gestalt psychologists identified several principles by which sensations are organized into meaningful perceptions; these include proximity, similarity, continuity, closure, and connectedness.

11. The visual cliff is a miniature cliff with an apparent drop-off on one side of a table. Gibson and Walk found that infants as young as 6 months of age refused to crawl out on the glass, despite their mother's coaxing. Newborn animals with virtually no visual experience respond similarly, thus indicating that the ability to perceive depth is innate.

12. Three-dimensional movies create the impression of depth by simulating retinal disparity. Each scene is photographed with two cameras placed a few inches apart. Viewers wear spectacles that allow each eye to see only the image from one camera. The perceived depth occurs as each eye focuses on one of the two-dimensional images and the brain integrates them in a single 3-D image.

    The binocular (two-eye) cues to depth include retinal disparity and convergence, and the monocular (one-eye) cues to depth include relative size, interposition, relative clarity, texture gradient, relative height, relative motion, linear perspective, and relative brightness.

13. Thanks to perceptual constancy we perceive familiar objects as having a constant form (shape constancy), size (size constancy), and brightness (lightness or brightness constancy), even when our retinal images of them change.

    There is a close interplay between an object's perceived size and its distance. As the retinal image of a familiar object decreases, we perceive its distance as increasing rather than its size as changing. This size-distance relationship partially explains the "moon illusion": Cues to objects' distances at the horizon make the moon behind them seem farther away, and seemingly larger, than when high in the sky. Similarly, one explanation of the Müller-Lyer illusion is that our experience with corners in our rectangularly carpentered world leads us to interpret a line segment ending in outward-pointing arrowheads as closer to us and therefore shorter than a line segment that ends in inward-pointing arrowheads.

14. On one side of the nature-nurture debate, the German philosopher Immanuel Kant maintained that knowledge comes from our inborn ways of organizing sensory experiences. On the other side, the British philosopher John Locke argued that we learn how to perceive the world through our experiences of it.

    In both humans and animals, infancy is a critical period during which normal visual stimulation must be experienced. Adults blinded with cataracts from birth, who later have their vision restored, are able to perceive figure, ground, and colors but are severely limited in their ability to recognize objects that were familiar by touch. Kittens and monkeys who were outfitted with goggles since infancy had similar visual impairments when the goggles were removed. Kittens raised in a restricted visual environment that allowed them to see only horizontal lines later had difficulty perceiving vertical lines. Research also shows that early visual experience is critical to the normal development of the feature detector cells of the brain.

15. Assumptions, expectations, schemas, and contexts may give us a perceptual set, or mental predisposition, that influences what we perceive. Perceptual sets, which are based on the concepts, or schemas, that we form through our experiences, help us organize and interpret unfamiliar or ambiguous information.

The immediate context of a stimulus also influences how it is perceived. For example, a person or object is more quickly recognized in an expected context than in a novel one. The effects of context and perceptual sets show how our experiences help us to construct meaningful perceptions from our sensory experiences.

Program Assignment

1. The task of all perception is to assign meaning to sensory experiences. *Distal stimulus* refers to the true identity of an object that stimulates the visual receptors. This perception is based on processing of the *proximal stimulus*, the object's stimulation of a sensory receptor in the body—in vision, the image formed on the retina. In order to do this for a visual stimulus, the brain must eliminate confusing signals, fill in missing information, give objects three dimensions, and put images in perspective. These transformations occur instantly and continuously.

2. Studies in which people and animals are given goggles that shift the world to the left, right, or even upside down demonstrate that vision is remarkably adaptable. After a relatively brief period of adjustment, most subjects are able to function normally in the distorted visual environment. When the goggles are first removed, subjects experience a brief perceptual aftereffect, as their perceptual systems continue to compensate for the shifted visual input.

3. To sense, perceive, and understand the world, two different processes are used. First, sensory receptors detect external sensory stimulation and send this raw data to the brain for processing. This is called *bottom-up processing*. *Top-down processing* in the brain then adds what we already know about such stimulation, what we remember about the context in which it usually appears, and how we label and classify it. In this way we give meaning to our perceptions.

4. These examples illustrate that our previous experience, expectations, interests, and biases are constantly giving rise to different perceptions. Research shows that young adults tend to see the young woman in the first ambiguous drawing, while older adults are more likely to perceive the older woman. Research on the "rat-man" illusion illustrates that prior exposure to drawings of either animal or human forms biases the viewer's perception of this ambiguous figure.

Progress Test

1. **d.** is the answer. (p. 152)

   a. "Sensory fatigue" is not a term in psychology.

   b. Accommodation refers to an adaptive change in shape by the lens of the eye.

   c. Sensory restriction refers to restricted sensory input because of sensory monotony or loss of a sense.

2. **d.** is the answer. (p. 155)

   a. The lens lies behind the pupil and focuses light on the retina.

   b. The retina lies at the back of the eyeball and contains the rods and cones.

   c. The cornea lies in front of the pupil and is the first structure that light passes through as it enters the eye.

3. **a.** is the answer. (p. 155)

b. Sensory adaptation is our diminishing sensitivity to an unchanging stimulus.

   c. Focusing is the process through which light converges onto the retina as a sharp image. The image is focused because the lens accommodates its shape.

   d. Transduction refers to the conversion of an environmental stimulus into a neural impulse by a receptor—a rod or a cone.

4. **c.** is the answer. The absolute threshold is the minimum stimulation needed to detect a stimulus. (video; p. 149)

   a. & b. The difference threshold, which is also known as the jnd, is the minimum difference between *two* stimuli that a person can detect. In this example, there is only one stimulus—the sight of the candle flame.

   d. Signal detection is a research task, not a sensory phenomenon.

5. **b.** is the answer. (video; p. 147)

   a. Both recognition and interpretation are examples of perception.

   c. This answer would have been correct if the question had read, "Perception is to sensation as _____ is to _____."

   d. Sensation and perception are important processes in both hearing and seeing.

6. **b.** is the answer. (p. 155)

   a. The iris controls the diameter of the pupil.

   c. The lens accommodates its shape to focus images on the retina.

   d. The optic nerve carries nerve impulses from the retina to the visual cortex.

7. **b.** is the answer. (p. 160)

   a. Feature detection is the process by which nerve cells in the brain respond to specific visual features of a stimulus, such as movement, angle, or shape.

   c. Accommodation is the process by which the lens changes its curvature to focus images on the retina.

   d. The opponent-process theory suggests that color vision depends on the response of brain cells to red-green, yellow-blue, and black-white opposing colors.

8. **b.** is the answer. (video; pp. 184–185)

   a. Top-down processing refers to how our knowledge and expectations influence perception.

   c. Parapsychology is the study of perception outside normal sensory input.

   d. Human factors psychology is concerned with how best to design machines and work settings to take into account human perception.

9. **a.** is the answer. Wavelength determines hue, or color. (p. 154)

   b. & d. The amplitude of light determines its brightness.

   c. Opponent processes are neural systems involved in color vision, not properties of light.

10. **c.** is the answer. (p. 152)

    a. The trichromatic theory cannot account for afterimages.

    b. & d. Afterimages are experienced as the complementary color of a stimulus. Green, rather than blue, is red's complement.

11. **c.** is the answer. (p. 155)

12. **b.** is the answer. Rods and cones enable vision in dim and bright light, respectively. If an animal is active only at night, it is likely to have more rods than cones in its retinas. (video; p. 157)

    d. Bipolar cells link both cones and rods to ganglion cells. There is no reason to expect that a nocturnal mammal would have more bipolar cells than a mammal active both during the day and at night. If anything, because several rods share a single bipolar cell, whereas many cones have their own, a nocturnal animal (with a visual system consisting mostly of rods) might be expected to have fewer bipolar cells than an animal active during the day (with a visual system consisting mostly of cones).

13. **c.** is the answer. Humans and certain animals, such as monkeys, are able to adjust to upside-down worlds and other visual distortions, figuring out the relationship between the perceived and the actual reality; lower animals, such as chickens and fish, are typically unable to adapt. (video; p. 196)

    a. Humans and certain animals are able to adapt quite well to distorted visual environments (and then to readapt).

    b. This answer is incorrect because humans are the most adaptable of creatures.

    d. Humans are able to adapt at any age to distorted visual environments.

14. **d.** is the answer. Feature detectors are cortical neurons and hence are located in the visual cortex. (video; p. 159)

    a. The fovea contains cones.

    b. The optic nerve contains neurons that relay nerve impulses from the retina to higher centers in the visual system.

    c. The iris is simply a ring of muscle tissue, which controls the diameter of the pupil.

15. **d.** is the answer. (pp. 149–150)

16. **c.** is the answer. (pp. 161–162)

    a. This answer is incorrect because separate red, green, and blue systems operate only in the retina.

    b. This answer is incorrect because opponent-process systems operate en route to the brain, after visual processing in the receptors is completed.

    d. This answer is incorrect because it reverses the correct order of the two stages of processing.

17. **c.** is the answer. (video)

    a. The frontal lobe is located at the front of the brain.

    b. The temporal lobes are located on the sides of the brain.

    d. The parietal lobe contains the sensory cortex.

18. **c.** is the answer. (video)

    a. & b. Whether the subjects perceived the image by breaking it into its component parts (analytic processing) or focusing on the image as a whole (holistic processing) had no bearing on the results.

19. **d.** is the answer. (p. 157)

    a. Feature detectors are nerve cells located in the visual cortex, not in the fovea of the retina.

    b. The proximity of rods and cones to the optic nerve does not influence their ability to resolve fine details.

c. Rods are concentrated in the peripheral regions of the retina, not in the fovea; moreover, several rods share a single bipolar cell.

20. **d.** is the answer. (p. 151)

    a. The absolute threshold refers to whether a single stimulus can be detected, not to whether two stimuli can be differentiated.

    b. Signal detection is a task in which one must determine whether a faint stimulus is present or not.

    c. A receptor threshold is a minimum amount of energy that will elicit a neural impulse in a receptor cell.

21. **d.** is the answer. Just as light strikes the film of a camera, visual images entering the eye are projected onto the retina. (p. 155)

    a. The pupil would be analogous to the aperture of a camera, since both control the amount of light permitted to enter.

    b. The lens of the eye performs a focusing function similar to the lens of the camera.

    c. The cornea would be analogous to a camera's lens cap in that both protect delicate inner structures.

22. **d.** is the answer. (video)

23. **a.** is the answer. (video)

    b. This describes any sensory neuron.

24. **b.** is the answer. (video)

    a. This defines proximal stimulus.

    c. This defines a feature detector.

    d. This is simply a visual illusion.

25. **b.** is the answer. (p. 157)

    a. & c. It is the cones, rather than the rods, that enable color vision.

    d. If the cones' threshold were lower than the available light intensity, they would be able to function and therefore detect the colors of the players' uniforms.

26. **c.** is the answer. In nearsightedness, objects converge in front of the retina; one cause of this is an eyeball longer than normal in relation to its lens. (p. 156)

    a. Inflexibility of the lens may cause the emergence of farsightedness as we get older.

    b. Thinness of the lens is unrelated to near- or farsightedness.

    d. A shorter-than-normal eyeball is related to farsightedness.

27. **d.** is the answer. Gestalt psychology, which developed in Germany at the turn of the century, was interested in how clusters of sensations are organized into whole perceptions. (p. 184)

    a. Parapsychology is the study of ESP and other paranormal phenomena

    b. & c. Behavioral and functional psychology were schools that developed later in the United States.

28. **c.** is the answer. Although we always differentiate a stimulus into figure and ground, those elements of the stimulus we perceive as figure and those as ground may change. In this way, the same stimulus can trigger more than one perception. (p. 185)

a. The idea of a figure-ground relationship has no bearing on the issue of whether perception is innate.

b. Perception cannot be simply a point-for-point representation of sensation, since in figure-ground relationships a single stimulus can trigger more than one perception.

d. Figure-ground relationships demonstrate the existence of general, rather than individual, principles of perceptual organization. Significantly, even the same person can see different figure-ground relationships when viewing a scene.

29. **d.** is the answer. The greater the retinal disparity, or difference between the images, the less the distance. (p. 187)

    a. Convergence is the extent to which the eyes move inward when looking at an object.

    b. Linear perspective is the monocular distance cue in which parallel lines appear to converge in the distance.

    c. Relative motion is the monocular distance cue in which objects at different distances change their relative positions in our visual image, with those closest moving most.

30. **a.** is the answer. (video)

    b. In holistic processing the person focuses on the image of an object as a whole.

    c. & d. These refer to perception that is driven by the senses (bottom-up) or the brain (top-down).

31. **a.** is the answer. Perception of constant shape, like perception of constant size, is part of the phenomenon of perceptual constancy. (p. 190)

    b. Relative motion is a monocular distance cue in which objects at different distances appear to move at different rates.

    c. Linear perspective is a monocular distance cue in which lines we know to be parallel converge in the distance, thus indicating depth.

    d. Continuity is the perceptual tendency to group items into continuous patterns.

32. **c.** is the answer. (p. 195)

    a. & b. The kittens had difficulty only with lines they had never experienced, and they never regained normal sensitivity.

    d. Both perceptual and feature-detector impairment resulted from visual deprivation.

33. **b.** is the answer. Because they have not had early visual experiences, these adults typically have great difficulty learning to perceive objects. (p. 195)

    a. Such patients typically could not visually recognize objects with which they were familiar by touch, and in some cases this inability persisted.

    c. Being able to perceive figure-ground relationships, patients *are* able to follow moving objects with their eyes.

    d. This answer is incorrect because eye-hand coordination is an acquired skill and requires much practice.

34. **a.** is the answer. The moon appears larger at the horizon than overhead in the sky because objects at the horizon provide distance cues that make the moon seem farther away and therefore larger. In the open sky, of course, there are no such cues. (p. 191)

35. **a.** is the answer. (video; pp. 184–185)

    b. Bottom-up processing refers to the physical characteristics of stimuli rather than their perceptual interpretation.

    c. Parapsychology is the study of perception outside normal sensory input.

    d. Human factors psychology is concerned with how best to design machines and work settings to take into account human perception.

36. **a.** is the answer. (video)

37. **c.** is the answer. We see a cloud as a figure against the background of sky. (p. 185)

    a., b., & d. The figure-ground relationship refers to the organization of the visual field into objects (figures) that stand out from their surroundings (ground).

38. **a.** is the answer. (p. 196)

    b. Retinal disparity is a binocular depth cue based on the fact that each eye receives a slightly different view of the world.

    c. Convergence is a binocular depth cue based on the fact that the eyes swing inward to focus on near objects.

    d. Visual capture refers to the tendency of vision to dominate the other senses.

39. **d.** is the answer. (p. 186)

40. **a.** is the answer. (pp. 191–192)

41. **c.** is the answer. In visual paradoxes, what we see contradicts what we know to be true, or possible. (video)

    a. The proximal stimulus is the sensory experience triggered by the image.

    d. Although paradoxical in these instances, the distal stimulus is nevertheless present.

Key Terms

Textbook Terms

1. **Sensation** is the process by which we detect physical energy from the environment and encode it as neural signals. (p. 147)

2. **Perception** is the process by which the brain organizes and interprets sensory information. (p. 147)

3. **Bottom-up processing** is analysis that begins with the sense receptors and works up to the brain's integration of sensory information. (p. 147)

4. **Top-down processing** is information processing guided by higher-level mental processes. (p. 147)

5. **Psychophysics** is the study of relationships between the physical characteristics of stimuli and our psychological experience of them. (p. 148)

6. The **absolute threshold** is the minimum stimulation needed to detect a stimulus 50 percent of the time. (p. 149)

7. **Signal detection theory** explains precisely how and when we detect the presence of a faint stimulus ("signal"). Detection depends partly on experience, expectation, motivation, and level of fatigue. (p. 149)

8. A stimulus that is **subliminal** is one that is below the absolute threshold for awareness. (p. 149)

Memory aid: Limen is the Latin word for "threshold." A stimulus that is **subliminal** is one that is *sub-* ("below") the *limen*, or threshold.

9. The **difference threshold**, or **just noticeable difference (jnd)**, is the minimum difference in two stimuli that a subject can detect 50 percent of the time. (p. 151)

10. **Weber's law** states that the just noticeable difference between two stimuli is a constant minimum proportion of the stimulus. (p. 152)

   Example: If a difference of 10 percent in weight is noticeable, **Weber's law** predicts that a person could discriminate 10- and 11-pound weights or 50- and 55-pound weights.

11. **Sensory adaptation** refers to the decreased sensitivity that occurs with continued exposure to an unchanging stimulus. (p. 152)

12. In the study of sensation, **transduction** refers to the process by which receptor cells in the eye, ear, skin, and nose convert environmental stimuli into neural impulses. (p. 153)

13. **Wavelength**, which refers to the distance from the peak of one light (or sound) wave to the next, gives rise to the perceptual experiences of **hue**, or color, in vision. (p. 154)

14. The **intensity** of light is determined by the amplitude of the waves and is experienced as brightness. (p. 154)

15. The **pupil** is the adjustable opening in the eye through which light enters. (p. 155)

16. The **iris** is a ring of muscle tissue that forms the colored part of the eye that controls the diameter of the pupil. (p. 155)

17. The **lens** is the transparent structure of the eye behind the pupil that changes shape to focus images on the retina. (p. 155)

18. **Accommodation** is the process by which the lens of the eye changes shape to focus near objects on the retina. (p. 155)

19. The **retina** is the light-sensitive, multilayered inner surface of the eye that contains the rods and cones, as well as neurons that form the beginning of the optic nerve. (p. 155)

20. Visual **acuity** refers to the sharpness of vision. (p. 156)

   Example: If your **acuity** is 20/10, you are able to see clearly at a distance of 20 feet a visual detail that most people cannot see beyond a distance of 10 feet.

21. **Nearsightedness** is a condition in which nearby objects are seen clearly but distant objects are blurred because light rays reflecting from them converge in front of the retina. (p. 156)

22. **Farsightedness** is a condition in which distant objects are seen clearly but nearby objects are blurred because light rays reflecting from them strike the retina *before* converging. (p. 156)

   Memory aid: To help you remember that farsightedness is caused by a shorter-than-normal eyeball, think of something falling "far short of the mark."

23. The **rods** and **cones** are visual receptors that transduce light into neural impulses. The rods are concentrated in the periphery of the retina, the cones in the fovea. The rods have poor sensitivity, detect black and white,

and function well in dim light. The cones have excellent sensitivity, enable color vision, and function best in daylight or bright light. (p. 156)

24. Comprised of the axons of retinal ganglion cells, the **optic nerve** carries neural impulses from the eye to the brain. (p. 156)

25. The **blind spot** is the region of the retina where the optic nerve leaves the eye. Because there are no rods or cones in this area, there is no vision here. (p. 156)

26. The **fovea** is the retina's point of central focus. It contains only cones; therefore, images focused on the fovea are the clearest. (p. 157)

27. **Feature detectors**, located in the visual cortex of the brain, are nerve cells that selectively respond to specific visual features, such as movement, shape, or angle. Feature detectors are evidently the basis of visual information processing. (p. 159)

28. **Parallel processing** is information processing in which several aspects of a stimulus, such as light or sound, are processed simultaneously. (p. 160)

29. The **Young-Helmholtz trichromatic (three-color) theory** maintains that the retina contains red-, green-, and blue-sensitive color receptors that in combination can produce the perception of any color. This theory explains the first stage of color processing. (p. 161)

30. The **opponent-process theory** maintains that color vision depends on pairs of opposing retinal processes (red-green, yellow-blue, and white-black). This theory explains the second stage of color processing. (p. 162)

31. **Color constancy** is the perception that familiar objects have consistent color despite changes in illumination that shift the wavelengths they reflect. (p. 163)

32. **Visual capture** is the tendency for vision to dominate the other senses. (p. 184)

33. **Gestalt** means "organized whole." The Gestalt psychologists emphasized our tendency to integrate pieces of information into meaningful wholes. (p. 184)

34. The **figure-ground** relationship refers to the organization of the visual field into two parts: the figure, which stands out from its surroundings, and the surroundings, or background. (p. 185)

35. **Grouping** is the perceptual tendency to organize stimuli in order to arrive at meaningful forms. Gestalt psychologists identified various principles of grouping. (p. 185)

36. **Depth perception** is the ability to see objects in three dimensions although the images that strike the retina are two-dimensional. (p. 186)

37. The **visual cliff** is a laboratory device for testing depth perception, especially in infants and young animals. In their experiments with the visual cliff, Gibson and Walk found strong evidence that depth perception is at least in part innate. (p. 186)

38. **Binocular cues** are depth cues that depend on information from both eyes. (p. 186)

   Memory aid: *Bi-* indicates "two"; *ocular* means something pertaining to the eye. **Binocular cues** are cues for the "two eyes."

39. **Monocular cues** are depth cues that depend on information from either eye alone. (p. 186)

Memory aid: *Mono-* means one; a monocle is an eyeglass for one eye. A **monocular cue** is one that is available to either the left or the right eye.

40. **Retinal disparity** refers to the differences between the images received by the left eye and the right eye as a result of viewing the world from slightly different angles. It is a binocular depth cue, since the greater the difference between the two images, the nearer the object. (p. 187)

41. **Convergence** is a binocular depth cue based on the extent to which the eyes converge, or turn inward, when looking at near or distant objects. The more the eyes converge, the nearer the objects. (p. 187)

42. The **phi phenomenon** is an illusion of movement created when two or more adjacent lights blink on and off in succession. (p. 190)

43. **Perceptual constancy** is the perception that objects have consistent lightness, color, shape, and size, even as illumination and retinal images change. (p. 190)

44. **Perceptual adaptation** refers to our ability to adjust to an artificially displaced or even inverted visual field. Given distorting lenses, we perceive things accordingly, but soon adjust by learning the relationship between our distorted perceptions and the reality. (p. 196)

45. **Perceptual set** is a mental predisposition to perceive one thing and not another. (p. 196)

Program Terms

46. A **proximal stimulus** is the actual stimulation of a sensory receptor by some form of environmental energy. In vision, for example, the proximal stimulus would be the image formed on the retina.

47. A **distal stimulus** is the actual source of a sensory experience (proximal stimulus). In vision, for example, objects in the environment that reflect light onto the retinas are distal stimuli.

PROGRAM 8

Learning

TEXTBOOK ASSIGNMENT: Chapter 8: Learning, pp. 243–267

ORIENTATION

No topic is closer to the heart of psychology than learning, a relatively permanent change in an organism's behavior due to experience. Program 8 covers the basic principles of two forms of learning: classical conditioning, in which we learn associations between events, and operant conditioning, in which we learn to engage in behaviors that are rewarded and to avoid behaviors that are punished. The reading assignment covers several other important issues, including the generality of principles of learning, the role of cognitive processes in learning, and the ways in which learning is constrained by the biological predispositions of different species—as well as a third type of learning, observational learning, in which we learn by observing and imitating others.

NOTE: Answer guidelines for all Program 8 questions begin on page 151.

GOALS

After completing your study of the program and reading assignment, you should be prepared to:

1. Identify three pioneers in the field of learning and discuss their contributions.

2. Explain the basic principles of classical and instrumental conditioning.

3. Describe several applications of principles of learning.

GUIDED STUDY

Textbook Assignment

The text chapter should be studied one section at a time. Before you read, preview each section by skimming it, noting headings and boldface items. Then read the appropriate section objectives from the following outline. Keep these objectives in mind and, as you read the chapter section, search for the information that will enable you to meet each objective. Once you have finished a section, write out answers for its objectives.

1. Discuss the importance of experience in learning and describe the role of association in learning.

Classical Conditioning (pp. 246–254)

2. Describe the nature of classical conditioning and show how it demonstrates associative learning.

3. Explain the processes of acquisition, extinction, spontaneous recovery, generalization, and discrimination.

4. Discuss the importance of cognitive processes and biological constraints in classical conditioning.

5. Discuss the importance of Pavlov's work in classical conditioning and explain how Pavlov paved the way for the behaviorist position.

Operant Conditioning (pp. 254–264)

6. Describe the process of operant conditioning, including the procedure of shaping.

7. Identify the different types of reinforcers and describe the four major schedules of partial reinforcement.

8. Discuss the effects of punishment on behavior.

9. Discuss evidence of the importance of cognitive and biological processes in operant conditioning.

10. Describe some major applications of operant conditioning.

Learning by Observation (pp. 265–267)

11. Describe the process of observational learning.

Program Assignment

Read the following objectives before you watch Program 8. As you watch, be alert for information that will help you answer each objective. Taking notes during the program will help you to formulate your answers later. After the program, write answers to the objectives. If you have access to the program on videotape, you may replay portions to refresh your memory.

1. Discuss the significance of biological reflexes and fixed action patterns in species survival.

2. Discuss the relative importance of learning to the survival of more highly evolved species.

3. Describe the experiment conducted by Ader and Cohen and discuss its results.

4. Discuss Edward Thorndike's contributions to behavioral psychology.

5. Describe the "Little Albert" experiment and discuss its results.

6. Explain B. F. Skinner's theory of behavior.

7. Discuss the example of behavioral therapy that appears in the program.

PROGRESS TEST

Circle your answers to the following questions and check them with the answers on page 154. If your answer is incorrect, read the explanation for why it is incorrect and then consult the appropriate pages of the text (in parentheses following the correct answer).

1. Learning is best defined as:
    a. any behavior emitted by an organism without being elicited.
    b. a change in the behavior of an organism.
    c. a relatively permanent change in the behavior of an organism due to experience.
    d. behavior based on operant rather than respondent conditioning.
    e. a perceived association between two or more events.

2. Which of the following statements concerning reinforcement is correct?
    a. Learning is most rapid with partial reinforcement, but continuous reinforcement produces the greatest resistance to extinction.
    b. Learning is most rapid with continuous reinforcement, but partial reinforcement produces the greatest resistance to extinction.
    c. Learning is fastest and resistance to extinction is greatest following continuous reinforcement.
    d. Learning is fastest and resistance to extinction is greatest following partial reinforcement.

3. A response that leads to the removal of an unpleasant stimulus is one being:
    a. positively reinforced.
    b. negatively reinforced.
    c. punished.
    d. extinguished.

4. Which of the following is an example of a fixed-action pattern?
    a. a dog salivating to the aroma of a steak being grilled
    b. a pigeon pecking a disk to earn food
    c. a person blinking at a speck of dust in the eye
    d. birds migrating in winter

5. One difference between classical and operant conditioning is that:
    a. in classical conditioning the responses operate on the environment to produce rewarding or punishing stimuli.
    b. in operant conditioning the responses are triggered by preceding stimuli.
    c. in classical conditioning the responses are automatically elicited by stimuli.
    d. in operant conditioning the responses are reflexive.

6. In Garcia and Koelling's studies of taste-aversion learning, rats learned to associate:
    a. taste with electric shock.
    b. sights and sounds with sickness.
    c. taste with sickness.
    d. taste and sounds with electric shock.
    e. taste and sounds with electric shock, then sickness.

7. "Survival of the fittest" refers specifically to:
    a. the ability of animals to adapt to environmental changes during their lifetimes.
    b. an organism's capacity for learning.
    c. the fact that animals who are the best equipped to survive, and manage to mate, will pass on their genes to the next generation.
    d. natural selection of aggressive behaviors.

8. Which of the following is true regarding the law of effect?
   a. Behaviors followed by satisfying outcomes tend to be repeated.
   b. Behaviors followed by unsatisfying outcomes are not repeated.
   c. both a. and b.
   d. neither a. nor b.

9. You always rattle the box of dog biscuits before giving your dog a treat. As you do so, your dog salivates. Rattling the box is a(n) _____ ; your dog's salivation is a(n) _____ .
   a. conditioned stimulus; conditioned response
   b. conditioned stimulus; unconditioned response
   c. unconditioned stimulus; conditioned response
   d. unconditioned stimulus; unconditioned response

10. Punishment is a controversial way of controlling behavior because:
    a. behavior is not forgotten and may return.
    b. punishing stimuli often create fear.
    c. punishment often increases aggressiveness.
    d. of all the above reasons.

11. Classical conditioning experiments by Rescorla and Wagner demonstrate that an important factor in conditioning is:
    a. the subject's age.
    b. the strength of the stimuli.
    c. the predictability of an association.
    d. the duration of the stimuli.
    e. all the above.

12. For the most rapid conditioning, a CS should be presented:
    a. about 1 second after the UCS.
    b. about one-half second before the UCS.
    c. about 15 seconds before the UCS.
    d. at the same time as the UCS.

13. Which of the following is an example of shaping?
    a. A dog learns to salivate at the sight of a box of dog biscuits.
    b. A new driver learns to stop at an intersection when the light changes to red.
    c. A parrot is rewarded first for making any sound, then for making a sound similar to "Laura," and then for speaking its owner's name.
    d. A psychology student reinforces a laboratory rat only occasionally, to make its behavior more resistant to extinction.

14. In Pavlov's studies of classical conditioning of a dog's salivary responses, spontaneous recovery occurred:
    a. during acquisition, when the CS was first paired with the UCS.
    b. during extinction, when the CS was first presented by itself.
    c. when the CS was reintroduced following extinction of the CR and a rest period.
    d. during discrimination training, when several conditioned stimuli were introduced.

15. In distinguishing between negative reinforcers and punishment, we note that:
    a. punishment, but not negative reinforcement, involves use of an aversive stimulus.
    b. in contrast to punishment, negative reinforcement decreases the likelihood of a response by the presentation of an aversive stimulus.
    c. in contrast to punishment, negative reinforcement increases the likelihood of a response by the presentation of an aversive stimulus.
    d. in contrast to punishment, negative reinforcement increases the likelihood of a response by the termination of an aversive stimulus.

16. Operant conditioning is to _____ as classical conditioning is to _____ .
    a. Pavlov; Watson
    b. Skinner; Bandura
    c. Pavlov; Skinner
    d. Skinner; Pavlov

17. In Pavlov's original experiment with dogs, the meat served as a(n):
    a. conditioned stimulus.
    b. conditioned response.
    c. unconditioned stimulus.
    d. unconditioned response.

18. Putting on your coat when it is cold outside is a behavior that is maintained by:
    a. discrimination learning.
    b. punishment.
    c. negative reinforcement.
    d. classical conditioning.
    e. positive reinforcement.

19. To be effective in promoting observational learning, models should be:
    a. perceived as similar to the observers.
    b. respected and admired.
    c. consistent in their actions and words.
    d. successful.
    e. any of the above.

20. After exploring a complicated maze for several days, a rat subsequently ran the maze with very few errors when food was placed in the goal box for the first time. This performance illustrates:
    a. classical conditioning.
    b. discrimination learning.
    c. observational learning.
    d. latent learning.

21. When a conditioned stimulus is presented without an accompanying unconditioned stimulus, _____ will soon take place.
    a. generalization
    b. discrimination
    c. extinction
    d. aversion
    e. spontaneous recovery

22. You teach your dog to fetch the paper by giving him a cookie each time he does so. This is an example of:
    a. operant conditioning.
    b. classical conditioning.
    c. secondary reinforcement.
    d. partial reinforcement.

23. In Pavlov's original experiment with dogs, salivation to meat was the:
    a. conditioned stimulus.
    b. conditioned response.
    c. unconditioned stimulus.
    d. unconditioned response.

24. Computer-assisted instruction (CAI) is an application of the operant conditioning principles of:
    a. shaping and immediate reinforcement.
    b. immediate reinforcement and punishment.
    c. shaping and primary reinforcement.
    d. continuous reinforcement and punishment.

25. Which of the following is the best example of a secondary reinforcer?
    a. putting on a coat on a cold day
    b. relief from pain after the dentist stops drilling your teeth
    c. receiving a cool drink after washing your mother's car on a hot day
    d. receiving an approving nod from the boss for a job well done
    e. having a big meal after going without food all day

26. Experiments on taste-aversion learning demonstrate that:
    a. for the conditioning of certain stimuli, the UCS need not immediately follow the CS.
    b. any perceivable stimulus can become a CS.
    c. all animals are biologically primed to associate illness with the taste of a tainted food.
    d. all the above are true.

27. Behavioral therapy:
    a. does not seek to determine the causes of an undesired behavior.
    b. seeks to determine the reinforcing consequences that are maintaining an undesired behavior.
    c. arranges new, positive consequences for desired behaviors.
    d. is characterized by all of the above.

28. In Watson and Rayner's experiment, the loud noise was the _____ and the white rat was the _____ .
    a. CS; CR
    b. UCS; CS
    c. CS; UCS
    d. UCS; CR
    e. UCR; CR

29. Classical conditioning may play a role in:
    a. emotional disorders.
    b. the body's immune response.
    c. how animals adapt to the environment.
    d. all the above.

30. You are expecting an important letter in the mail. As the regular delivery time approaches you glance more and more frequently out the window, searching for the letter carrier. Your behavior in this situation typifies that associated with which schedule of reinforcement?
    a. fixed-ratio
    b. variable-ratio
    c. fixed-interval
    d. variable-interval

31. Jack finally takes out the garbage in order to get his father to stop pestering him. Jack's behavior is being influenced by:
    a. positive reinforcement.
    b. negative reinforcement.
    c. primary reinforcement.
    d. punishment.

32. A pigeon can easily be taught to flap its wings in order to avoid shock but not to acquire food reinforcement. According to the text, this is most likely so because:
    a. pigeons are biologically predisposed to flap their wings in order to escape aversive events and to use their beaks to obtain food.
    b. shock is a more motivating stimulus for birds than food is.
    c. hungry animals have difficulty delaying their eating long enough to learn any new skill.
    d. of all the above reasons.

33. From a casino owner's viewpoint, which of the following jackpot-payout schedules would be the most desirable for reinforcing customer use of a slot machine?
    a. variable-ratio
    b. fixed-ratio
    c. variable-interval
    d. fixed-interval

34. After discovering that her usual route home was closed due to road repairs, Sharetta used her knowledge of the city and sense of direction to find an alternate route. Her behavior is an example of:
    a. latent learning.
    b. observational learning.
    c. shaping.
    d. using a cognitive map.
    e. discrimination.

35. In Ader and Cohen's experiment, several rats that acquired a conditioned taste aversion died because:
    a. they refused to take water and became dehydrated.
    b. the drug that was used to establish the aversion also suppressed their immune systems, making them more susceptible to disease.
    c. the experiment triggered stress-related heart attacks.
    d. the researchers failed to provide adequate supplements to the animals' diets.

36. Which of the following would be most likely to result in the overjustification effect?
    a. Each day that her son fails to clean his room, Mrs. Shih adds an additional chore he must complete.
    b. Kim's mother decides to reward her daughter's enjoyment of karate by paying her 75 cents for each hour that she practices.
    c. The manager of a shoe store decides to give a bonus to the employee who sells the most shoes each week.
    d. After her soccer team's poor performance, the coach scolds the players.
    e. Greg "pays" himself $2 a day for not smoking.

37. Two groups of rats receive classical conditioning trials in which a tone and electric shock are presented. For Group 1 the electric shock always follows the tone. For Group 2 the tone and shock occur randomly. Which of the following is likely to result?
    a. The tone will become a CS for Group 1 but not for Group 2.
    b. The tone will become a CS for Group 2 but not for Group 1.
    c. The tone will become a CS for both groups.
    d. The tone will not become a CS for either group.

38. Reggie's mother tells him that he can watch TV after he cleans his room. Evidently, Reggie's mother is attempting to use _____ to increase room cleaning.
    a. operant conditioning
    b. secondary reinforcement
    c. positive reinforcement
    d. all of the above

39. Lars is paid for his job every two weeks, whereas Tom receives a commission for each pair of shoes he sells. Evidently, Lars is paid on a _____ schedule of reinforcement, and Tom on a _____ schedule of reinforcement.
    a. fixed-ratio; fixed-interval
    b. continuous; intermittent
    c. fixed-interval; fixed-ratio
    d. variable-interval; variable-ratio

40. In Pavlov's original experiment with dogs, the tone was initially a(n) _____ stimulus; after it was paired with meat, it became a(n) _____ stimulus.
    a. conditioned; neutral
    b. neutral; conditioned
    c. conditioned; unconditioned
    d. unconditioned; conditioned

41. The primary purpose of the Skinner box is to:
    a. study classical conditioning.
    b. keep subjects safe and comfortable.
    c. provide a simple, controlled research environment.
    d. free researchers from tedious observation

KEY TERMS

Using your own words, write a brief definition or explanation of each of the following terms.

Textbook Terms

1. learning

2. associative learning

3. behaviorism

4. classical conditioning

5. unconditioned response (UCR)

6. unconditioned stimulus (UCS)

7. conditioned response (CR)

8. conditioned stimulus (CS)

9. acquisition

10. extinction

11. spontaneous recovery

12. generalization

13. discrimination

14. operant conditioning

15. respondent behavior

16. operant behavior

17. Skinner box

18. shaping

19. reinforcer

20. primary reinforcers

21. secondary reinforcers

22. continuous reinforcement

23. partial reinforcement

24. fixed-ratio schedule

25. variable-ratio schedule

26. fixed-interval schedule

27. variable-interval schedule

28. punishment

29. cognitive map

30. latent learning

31. overjustification effect

32. observational learning

33. modeling

34. prosocial behavior

Program Terms

35. fixed-action pattern

36. law of effect

ANSWERS

Guided Study

The following guidelines provide the main points that your answers should have touched upon.

Textbook Assignment

1. Experience is the key to learning, which is defined as a relatively permanent change in an organism's behavior due to experience. This ability to learn from experience is the foundation for adaptability—the capacity to learn new behaviors that enable humans and animals to cope with ever-changing circumstances.

    As such philosophers as Aristotle, Locke, and Hume noted, our minds naturally link events that we have experienced together. This is the basis for associative learning, in which two stimuli (as in classical conditioning) or a response and a rewarding or punishing stimulus (as in operant conditioning) become linked because of their co-occurrence.

2. In associative learning, organisms learn that certain events occur together. Through classical conditioning, organisms learn to anticipate and prepare for significant events, such as the delivery of food or a painful stimulus. In other words, they learn to associate two events. Classical conditioning occurs when a neutral stimulus becomes associated with an unconditioned stimulus (UCS). By itself, the UCS will automatically trigger a reflexive, unconditioned response (UCR). If the association between the CS and UCS is predictable, conditioning will occur and the CS alone will eventually elicit a conditioned response (CR) similar to the UCR.

3. Acquisition refers to the initial stage of learning, during which the CR is established and gradually strengthened. Extinction refers to the diminishing of a CR when the CS is repeatedly presented without a UCS. Spontaneous recovery refers to the reappearance, after a period of rest, of a weakened CR. Generalization is the tendency for stimuli similar to the CS to evoke a CR. Discrimination is the ability to distinguish between an actual CS and similar stimuli that have not been associated with the UCS.

4. Pavlov, Watson, and the early behaviorists underestimated the importance of cognitive processes and biological constraints on learning.

    Research by Rescorla and Wagner demonstrated that classical conditioning occurs best when the association between a CS and UCS is predictable. This indicates that subjects develop a cognitive expectancy, or an awareness of how likely it is that the UCS will follow the CS.

    Garcia and Koelling's studies of conditioned taste aversion demonstrated that animals are biologically primed to learn to associate certain CSs with certain UCSs. Rats, for example, develop aversions to the taste, but not the appearance, of tainted foods. In contrast, birds are biologically primed to develop aversions to the sight of tainted food. This violates the behaviorist tenet that any perceivable stimulus can become a CS.

5. Pavlov's work showed that virtually all organisms can learn to adapt to their environment. It also showed how a significant internal process, such as learning, could be studied objectively. Finally, Pavlov's findings also provided a basis for the behaviorist idea that human behavior consists, in part, of stimulus-response connections.

    The original behaviorist philosophy, as stated by John Watson, was that psychology should be an objective science that studied only observable behaviors and avoided references to all mental processes. Watson argued that by studying how organisms respond to stimuli in their environments, psychologists would eventually become able to understand, predict, and control behavior.

6. In contrast to classical conditioning, which works on automatic responses to stimuli, *operant* conditioning works on behaviors that *operate* on the environment to produce consequences that influence the future occurrence of those behaviors. Behaviors followed by favorable events (reinforcers) tend to be repeated. Behaviors followed by unpleasant stimuli (punishers) tend not to be repeated.

    Shaping is a systematic technique for establishing a new response in which successive approximations of a desired behavior are reinforced.

7. A positive reinforcer is a stimulus that strengthens a response that leads to its presentation. A negative reinforcer is an aversive stimulus that strengthens a response that leads to its removal. Primary reinforcers are innately reinforcing stimuli that satisfy biological needs. Secondary reinforcers acquire their effectiveness by being associated with primary reinforcers.

    Fixed-ratio schedules deliver reinforcement after a set number of responses. Variable-ratio schedules deliver reinforcement after an unpredictable number of responses. Fixed-interval schedules deliver reinforcement for the first response that follows a specified amount of time. Variable-interval schedules deliver reinforcement for a response that follows an unpredictable time interval.

8. A punisher is any consequence that decreases the frequency of a behavior that it follows. Although punishment may be effective in the short run, it has its drawbacks. Because punished behavior is merely suppressed rather than forgotten, it may reappear in safe settings. Punishment may also promote aggressiveness as a way of coping with problems; fear of the person who administers it; fear of the situation in which it occurs; or, when it is unpredictable, a sense that events are beyond the person's control. Because punishment does not teach positive behaviors, it is usually more effective when used in combination with positive reinforcement.

9. Latent learning is learning that occurs without reinforcement. Rats allowed to explore a maze without reinforcement nevertheless acquire a cognitive map of its layout. When they later are rewarded, they immediately perform as well as rats that have been reinforced with food all along.

    Overjustification occurs when people who are offered a reward for a task they already enjoy lose their intrinsic motivation for the task.

    Latent learning and overjustification demonstrate that there is more to learning than the association of a response with a reinforcer. Cognitive processes must be taken into consideration.

    Evidence for biological processes in operant conditioning comes from studies demonstrating that animals have biologically predisposed response patterns that influence the effectiveness of operant procedures with certain behaviors.

10. Operant principles of shaping and immediate reinforcement have been applied in school settings through the use of computer-assisted instruction for some drill and practice tasks. Reinforcement principles have been used to enhance sports abilities, especially in golf and baseball. Operant principles have also helped business managers increase productivity among their employees. Operant principles also have helped people take charge of their own behavior by creating self-management programs to stop smoking, lose weight, study, or exercise.

11. Observational learning, in which people observe and imitate, or model, others' behaviors, explains how many social behaviors are acquired. Research studies have shown that children will imitate both antisocial and prosocial models. Models are most effective when their actions and words are consistent. We are most likely to imitate people we respect, those we perceive as similar to ourselves, and those we perceive as successful.

Program Assignment

1. Animals who are the best equipped to survive, and manage to mate, will pass on their genes to the next generation. Nature lends a helping hand by providing animals with a set of built-in, inherited skills called *reflexes*. Some reflexes, like sucking, provide necessary biological supports; others are swift reactions to stimuli that pose a potential threat. Nature also provides more complex *fixed-action patterns*, which are sequences of behavior triggered automatically by particular environmental and biological events. Examples of fixed-action patterns include bird migration and spawning in fish.

2. In more highly evolved animals, behavior is more variable from individual to individual. Because of their capacity for learning, their behavior is more adaptable to changing circumstances—they can acquire new habits and even change the environment. Learning is the way that a species profits from its experience. Learning allows species to do two important things in the quest for survival: (a) to anticipate the future from past experience; and (b) to control a complex and ever-changing environment.

3. Classical conditioning can be so powerful that it can actually make us sick by suppressing the immune system. The immune system defends against disease by releasing antibodies that destroy bacteria, viruses, and other invaders. Ader and Cohen paired sweet-tasting water with a drug that produced stomach upset in laboratory rats. The animals quickly developed an aversion to the saccharin-laced water. Unbeknownst to the researchers, the drug also suppressed immune system activity in the animals. Because their ability to defend against disease was reduced, several of the animals died. The researchers concluded that at the same time they were conditioning an aversion to saccharin, they were conditioning the immune-suppressing effects of the drug.

4. Around the turn of the century, Edward Thorndike was investigating trial-and-error learning in animals. This research led to his formulating the *law of effect*, which states that learning is controlled by the environmental consequences of specific behaviors. Behaviors followed by favorable consequences are repeated while those followed by unfavorable consequences, or no consequences at all, are not repeated. Thorndike's experiments led to the conclusion that learning is controlled by its consequences. This became known as instrumental conditioning.

5. In this experiment, John Watson and Rosalie Rayner used classical and instrumental conditioning to condition an infant to fear a white rat. Each time the rat was presented, a gun was fired. Albert soon came to fear the rat, which had become a conditioned stimulus associated with the noise of the gun. When the child crawled away from the rat, the behavior was instrumentally rewarded by a reduction in the child's fear. The infant's fear of the rat generalized to other animals and furry objects, including coats and masks. This experiment was highly controversial, however, because of its treatment of human infants. A few years later, an associate of Watson named Mary Carver Jones became the first behavior therapist by developing techniques for removing conditioned fears in children.

6. For many psychologists, behavior is explained as the product of internal mental and neural processes. Skinner's theory views behavior as the product of environmental variables that precede and follow specific responses which Zimbardo refers to as the ABCs of learning: (antecedent → behavior → consequence). In Skinner's view, any behavior that is followed by a consequence will change in its rate of occurrence in direct relationship to changes in the consequence. According to this view, searching for internal explanations for behavior is unnecessary. Skinner's principles of operant conditioning have been applied in many settings outside the laboratory, including schools, businesses, and behavioral therapy. His basic experimental device, the Skinner box, has become the symbol of behaviorism.

7. In the program, behavioral therapy based on principles of operant conditioning is used to help a woman suffering from agoraphobia. The unique feature of this approach is its pragmatic focus on directly changing the problem behavior. There is no attempt to find out what caused the behavior, only to identify and change the sources of reinforcement that are maintaining it. The problem is treated by arranging new, positive consequences for the desired behavior.

Progress Test

1. **c.** is the answer. (p. 243)

    a. This answer is incorrect because it simply describes any behavior that is voluntary rather than triggered, or elicited, by a specific stimulus.

    b. This answer is too general, since behaviors can change for reasons other than learning.

    d. Respondently conditioned behavior also satisfies the criteria of our definition of learning.

    e. This answer is incorrect because it is unclear whether the association emerged as a result of experience.

2. **b.** is the answer. A continuous association will naturally be easier to learn than one that occurs on only some occasions, so learning is most rapid with continuous reinforcement. Yet once the continuous association is no longer there, as in extinction training, extinction will occur more rapidly than it would have had the organism not always experienced reinforcement. (p. 257)

3. **b.** is the answer. (p. 256)

    a. Positive reinforcement involves presenting a favorable stimulus following a response.

    c. Punishment involves *presenting* an unpleasant stimulus following a response.

    d. In extinction, a previously reinforced response is no longer followed by reinforcement. In this situation, a response causes a stimulus to be terminated or removed.

4. **d.** is the answer. (video)

    a. This is an example of a classically conditioned response.

    b. This is an example of an operantly conditioned response.

    c. This is an example of an unconditioned response.

5. **c.** is the answer. (p. 254)

    a. In *operant* conditioning the responses operate on the environment.

b. In *classical* conditioning responses are triggered, or elicited, by preceding stimuli.

d. In *classical* conditioning responses are reflexive.

6. **c.** is the answer. (pp. 250–251)

    a., d., & e. These studies also indicated that rats are biologically predisposed to associate visual and auditory stimuli, but not taste, with shock.

    b. Rats are biologically predisposed to associate taste with sickness.

7. **c.** is the answer. (video)

8. **c.** is the answer. (video; p. 255)

9. **a.** is the answer. Your dog had to learn to associate the rattling sound with the food. Rattling is therefore a conditioned, or learned, stimulus, and salivation in response to this rattling is a learned, or conditioned, response. (video; pp. 246–247)

10. **d.** is the answer. (p. 259)

11. **c.** is the answer. (p. 250)

    a., b., & d. Rescorla and Wagner's research did not address the importance of these factors in classical conditioning.

12. **b.** is the answer. (p. 248)

    a. Backward conditioning, in which the UCS precedes the CS, is ineffective.

    c. This interval is longer than is optimum for the most rapid acquisition of a CS-UCS association.

    d. Simultaneous presentation of CS and UCS is ineffective because it does not permit the subject to anticipate the UCS.

13. **c.** is the answer. The parrot is reinforced for making successive approximations of a goal behavior. This defines shaping. (video; p. 256)

    a. Shaping is an operant conditioning procedure; salivation at the sight of dog biscuits is a classically conditioned response.

    b. Shaping involves the systematic reinforcement of successive approximations of a more complex behavior. In this example, there is no indication that the response of stopping at the intersection involved the gradual acquisition of simpler behaviors.

    d. This is an example of the partial reinforcement of an established response, rather than the shaping of a new response.

14. **c.** is the answer. (video; p. 248)

    a., b., & d. Spontaneous recovery occurs after a CR has been extinguished, and in the absence of the UCS. The situations described here all involve the continued presentation of the UCS and, therefore, the further strengthening of the CR.

15. **d.** is the answer. (pp. 256, 258)

    a. Both involve an aversive stimulus.

    b. All reinforcers, including negative reinforcers, increase the likelihood of a response.

    c. In negative reinforcement an aversive stimulus is withdrawn following a desirable response.

16. **d.** is the answer. (video; pp. 246, 255)

a. Pavlov and Watson are both associated with respondent conditioning.

b. Skinner is associated with operant conditioning, and Bandura is associated with observational learning.

17. **c.** is the answer. Meat automatically triggers the response of salivation and is therefore an unconditioned stimulus. (video; p. 246)

    a. A conditioned stimulus acquires its response-eliciting powers through learning. A dog does not learn to salivate to meat.

    b. & d. Responses—in this case the dog's salivation—are behaviors elicited in the organism. The meat is a stimulus.

18. **c.** is the answer. By learning to put on your coat before going outside, you have learned to reduce the aversive stimulus of the cold. (p. 256)

    a. Discrimination learning involves learning to make a response in the presence of the appropriate stimulus and not other stimuli.

    b. Punishment is the suppression of an undesirable response by the presentation of an aversive stimulus.

    d. Putting on a coat is a response that is willfully emitted by the person. Therefore, this is an example of operant, not classical, conditioning.

    e. Positive reinforcement involves the *presentation* of a stimulus.

19. **e.** is the answer. (p. 266)

20. **d.** is the answer. The rat had learned the maze but did not display this learning until reinforcement became available. (p. 260)

    a. Negotiating a maze is clearly operant behavior.

    b. This example does not involve learning to distinguish between stimuli.

    c. This is not observational learning because the rat has no one to observe!

21. **c.** is the answer. In this situation, the conditioned response will decline, a phenomenon known as extinction. (video; p. 248)

    a. Generalization occurs when the subject makes a conditioned response to stimuli similar to the original conditioned stimulus.

    b. Discrimination is when the subject does not make a conditioned response to stimuli other than the original conditioned stimulus.

    d. An aversion is a conditioned response to a conditioned stimulus that has been associated with an unpleasant event (an unconditioned stimulus), such as shock or a nausea-producing drug.

    e. Spontaneous recovery is the reappearance, after a rest period, of a conditioned response.

22. **a.** is the answer. You are teaching your dog by rewarding him when he produces the desired behavior. (video; p. 254)

    b. This is not classical conditioning because the cookie is a primary reinforcer presented after the operant behavior of the dog's fetching the paper.

    c. Food is a primary reinforcer; it satisfies an innate need.

    d. Because you reward your dog each time he fetches the paper, this is continuous reinforcement.

23. **d.** is the answer. A dog does not have to learn to salivate to food; therefore, this response is unconditioned. (video; p. 260)

24. **a.** is the answer. CAI applies operant principles such as reinforcement, immediate feedback, and shaping to the teaching of new skills. (p. 264)

b. & d. CAI provides immediate, and continuous, reinforcement for correct responses but does not make use of aversive control procedures such as punishment.

c. CAI is based on feedback for correct responses; this feedback constitutes secondary, rather than primary, reinforcement.

25. **d.** is the answer. An approving nod from the boss is a secondary reinforcer in that it doesn't satisfy an innate need but has become linked with desirable consequences. Cessation of cold, cessation of pain, and a drink are all primary reinforcers, which meet innate needs. (p. 257)

26. **a.** is the answer. Taste-aversion experiments demonstrate conditioning even with CS-UCS intervals as long as several hours. (p. 251)

    b. Despite being perceivable, a visual or auditory stimulus cannot become a CS for illness in some animals, such as rats.

    c. Some animals, such as birds, are biologically primed to associate the *appearance* of food with illness.

27. **d.** is the answer. (video)

28. **b.** is the answer. The loud noise automatically elicited Albert's fear and therefore functioned as an unconditioned stimulus. After being associated with the unconditioned stimulus, the white rat acquired the power to elicit fear and thus became a conditioned stimulus. (video; p. 253)

29. **d.** is the answer. (video)

30. **c.** is the answer. Reinforcement (the letter) comes after a fixed interval, and as the likely end of the interval approaches, your behavior (glancing out the window) becomes more frequent. (p. 258)

    a. & b. These answers are incorrect because with ratio schedules, reinforcement is contingent upon the number of responses rather than on the passage of time.

    d. Assuming that the mail is delivered at about the same time each day, the interval is fixed rather than variable. Your behavior reflects this, since you glance out the window more often as the delivery time approaches.

31. **b.** is the answer. By taking out the garbage, Jack terminates an aversive stimulus, his father's nagging. (p. 256)

    a. Positive reinforcement would involve a desirable stimulus that increases the likelihood of the response that preceded it.

    c. This answer would have been correct if Jack's father had rewarded Jack for taking out the garbage by providing his favorite food.

    d. Punishment suppresses behavior; Jack is emitting a behavior in order to obtain reinforcement.

32. **a.** is the answer. As in this example, conditioning must be consistent with the particular organism's biological predispositions. (p. 261)

    b. Some behaviors, but certainly not all, are acquired more rapidly than others when shock is used as negative reinforcement.

    c. Pigeons are able to acquire many new behaviors when food is used as reinforcement.

33. **a.** is the answer. Ratio schedules maintain higher rates of responding—gambling in this example—than do interval schedules. Furthermore, variable schedules are not associated with the pause in responding following reinforcement that is typical of fixed schedules. The slot machine would there-

fore be used more often, and more consistently, if jackpots were scheduled according to a variable-ratio schedule. (p. 258)

34. **d.** is the answer. Sharetta is guided by her mental representation of the city, or cognitive map. (p. 260)

    a. & e. Latent learning, or learning in the absence of reinforcement that is demonstrated when reinforcement becomes available, has no direct relevance to the example. The same is true of discrimination.

    b. Observational learning refers to learning from watching others.

    c. Shaping is the technique of reinforcing successive approximations of a desired behavior.

35. **b.** is the answer. (video)

36. **b.** is the answer. Paying a person for doing what he or she already enjoys may undermine the person's intrinsic motivation for the task and lead to the overjustification effect. (p. 261)

    a. This negative reinforcement of room cleaning may motivate the son to get the job done, but since the job apparently is not intrinsically rewarding, it is doubtful that Mrs. Shih's additional incentives will lead to an overjustification effect.

    c. Presumably, the salespeople work in order to make money; a bonus should therefore serve as additional positive reinforcement for selling shoes.

    d. The coach's scolding may make soccer less enjoyable for the players, but not as a result of overjustification provided by additional reinforcement.

    e. This answer is incorrect because it is unclear whether Greg enjoys not smoking.

37. **a.** is the answer. Classical conditioning proceeds most effectively when the CS and UCS are reliably paired and therefore appear predictably associated. Only for Group 1 is this likely to be true. (p. 248)

38. **d.** is the answer. By making a more preferred activity (watching TV) contingent on a less preferred activity (room cleaning), Reggie's mother is employing the operant conditioning technique of positive reinforcement. Since TV is not an innate need, it provides secondary reinforcement. (pp. 254, 256–257)

39. **c.** is the answer. Whereas Lars is paid (reinforced) after a fixed period of time (fixed-interval), Tom is reinforced for each sale (fixed-ratio) he makes. (p. 258)

    b. Lars and Tom are both being reinforced intermittently.

    d. In this example Lars's pay interval and Tom's work ratio are both fixed, rather than variable.

40. **b.** is the answer. Prior to its pairing with meat, the tone did not elicit salivation and was therefore a neutral stimulus. Afterward, the tone elicited salivation and was therefore a conditioned stimulus. (video; p. 247)

    c. & d. Unconditioned stimuli, such as meat, innately elicit responding. Pavlov's dogs had to learn to associate the tone with the food.

41. **c.** is the answer. (video; p. 255)

Key Terms

Textbook Terms

1. **Learning** is any relatively permanent change in an organism's behavior due to experience. (p. 243)

2. In **associative learning**, organisms learn that certain events occur together. Two variations of associative learning are classical conditioning and operant conditioning. (p. 244)

3. **Behaviorism** is the school of thought maintaining that psychology should be an objective science, study only observable behaviors, and avoid references to mental processes. (p. 246)

    Example: Because he was an early advocate of the study of observable behavior, John Watson is often called the father of **behaviorism**.

4. Also know as Pavlovian conditioning, **classical conditioning** is a type of learning in which a neutral stimulus becomes capable of eliciting a conditioned response after having become associated with an unconditioned stimulus. (p. 246)

5. In classical conditioning, the **unconditioned response (UCR)** is the unlearned, involuntary response to the unconditioned stimulus. (p. 246)

6. In classical conditioning, the **unconditioned stimulus (UCS)** is the stimulus that naturally and automatically elicits the reflexive unconditioned response. (p. 246)

7. In classical conditioning, the **conditioned response (CR)** is the learned response to a previously neutral conditioned stimulus, which results from the acquired association between the CS and UCS. (p. 247)

8. In classical conditioning, the **conditioned stimulus (CS)** is an originally neutral stimulus that comes to elicit a CR after association with an unconditioned stimulus. (p. 247)

9. In classical conditioning, **acquisition** refers to the initial stage of conditioning in which the new response is established and gradually strengthened. In operant conditioning, it is the strengthening of a reinforced response. (p. 248)

10. **Extinction** in classical conditioning refers to the weakening of a CR when the CS is no longer followed by the UCS; in operant conditioning extinction occurs when a response is no longer reinforced. (p. 248)

11. **Spontaneous recovery** is the reappearance of an extinguished CR after a rest period. (p. 248)

12. **Generalization** refers to the tendency, once a response has been conditioned, for stimuli similar to the original CS to evoke a CR. (p. 249)

13. **Discrimination** in classical conditioning refers to the ability to distinguish the CS from similar stimuli that do not signal a UCS. In operant conditioning, responding differently to stimuli that signal a behavior will be reinforced or will not be reinforced. (p. 250)

14. **Operant conditioning** is a type of learning in which behavior is strengthened if followed by reinforcement or diminished if followed by punishment. (p. 254)

Example: Unlike classical conditioning, which works on automatic behaviors, **operant conditioning** works on behaviors that are willfully emitted by an organism.

15. **Respondent behavior** is that which occurs as an automatic response to some stimulus. (p. 255)

    Example: In classical conditioning, conditioned and unconditioned responses are examples of **respondent behavior** in that they are automatic responses elicited by specific stimuli.

16. **Operant behavior** is behavior the organism emits that operates on the environment to produce reinforcing or punishing stimuli. (p. 255)

17. A **Skinner box** is an experimental chamber for the operant conditioning of an animal such as a pigeon or rat. The controlled environment enables the investigator to present visual or auditory stimuli, deliver reinforcement or punishment, and precisely measure simple responses such as bar presses or key pecking. (p. 255)

18. **Shaping** is the operant conditioning procedure for establishing a new response by reinforcing successive approximations of the desired behavior. (p. 255)

19. In operant conditioning, a **reinforcer** is any event that strengthens the behavior it follows. (p. 256)

20. The powers of **primary reinforcers** are inborn and do not depend on learning. (p. 257)

21. **Secondary reinforcers** are stimuli that acquire their reinforcing power through their association with a primary reinforcer. (p. 257)

22. **Continuous reinforcement** is the operant procedure of reinforcing the desired response every time it occurs. In promoting the acquisition of a new response it is best to use continuous reinforcement. (p. 257)

23. **Partial reinforcement** is the operant procedure of reinforcing a response intermittently. A response that has been partially reinforced is much more resistant to extinction than one that has been continuously reinforced. (p. 257)

24. In operant conditioning, a **fixed-ratio schedule** is one in which reinforcement is presented after a set number of responses. (p. 258)

    Example: Continuous reinforcement is a special kind of **fixed-ratio schedule**: Reinforcement is presented after *each* response, so the ratio of reinforcements to responses is one to one.

25. In operant conditioning, a **variable-ratio schedule** is one in which reinforcement is presented after a varying number of responses. (p. 258)

26. In operant conditioning, a **fixed-interval schedule** is one in which a response is reinforced after a specified time has elapsed. (p. 258)

27. In operant conditioning, a **variable-interval schedule** is one in which responses are reinforced after varying intervals of time. (p. 258)

28. In operant conditioning, **punishment** is the presentation of an aversive stimulus, such as shock, which decreases the behavior it follows. (p. 258)

    Memory aid: People often confuse negative reinforcement and **punishment**. The former strengthens behavior, while the latter weakens it.

29. A **cognitive map** is a mental picture of one's environment. (p. 260)

30. **Latent learning** is learning that occurs in the absence of reinforcement but only becomes apparent when there is an incentive to demonstrate it. (p. 260)

31. The undermining effect of being rewarded for something enjoyable is called the **overjustification effect**. (p. 261)

32. **Observational learning** is learning by watching and imitating the behavior of others. (p. 265)

33. **Modeling** is the process of watching and then imitating a specific behavior and is thus an important means through which observational learning occurs. (p. 265)

34. The opposite of antisocial behavior, **prosocial behavior** is positive, helpful, and constructive, and is subject to the same principles of observational learning as is undesirable behavior, such as aggression. (p. 266)

Program Terms

35. **Fixed action patterns** are complex sequences of behavior triggered automatically by particular environmental and biological events. Examples of fixed action patterns include bird migration and spawning in fish.

36. Edward Thorndike's **law of effect** states that learned behavior is controlled by its consequences. Behaviors that are followed by favorable consequences are repeated while those that are followed by unfavorable consequences are not. (See also text p. 255.)

PROGRAM 9

Remembering and Forgetting

TEXTBOOK ASSIGNMENT: Chapter 7: Memory, 269–303

ORIENTATION

Program 9 explores human memory as a system that processes information in three steps. Encoding refers to the process of putting information into the memory system. Storage is the purely passive mechanism by which information is maintained in memory. Retrieval is the process by which information is accessed from memory through recall or recognition. The reading assignment and program also discuss the importance of imagery, order, and organization in encoding new memories, the physical representation of memory in the brain, and forgetting as the result of failure to encode or store information or to find appropriate retrieval cues. The reading assignment also includes a complete section on memory construction, focusing on its relationship to the recovery of supposedly long-repressed memories. As you study, try applying some of the memory and study tips discussed in the program and text.

NOTE: Answer guidelines for all Program 9 questions begin on page 175.

GOALS

After you have read the text and viewed the program, you should be prepared to:

1. Explain how new memories are formed and then retrieved for later use.
2. Discuss research on how memories are physically represented in the nervous system.
3. Discuss various reasons for forgetting.
4. Discuss the constructive nature of memory.

GUIDED STUDY

Textbook Assignment

The text chapter should be studied one section at a time. Before you read, preview each section by skimming it, noting headings and boldface items. Then read the appropriate section objectives from the following outline. Keep these objectives in mind and, as you read the chapter section, search for the information that will enable you to meet each objective. Once you have finished a section, write out answers for its objectives.

The Phenomenon of Memory (pp. 269–272)

1. Explain memory in terms of information processing.

Encoding: Getting Information In (pp. 273–280)

2. Explain the process of encoding and distinguish between automatic and effortful processing.

3. Discuss the importance of rehearsal, spacing, and serial position in encoding.

4. Explain the importance of meaning, imagery, and organization in the encoding process.

5. Discuss forgetting as a form of encoding failure.

Storage: Retaining Information (pp. 280–288)

6. Distinguish between iconic and echoic memory.

7. Describe memory capacity and duration.

8. Discuss research findings on the physical basis of memory.

9. Discuss what research with amnesics reveals about memory.

Retrieval: Getting Information Out (pp. 288–294)

10. Contrast recall, recognition, and relearning measures of memory and describe the importance of retrieval cues.

11. Discuss the role of interference in the process of forgetting.

12. Describe motivated forgetting and explain the concept of repression.

Memory Construction (pp. 294–301)

13. Discuss the evidence for memory's being constructive.

14. Explain why memory researchers are suspicious of claims of long-repressed memories "recovered" with the aid of a therapist.

15. Discuss whether children are reliable witnesses.

Improving Memory (pp. 302–303)

16. Discuss strategies for improving memory.

Program Assignment

Read the following objectives before you watch Program 9. As you watch, be alert for information that will help you answer each objective. Taking notes during the program will help you to formulate your answers later. After the program, write answers to the objectives. If you have access to the program on videotape, you may replay portions to refresh your memory.

1. Discuss Hermann Ebbinghaus's contributions to our understanding of the nature of memory.

2. Explain the concept of associative networks in long-term memory.

3. Discuss Sigmund Freud's contributions to our understanding of memory.

4. Discuss the constructive nature of memory and explain the concept of schemas.

5. Explain the concept of the engram, noting the different types of memories in storage.

6. Discuss Richard Thompson's findings regarding the brain circuitry involved in classical conditioning.

7. Differentiate two forms of amnesia.

PROGRESS TEST

Circle your answers to the following questions and check them with the answers on page 179. If your answer is incorrect, read the explanation for why it is incorrect and then consult the appropriate pages of the text (in parentheses following the correct answer).

1. The three steps in memory information processing are:
    a. input, processing, output.
    b. input, storage, output.
    c. input, storage, retrieval.
    d. encoding, storage, retrieval.
    e. encoding, retrieval, storage.

2. Iconic memories fade after approximately:
    a. 1 hour.
    b. 1 minute.
    c. 1 second.
    d. 1/10th of a second.
    e. 3 to 4 seconds.

3. Our short-term memory span is approximately _____ items.
   a. 2
   b. 5
   c. 7
   d. 15

4. Memory techniques such as the method of loci, acronyms, and the peg-word system are called:
   a. consolidation techniques.
   b. imagery techniques.
   c. encoding strategies.
   d. mnemonic devices.

5. One way to increase the amount of information in memory is to group it into larger, familiar units. This process is referred to as:
   a. consolidating.
   b. organization.
   c. memory construction.
   d. encoding.
   e. chunking.

6. Kandel and Schwartz have found that when learning occurs, more of the neurotransmitter _____ is released into synapses.
   a. ACh
   b. dopamine
   c. serotonin
   d. noradrenaline.

7. In a study on context cues, people learned words while on land or when they were underwater. In a later test of recall, those with the best retention had:
   a. learned the words on land, that is, in the more familiar context.
   b. learned the words under water, that is, in the more exotic context.
   c. learned the words and been tested on them in different contexts.
   d. learned the words and been tested on them in the same context.

8. Richard Thompson has found an area in the _____ of the rabbit brain that is involved in storing classically conditioned memories.
   a. cortex
   b. cerebellum
   c. amygdala
   d. thalamus
   e. hypothalamus

9. In Sperling's memory experiment, subjects were shown three rows of three letters, followed immediately by a low-, medium-, or high-pitched tone. The subjects were able to report:
   a. all three rows with perfect accuracy.
   b. only the top row of letters.
   c. only the middle row of letters.
   d. any one of the three rows of letters.
   e. none of the letters; the tone retroactively interfered with their memory.

10. Studies of victims of amnesia suggest that:
    a. memory is a single, unified system.
    b. there are two distinct types of memory.
    c. there are three distinct types of memory.
    d. memory losses following brain trauma are unpredictable.
    e. brain trauma eliminates the person's ability to learn.

11. When Gordon Bower presented subjects with words grouped by category or in random order, recall was:
    a. the same for all words.
    b. better for the categorized words.
    c. better for the random words.
    d. improved when subjects developed their own mnemonic devices.

12. Research on constructive memory reveals that memories:
    a. are stored as exact copies of experience.
    b. reflect a person's biases and assumptions.
    c. can be chemically transferred from one organism to another.
    d. even if long term, usually decay within about five years.

13. Memory for skills is called:
    a. explicit memory.
    b. declarative memory.
    c. episodic memory.
    d. implicit memory.

14. Which of the following has been proposed as a neurophysiological explanation of infantile amnesia?
    a. The slow maturation of the hippocampus leaves the infant's brain unable to store images and events.
    b. The deficient supply of serotonin until about age 3 makes encoding very limited.
    c. The limited availability of association areas of the cortex until about age 3 impairs encoding and storage.
    d. All of the above explanations have been proposed.

15. Hypnotically "refreshed" memories may prove inaccurate—especially if the hypnotist asks leading questions—because of:
    a. encoding failure.
    b. state-dependent memory.
    c. proactive interference.
    d. memory construction.
    e. repression.

16. Jenkins and Dallenbach found that memory was better in subjects who were _____ during the retention interval, presumably because _____ was reduced.
    a. awake; decay
    b. asleep; decay
    c. awake; interference
    d. asleep; interference

17. Which of the following best describes the typical forgetting curve?
    a. a steady, slow decline in retention over time
    b. a steady, rapid decline in retention over time
    c. a rapid, initial decline in retention, becoming stable thereafter
    d. a slow, initial decline in retention, becoming rapid thereafter

18. Lashley's studies, in which rats learned a maze and then had various parts of their brains surgically removed, showed that the memory:
    a. was lost when surgery took place within 1 hour of learning.
    b. was lost when surgery took place within 24 hours of learning.
    c. was lost when any region of the brain was removed.
    d. remained no matter which area of the brain was tampered with.

19. Elderly Mr. Flanagan can easily recall his high school graduation, but he can't remember the name of the president of the United States. Evidently, Mr. Flanagan's _____ memory is better than his _____ memory.
    a. implicit; explicit
    b. explicit; implicit
    c. episodic; semantic
    d. semantic; episodic

20. Amnesics typically have experienced damaged to the brain's _____ .
    a. frontal lobes
    b. cerebellum
    c. thalamus
    d. hippocampus
    e. cortex

21. According to the serial position effect, when recalling a list of words you should have the greatest difficulty with those:
    a. at the beginning of the list.
    b. at the end of the list.
    c. at the end and in the middle of the list.
    d. at the beginning and end of the list.
    e. in the middle of the list.

22. Lewis cannot remember the details of the torture he experienced as a prisoner of war. Lewis's failure to remember these painful memories is an example of:
    a. repression.
    b. retrieval failure.
    c. state-dependent memory.
    d. flashbulb memory.
    e. implicit memory.

23. The chief cause of functional amnesia is:
    a. alcohol addiction.
    b. disease.
    c. injury to the brain.
    d. severe anxiety.
    e. any of the above.

24. Craik and Tulving had subjects process words visually, acoustically, or semantically. In a subsequent recall test, which type of processing resulted in the greatest retention?
    a. visual
    b. acoustic
    c. semantic
    d. Acoustic and semantic processing were equally beneficial.

25. Schemas are:
    a. mnemonic devices used to facilitate memory.
    b. frameworks of our basic ideas and preconceptions about people, objects, and situations.
    c. structural defects in the brain neurons involved in memory.
    d. examples of motivated forgetting.

26. How long can unrehearsed information normally remain in short-term memory?
    a. about 7 seconds
    b. about 30 seconds
    c. about 1 hour
    d. about 24 hours
    e. indefinitely

27. *Long-term potentiation* refers to:
    a. the disruptive influence of old memories on the formation of new memories.
    b. the disruptive influence of recent memories in the retrieval of old memories.
    c. our tendency to recall experiences that are consistent with our current mood.
    d. the increased efficiency of synaptic transmission between certain neurons following learning.
    e. our increased ability to recall long-ago events as we grow older.

28. Studies by Loftus and Palmer, in which subjects were quizzed about a film of an accident, indicate that:
    a. when quizzed immediately, subjects can recall very little, due to the stress of witnessing an accident.
    b. when questioned as little as one day later, their memory was very inaccurate.
    c. most subjects had very accurate memories as much as 6 months later.
    d. subjects' recall may easily be affected by misleading information.

29. Amnesic patients typically experience disruption of:
    a. implicit memories.
    b. explicit memories.
    c. iconic memories.
    d. echoic memories.
    e. all of the above.

30. Information is maintained in short-term memory only briefly unless it is:
    a. encoded.
    b. rehearsed.
    c. iconic or echoic.
    d. retrieved.

31. Textbook chapters are often organized into _____ in order to facilitate information processing.
    a. mnemonic devices
    b. chunks
    c. hierarchies
    d. recognizable units

32. In an experiment, subjects briefly examined the contents of an office. When they were later asked to recall what they had seen, they were most likely to remember those objects that:
    a. were unusual in a typical office.
    b. were similar to ones they themselves owned.
    c. fit into their existing office schema.
    d. had been placed into their short-term memories.

33. The information-processing model of memory arose in response to:
    a. the computer revolution of the 1960s.
    b. studies of amnesics.
    c. evidence that memories are physically represented in the brain.
    d. all of the above

34. It is easier to recall information that has just been presented when the information:
    a. consists of random letters rather than words.
    b. is seen rather than heard.
    c. is heard rather than seen.
    d. is experienced in an unusual context.

35. PET scans taken when a person is truly or falsely recalling a word reveal different patterns of activity in an area of the:
    a. hippocampus.
    b. left temporal lobe.
    c. cerebellum.
    d. thalamus.

36. After finding her old combination lock, Janice can't remember its combination because she keeps confusing it with the combination of her new lock. She is experiencing:
    a. proactive interference.
    b. retroactive interference.
    c. encoding failure.
    d. storage failure.
    e. repression.

37. Being in a bad mood after a hard day of work, Susan could think of nothing positive in her life. This is best explained as an example of:
    a. priming.
    b. memory construction.
    c. mood-congruent memory.
    d. retrieval failure.

38. Walking through the halls of his high school 10 years after graduation, Tom experienced a flood of old memories. Tom's experience showed the role of:
    a. state-dependent memory.
    b. context effects.
    c. retroactive interference.
    d. echoic memory.
    e. iconic memory.

39. Which of the following is the best example of a flashbulb memory?
    a. suddenly remembering to buy bread while standing in the checkout line at the grocery store
    b. recalling the name of someone from high school while looking at his or her yearbook snapshot
    c. remembering to make an important phone call
    d. remembering what you were doing the day the federal building in Oklahoma City was bombed

40. At your high school reunion you cannot remember the last name of your homeroom teacher. Your failure to remember is most likely the result of:
    a. encoding failure.
    b. storage failure.
    c. retrieval failure.
    d. state-dependent memory.

KEY TERMS

Using your own words, write a brief definition or explanation of each of the following terms.

Textbook Terms

1. memory

2. flashbulb memory

3. encoding

4. storage

5. retrieval

6. long-term memory

7. short-term memory

8. automatic processing

9. effortful processing

10. rehearsal

11. spacing effect

12. serial position effect

13. semantic encoding

14. acoustic encoding

15. visual encoding

16. imagery

17. mnemonics

18. chunking

19. sensory memory

20. iconic memory

21. echoic memory

22. long-term potentiation (LTP)

23. amnesia

24. implicit memory

25. explicit memory

26. hippocampus

27. recall

28. recognition

29. relearning

30. priming

31. déjà vu

32. mood-congruent memory

33. proactive interference

34. retroactive interference

35. repression

36. misinformation effect

37. source amnesia

Program Terms

38. functional amnesia

38. organic amnesia

39. episodic memory

40. semantic memory

41. procedural memory

ANSWERS

Guided Study

The following guidelines provide the main points that your answers should have touched upon.

Textbook Assignment

1. To remember any event requires that we somehow get information into our brain (encoding), retain it (storage) as short- or long-term memory, and get it back out (retrieval). These three steps apply not only to human memory but also to other information-processing systems, such as computers.

2. Encoding is the process by which sensory information is transferred into the memory system. Information about space, time, and frequency, as well as well-learned information, is encoded with little or no effort (automatic processing). Encoding of most other types of information requires attention and conscious rehearsal (effortful processing).

3. Ebbinghaus demonstrated that the amount of material remembered depends on the time spent rehearsing it. Even after material is learned, additional rehearsal (overlearning) increases retention.
   Experiments show that distributed study yields better long-term retention than cramming (spacing effect).
   The serial position effect refers to the finding that people often remember the first and last items in a list better than they do middle items.

4. Studies by Craik and Tulving demonstrate that the processing of meaning (semantic encoding) yields better memory of verbal information than does the processing of images (visual encoding) or sounds (acoustic encoding). Recall of information we relate to ourselves is particularly good.
   The imagery principle—that people have excellent memory for pictures and picture-evoking words—is at the heart of memory-enhancing mnemonic devices. In the method of loci and the "peg-word" system, we associate to-be-remembered items with visual codes.
   Organizing information into meaningful units, or chunks, also improves memory. The use of acronyms and hierarchies, for example, can facilitate

both retention and retrieval.

5. We sense so much during a lifetime that it is fortunate that we forget some things. Much of the material we think of as having been forgotten was never "remembered." Although it was sensed, it never entered the memory system because it was not encoded; therefore, its "loss" can be attributed to encoding failure.

6. Iconic memory is momentary photographic memory in which the eyes register an exact representation of a scene. George Sperling first demonstrated the existence of this type of sensory memory, which lasts for only about a few tenths of a second. Sensory memory for sound, called echoic memory, disappears after 3 or 4 seconds.

7. Studies by Peterson and Peterson demonstrate that short-term memory stores approximately seven chunks of information. This type of memory is slightly better for random digits than for random letters and is slightly better for information we hear rather than see.

    Our capacity for storing long-term memories is essentially limitless. Ebbinghaus's famous "forgetting curve" studies and Bahrick's study of long-term retention of Spanish vocabulary showed that most forgetting occurs relatively soon after learning. Two possible explanations for the forgetting curve are that new experiences interfere with retrieval and that the physical memory trace gradually decays.

8. Lashley's studies demonstrated that memories do not reside in single, specific parts of the cortex. Gerard demonstrated that lowering animals' body temperatures until their brains' electrical activity ceased did not disrupt long-term memories. Kandel and Schwartz found that when learning occurs in sea snails, more of the neurotransmitter serotonin is released at certain synapses, and neural transmission is more efficient. This increased efficiency, called long-term potentiation, may be the neural basis for learning and memory. Other studies have shown that when neurotransmitters are blocked by alcohol or other drugs, memory formation is disrupted. Conversely, learning and retention are boosted by emotion-triggered hormonal changes.

9. Although amnesics often can't recall new facts or recent experiences, most are capable of learning new skills. This suggests that there are two distinct types of memory: implicit (or nondeclarative) memory of skills, preferences, and dispositions; and explicit (declarative) memory of facts and experiences that are consciously known.

    The fact that most amnesics have suffered damage to the hippocampus suggests that this limbic structure plays a crucial role in the processing of explicit memories. Because older memories remain intact in amnesics, the hippocampus cannot be the permanent storehouse for such memories. It is likely that the hippocampus functions as a relay station that feeds new information to other brain circuits for permanent storage.

10. Recall is the ability to retrieve information not in conscious awareness. Recognition is a measure of memory in which one need only identify previously learned information. Relearning measures the amount of time saved when previously learned information is learned for a second time. Tests of recognition and relearning typically reveal that people remember more than they can recall.

    Recognition tests of memory are "easier" because they provide retrieval cues that serve as reminders of information that could not otherwise be recalled. Priming and context effects, too, indicate the importance of retrieval cues in memory. Emotions also trigger memories. State-dependent memory is the phenomenon that things learned in one emotional state are more easily recalled when we are again in the same state. Another aspect of this phenomenon is that our current mood influences our retrieval of past experiences. Mood also influences how we interpret other people's behavior and how attentive we are to new information.

11. Proactive interference refers to the disruptive effect of previous learning on the recall of new information. Retroactive interference refers to the disruptive effect of new information on the recall of previous information. Jenkins and Dallenbach's classic study demonstrated that retroactive interference was reduced when subjects slept following a learning episode, presumably because the number of potentially interfering events was minimized.

12. Motivated forgetting refers to the irretrievability of memories that are embarrassing to remember. Similarly, with his concept of repression Freud proposed that memory is self-censoring. According to this viewpoint, repressed memories remain intact and may be retrieved at some later time.

13. Memory retrieval does not consist merely of a literal reporting of stored information. Instead, memories are constructed as we encode them, then alter them in the face of new experiences. Loftus and Palmer have shown that after exposure to subtle misinformation, eyewitnesses to an incident incorrectly recalled the actual incident (the misinformation effect). Another phenomenon, *source amnesia*, is at the heart of many false memories. This occurs whenever we misattribute an event that we experienced, read about, or imagined to the wrong source. Memory construction also explains why "hypnotically refreshed" memories often incorporate false information.

14. Researchers are skeptical of such claims because, although recovered memories are commonplace, memories of things happening before age 3, as well as those "recovered" under hypnosis or the influence of drugs, are unreliable. In addition, the "recovery" of painful memory rests on the assumption that the human mind commonly represses traumatic experiences—an assumption that increasingly is being challenged by contemporary researchers.

15. Recent studies of eyewitness memory demonstrate that young children are more suggestible to memory plants than older children or adults. Children do not, however, *routinely* confuse reality with fantasy. They are especially credible when questioned by a neutral person who asks nonleading questions.

16. Suggestions for improving memory include rehearsing material over many separate and distributed study sessions with the objective of overlearning material. Studying should also involve active rehearsal, rather than mindless repetition of information. Organizing information, relating material to what is already known, developing numerous retrieval cues, and using mnemonic devices that incorporate vivid imagery are helpful too. Frequent activation of retrieval cues, such as the context and mood in which the original learning occurred, can also help strengthen memory, as can recalling events while they are fresh, before possible misinformation is encountered. Studying should also be arranged to minimize potential sources of interference. Finally, self-tests in the same format (recall or recognition) that will later be used on the actual test are useful. (The PRTR technique described in the Introduction of the text incorporates several of these strategies.)

Program Assignment

1. Modern memory research began about 100 years ago with the work of German psychologist Hermann Ebbinghaus. Ebbinghaus's procedure consisted of memorizing a list of nonsense syllables and then trying to retain the list in memory while distracting himself by learning other lists. He then measured his memory of the original list by determining how many times he had to reread it before remembering it perfectly. Ebbinghaus's findings reveal a standard forgetting curve, in which there is an initial rapid loss of memory, followed by a more gradual decline over the next month. Ebbinghaus's rapid initial memory loss was due in part to his use of essentially meaningless material. With such material, he unwittingly stripped himself of one of the most powerful memory strategies of the mind: discovering meaning, order, and organization in the information we encounter.

2. Some researchers believe that long-term memories are stored in the form of associative networks in which each piece of information is linked to a family of others that share common properties. Activating any of the concepts in the network activates the others associated with it. This activation spreads automatically and rapidly.

3. Sigmund Freud was the first to recognize that what we remember and what we choose to forget can help maintain our sense of integrity and self-esteem. Freud labeled the process *repression*, in which the ego defends against unacceptable thoughts by pushing them out of awareness into the unconscious. Freud maintained that repressed thoughts often resurface in disguised form in dreams, slips of the tongue, and symptoms of mental distress.

4. Memories are made more meaningful through the constructive process of remembering. To make new information fit better with what we already know and believe, we accentuate some details, eliminate some, and reinterpret others. In this way we construct consistent themes and coherent stories, even when the information is inconsistent and ambiguous. Constructive memory highlights a central principle of memory: How and what you remember is determined by who you are and what you already know. All the new information we learn is organized by relating it to existing schemas. Schemas are frameworks of our basic ideas and preconceptions about people, objects, and situations. Many of our constructions and distortions of memory arise as we try to fit new information into old schemas.

5. Memory traces in neurons, called *engrams*, make up the biological substrate of human memory. One set of engrams forms the foundation of everything we know *how* to do; this is the procedural knowledge (referred to as "implicit memory" in the text) that lies behind every skilled action. Another set of engrams forms the foundation of semantic or declarative knowledge (referred to as "explicit memory" in the text), which embodies *what* we know, including concepts, ideas, and things. Another batch of engrams works in the service of our episodic memory, our diary of personal experiences, each tagged with a time and place. (See also Figure 9.15, text p. 286, which diagrams the relationships among these types of memories.)

6. Richard Thompson has traced the circuitry involved in the classically conditioned eye-blink response of rabbits. In Thompson's experiment, a tone was presented just before a puff of air struck the rabbit's eye. By recording the electrical activity of brain cells during training, Thompson identified an area of the cerebellum (the interpositus nucleus) that seemed to store the memory of the conditioned response. Destroying this area with a small lesion completely abolished the conditioned eye-blink response.

7. People who lose their memories provide important information about memory. The best known type of memory loss is called *functional amnesia*, or memory loss caused by psychological factors. It is typically found in people who are in an extreme state of anxiety or hysteria who subconsciously escape by blocking off all memories. This memory block can often be removed through psychotherapy and hypnosis. Most permanent memory loss results from destruction of brain tissue. *Organic amnesia* can be caused by injury to the brain, disease, alcohol addiction, chemical poisoning, and senility. In Alzheimer's disease, brain tissue atrophies.

Progress Test

1. **d.** is the answer. Information must be encoded, or put into appropriate form; stored, or retained over time; and retrieved, or located and gotten out when needed. (p. 272)
2. **c.** is the answer. Echoic memories last 3 to 4 seconds. (p. 281)
3. **c.** is the answer. (video; p. 282)
4. **d.** is the answer. (video; p. 277)

    a. There is no such term as "consolidation techniques."

    b. & c. Imagery and encoding strategies are important in storing new memories, but mnemonic device is the general designation of techniques that facilitate memory, such as acronyms and the peg-word system.

5. **e.** is the answer. (video; p. 278)

    a. There is no such process of "consolidating."

    b. Organization *does* enhance memory but it does so through hierarchies, not grouping.

    c. Memory construction refers to the ways in which memories are altered by the individual's basic assumptions and experiences.

    d. Encoding refers to the processing of information into the memory system.

6. **c.** is the answer. Kandel and Schwartz found that when learning occurred in sea snails, serotonin was released at certain synapses, which then became more efficient at signal transmission. (p. 284)

7. **d.** is the answer. In general, being in a context similar to that in which you experienced something will tend to help you recall the experience. (p. 289)

    a. & b. The learning environment per se—and its familiarity or exoticness—had no effect on retention.

8. **b.** is the answer. (video)

9. **d.** is the answer. When asked to recall all the letters, subjects could recall only about half; however, if immediately after the presentation they were signaled to recall a particular row, their recall was near perfect. This showed that they had a brief photographic memory, so brief that it faded in less time than it would have taken to say all nine letters. (p. 281)

10. **b.** is the answer. Because amnesics lose their fact (explicit) memories but not their skill (implicit) memories or their capacity to learn, it appears that human memory can be divided into two distinct types. (p. 286)

    d. As studies of victims of amnesia show, memory losses following damage to the hippocampus are quite predictable.

11. **b.** is the answer. When the words were organized into categories, recall was two to three times better, indicating the benefits of hierarchical organization in memory. (p. 279)

    d. This study did not examine the use of mnemonic devices by subjects.

12. **b.** is the answer. In essence, we construct our memories, bringing them into line with our biases and assumptions, as well as with our subsequent experiences. (video; pp. 294–295)

    a. If this were true, it would mean that memory construction does not occur. Through memory construction, memories may deviate significantly from the original experiences.

    c. There is no evidence that such chemical transfers occur.

    d. Many long-term memories are apparently unlimited in duration.

13. **d.** is the answer. (video; p. 286)

    a. & b. Explicit memory (also called declarative memory) is memory of facts and experiences that one can consciously know and declare.

    c. Episodic memory is explicit memory for personally experienced events.

14. **a.** is the answer. We remember skills acquired in infancy, as such memories are recorded in earlier developing brain regions, but declarative memories involve the hippocampus. (p. 288)

    b., c., & d. There is no evidence that serotonin levels or association areas are deficient until age 3. Moreover, such proposals are unlikely, as they wouldn't explain why we remember skills learned in infancy while forgetting events experienced.

15. **d.** is the answer. It is in both encoding and retrieval that we construct our memories, and as Loftus's studies showed, leading questions affect people's memory construction. (p. 295)

    a. The memory encoding occurred at the time of the event in question, not during questioning by the hypnotist.

    b. State-dependent memory refers to the influence of one's own emotional or physiological state on encoding and retrieval, and would not apply here.

    c. Proactive interference is the interfering effect of prior learning on the recall of new information.

    e. Repression is the suppression of emotionally painful memories.

16. **d.** is the answer. (p. 292)

    a. & b. This study did not find evidence that memories fade (decay) with time.

    c. When one is awake, there are many *more* potential sources of memory interference than when one is asleep.

17. **c.** is the answer. As Ebbinghaus and Bahrick both showed, most of the forgetting that is going to occur happens soon after learning. (video; p. 282)

18. **d.** is the answer. Surprisingly, Lashley found that no matter where he cut, the rats had at least a partial memory of how to solve the maze. (video; p. 284)

    a. & b. Lashley's studies did not investigate the significance of the interval between learning and cortical lesioning.

19. **c.** is the answer. Episodic memory is memory for personal life experiences, such as a high school graduation; semantic memory is memory for facts, such as the name of the president. (video; p. 286)

    a. & b. Implicit memories are memories for skills. Both of these examples involve explicit memory, which is memory for facts and experiences.

20. **d.** is the answer. (p. 287)

21. **e.** is the answer. According to the serial position effect, items at the beginning and end of a list tend to be remembered best. (pp. 274–275)

22. **a.** is the answer. (p. 294)

    b. Although Lewis's difficulty in recalling these memories could be considered retrieval failure, it is caused by repression, which is therefore the *best* explanation.

    c. This answer is incorrect because it is clear that Lewis fails to remember these experiences because they are painful memories and not because he is in a different emotional or physiological state.

    d. Flashbulb memories are especially *vivid* memories for emotionally significant events. Lewis has no memory at all.

    e. Implicit memories are memories of skills.

23. **d.** is the answer. (video)

    a., b., & c. These are causes of organic amnesia.

24. **c.** is the answer. Processing a word in terms of its meaning (semantic encoding) produces much better retention than does visual or acoustic encoding. (p. 275)

25. **b.** is the answer. (video)

26. **b.** is the answer. (video)

27. **d.** is the answer. (p. 285)

28. **d.** is the answer. When misled by the phrasing of questions, subjects incorrectly recalled details of the film and even "remembered" objects that weren't there. (p. 295)

    a., b., & c. These were not findings of Loftus and Palmer.

29. **b.** is the answer. Amnesics typically have suffered damage to the hippocampus, a brain structure involved in processing explicit memories for facts. (p. 286)

    a. Amnesics do retain implicit memories for how to do things; these are processed in the more ancient parts of the brain.

    c. & d. Amnesics generally do not experience impairment in their iconic and echoic sensory memories.

30. **b.** is the answer. (p. 272)

    a. Information in short-term memory has *already* been encoded.

    c. Iconic and echoic are types of *sensory* memory.

    d. Retrieval is the process of getting material out of storage and into conscious, short-term memory. Thus, all material in short-term memory has either already been retrieved, or is about to be placed in storage.

31. **c.** is the answer. By breaking concepts down into subconcepts and yet smaller divisions and showing the relationships among these, hierarchies facilitate information processing. Use of main heads and subheads is an example of the organization of textbook chapters into hierarchies. (p. 279)

    a. Mnemonic devices are the method of loci, acronyms, and other memory *techniques* that facilitate retention.

    b. Chunks are organizations of knowledge into familiar, manageable units.

    d. Recognition is a measure of retention.

32. **c.** is the answer. (video)

33. **a.** is the answer. In fact, this model of memory uses the computer as a metaphor for the mind. (video)

34. **c.** is the answer. Short-term recall is slightly better for information we hear rather than see, because echoic memory momentarily outlasts iconic memory. (p. 281)

a. Meaningful stimuli, such as words, are usually remembered more easily than meaningless stimuli, such as random letters.

b. Iconic memory does not last as long as echoic memory in short-term recall.

d. Although context is a powerful retrieval cue, there is no general facilitation of memory in an unusual context.

35. **b.** is the answer. (p. 297)

a. In fact, brain activity in the hippocampus does *not* differentiate true and false word recognition memories.

c. & d. These brain areas are not implicated in this type of memory.

36. **b.** is the answer. Retroactive interference is the disruption by new information of something you once learned. (p. 292)

a. Proactive interference occurs when old information makes it difficult to correctly remember new information.

c. & d. Interference produces forgetting even when the forgotten material was effectively encoded and stored. Janice's problem is at the level of retrieval.

e. There is no reason to believe that Janice's old locker combination is a painful memory.

37. **c.** is the answer. Susan's memories are affected by her state, in this case her bad mood. (p. 291)

a. Priming refers to the conscious or unconscious activation of particular associations in memory.

b. Memory construction refers to changes in memory as new experiences occur.

d. Although Susan's difficulty in recalling the good could be considered retrieval failure, it is caused by the state-dependent effect, which is therefore the best explanation.

e. Repression involves the suppression of *painful* memories.

38. **b.** is the answer. Being back in the context in which the original experiences occurred triggered memories of these experiences. (p. 290)

a. The memories were triggered by similarity of place, not mood.

c. Retroactive interference would involve difficulties in retrieving old memories.

d. Echoic memory refers to momentary memory of auditory stimuli.

e. Iconic memory refers to momentary memory of visual stimuli.

39. **d.** is the answer. Flashbulb memories are unusually clear memories of emotionally significant moments in life. (p. 270)

40. **c.** is the answer. (p. 288)

a. & b. The name of your homeroom teacher, which you probably heard at least once each day of school, was surely processed into memory (encoded) and maintained there for some time (stored).

d. State-dependent memory is the tendency to recall information best in the same state as when the information was learned. It is unlikely that any single state was associated with learning your homeroom teacher's name.

Key Terms

Textbook Terms

1. **Memory** is the persistence of learning over time via the storage and retrieval of information. (p. 269)
2. A **flashbulb memory** is an unusually vivid memory of an emotionally important moment in one's life. (p. 270)
3. **Encoding** is the first step in memory; information is translated into some form that enables it to enter our memory system. (p. 272)
4. **Storage** is the passive process by which encoded information is maintained over time. (p. 272)
5. **Retrieval** is the process of bringing to consciousness information from memory storage. (p. 272)
6. **Long-term memory** is the relatively permanent and unlimited capacity memory system into which information from short-term memory may pass. (p. 272)
7. **Short-term memory** is conscious memory, which can hold about seven items for a short time. (p. 272)
8. **Automatic processing** refers to our unconscious encoding of incidental information such as space, time, and frequency, and of well-learned information. (p. 273)
9. **Effortful processing** is encoding that requires attention and some degree of conscious effort. (p. 273)
10. **Rehearsal** is the conscious, effortful repetition of information that you are trying either to maintain in consciousness or to encode for storage. (p. 273)
11. The **spacing effect** is the tendency for distributed practice to yield better long-term retention than massed practice, or cramming. (p. 274)
12. The **serial position effect** is the tendency for items at the beginning and end of a list to be more easily retained than those in the middle. (pp. 274–275)
13. **Semantic encoding** is the processing of information into memory according to its meaning. (p. 275)
14. **Acoustic encoding** is the processing of information into memory according to its sound. (p. 275)
15. **Visual encoding** is the use of imagery to process information into effortful processing. (p. 275)
16. **Imagery** refers to mental pictures and can be an important aid to effortful processing. (p. 276)
17. **Mnemonics** are memory aids (the method of loci, acronyms, peg-words, etc.), which often use visual imagery. (p. 277)
18. **Chunking** is the memory technique of organizing material into familiar, meaningful units. (p. 278)
19. **Sensory memory** is the immediate, initial recording of sensory information in the memory system. (p. 281)
20. **Iconic memory** is the visual sensory memory consisting of a perfect photographic memory, which lasts no more than a few tenths of a second. (p. 281)

Memory aid: *Icon* means "image" or "representation." **Iconic memory** consists of brief visual images.

21. **Echoic memory** is the momentary sensory memory of auditory stimuli, lasting about 3 or 4 seconds. (p. 281)

22. **Long-term potentiation (LTP)** is an increase in a synapse's firing potential following brief, rapid stimulation. LTP is believed to be the neural basis for learning and memory. (p. 285)

23. **Amnesia** is the loss of memory. (p. 286)

24. **Implicit memories** are memories of skills, preferences, and dispositions. These memories are evidently processed, not by the hippocampus, but by a more primitive part of the brain, the cerebellum. They are also called nondeclarative memories. (p. 286)

25. **Explicit memories** are memories of facts, including names, images, and events. They are also called declarative memories. (p. 286)

26. The **hippocampus** is a neural region within the limbic system that is important in the processing of explicit memories for storage. (p. 287)

27. **Recall** is a measure of retention in which the person must remember, with few retrieval cues, information learned earlier. (p. 288)

28. **Recognition** is a measure of retention in which one need only identify, rather than recall, previously learned information. (p. 288)

29. **Relearning** is also a measure of retention in that the less time it takes to relearn information, the more that information has been retained. (p. 288)

30. **Priming** is the activation, often unconscious, of a web of associations in memory in order to retrieve a specific memory. (p. 289)

31. **Déjà vu** is the false sense that you have already experienced a current situation. (p. 290)

32. **Mood-congruent memory** is the tendency to recall experiences that are consistent with our current mood. (p. 291)

33. **Proactive interference** is the disruptive effect of something you already have learned on your efforts to learn or recall new information. (p. 292)

34. **Retroactive interference** is the disruptive effect of something recently learned on old knowledge. (p. 292)

Memory aid: *Retro* means "backward." **Retroactive interference** is "backward-acting" interference.

35. **Repression** is an example of motivated forgetting in that painful and unacceptable memories are prevented from entering consciousness. (p. 294)

36. The **misinformation effect** is the tendency of eyewitnesses to an event to incorporate misleading information about the event into their memories. (p. 295)

37. At the heart of many false memories, **source amnesia** refers to misattributing an event to the wrong source. (p. 296)

Program Terms

38. **Functional amnesia** is memory loss caused by severe anxiety or intolerable stress.

39. **Organic amnesia** is memory loss caused by injury to the brain, disease, or alcohol addiction.

40. **Episodic memory** is memory for chronological, or temporally dated, personal experiences (a type of explicit memory).

41. **Semantic memory** is general knowledge that is not tied to the time when information was learned (a type of explicit memory).

42. **Procedural memory** is memory for actions, skills, and operations (a type of implicit memory).

PROGRAMS *10 & 11*

Cognitive Processes
Judgment and Decision Making

TEXTBOOK ASSIGNMENT: Chapter 10: Thinking and Language, pp. 305–319

ORIENTATION

Programs 10 and 11 deal with thinking and decision making. In Program 10, the emphasis is on basic thought processes—formulating mental representations, categorizing, creating hierarchies, and using algorithms and heuristics, for example. Program 11 explores the tendency of people, as individuals and in groups, to lapse into irrational thinking in part because they apply inappropriate mental strategies that are better suited to other situations.

Program 10 discusses several common obstacles to problem solving, including fixations that prevent us from taking a fresh perspective on a problem and our bias to seek information that confirms rather than challenges existing hypotheses. The reading assignment and program also explore how the new generation of computer systems has been constructed to simulate the neural networks of the human brain. By mimicking the ways in which human neural networks interconnect, computers enable scientists to study how human systems process sensations and memories and how the thought process works.

Program 11 introduces the new science of risk assessment, which reveals that although people avoid risks when seeking gains they choose risks to avoid sure losses. Another new field is the psychology of negotiation. Research in this field demonstrates several pitfalls to effective negotiations.

NOTE: Answer guidelines for all questions for Programs 10 and 11 begin on page 200.

GOALS

After completing your study of the program and reading assignment, you should be prepared to:

1. Describe the range of phenomena investigated by cognitive psychologists.

2. Explain several strategies and obstacles in efficient problem solving and reasoning.

3. Discuss the use of the computer as a metaphor for the mind.

4. Explain how thinking strategies can result in irrational decision making.

5. Discuss findings from research studies of risk assessment and negotiation.

6. Discuss the symptoms and prevention of groupthink.

Programs 10 & 11: Cognitive Processes and Judgment and Decision Making

GUIDED STUDY

Textbook Assignment

The text chapter should be studied one section at a time. Before you read, preview each section by skimming it, noting headings and boldface items. Then read the appropriate section objectives from the following outline. Keep these objectives in mind and, as you read the chapter section, search for the information that will enable you to meet each objective. Once you have finished a section, write out answers for its objectives.

Thinking (pp. 306–319)

1. Describe the nature, function, and formation of concepts.

2. Discuss the major problem-solving strategies and describe the nature of insight.

3. Identify obstacles to problem solving.

4. Describe the heuristics that guide decision making and explain how overconfidence and framing can affect judgment.

5. Describe how our beliefs influence our logical reasoning.

6. Contrast the human mind and the computer as information processors and describe recent advances in artificial intelligence.

Program Assignment

Read the following objectives before you watch Programs 10 and 11. As you watch, be alert for information that will help you answer each objective. Taking notes during the programs will help you to formulate your answers later. After the programs, write answers to the objectives. If you have access to the programs on videotape, you may replay portions to refresh your memory.

Program 10

1. Trace the development of the field of cognitive psychology and discuss its subject matter.

2. State the contributions of Donald Broadbent to the field of cognitive psychology.

3. Describe how researchers study the relationship between brain physiology and cognition.

4. Discuss how cognitive psychologists are attempting to apply cognitive science to the field of education.

Program 11

5. Discuss two explanations for the irrationality of human thinking.

6. Contrast two approaches to the study of decision making and describe several potential obstacles to rational thinking.

7. Discuss factors involved in risk taking.

8. Identify the symptoms of groupthink and cite steps leaders can take to prevent its development.

9. Describe the goals of the psychology of negotiation and identify five common cognitive mistakes made by negotiators.

10. Explain the theory of cognitive dissonance and describe the classic Festinger and Carlsmith study.

PROGRESS TEST

Circle your answers to the following questions and check them with the answers on page 202. If your answer is incorrect, read the explanation for why it is incorrect and then consult the appropriate pages of the text (in parentheses following the correct answer).

1. The text defines cognition as:
   a. silent speech.
   b. all mental activity.
   c. mental activity associated with processing, understanding, and communicating knowledge.
   d. logical reasoning.
   e. problem solving.

2. Confirmation bias refers to the tendency to:
   a. allow preexisting beliefs to distort logical reasoning.
   b. cling to one's initial conceptions after the basis on which they were formed has been discredited.
   c. search randomly through alternative solutions when problem solving.
   d. look for information that is consistent with one's beliefs.

3. *Cognition* is the general term that refers to *all* forms of:
   a. knowing.
   b. remembering.
   c. feeling.
   d. sensing.

4. Dr. Mendoza is studying the mental strategies people use when solving problems. Dr. Mendoza is clearly a(n):
   a. cognitive psychologist.
   b. experimental psychologist.
   c. organizational psychologist.
   d. developmental psychologist.

5. Cognitive psychology emerged partly as a reaction against _____ , which chose to focus on observable behaviors rather than internal processes.
   a. psychoanalysis
   b. behaviorism
   c. humanistic psychology
   d. information processing

6. Mental set and functional fixedness are two types of:
   a. algorithms.
   b. heuristics.
   c. fixation.
   d. insight.

7. Which of the following is an example of the use of heuristics?
   a. trying every possible letter ordering when unscrambling a word
   b. considering each possible move when playing chess
   c. using the formula area = length × width to find the area of a rectangle
   d. playing chess using a defensive strategy that has often been successful for you

8. The chimpanzee Sultan used a short stick to pull a longer stick that was out of reach into his cage. He then used the longer stick to reach a piece of fruit. Researchers hypothesized that Sultan's discovery of the solution to his problem was the result of:
   a. trial and error.
   b. heuristics.
   c. functional fixedness.
   d. mental set.
   e. insight.

9. Cognitive psychology developed:
   a. with the writings of Descartes in the seventeenth century.
   b. at the beginning of the twentieth century.
   c. after World War II.
   d. during the 1970s.

10. Donald Broadbent was the first psychologist to:
    a. use the information-processing approach to model human thought processes.
    b. create a "thinking machine."
    c. use brain-imaging techniques to investigate the physiology of thinking.
    d. apply cognitive science to the field of education.

11. You hear that one of the Smith children is an outstanding Little League player and immediately conclude it's their one son rather than any of their four daughters. You reached your quite possibly erroneous conclusion as the result of:
    a. the confirmation bias.
    b. the availability heuristic.
    c. the representativeness heuristic.
    d. belief perseverance.

12. Because of their lightning speed, computers can retrieve and manipulate stored data faster than people can, but the human brain beats the computer hands down when it comes to:
    a. using heuristics.
    b. following algorithms.
    c. serial processing.
    d. simultaneous processing.

13. Neural networks are:
    a. computer circuits that mimic the brain's neural circuitry.
    b. obstacles to effective problem solving.
    c. heuristics that make problem solving more efficient.
    d. biologically programmed synaptic connections that enable simple responses.

14. A common problem in everyday reasoning is our tendency to:
    a. accept as logical those conclusions that agree with our own opinions.
    b. accept as logical those conclusions that disagree with our own opinions.
    c. underestimate the accuracy of our knowledge.
    d. accept as logical those conclusions that involve unfamiliar concepts.

15. According to Herbert Simon, the computer equivalent of a neuron in representing information is:
    a. the video display unit.
    b. a printer.
    c. a punch card.
    d. a keyboard.

16. A mental grouping of similar things, events, or people is called a(n):
    a. prototype.
    b. concept.
    c. algorithm.
    d. heuristic.
    e. mental set.

17. Representativeness and availability are examples of:
    a. mental sets.
    b. belief bias.
    c. algorithms.
    d. fixation.
    e. heuristics.

18. Which of the following describes artificial intelligence?
    a. the science of low-temperature phenomena
    b. the study of animal behavior in its natural habitat
    c. the study of control processes in electronic and biological systems
    d. the science that explores human thought by attempting to model it on the computer
    e. the best example of a category

19. Assume that Congress is considering revising its approach to welfare and to this end is hearing a range of testimony. A member of Congress who uses the availability heuristic would be most likely to:
    a. want to experiment with numerous possible approaches to see which of these seems to work best.
    b. want to cling to approaches to welfare that seem to have had some success in the past.
    c. refuse to be budged from his or her beliefs despite persuasive testimony to the contrary.
    d. base his or her ideas on the most vivid, memorable testimony, even though many statistics presented run counter to this testimony.

20. According to cognitive dissonance theory, dissonance is most likely to occur when:
    a. a person's behavior is not based on strongly held attitudes.
    b. two people who have conflicting attitudes disagree.
    c. an individual does something that is personally disagreeable.
    d. an individual is coerced into doing something that he or she does not want to do.

21. Which of the following is most likely to promote groupthink?
    a. The group leader fails to take a firm stance on an issue.
    b. A minority faction holds to its position.
    c. The group consults with various experts.
    d. Group isolation is evident.

22. Before she gave a class presentation favoring gun control legislation, Wanda opposed it. Her present attitude favoring such legislation can best be explained by:
    a. the normative model of decision making.
    b. cognitive dissonance theory.
    c. social exchange theory.
    d. the descriptive model of decision making.

23. Neural network computers:
    a. can be programmed to mimic excitatory and inhibitory neural messages.
    b. have a greater capacity than conventional computers to learn from experience.
    c. are not limited to serial processing.
    d. can do all of the above.
    e. can do none of the above.

24. Which of the following illustrates belief perseverance?
    a. Your belief remains intact even in the face of evidence to the contrary.
    b. You refuse to listen to arguments counter to your beliefs.
    c. You tend to become flustered and angry when your beliefs are refuted.
    d. You tend to search for information that supports your beliefs.
    e. Your beliefs tend to distort logical reasoning.

25. When we distinguish objects on the basis of their shape or color, we are performing the cognitive process of:
    a. schema formation.
    b. prototyping.
    c. categorizing.
    d. assimilation.

26. The basic units of cognition are:
    a. phonemes.
    b. concepts.
    c. prototypes.
    d. morphemes.

27. Complete the following analogy: Rose is to flower as:
    a. concept is to prototype.
    b. prototype is to concept.
    c. concept is to hierarchy.
    d. hierarchy is to concept.

28. The board members of Acme Truck Company are so afraid of contradicting the chairman and breaking the "team spirit" that they often conceal their true opinions. This group is a victim of:
    a. reasoning by representativeness.
    b. cognitive dissonance.
    c. the anchoring effect.
    d. groupthink.

29. Which of the following situations should produce the *greatest* cognitive dissonance?
    a. A soldier is forced to carry out orders that he finds disagreeable.
    b. A student who loves animals has to dissect a cat in order to pass biology.
    c. As part of an experiment, a subject is directed to deliver electric shocks to another person.
    d. A student volunteers to debate an issue, taking the side he personally disagrees with.

30. According to Program 10, we are likely to assume that Montreal is north of Seattle because:
    a. Montreal is a prototype for the concept "north."
    b. we initially encoded this incorrect information.
    c. in our mental map of America, all of Canada is north of the United States.
    d. we are less familiar with Canadian cities than with cities in the United States.

31. Unlike computers, which process information _____ , we often process information according to _____ .
    a. sequentially; the particular meaning it has for us
    b. randomly; our personal schemas
    c. schematically; the order in which we perceive it
    d. rationally; irrational ideas

32. Your stand on an issue such as the use of nuclear power involves personal judgment. In such a case, one memorable occurrence can weigh more heavily than a bookful of data, thus illustrating:
    a. belief perseverance.
    b. confirmation bias.
    c. the representativeness heuristic.
    d. the availability heuristic.
    e. belief bias.

33. In Program 11, various people were asked whether the Mississippi River is longer or shorter than 500 miles. Others were asked whether it is longer or shorter than 5000 miles. How did the estimates of the two groups compare?
    a. They were essentially the same.
    b. The first group made a slightly larger estimate.
    c. The second group made a slightly larger estimate.
    d. The second group made a substantially larger estimate.

34. Karen is terrified of nuclear accidents but never thinks twice about the dangers of jaywalking. Evidently, Karen is under the influence of:
    a. risk aversion.
    b. the dread factor.
    c. an anchoring effect.
    d. cognitive dissonance.

35. A dessert recipe that gives you the ingredients, their amounts, and the steps to follow is an example of a(n):
    a. prototype.
    b. algorithm.
    c. heuristic.
    d. mental set.

36. Marilyn was asked to solve a series of five math problems. The first four problems could only be solved by a particular sequence of operations. The fifth problem could also be solved following this sequence; however, a much simpler solution was possible. Marilyn did not realize this simpler solution existed, and she solved the problem in the way she had solved the first four. Her problem-solving strategy was hampered by:
    a. functional fixedness.
    b. the overconfidence phenomenon.
    c. mental set.
    d. her lack of a prototype for the solution.

37. A cognitive illusion is:
    a. the tendency to consider events that come readily to mind as highly likely.
    b. the tendency to reason from personal stereotypes about events and people.
    c. the impact of initial impressions on problem solving.
    d. a systematic way of thinking that causes an error in reasoning.

38. According to Sigmund Freud, people sometimes make irrational decisions because:
    a. they are driven by primitive needs.
    b. of the impact of other people, particularly when they are in a crowd, on their thinking.
    c. of normal flaws in their everyday powers of reasoning.
    d. of all the above reasons.

39. Automaticity:
    a. refers to the computer's tremendous advantage over humans in terms of the speed at which information is processed.
    b. frees human memory from having to focus on lower-level processes.
    c. usually is a hindrance to problem solving because it prevents us from thinking logically about pertinent issues.
    d. is the process by which environmental information is consciously attended to.

40. When Michael Posner conducted PET scans of people reading words, he found that:
   a. specific regions of the brain were more active than others.
   b. processing tended to be localized in specific regions of the brain in subjects who had poor reading skills.
   c. processing was not localized in specific regions of the brain in subjects who had poor reading skills.
   d. the brain regions activated in women and men were very different.

41. In one experiment people were shown a model boat and later asked whether the boat had a windshield or an anchor. The results indicated that the subjects:
   a. used their preexisting schemas in order to form their answers.
   b. based their answers on their prototype of the concept "boat."
   c. were overconfident in the accuracy of their answers.
   d. scanned mental images of the boat in order to answer.

42. When people were faced with a choice of a sure loss of 85 dollars or an 85 percent chance of losing 100 dollars, they:
   a. chose the sure loss of 85 dollars.
   b. refused to make a choice.
   c. became quite agitated.
   d. chose the 85 percent chance of losing 100 dollars.

43. Boris the chess master selects his next move by considering moves that would threaten his opponent's queen. His opponent, a chess-playing computer, selects its next move by considering all possible moves. Boris is using a(n) _____ and the computer is using a(n) _____ .
   a. algorithm; heuristic
   b. prototype; mental set
   c. mental set; prototype
   d. heuristic; algorithm

44. During a televised political debate, the Republican and Democratic candidates each argued that the results of a recent public opinion poll supported their party's platform. Because both candidates saw the information as supporting their belief, it is clear that both were victims of:
   a. functional fixedness.
   b. mental set.
   c. belief bias.
   d. confirmation bias.

45. Experts in a field prefer heuristics to algorithms because heuristics:
   a. guarantee solutions to problems.
   b. prevent mental sets.
   c. often save time.
   d. prevent fixation.
   e. do all of the above.

46. Rudy is 6 feet 6 inches tall, weighs 210 pounds, and is very muscular. If you think that Rudy is more likely to be a professional basketball player than a computer programmer, you are a victim of:
   a. belief bias.
   b. the availability heuristic.
   c. mental set.
   d. functional fixedness.
   e. the representativeness heuristic.

47. Failing to see that an article of clothing can be inflated as a life preserver is an example of:
    a. belief bias.
    b. the availability heuristic.
    c. the representativeness heuristic.
    d. functional fixedness.

48. Connie is placing a bet at the race track. She prefers to bet on a small sure gain over a probable larger gain. Connie is evidently subject to the psychological principle of:
    a. risk seeking.
    b. risk aversion.
    c. anchoring bias.
    d. cognitive dissonance.

49. What was Irving Janis's advice for preventing the development of groupthink?
    a. Groups should make their decisions in isolation.
    b. Dissenting opinions from the majority's decision should be discouraged.
    c. The group leader should encourage views that oppose the majority's position.
    d. members of the group should be guarded from any information that might lead them to change their mind or raise questions about their decision.

50. A "zero-sum game" is one in which:
    a. both parties in a negotiation "win" when agreement is reached.
    b. neither party in a negotiation "wins."
    c. negotiators believe that one party must "win" and the other "lose."
    d. the members of a group forge a "team spirit" that leads to irrational decision making.

51. Airline reservations typically decline after a highly publicized airline crash because people overestimate the incidence of such disasters. In such instances, people's decisions are being influenced by:
    a. belief bias.
    b. the availability heuristic.
    c. the representativeness heuristic.
    d. functional fixedness.

52. Most people tend to:
    a. accurately estimate the accuracy of their knowledge and judgments.
    b. underestimate the accuracy of their knowledge and judgments.
    c. overestimate the accuracy of their knowledge and judgments.
    d. lack confidence in their decision-making strategies.

53. In relation to ground beef, consumers respond more positively to an ad describing it as 75 percent lean than to one referring to its 25 percent fat content. This is an example of:
    a. the framing effect.
    b. confirmation bias.
    c. mental set.
    d. overconfidence.

54. Which of the following is *not* a common cognitive mistake made by negotiators?
    a. failing to consider the judgments of the other side in negotiation
    b. escalating conflict by increasing commitment to a previous course of action

c. having a very limited frame in their perspective to conflict
d. lacking confidence that the negotiation will be successful

55. Researcher A is investigating techniques that ensure rational decision making, while Researcher B studies how people typically make decisions. Researcher A is using the _____ approach and Researcher B the _____ approach.
   a. heuristic; algorithmic
   b. descriptive; normative
   c. normative; descriptive
   d. normative; algorithmic

KEY TERMS

Using your own words, write a brief definition or explanation of each of the following terms.

Textbook Terms

1. cognition

2. concept

3. prototype

4. algorithm

5. heuristic

6. insight

7. confirmation bias

8. fixation

9. mental set

10. functional fixedness

11. representativeness heuristic

12. availability heuristic

13. overconfidence

14. framing

15. belief bias

16. belief perseverance

17. artificial intelligence (AI)

18. neural networks

Program Terms
Program 10
19. automaticity

Program 11

20. cognitive illusion

21. normative approach

22. descriptive approach

23. anchoring effect

24. dread factor

25. risk aversion

26. illusion of invulnerability

27. mind-guarding

28. cognitive dissonance

29. psychology of negotiation

30. zero-sum

ANSWERS

Guided Study

The following guidelines provide the main points that your answers should have touched upon.

Textbook Assignment

1. Concepts are mental groupings of similar objects, events, and people. Because they provide a great deal of information with minimal cognitive effort, concepts are the basic units of thinking. Most concepts are formed around a best example, or prototype, of a particular category. Concepts are often organized into hierarchies that further increase cognitive efficiency.

2. Trial and error is a haphazard strategy for solving problems, in which one solution after another is tried until success is achieved. Algorithms are methodical and logical rules for solving problems; they often are laborious and inefficient. Heuristics are based on rules of thumb. Although formally not a problem-solving strategy, a sudden flash of inspiration (insight) often helps us to solve problems. Insight has been observed in chimpanzees who are given challenging problems to solve.

3. The confirmation bias is an obstacle to problem solving in which people search for information that confirms their preconceptions. Another common obstacle to problem solving is fixation, an inability to approach a familiar problem in a new way. One example of fixation is the tendency to continue applying a particular problem-solving strategy even when it is no longer useful (mental set). Another example is functional fixedness, whereby a person is unable to perceive unusual functions for familiar objects.

4. The representativeness heuristic is the tendency to judge the likelihood of things in terms of how well they represent particular prototypes. With the availability heuristic, we base our judgments on how readily information comes to mind.

    The overconfidence phenomenon is the tendency of people to overestimate the accuracy of their knowledge and judgments. Although overconfidence may blind us to our vulnerability to error in reasoning, it has adaptive value in that it makes decision making somewhat easier.

    Framing refers to the way an issue or question is posed, which can greatly influence our perception of the issue or answer to the question.

5. Belief bias is the tendency for our beliefs to distort logical reasoning. An example of this common error is our tendency to accept as logical those conclusions that agree with our opinions. Belief perseverance is our tendency to cling to our beliefs even in the face of contrary evidence. Once beliefs are formed, it takes stronger evidence to change them than it did to create them.

6. Although both the mind and the computer process input from the environment, only humans truly think and feel. Computers excel at tasks that require the manipulation of large amounts of data. Unlike the human brain, which can process unrelated bits of information simultaneously, most computers process information serially (in sequence). A new generation of computer neural networks has been designed to more closely simulate the brain's interconnected neural units and their functions. Compared with conventional artificial intelligence systems, neural network computers show greater capacity for parallel processing and "learning" from experience.

Program Assignment

1. Cognitive psychologists study how people take in, store, and manipulate information through the processes of remembering, deciding, planning, and problem solving. In the 1930s and 1940s, behaviorism dominated psychology. Its influence was such that cognitive processes were ignored in favor of studying only observable behaviors. With the advent of the computer industry after World War II, scientists from various disciplines, including

psychology, philosophy, artificial intelligence, and linguistics, began to consider the human mind as a computer-like information-processing device. Cognitive psychologists perceive the behaviorist approach to human cognition as a dead end. In their view, human cognition cannot be understood without reference to internal processes such as ideas, images, and concepts.

2. In 1958, Donald Broadbent was the first psychologist to use the information-processing approach to model human thought processes. Broadbent developed a flow chart to describe what happens to information as it is received by the senses, selectively attended to, and then stored as memory. This model, which interprets the workings of the mind as if it were a computer, has proven extremely valuable because it analyzes cognitive processes as a sequence of ordered stages.

3. With the current technology, cognitive psychologists have recently been able to investigate how the physiology of the brain enables thinking, memory, and problem solving. Michael Posner of the University of Oregon, for example, uses brain-imaging techniques to identify which parts of the brain are used in specific cognitive tasks such as reading. In particular, positron emission tomography allows one to analyze cerebral blood flow in normal people as they perform cognitive tasks (see also text p. 53). Posner has found that different parts of the brain become active as people perform different cognitive tasks, such as stating the use of an object or attending to the association between a word and its meaning.

4. Some cognitive psychologists are attempting to apply cognitive science to everyday concerns, such as those of educators. Robert Glaser of the University of Pittsburgh, for example, studies the nature of learning in its various forms. This includes investigating the idea of the relationship between conscious and unconscious processes, such as the relationship between basic reading skills and the higher-level processes involved in reading *comprehension*, for instance. Glaser thinks of intelligence as a set of cognitive skills that include the abilities to learn and to solve problems. He believes that the more we learn about these skills, the more we will be able to increase people's proficiency in these skills and their ability to function effectively in their everyday lives. Other researchers study expert teaching in order to improve classroom instruction and motivate students.

5. Psychological research has cast grave doubts on the rationality of human decision making. People may lapse into irrational decision making for two reasons: The first is the influence of crowds. As part of a mob, the individual can no longer think independently or clearly. Sigmund Freud and others have argued that people stop being rational when they are driven by primitive needs, such as those for sex and aggression, that demand immediate gratification. Today, cognitive psychologists look to the origins of irrationality within the everyday processes of the mind.

6. The normative approach seeks to uncover the nature of rational decision making. The descriptive approach, on the other hand, asks not how we ought to make decisions, but how decisions are actually made in practice.
    Although our intuitions are often correct, they are just as often predictably wrong. The availability heuristic occurs when we base our judgments on how readily certain information comes to mind. In reasoning by representativeness we tend to judge the likelihood of things in terms of how well they represent particular stereotypes. In the anchoring effect, an initial impression biases later judgments in its direction.

7. Most people are subject to risk aversion and are willing to risk a potentially greater loss in order to avoid a certain loss. People are also subject to the

dread factor: they tend to judge risks that are unfamiliar and potentially catastrophic as more severe than risks that are more familiar. Risks that have immediate consequences also tend to be judged as more severe than those that have delayed consequences.

8. Groupthink, first described by Irving Janis, occurs when a decision-making group is dominated by a desire to preserve the harmony of the group. One of the main symptoms of groupthink is self-censorship of doubts. Another is a sense of unanimity of the group that is based on the false assumption that silence means consent. Another is the illusion of invulnerability, which is the tendency of the members of the group to feel that they are powerful and clever enough to succeed at solving difficult problems at which others have failed. Another symptom, called mind-guarding, involves various members of the group guarding the group from any information that might lead them to change their minds or raise questions about their decision.

    Janis has outlined procedures that group leaders can follow to prevent groupthink from developing. One is having a devil's advocate appointed by the leader. Another is to ensure that the group is not isolated from others that ought to have input into the decisions being made.

9. The psychology of negotiation seeks to help people avoid the costs of bad decision making. Research in this field studies why negotiations sometimes fail and how the process of negotiation can be improved to the benefit of both parties. Max Bazerman has identified the five most common cognitive mistakes made by negotiators: (a) failing to consider the judgments of the other side in negotiation, (b) escalating conflict by increasing one's commitment to a previous course of action, (c) having a very limited frame in one's perspective to conflict, (d) feeling overconfident that one will prevail in a negotiation, and (e) viewing negotiations in a zero-sum manner.

10. Cognitive dissonance occurs whenever we choose to do something that conflicts with our prior beliefs or values. This uncomfortable tension motivates us to take action to reduce the dissonance. We may change the way we think about the decision; we may try to change the behavior of others so that they will support our decision; or we may change some aspect of our behavior so that the decision seems more in keeping with our character.

    Festinger and Carlsmith had students perform an extremely boring task and then asked them to persuade other students that the task was really quite interesting. Half the students received $20 for lying; the other half received $1 for lying. The dissonance came from the fact that the experiment was actually boring and $1 was insufficient reward for lying. Many of the $1 subjects who agreed to the request later changed their attitude about the experiment. Festinger believes that they did so in order to reduce the dissonance between their initial attitude and later behavior. The $20 subjects felt no dissonance because they were comfortable lying for the large reward.

Progress Test

1. **c.** is the answer. (p. 306)
2. **d.** is the answer. It is a major obstacle to problem solving. (p. 308)
    a. & b. These refer to belief bias and belief perseverance, respectively.
    c. This is trial-and-error problem solving.
3. **a.** is the answer. (video; p. 306)
    b., c., & d. These are all aspects of cognition.

4. **a.** is the answer. Cognitive psychologists study how we process, understand, and communicate knowledge. Problem solving involves processing information and is therefore a topic explored by cognitive psychologists. (video; p. 306)

   b. Cognitive psychologists often use experimentation to study phenomena, but, because not all experimental psychologists study cognition, a. is the best answer.

   c. Organizational psychologists study behavior in the workplace.

   d. Developmental psychologists study the ways in which behavior changes over the life span.

5. **b.** is the answer. (video)

   a. & c. Psychoanalysis and humanistic psychology emphasize internal thoughts, feelings and processes.

   d. The information-processing model has played a major role in the development of cognitive psychology.

6. **c.** is the answer. Both are examples of failing to see a problem from a new perspective. (pp. 309–310)

   a. & b. Algorithms and heuristics are problem-solving strategies.

   d. Insight is the sudden realization of a problem's solution.

7. **d.** is the answer. Heuristics are rule-of-thumb strategies, such as playing chess defensively, that are based on past successes in similar situations. (video; p. 307)

   a., b., & c. These are all algorithms.

8. **e.** is the answer. Sultan suddenly arrived at a novel solution to his problem, thus displaying apparent insight. (p. 307)

   a. Sultan did not randomly try various strategies of reaching the fruit; he demonstrated the light bulb reaction that is the hallmark of insight.

   b. Heuristics are rule-of-thumb strategies.

   c. & d. Functional fixedness and mental set are impediments to problem solving. Sultan obviously solved his problem.

9. **c.** is the answer. (video)

10. **a.** is the answer. (video)

    b. This describes the research of Herbert Simon.

    c. This describes the research of scientists such as Michael Posner.

    d. This describes the work of scientists such as Robert Glazer.

11. **c.** is the answer. Your conclusion is based on sex-role stereotypes, that is, athletic ability and participation are for you more *representative* of boys. Your conclusion is by no means necessarily right, however, especially since the Smiths have four daughters and only one son. (pp. 310–311)

    a. The confirmation bias is the tendency to look for information that confirms one's preconception.

    b. The availability heuristic involves judging the probability of an event in terms of how readily it comes to mind.

    d. Belief perseverance is the tendency to cling to beliefs, even when the evidence has shown that they are wrong.

12. **d.** is the answer. People can process millions of different bits of information at the same time; computers must generally process information one step at a time. (p. 317)

    a., b., & c. Both computers and people are capable of these.

13. **a.** is the answer. (pp. 317–318)
14. **a.** is the answer. Reasoning in daily life is often distorted by our beliefs, which may lead us, for example, to accept conclusions that haven't been arrived at logically. (video; p. 315)

    b., c., & d. These are just the opposite of what we tend to do.
15. **c.** is the answer. Both the punch card and the neuron store patterns of information that can be processed further. (video)
16. **b.** is the answer. (video; p. 306)

    a. A prototype is the best example of a particular category, or concept.

    c. & d. Algorithms and heuristics are problem-solving strategies.

    e. Mental set is an obstacle to problem solving.
17. **e.** is the answer. Both are rule-of-thumb strategies that allow us to make quick judgments. (pp. 310–311)

    a. & d. Mental sets and fixation are obstacles to problem solving, in which the person tends to repeat solutions that have worked in the past and is unable to conceive of other possible solutions.

    b. Belief bias is the tendency for preexisting beliefs to distort logical reasoning.

    c. Algorithms are methodical strategies that guarantee a solution to a particular problem.
18. **d.** is the answer. Artificial intelligence researchers attempt to design and program computers to do things that appear "intelligent." (p. 317)
19. **d.** is the answer. If we use the availability heuristic, we base judgments on the availability of information in our memories, and more vivid information is often the most readily available. (p. 311)

    a. This would exemplify use of the trial-and-error approach to problem solving.

    b. This would exemplify a mental set.

    c. This would exemplify belief perseverance.
20. **c.** is the answer. Cognitive dissonance is the tension we feel when we are aware of a discrepancy between our thoughts and actions, as would occur when we do something we find distasteful. (video; see also text Chapter 18, p. 554)

    a. Dissonance requires strongly held attitudes, which must be perceived as not fitting behavior.

    b. Dissonance is a personal cognitive process.

    d. In such a situation, the person is unlikely to experience dissonance because the action can be attributed to "having no choice."
21. **d.** is the answer. (video; see also text Chapter 18, p. 563)

    a. Groupthink is more likely when a leader highly favors an idea, which may make members reluctant to disagree.

    b. A strong minority faction would probably have the opposite effect, in that it would diminish group harmony while promoting critical thinking.

    c. Consulting with experts would discourage groupthink by exposing the group to other opinions.
22. **b.** is the answer. Dissonance theory focuses on what happens when our actions contradict our attitudes. (video; see also text Chapter 18, p. 554)

    a. The normative approach to the study of decision making investigates how people can reason most effectively and rationally.

c. This theory was not discussed.

d. The descriptive approach investigates how people typically reason when making decisions.

23. **d.** is the answer. (pp. 317–318)
24. **a.** is the answer. (p. 315)

    b. & c. These may very well occur, but they do not define belief perseverance.

    d. This is the confirmation bias.

    e. This is belief bias.

25. **c.** is the answer. (video; p. 306)

    a. Schemas are mental concepts that help organize existing and new information.

    b. A prototype is the best example of a particular category, or concept.

    d. Assimilation refers to the interpretation of new information in light of existing cognitive schemas.

26. **b.** is the answer. (video; p. 306)

    a. & d. These are linguistic structures (see Program 6).

    c. Prototypes are the best examples of specific categories.

27. **b.** is the answer. A rose is a prototypical example of the concept *flower*. (video; p. 306)

    c. & d. Hierarchies are organized clusters of concepts. In this example, there is only the single concept *flower*.

28. **d.** is the answer. (video; see also text Chapter 18, p. 563)

    a. This is the tendency to judge the likelihood of things in terms of how well they conform to stereotypes.

    b. Cognitive dissonance occurs when our actions contradict our beliefs.

    c. An anchoring effect occurs in reasoning when our initial impression of an issue biases our thinking about it.

29. **d.** is the answer. In this situation, the counter-attitudinal behavior is performed voluntarily and cannot be attributed to the demands of the situation. (video; see also text Chapter 18, p. 554)

    a., b., & c. In these situations, the counter-attitudinal behaviors should not arouse much dissonance, since they can be attributed to the demands of the situation.

30. **c.** is the answer. (video)
31. **a.** is the answer. (video)

    b. & c. Computers are not limited to random or schematic processing of information.

    d. Rationality is not a term applied to computers.

32. **d.** is the answer. The availability heuristic is the judgmental strategy that estimates the likelihood of events in terms of how readily they come to mind, and the most vivid information is often the most readily available. (p. 311)

33. **d.** is the answer. (video)

34. **b.** is the answer. The dread factor occurs because unfamiliar incidents seem more potentially catastrophic. (video)

35. **b.** is the answer. Follow the directions precisely and you can't miss! (p. 307)

    a. A prototype is the best example of a concept.

c. Heuristics are rules of thumb that help solve problems but, in contrast to a recipe that is followed precisely, do not guarantee success.

d. A mental set is a tendency to approach a problem in a way that has been successful in the past.

36. **c.** is the answer. By simply following a strategy that has worked well in the past, Marilyn is hampered by the type of fixation called mental set. (p. 309)

a. Functional fixedness is being unable to conceive of an unusual function for an object.

b. Overconfidence is exhibited by the person who overestimates the accuracy of his or her judgments.

d. Prototypes are best examples of categories, not strategies for solving problems.

37. **d.** is the answer. (video)

a. This describes the availability heuristic.

b. This describes reasoning from representativeness.

c. This describes the anchoring effect.

38. **a.** is the answer. (video)

b. This is a classic, social-psychological explanation for irrational thinking.

c. This describes the view of many contemporary cognitive psychologists.

39. **b.** is the answer. (video)

a., c., & d. Automaticity is an unconscious human skill that improves thinking and problem solving.

40. **a.** is the answer. (video)

b., c., & d. Posner did not find evidence that brain functioning varied with the skill level or gender of his subjects.

41. **d.** is the answer. (video)

42. **d.** is the answer. (video)

43. **d.** is the answer. (p. 307)

b. & c. If Boris always attacks his opponent's queen when playing chess, he is a victim of mental set; prototypes have nothing to do with chess playing.

44. **d.** is the answer. The confirmation bias is the tendency to search for information that confirms ones preconceptions. In this example, the politicians' preconceptions are biasing their interpretation of the survey results. (p. 308)

a. Functional fixedness is the inability to perceive an unusual use for a familiar object.

b. Mental set is the tendency to approach a problem in a particular way. There is no problem per se in this example.

c. Belief bias is the tendency for one's preexisting beliefs to distort logical reasoning. This answer is incorrect because it is not clear, in this example, whether either politician is reasoning illogically.

45. **c.** is the answer. (p. 307)

a., b., & d. Heuristics do not guarantee solutions; nor do they prevent mental sets or fixation.

46. **e.** is the answer. Your conclusion is based on the stereotype that muscular build is more *representative* of athletes than computer programmers. (p. 310)

a. Belief bias is the tendency for one's preexisting beliefs to distort logical reasoning.

Programs 10 & 11: Cognitive Processes and Judgment and Decision Making 207

      b. The availability heuristic involves judging the probability of an event in terms of how readily it comes to mind.

      c. Mental set is the tendency to repeat solutions that have worked in the past.

      d. Functional fixedness is the tendency to think of things only in terms of their usual functions.

47. **d.** is the answer. (pp. 309–310)

48. **b.** is the answer. (video)

      a. An example of risk seeking would be preferring a gamble over a sure loss.

      c. This occurs when the framing of a question biases a person's answer.

      d. This occurs when our behavior contradicts our beliefs.

49. **c.** is the answer. (video; see also text Chapter 18, p. 563)

      a., b., & d. These would promote groupthink.

50. **c.** is the answer. (video)

51. **b.** is the answer. The publicity surrounding disasters makes such events vivid and seemingly more probable than they actually are. (p. 311)

      a. The belief bias is the tendency for preexisting beliefs to distort logical thinking.

      c. The representativeness heuristic operates when we judge the likelihood of things in terms of how well they represent particular prototypes. This example does not involve such a situation.

      d. Functional fixedness operates in situations in which effective problem solving requires using an object in an unfamiliar manner.

52. **c.** is the answer. This is referred to as overconfidence. (p. 313)

53. **a.** is the answer. In this example, the way the issue is posed, or framed, has evidently influenced consumers' judgments. (p. 314)

      b. Confirmation bias is the tendency to search for information that confirms one's preconceptions.

      c. Mental set is the tendency to approach a problem in a particular way.

      d. Overconfidence is the tendency to be more confident than correct.

54. **d.** is the answer. In fact, most people tend to be overly confident in their ability to prevail in a negotiation. (video)

55. **c.** is the answer. (video)

      a. & d. Algorithms are methodical problem-solving strategies that guarantee success.

Key Terms

Textbook Terms

1. Thinking, or **cognition**, refers to the mental activity associated with processing, understanding, and communicating information. (p. 306)

2. A **concept** is a mental grouping of similar objects, events, or people. (p. 306)

3. A **prototype** is the best example of a particular category. (p. 306)

4. An **algorithm** is a methodical, logical procedure that, while sometimes slow, guarantees success. (p. 307)

5. A **heuristic** is any problem-solving strategy based on rules of thumb. Although heuristics are more efficient than algorithms, they do not guarantee success and sometimes even impede problem solving. (p. 307)

6. **Insight** is a sudden and often novel realization of the solution to a problem. Insight contrasts with trial and error and, indeed, may often follow an unsuccessful episode of trial and error. (p. 307)

7. The **confirmation bias** is an obstacle to problem solving in which people tend to search for information that validates their preconceptions. (p. 308)

8. **Fixation** is an inability to approach a problem in a new way. (p. 309)

9. **Mental set** refers to the tendency to continue applying a particular problem-solving strategy even when it is no longer helpful. (p. 309)

10. **Functional fixedness** is a type of fixation in which a person can think of things only in terms of their usual functions. (pp. 309–310)

11. The **representativeness heuristic** is the tendency to judge the likelihood of things in terms of how well they conform to one's prototypes. (p. 310)

12. The **availability heuristic** is based on estimating the probability of certain events in terms of how readily they come to mind. (p. 311)

13. Another obstacle to problem solving, **overconfidence** refers to the tendency to overestimate the accuracy of one's beliefs and judgments. (p. 313)

14. **Framing** refers to the way an issue or question is posed. It can affect people's perception of the issue or answer to the question. (p. 314)

15. **Belief bias** is the tendency for a person's preexisting beliefs to distort his or her logical reasoning. (p. 315)

16. **Belief perseverance** is the tendency for people to cling to a particular belief even after the information that led to the formation of the belief is discredited. (p. 315)

17. **Artificial intelligence (AI)** is the science of designing and programming computers to do "intelligent" things and to simulate human thought processes. (p. 317)

18. **Neural networks** are computer circuits that simulate the brain's interconnected nerve cells and perform tasks such as learning to recognize visual patterns. (p. 317)

Program Terms

19. **Automaticity** refers to the unconscious performance of basic skills that are well learned. The automatic processing of word meaning, for example, facilitates the reader's comprehension of sentences, paragraphs, and chapters.

20. A **cognitive illusion** occurs when a systematic way of thinking is responsible for an error in judgment.

21. The **normative approach** to the study of decision making investigates how people can reason most effectively and rationally.

22. The **descriptive approach** investigates how people actually reason when making decisions.

23. An **anchoring effect** occurs in reasoning when our initial impression of an issue biases our thinking about it.

24. The **dread factor** refers to the tendency of people to judge risks that are unfamiliar and potentially catastrophic as greater than risks that are more familiar.

25. Most people are subject to **risk aversion**: They are unwilling to risk a certain loss. Thus, they risk a potentially greater loss in order to avoid a certain loss.

26. The **illusion of invulnerability** is the tendency of group members to feel that they are powerful and clever enough to succeed at solving difficult problems where others may have failed.

27. **Mind-guarding** is a symptom of groupthink in which members of the group guard the group from any information that might lead them to change their mind or raise questions about their decision.

28. **Cognitive dissonance** is the uncomfortable tension we feel whenever we choose to do something that conflicts with our prior beliefs or values.

29. The **psychology of negotiation** is a subfield of psychology that investigates why negotiations between two parties sometimes fail and how the process of negotiation can be improved.

30. **Zero-sum** refers to a cognitive mistake made by negotiators who assume that in order for one "side" to "win" in a negotiation, the other must "lose."

PROGRAM 12

Motivation and Emotion

TEXTBOOK ASSIGNMENT: Chapter 12: Motivation, pp. 363–366, 368–384
Chapter 13: Emotion, pp. 393–417

ORIENTATION

Perhaps no topic is more fundamental to psychology than motivation—the forces that energize and direct our behavior. The text chapter discusses various theories of motivation and looks closely at two motives: hunger and sex. Research on hunger points to the interplay between physiological and psychological (internal and external) factors in motivation. Human sexual motivation is triggered less by physiological factors and more by external incentives. The program contrasts several major theories of motivation, including those of Freud, Rogers, and Maslow. It also discusses how evolution and culture influence motivation.

Emotions are responses of the whole individual, involving physiological arousal, expressive reactions, and conscious feelings and thoughts. The text examines each of these components in detail, particularly as they relate to three specific emotions: fear, anger, and happiness. In addition, it discusses several theoretical controversies concerning the relationship between and the sequence of the components of emotion. Primary among these are whether body response to a stimulus causes the emotion that is felt and whether thinking is necessary to and must precede the experience of emotion. The program also presents the views of Robert Plutchik and Martin Seligman regarding human emotion. Plutchik proposes that there are eight basic emotions made up of four pairs of opposites, such as joy and sadness; combinations of the basic emotions produce the wide range of other emotions. Seligman emphasizes the role of cognitive appraisal in emotion, suggesting that a key factor in our emotional states is how we view failure and success.

NOTE: Answer guidelines for all Program 12 questions begin on page 225.

GOALS

After completing your study of the program and reading assignment, you should be able to:

1. Differentiate drive-reduction, instinct, psychoanalytic, and humanistic theories of motivation.

2. Discuss the motivational basis for hunger and sex, focusing on the interplay between physiological and psychological factors.

3. Discuss the role of physiological arousal, expressive reactions, and conscious feelings and thoughts in emotion, particularly as they relate to fear, anger, and happiness.

GUIDED STUDY

Textbook Assignment

The text chapter should be studied one section at a time. Before you read, preview each section by skimming it, noting headings and boldface items. Then read the appropriate section objectives from the following outline. Keep these objectives in mind and, as you read the chapter section, search for the information that will enable you to meet each objective. Once you have finished a section, write out answers for its objectives.

Motivational Concepts (pp. 364–366)

1. Define motivation and discuss the three perspectives that have influenced our understanding of motivation.

Hunger (pp. 368–373)

2. Discuss the basis of hunger in terms of both physiology and external incentives and explain how taste preferences are determined.

3. Describe the symptoms and possible causes of anorexia nervosa and bulimia nervosa.

Sexual Motivation (pp. 374–384)

4. Discuss whether survey research has contributed to our understanding of sexual behavior and describe the human sexual response cycle.

5. Discuss the basis of sexual motivation in terms of both internal physiology and external incentives.

6. Identify some common sexual disorders and their possible treatment.

7. Discuss gender differences in sexual attitudes and behaviors.

8. Describe research findings on the nature and dynamics of sexual orientation.

The Physiology of Emotion (pp. 394–398)

9. Identify the three components of emotion and describe the physiological changes that occur during emotional arousal, including the relationship between arousal and performance.

10. Discuss the research findings on the relationship between body states and specific emotions.

Expressing Emotion (pp. 398–403)

11. Discuss the extent to which nonverbal expressions of emotion are universally understood and describe the effects of facial expressions on emotion.

Experiencing Emotion (pp. 403–413)

12. Identify three dimensions of emotional experience; discuss the significance of biological and environmental factors in the acquisition of fear.

13. Discuss the catharsis hypothesis and identify some of the advantages and disadvantages of openly expressing anger.

14. Identify some potential causes and consequences of happiness and discuss reasons for the relativity of happiness.

15. (Close-Up) Explain the opponent-process theory of emotion.

Theories of Emotion (pp. 413–417)

16. Contrast and critique the James-Lange and Cannon-Bard theories of emotion.

17. Describe Schachter's two-factor theory of emotion and discuss evidence suggesting that some emotional reactions involve no conscious thought.

Program Assignment

Read the following objectives before you watch Program 12. As you watch, be alert for information that will help you answer each objective. Taking notes during the program will help you to formulate your answers later. After the program, write answers to the objectives. If you have access to the program on videotape, you may replay portions to refresh your memory.

1. Define the concept of motivation and, using the example of aggression, identify the various factors that underlie motivation.

2. Discuss how evolution and culture influence motivation.

3. Explain Freud's views regarding motivation.

4. Contrast Freud's view of motivation with those of Rogers and Maslow.

5. Explain why sexual activity is more pleasurable, and more adaptive, for some species than for others.

6. Identify the "problems" that animals confront in attempting to achieve successful reproduction and explain nature's solutions to these problems.

7. Discuss Norman Adler's findings regarding the interaction of biology and behavior in reproduction.

8. Discuss the nature of sexuality and romantic love in humans.

9. Discuss the views of Charles Darwin and Robert Plutchik regarding human emotion.

10. Discuss Martin Seligman's explanatory style theory of optimism and pessimism.

PROGRESS TEST

Circle your answers to the following questions and check them with the answers on page 231. If your answer is incorrect, read the explanation for why it is incorrect and then consult the appropriate pages of the text (in parentheses following the correct answer).

1. Which of the following is a difference between a drive and a need?
   a. Needs are learned; drives are inherited.
   b. Needs are physiological states; drives are psychological states.
   c. Drives are generally stronger than needs.
   d. Needs are generally stronger than drives.

2. One problem with the idea of motivation as drive reduction is that:
   a. because some motivated behaviors do not seem to be based on physiological needs, they cannot be explained in terms of drive reduction.
   b. it fails to explain any of human motivation.
   c. it cannot account for homeostasis.
   d. it does not explain the hunger drive.

3. Two rats have escaped from their cages in the neurophysiology laboratory. The technician needs your help in returning them to their proper cages. One rat is grossly overweight; the other is severely underweight. You confidently state that the overweight rat goes in the "_____-lesion" cage, while the underweight rat goes in the "_____-lesion" cage.
   a. hippocampus; amygdala
   b. amygdala; hippocampus
   c. lateral hypothalamus; ventromedial hypothalamus
   d. ventromedial hypothalamus; lateral hypothalamus

4. Rodin found that, in response to the sight and smell of a steak being grilled:
   a. overweight people had a greater insulin response than people of normal weight.
   b. people of normal weight had a greater insulin response than overweight people.
   c. externals had a greater insulin response than internals.
   d. internals had a greater insulin response than externals.

5. Motivation is best understood as a process that:
   a. reduces a drive.
   b. aims at satisfying a biological need.
   c. initiates, maintains, and stops behavior.
   d. directs behavior.

6. Much of life involves a struggle between the basic motivation to _____ and the constraints of _____ , which direct us to restrain ourselves.
   a. seek pleasure and avoid pain; society
   b. feel safe; our conscious
   c. survive; our unconscious
   d. achieve; the id

7. According to Freud, the two primary motives are to:
   a. seek transcendence and develop integrity.
   b. feel both creative and loved.
   c. seek sexual satisfaction and battle those who thwart us in our pursuit of pleasure.
   d. love and work.

8. The correct order of the stages of Masters and Johnson's sexual response cycle is:
   a. plateau; excitement; orgasm; resolution.
   b. excitement; plateau; orgasm; resolution.
   c. excitement; orgasm; resolution; refractory.
   d. plateau; excitement; orgasm; refractory.
   e. excitement; orgasm; plateau; resolution.

9. Few human behaviors are sufficiently automatic to qualify as:
   a. needs.
   b. drives.
   c. instincts.
   d. incentives.

10. Kathy has been undergoing treatment for bulimia. There is an above-average probability that one or more members of Kathy's family are:
    a. high-achieving.
    b. overprotective.
    c. alcoholic.
    d. all of the above.

11. Kinsey's studies of sexual behavior showed that:
    a. males enjoy sex more than females.
    b. females enjoy sex more than males.
    c. premarital sex is less common than is popularly believed.
    d. sexual behavior is enormously varied.

12. Freud believed that our unconscious motives are revealed by:
    a. our anxieties.
    b. slips of the tongue.
    c. our dreams and fantasies.
    d. all of the above.

13. Compared with Freud's view of motivation, the views of Maslow and Rogers are more _____ , partly because these theorists studied _____ .
    a. negative; neurotic patients
    b. biologically based; animals
    c. optimistic; healthy individuals
    d. cognitive in nature; unconscious mental processes

14. Although the cause of eating disorders is still unknown, explanations that have been proposed focus on all of the following *except*:
    a. metabolic factors.
    b. genetic factors.
    c. family background factors.
    d. cultural factors.

15. Which of the following statements concerning homosexuality is true?
    a. Homosexuals have abnormal hormone levels.
    b. As children, most homosexuals were molested by an adult homosexual.
    c. Homosexuals had a domineering opposite-sex parent.
    d. New research indicates that sexual orientation may be at least partly physiological.

16. According to Maslow's theory:
    a. the most basic motives involve psychological needs.
    b. needs are satisfied in an unspecified order.
    c. the highest motives relate to self-actualization.
    d. all of the above are true.

17. Animals that live in _____ environments tend to reproduce by non-sexual means.
    a. unstable
    b. stable
    c. hot
    d. cold

18. Sexual reproduction:
    a. promotes healthier offspring.
    b. ensures that offspring will be nurtured.
    c. helps a species survive by adapting to changing conditions.
    d. does all of the above.

19. Investigations of men's and women's view of body image found that:
    a. men and women alike expressed significant self-dissatisfaction.
    b. men and women alike accurately assessed the body weight for their own sex that the other sex preferred.
    c. men tended to rate their current weight as corresponding both to their ideal weight and to women's ideal weight for men.
    d. women tended to be satisfied with their current body weight but to think that men preferred a thinner body shape for women.

20. The power of external stimuli in sexual motivation is illustrated in Julia Heiman's experiment, in which subjects' responses to various romantic, erotic, or neutral audiotapes were recorded. Which of the following was among the findings of her research?
    a. The women were more aroused by the romantic tape; the men were more aroused by the sexually explicit tape.
    b. The sexually experienced subjects reported greater arousal when the tape depicted a sexual encounter in which a woman is overpowered by a man and enjoys being dominated.
    c. Whereas the men's physical arousal was both obvious and consistent with their verbal reports, the women's verbal reports did not correspond very directly with their measured physical arousal.
    d. Both men and women were aroused most by the sexually explicit tape.

21. Lucille has been sticking to a strict diet but can't seem to lose weight. What is the most likely explanation for her difficulty?
    a. Her body has a very low set point.
    b. Her prediet weight was near her body's set point.
    c. Her weight problem is actually caused by an underlying eating disorder.
    d. Lucille is an "external."

22. Which of the following is *not* an example of homeostasis?
    a. perspiring in order to restore normal body temperature
    b. feeling hungry and eating to restore the level of blood glucose to normal.
    c. feeling hungry at the sight of an appetizing food
    d. All of the above are examples of homeostasis.

23. Animal behaviors, such as the peacock's display of its feathers, enable the _____ of the species to _____ .
    a. male; select a healthy mate
    b. female; select a mate with good genes
    c. male; suppress his sexual drive
    d. young; practice adult behaviors

24. Concerning emotions and their accompanying body responses, which of the following appears to be true?
    a. Each emotion has its own body response and underlying brain activity.
    b. All emotions involve the same body response as a result of the same underlying brain activity.
    c. Many emotions involve similar body response but have different underlying brain activity.
    d. All emotions have the same underlying brain activity but different body responses.

25. The Cannon-Bard theory of emotion states that:
    a. emotions have two ingredients: physical arousal and a cognitive label.
    b. the conscious experience of an emotion occurs at the same time as the body's physical reaction.
    c. emotional experiences are based on an awareness of body responses to an emotion-arousing stimulus.
    d. emotional ups and downs tend to balance in the long run.

26. The body's response to danger is triggered by the release of _____ by the _____ glands.
    a. acetylcholine; adrenal
    b. epinephrine and norepinephrine; adrenal
    c. acetylcholine; pituitary
    d. epinephrine and norepinephrine; pituitary

27. A male rat may mount a female 10 to 15 times within a period of several minutes. The purpose of these mountings is to:
    a. convince the female that the male is a worthy mate.
    b. trigger ovulation by the female.
    c. help the sperm find their way to the female's uterus.
    d. trigger the secretion of progesterone in the female.

28. Romantic love can best be described as a(n):
    a. intense state of euphoria.
    b. intensely positive state of longing.
    c. potent mix of positive and negative emotions.
    d. enduring, deep attachment to another person.

29. Darwin believed that:
    a. the expression of emotions helped our ancestors to survive.
    b. all humans express basic emotions using similar facial expressions.
    c. human facial expressions of emotion retain elements of animals' emotional displays.
    d. all of the above are true.

30. Which of the following was *not* raised as a criticism of the James-Lange theory of emotion?
    a. The body's responses are too similar to trigger the various emotions.
    b. Emotional reactions occur before the body's responses can take place.
    c. The cognitive activity of the cortex plays a role in the emotions we experience.
    d. People with spinal cord injuries at the neck typically experience less emotion.

31. In the Schachter-Singer experiment, which subjects reported feeling an emotional change in the presence of the experimenter's highly emotional confederate?
    a. those receiving epinephrine and expecting to feel physical arousal
    b. those receiving a placebo and expecting to feel physical arousal
    c. those receiving epinephrine and not expecting to feel physical arousal
    d. those receiving a placebo and not expecting to feel physical arousal

32. Which of the following is true?
    a. People with more education tend to be happier.
    b. Whites tend to be happier than Latinos.
    c. Women tend to be happier than men.
    d. People with children tend to be happier.
    e. People who are socially outgoing or who exercise regularly tend to be happier.

33. Catharsis will be most effective in reducing anger toward another person if:
    a. you wait until you are no longer angry before confronting the person.
    b. the target of your anger is someone you feel has power over you.
    c. your anger is directed specifically toward the person who angered you.
    d. the other person is able to retaliate by also expressing anger.

34. According to Robert Plutchik, humans are born with _____ basic emotions, divided into _____ .
    a. 4; categories of positive and negative feelings
    b. 6; 3 categories
    c. 8; 4 pairs of opposites
    d. 12; 6 categories

35. Research on nonverbal communication has revealed that:
    a. it is easy to hide your emotions by controlling your facial expressions.
    b. facial expressions tend to be the same the world over, while gestures vary from culture to culture.
    c. most authentic expressions last between 7 and 10 seconds.
    d. most gestures have universal meanings; facial expressions vary from culture to culture.

36. Which of the following is *not* one of the basic dimensions of emotion?
    a. duration   c. pleasantness
    b. intensity   d. specificity

37. Schachter's two-factor theory emphasizes that emotion involves both:
    a. the sympathetic and parasympathetic divisions of the nervous system.
    b. verbal and nonverbal expression.
    c. physical arousal and a cognitive label.
    d. universal and culture-specific aspects.

38. Which of the following was *not* presented in the text as evidence that some emotional reactions involve no deliberate, rational thinking?
    a. Some of the neural pathways involved in emotion are separate from those involved in thinking and memory.
    b. Emotional reactions are sometimes quicker than our interpretations of a situation.
    c. People can develop an emotional preference for visual stimuli to which they have been unknowingly exposed.
    d. Arousal of the sympathetic nervous system will trigger an emotional reaction even when artificially induced by an injection of epinephrine.

39. Which of the following is *not* a dimension of people's explanatory style, as described by Martin Seligman?
    a. active/passive   c. stable/unstable
    b. internal/external   d. specific/global

40. Several studies have shown that physical arousal can intensify just about any emotion. For example, when people who have been physically aroused by exercise are insulted, they often misattribute their arousal to the insult. This finding illustrates the importance of:
    a. cognitive labels of arousal in the conscious experience of emotions.
    b. a minimum level of arousal in triggering emotional experiences.
    c. the simultaneous occurrence of physical arousal and cognitive labeling in emotional experience.
    d. all of the above.

41. In cultures that emphasize social interdependence:
    a. emotional displays are typically intense.
    b. emotional displays are typically prolonged.
    c. negative emotions are more rarely displayed.
    d. all of the above are true.

42. You are on your way to school to take a big exam. Suddenly, on noticing that your pulse is racing and that you are sweating, you feel nervous. With which theory of emotion is this experience most consistent?
    a. Cannon-Bard theory
    b. James-Lange theory
    c. opponent-process theory
    d. adaptation-level theory

43. The candidate stepped before the hostile audience, panic written all over his face. It is likely that the candidate's facial expression caused him to experience:
    a. a lessening of his fear.
    b. an intensification of his fear.
    c. a surge of digestive enzymes in his body.
    d. increased body temperature.

44. After hitting a grand-slam home run, Mike noticed that his heart was pounding. Later that evening, after nearly having a collision while driving on the freeway, Mike again noticed that his heart was pounding. That he interpreted this reaction as fear, rather than as ecstacy, can best be explained by the:
    a. James-Lange theory.
    b. Cannon-Bard theory.
    c. opponent-process theory.
    d. two-factor theory.
    e. adaptation-level theory.

45. As part of her job interview, Jan is asked to take a lie-detector test. Jan politely refuses and points out that:
    a. a guilty person can be found innocent by the polygraph.
    b. an innocent person can be found guilty.
    c. a liar can learn to fool a lie-detector test.
    d. these tests err one-third of the time.
    e. all of the above are true.

46. When Professor Simon acquired a spacious new office, he was overjoyed. Six months later, however, he was taking the office for granted. His behavior illustrates the:
    a. relative deprivation principle.
    b. adaptation-level principle.
    c. opponent-process theory.
    d. optimum arousal principle.

47. After Brenda scolded her brother for forgetting to pick her up from school, the physical arousal that had accompanied her anger diminished. Which division of her nervous system mediated her physical *relaxation*?
    a. sympathetic division
    b. parasympathetic division
    c. skeletal division
    d. peripheral nervous system

48. The first time Rosalina used cocaine she enjoyed it. After taking the drug several times a day for several months, she no longer enjoys its effects; she continues to take it, however, in order not to feel shaky and depressed. Which theory best accounts for her behavior?
    a. James-Lange theory
    b. Cannon-Bard theory
    c. opponent-process theory
    d. two-factor theory

49. When the scientist electrically stimulated one area of a monkey's brain, the monkey became enraged. When another electrode was activated, the monkey cowered in fear. The electrodes were most likely implanted in the:
    a. pituitary gland.
    b. adrenal glands.
    c. limbic system.
    d. right hemisphere.

50. Research has found that:
    a. children who typically make stable, internal, and global explanations of failure are more immune to depression than those who have a pessimistic explanatory style.
    b. those whose explanatory style tends to be specific, external, and unstable are pessimists.
    c. those who habitually make stable, internal, and global explanations of undesirable events are pessimists.
    d. those whose explanatory style tends to be specific, external, and unstable are at increased risk for chronic illness.

KEY TERMS

Using your own words, write a brief definition or explanation of each of the following terms.

Textbook Terms

1. motivation

2. instinct

3. drive-reduction theory

4. homeostasis

5. incentives

6. hierarchy of needs

7. glucose

8. set point

9. metabolic rate

10. anorexia nervosa

11. bulimia nervosa

12. sexual response cycle

13. refractory period

14. estrogen

15. sexual disorder

16. sexual orientation

17. emotion

18. catharsis

19. feel-good, do-good phenomenon

20. subjective well-being

21. adaptation-level phenomenon

22. relative deprivation

23. James-Lange theory

24. Cannon-Bard theory

25. two-factor theory

Program Terms
26. attributional style

27. optimism

28. pessimism

ANSWERS

Guided Study

The following guidelines provide the main points that your answers should have touched upon.

Textbook Assignment

1. Motivation is a need or desire that energizes behavior and directs it toward a goal. The earliest theory classified motivated behavior as instinctive and unlearned; more recently, the evolutionary perspective contends that genes predispose species-typical behavior. Drive-reduction theory argues that a physiological need—not necessarily an instinct—creates a psychological state. People are not only pushed by the need to reduce drives but also pulled by incentives. Arousal theory emphasizes the urge for an optimum level of stimulation.

2. Although stomach pangs correlate with feelings of hunger, they are not the only source. Hunger also increases when increases in insulin diminish the secretion of glucose into the bloodstream. Blood chemistry is monitored by the lateral and ventromedial areas of the hypothalamus, which therefore control body weight. Animal research shows that when the LH is electrically stimulated, hunger increases; when the LH is destroyed, hunger decreases. Stimulation of the VMH depresses hunger, while its destruction will increase hunger and trigger rapid weight gain. The body also adjusts its metabolic rate to maintain its weight set point.

    Our preferences for sweet and salty tastes are genetic and universal. Culture and learning also affect taste, as when people given highly salted foods or foods common only in certain societies develop preferences for these tastes. Studies by Judith Rodin indicate that, especially in "external" people, the sights and smells of food can increase hunger, in part because these stimuli trigger increases in blood levels of insulin.

3. Anorexia nervosa is a disorder in which a person becomes significantly underweight yet feels fat. The disorder usually develops in adolescent females. Anorexia patients tend to come from high-achieving and protective families.

    Bulimia nervosa is a more common disorder characterized by repeated episodes of overeating followed by vomiting or using a laxative ("binge-purge" episodes). The families of bulimia patients have a higher than usual incidence of alcoholism, obesity, and depression.

    Several factors may contribute to these eating disorders—for example, genetics or the presence of abnormal supplies of certain neurotransmitters may be implicated. Socially, a factor may be the increasingly stringent cultural standards of thinness for women. In addition, studies have demonstrated that, in Western societies such as the United States, women's self-reported ideal weights tend to be lighter than their current weights and that women tend to think that men prefer them to weigh less than the weight men actually prefer. Another indication of the impact of psychological factors is evidence that women with low self-esteem are especially vulnerable to eating disorders.

4. Biologist Alfred Kinsey interviewed 18,000 men and women in an effort to describe human sexual behavior. Although Kinsey's sample was not random, his statistics showed that sexual behavior is enormously varied. Other sex reports have been prepared, but because they were based on biased samples of people, they cannot be taken seriously. Better information is only now starting to become available.

    Masters and Johnson outlined four stages in the sexual response cycle. During the initial excitement phase, the genital areas become engorged with blood, causing the penis and clitoris to swell and the vagina to expand and secrete lubricant. In the plateau phase, breathing, pulse, and blood pressure rates increase along with sexual excitement. During orgasm, rhythmic genital contractions create a pleasurable feeling of sexual release. During the resolution phase, the body gradually returns to its unaroused state and males enter a refractory period during which they are incapable of another orgasm.

5. Sex hormones direct the development of male and female sex characteristics and (especially in nonhuman animals) they activate sexual behavior. In most mammals, sexual activity coincides with ovulation and peak level of estrogen in the female. Sexual behavior in male animals is directly related to the level of testosterone in their bodies.

    In humans, normal fluctuations in hormone levels have little effect on sex drive once the pubertal surge in sex hormones has occurred. In later life, however, the frequency of intercourse decreases as sex hormone levels decline.

    External stimuli, such as touch and erotic material, can trigger sexual arousal in both men and women, although sexually explicit materials may lead people to devalue their partners. Our imagination—in dreams and fantasies—can also lead to arousal.

6. Sexual disorders are problems that consistently impair sexual arousal or functioning, such as premature ejaculation, the inability to have or maintain an erection (impotence), or infrequent orgasms (orgasmic disorder).

    Sexual disorders do not appear to be linked to personality disorders; it is therefore not surprising that traditional psychotherapy is ineffective in treating them. Sexual disorders are most effectively treated by methods that assume that people can learn and therefore modify their sexual responses.

7. Males are more likely than females to initiate sexual activity, they are more accepting of casual sex, and they report masturbating much more often. Men also have a lower threshold for perceiving someone's warmth as a sexual come-on.

    There may be an evolutionary explanation for these differences. Because sperm are much more plentiful than eggs, natural selection may have favored different mating strategies and attitudes toward sex in males and females.

8. Sexual orientation is an individual's enduring sexual attraction toward members of a particular sex. Although virtually all cultures in all times have been predominantly heterosexual, studies suggest that 3 or 4 percent of men and 1 percent of women are exclusively homosexual.

Most homosexuals report first being aware of same-gender sexual feelings around puberty, but they typically do not think of themselves as gay or lesbian until nearer their twenties. The ostracism homosexuals often face may cause them to struggle with their sexual motivation. Because sexual orientation is neither willfully chosen nor willfully changed, however, homosexual feelings generally persist.

There are many myths about the causes of homosexuality, including that it is linked with levels of sex hormones; as a child, being molested or seduced by an adult homosexual; having a domineering mother and an ineffectual father; or fearing or hating members of the opposite sex. Recent evidence suggests genetic influence plays a role, possibly through the inheritance of a particular gene. In animals and some exceptional human cases, sexual orientation has been altered by abnormal prenatal hormone conditions, leading some researchers to suggest that exposure to hormone levels typical of females during a critical period of brain development may predispose the individual to become attracted to males.

The consistency of genetic, prenatal, and brain research findings has caused most psychiatrists to now believe that nature more than nurture predisposes sexual orientation.

9. Emotions involve a mixture of physiological arousal, expressive behaviors, and conscious experience. Physiological arousal occurs when the sympathetic nervous system directs the adrenal glands to release epinephrine and norepinephrine. These hormones trigger increased heart rate, blood pressure, and blood sugar levels.

    Our performance on a task is usually best when arousal is moderate. However, the difficulty of the task affects optimum arousal level. A relatively high level of arousal is best on easy or well-learned tasks; a relatively low level of arousal is best on difficult or unrehearsed tasks.

10. The heart rate, blood pressure, and breathing patterns that accompany the different emotions often are not different. However, different brain circuits underlie different emotions. Limbic stimulation, for example, will trigger rage or terror in an animal. These emotions are also accompanied by different finger temperatures and hormone secretions. Negative emotions and positive emotions tend to be accompanied by greater activity in the right and left hemispheres, respectively. Infants and adults with greater activity in their left frontal lobes tend to be more cheerful than those with more active right frontal lobes.

11. People differ in their abilities to detect nonverbal expressions of emotion; introverts and women are better at reading others' emotions, and extraverts are easier to read. Women express happiness best, but men are better at expressing anger. Although there are many cultural variations in the meaning of gestures, facial expressions have universal meaning. Cultures differ in how and how much they use nonverbal expressions, however. In cultures that encourage individuality, emotional displays often are more intense and prolonged than in communal cultures that value interdependence.

    Research demonstrates that facial expressions intensify emotions and also trigger physiological changes in the autonomic nervous system.

12. People place emotions along three dimensions: pleasantness, intensity, and duration.

    Fear is an adaptive response that prepares the body to flee from danger, protects us from harm, and constrains us from harming other people. Although most fears are the product of learning (either directly or through observation), we are biologically prepared to acquire certain fears, such as those that probably helped our ancestors to survive. Biological factors also influence specific emotional tendencies, such as a person's level of fearfulness. The amygdala in the brain plays an important role in associating various emotions with certain situations. Following fear conditioning, subjects who have suffered amygdala damage will *remember* the conditioning but no longer show the emotional reaction. If the hippocampus is damaged, however, subjects will show the emotional reaction but won't remember the conditioning trials.

13. The catharsis hypothesis maintains that expressing emotion results in emotional release. Research shows that the cathartic expression of anger is most likely to reduce anger *temporarily* when it is specifically directed against the provoker, when it is justifiable, and when the provoker is not intimidating. Other studies show that openly expressing anger can have the opposite effect and amplify underlying hostility. Angry outbursts may also be habit-forming if they temporarily calm the individual.

    Anger experts recommend that the best way to handle anger is: first, bring down the level of physiological arousal by waiting; then, deal with the anger in a way that involves neither being chronically angry nor passively sulking.

14. People who are happy perceive the world as safer, make decisions more easily, rate job applicants more favorably, report greater satisfaction with their lives, and are more willing to help others. Factors that predict happiness include having high self-esteem, a close friendship or a satisfying marriage, a meaningful religious faith, being optimistic and outgoing, sleeping well, exercising, and engaging in challenging work and leisure activities.

    The effect of dramatically positive or negative events on happiness is typically temporary. Happiness is also relative to our recent experiences (adaptation-level phenomenon) and to how we compare ourselves with others (relative deprivation principle). These principles help explain why middle- and upper-income people in a given country tend to be slightly more satisfied with life than the relatively poor, even though happiness does not directly increase with affluence.

15. (Close-Up) According to the opponent-process theory, every emotion triggers an opposing emotion that causes our emotions to balance. Repetitions of the event that arouses the primary emotion strengthen the opposing emotion and weaken the experience of the primary emotion, explaining why with repetition the afterreaction, such as the pain of drug withdrawal, becomes stronger.

16. According to the James-Lange theory, the experience of emotion results from awareness of the physiological responses to emotion-arousing stimuli. According to the Cannon-Bard theory, an emotion-arousing stimulus is simultaneously routed to the cortex, which causes the subjective experience of emotion, and to the sympathetic nervous system, which causes the body's physiological arousal.

    In criticizing the James-Lange theory, Walter Cannon argued that the body's responses were not sufficiently distinct to trigger the different emotions. The James-Lange theory has recently received support from evidence showing that there are physiological distinctions among the emotions and that emotions are diminished when the brain's awareness of the body's reactions is reduced. However, many researchers continue to agree with Cannon and Bard that the experience of emotion also involves cognitive activity.

17. Schachter's two-factor theory of emotion proposes that emotions have two components: physical arousal and a cognitive label. Like the James-Lange

theory, the two-factor theory presumes that our experience of emotion stems from our awareness of physical arousal. Like the Cannon-Bard theory, the two-factor theory presumes that emotions are physiologically similar and require a conscious interpretation of the arousal.

Although complex emotions, such as guilt, happiness, and love, clearly arise from conscious thought, there is evidence that some simple emotional responses may not involve conscious thinking. When people repeatedly view stimuli they are not consciously aware of (subliminal stimuli), for example, they come to prefer those stimuli. Furthermore, some neural pathways involved in emotion, such as the one that links the eye to the amygdala, bypass cortical areas involved in thinking and enable an automatic emotional response.

Program Assignment

1. *Motivation* is the general term for all the physical and psychological processes that start, maintain, and stop behavior. When studying motivation, psychologists attempt to separate environmental causes for behaviors from internal causes. An act of aggression, for example, might be triggered by environmental factors such as political upheaval, the heat, or a hostile crowd. Or it might be caused by psychological factors within the individual, such as hostility or frustration, or by physical causes, such as a brain disorder.

2. Evolution generally has favored individuals who are strongly motivated to survive. Usually, if something is pleasurable, we are motivated toward it; if something is painful, we are motivated to avoid it. This principle of hedonism is, in most cases, an effective survival mechanism. However, culture, family, and personal experience also influence our perception of what is desirable and what is not. We feel conflict when pleasurable things, such as drugs, alcohol, and tobacco, are bad for us—or when things that are good for us, like studying hard, are painful. Much of life involves a struggle between the basic motivation to seek pleasure and the constraints of society which direct us to restrain ourselves. A vital part of growing up involves training in how to resolve the tensions between desire and restraint.

3. Freud felt that our basic biological desires never disappear, no matter how strong the personal and societal restraints against them. Freud analyzed behavior in terms of unconscious motivations and identified two primary motivations that have to be repressed. First, beginning in infancy we desire sexual satisfaction or pleasurable physical contact. Second are our aggressive urges against those who thwart us in our pursuit of pleasure. Freud believed that no matter how much effort we put into restraining these urges, they still find a way to break through to consciousness. Our concealed motives are revealed through our anxieties, slips of the tongue, dreams, and fantasies.

4. Freud had a restricted, negative view of motivation, based largely on his neurotic patients. Later theorists, such as Carl Rogers and Abraham Maslow, added a more positive dimension to the study of motivation by focusing on normal, healthy people and the interplay between human nature and society. Maslow proposed the existence of a hierarchy of needs that dominates the individual's motivation; they are the basic needs, then the attachment, esteem, cognitive, aesthetic, self-actualization, and esoteric needs. As each level is adequately satisfied, the higher needs occupy the individual's effort and attention.

5. Because the survival of many species depends on sexual reproduction, nature made sexual stimulation intensely pleasurable. Nature also arranged things so that any event regularly associated with sexual arousal can become a sexual motivator and a learned reinforcer. Some animals, like jellyfish, reproduce by nonsexual means because they live in highly stable environments. They need only the same genes as their parents to adapt to the same conditions. In a changing, variable environment, however, there is an advantage to having offspring that are the product of a mixed set of genes from two parents. Genetic variability ensures that the offspring will not be carbon copies of their parents and that some will survive by adapting to changing conditions.

6. The first problem to be solved is how to synchronize the activities of males and females so that their sperm and egg meet under the right conditions. First, a sexually mature partner must be selected from the same species, ideally a partner that can provide the best genes for the new generation. Males of many species "strut their stuff" so that females can select from among them. Next, the male and female have to pick the right time and place. Most animals produce offspring only in the spring and summer, when the environment can provide enough food and warmth for the young. The mating place must be safe from predators and natural disasters; to find such a place the animals may have to migrate long distances. Finally, certain mating behaviors are necessary to direct the animals toward fertilization. Courtship rituals increase the female's readiness to accept the male and excite the male to focus attention on the matter at hand. Built in reflexes aid in orienting males and females so that copulation can occur.

7. In many species, behavior triggers and synchronizes reproductive processes in males and females. Norman Adler (University of Pennsylvania) has studied reproduction in rats. In female rats, progesterone (the hormone necessary for pregnancy) is not automatically secreted after ovulation. With the male's stimulation during copulation, however, the secretion of progesterone is triggered, thereby making pregnancy possible. The mating ritual begins with a series of behavioral signals that signify readiness to mate. The female has a solicitation posture that attracts the male, causing him to emit a series of vocalizations. If all goes well, the male mounts the female as many as 10 to 15 times within a period of several minutes. On some occasions, the male inserts the penis into the female, stimulating nerves in her cervix. This stimulation triggers hormonal secretions in the female. On the last intromission, the male ejaculates sperm into the female along with a coagulant that plugs the cervix for a few minutes, allowing the sperm to find their way to the uterus. The change in the female's hormonal status is therefore a function of the male's behavior. In this example, not only does physiology control behavior, but the stimuli produced by the behavior also influence physiology.

8. In humans, sexuality is a way of using the body to satisfy personal desires. Sexual motivation often finds its expression in romantic love—intense emotions and thoughts, physiological arousal, and a strong attraction toward another person. This love embodies a potent mix of positive and negative emotions. Our need to be understood, accepted, and sexually satisfied can create tension as well as harmony. We may become jealous, frustrated, or angry due to the pain and uncertainty created by such an intense relationship. Romantic love tends to be short-lived and fragile, and not always sensible.

9. Charles Darwin believed that emotions were innate, evolutionary remnants of once adaptive behaviors, such as fighting. He also believed that some

human facial expressions are similar to those of animals in comparable situations. At birth all infants show similar expressions of emotion. Robert Plutchik has proposed that humans are born with eight basic emotions, divided into four pairs of opposites. All other emotions are blends of these basic emotions. Love, for example, is believed to be a blend of joy and acceptance. Paul Ekman's cross-cultural research has revealed a remarkable universality in facial expressions of emotion. Furthermore, people all over the world show similar changes in the brain activity, muscles, and thoughts that accompany various emotions.

10. Martin Seligman (University of Pennsylvania) proposes that how we view or explain failure and success strongly influences our motivations and emotional states. In explaining why bad events occur, for example, three dimensions are believed to be important. The first concerns whether the event is attributed to an internal or external cause. The second, stability/instability, addresses whether the perceived cause of the event is temporary (unstable) or permanent (stable). The third dimension, specific/global, involves perceiving the cause of the undesirable event as limited (specific) or pervasive (global) in its influence on the person's life. Those people who habitually make stable, internal, and global explanations are pessimists. Those whose explanatory style is more specific, external, and unstable are optimists.

Seligman has explored optimism and pessimism in three areas: depression, achievement, and health. He has found that children who have an optimistic explanatory style are more immune to depression, and he has identified three clues to the origin of optimism or pessimism: from the mother, from criticisms of teachers, and from the first major event that triggered optimism or pessimism. He also found that optimistic college students achieve more than those who are pessimists. Finally, Seligman found that, starting in middle age, pessimists are at increased risk for chronic illness.

Progress Test

1. **b.** is the answer. A drive is the psychological consequence of a physiological need. (p. 363)

    a. Needs are unlearned states of deprivation.

    c. & d. Since needs are physical and drives psychological, their strengths cannot be compared directly.

2. **a.** is the answer. The curiosity of a child or a scientist is an example of behavior apparently motivated by something other than a physiological need. (p. 365)

    b. & d. Some behaviors, such as thirst and hunger, are partially explained by drive reduction.

    c. Drive reduction is directly based on the principle of homeostasis.

3. **d.** is the answer. Lesions of the ventromedial hypothalamus produce overeating and rapid weight gains. Lesions of the lateral hypothalamus suppress hunger and produce weight loss. (p. 369)

    a. & b. The hippocampus and amygdala are not involved in regulating eating behavior.

4. **c.** is the answer. Externals—those whose eating is especially triggered by food stimuli—showed a greater insulin response than did internals. (p. 371)

    a. & b. The greater insulin response occurred in people who were especially sensitive to external cues, regardless of whether they were overweight.

    d. Blood insulin levels rose less in internal subjects.

5. **c.** is the answer. (video)

   a. & b. Although motivation is often aimed at reducing drives and satisfying biological needs, this is by no means always the case, as achievement motivation and curiosity illustrate.

   d. Motivated behavior is not only directed at but also energized by a goal.

6. **a.** is the answer. (video)

   b. "Feeling safe" is a manifestation of the more basic feeling of pleasure.

   c. & d. "Unconscious" and "id" reflect a Freudian analysis of motivated behavior; this analysis is by no means widely accepted.

7. **c.** is the answer. (video)

8. **b.** is the answer. (p. 375)

9. **c.** is the answer. (p. 364)

   a. & b. Needs and drives are biologically based states that stimulate behaviors but are not themselves behaviors.

   d. Incentives are the external stimuli that motivate behavior.

10. **c.** is the answer. (p. 372)

    a. & b. These are more typical of the families of anorexia patients.

11. **d.** is the answer. (p. 374)

    a., b., & c. Kinsey's data do not support any of these statements.

12. **d.** is the answer. (video)

13. **c.** is the answer. (video; p. 366 for Maslow)

    a. This describes Freud's view of motivation.

    b. None of these theorists focused their research on animals.

    d. The theories of Maslow and Rogers, which are most definitely cognitive in nature, emphasized conscious rather than unconscious mental processes.

14. **a.** is the answer. The text does not indicate whether their metabolism is higher or lower than most. (p. 372)

    b., c., & d. Genetics, family background, and cultural influence have all been proposed as factors in eating disorders.

15. **d.** is the answer. Researchers have not been able to find any clear differences, psychological or otherwise, between homosexuals and heterosexuals. Thus, the basis for sexual orientation remains unknown, although recent evidence points more to a physiological basis. (p. 381)

16. **c.** is the answer. (video; p. 366)

    a. The most basic needs in Maslow's theory are physiological.

    b. In Maslow's theory, needs are satisfied in a *specific* order.

17. **b.** is the answer. (video)

    a. Animals that live in unstable environments tend to reproduce by sexual means.

    c. & d. It is stability of the environment rather than temperature that predicts the most adaptive mating strategy for a species.

18. **c.** is the answer. (video)

19. **c.** is the answer. (p. 373)

a. It has been found that women tend to express greater dissatisfaction with their body image than do men.

b. Men tend to judge more accurately the body weight they think women prefer.

d. Women tend to be dissatisfied with their body weight and to think, erroneously, that men would prefer them thinner.

20. **d.** is the answer. (p. 377)

21. **b.** is the answer. The body acts to defend its set point, or the weight to which it is predisposed. If Lucille was already near her set point, weight loss would prove difficult. (p. 370)

    a. If the weight level to which her body is predisposed is low, weight loss upon dieting should not be difficult.

    c. The eating disorders relate to eating behaviors and psychological factors and would not explain a difficulty with weight loss.

    d. Externals might have greater problems losing weight, since they tend to respond to food stimuli, but this can't be the explanation in Lucille's case, since she has been sticking to her diet.

22. **c.** is the answer. This is an example of salivating in response to an incentive rather than to maintain a balanced internal state. (p. 365)

    a. & b. Both of these are examples of behavior that maintains a balanced internal state (homeostasis).

23. **b.** is the answer. (video)

    a. & c. These behaviors demonstrate the behaviors of male animals toward females, who then select from among the males.

    d. Behavioral rituals such as these occur primarily in sexually mature members of the species.

24. **c.** is the answer. Although many emotions have the same general body arousal, resulting from activation of the sympathetic nervous system, they appear to be associated with different brain circuits. (p. 398)

25. **b.** is the answer. (p. 413)

    a. This expresses the two-factor theory.

    c. This expresses the James-Lange theory.

    d. This expresses the opponent-process theory.

26. **b.** is the answer. (p. 394)

    a. & c. Acetylcholine, a neurotransmitter involved in motor responses, is not a hormone and therefore is not secreted by a gland.

27. **d.** is the answer. (video)

    a. This has already been decided by the time the male mounts the female.

    b. Ovulation is triggered biologically, according to the female's 4-day cycle.

    c. The male ejaculates only during the final mount.

28. **c.** is the answer. (video)

    a. & b. Romantic love often entails negative feelings such as jealousy.

    d. Romantic love is generally short-lived.

29. **d.** is the answer. (video; p. 401)

30. **d.** is the answer. The finding that people whose brains can't sense the body's responses experience considerably less emotion in fact supports the James-Lange theory, which claims that experienced emotion follows from body response. (p. 414)

    a., b., & c. All these statements go counter to the theory's claim that experienced emotion is essentially just an awareness of the body's response.

31. **c.** is the answer. Subjects who received epinephrine without an explanation felt arousal and experienced this arousal as whatever emotion the experimental confederate in the room with them was displaying. (pp. 414–415)

    a. Epinephrine recipients who expected arousal attributed their arousal to the drug and reported no emotional change in reaction to the confederate's behavior.

    b. & d. In addition to the two groups discussed in the text, the experiment involved placebo recipients; these subjects were not physically aroused and did not experience an emotional change.

32. **e.** is the answer. Education level, race, gender, and whether one has children seem unrelated to happiness. (p. 412)

33. **c.** is the answer. (p. 406)

    a. This would not be an example of catharsis, since catharsis involves releasing, rather than suppressing, aggressive energy.

    b. Expressions of anger in such a situation tend to cause the person anxiety and thus tend not to be effective.

    d. One of the dangers of expressing anger is that it will lead to retaliation and an escalation of anger.

34. **c.** is the answer. (video)

35. **b.** is the answer. (pp. 400–401)

    a. The opposite is true; relevant facial muscles are hard to control voluntarily.

    c. Authentic facial expressions tend to fade within 4 or 5 seconds.

    d. Facial expressions are generally universal; many gestures vary from culture to culture.

36. **d.** is the answer. (p. 403)

37. **c.** is the answer. According to Schachter, the two factors in emotion are (1) body arousal and (2) conscious interpretation of the arousal. (p. 414)

38. **d.** is the answer. As the Schachter-Singer study indicated, physical arousal is not always accompanied by an emotional reaction. Only when arousal was attributed to an emotion was it experienced as such. The results of this experiment, therefore, support the viewpoint that conscious interpretation of arousal must precede emotion . (pp. 414–415)

39. **a.** is the answer. (video)

40. **a.** is the answer. That physical arousal can be misattributed demonstrates that it is the cognitive interpretation of arousal, rather than the intensity or specific nature of the body's arousal, that determines the conscious experience of emotions. (p. 414–415)

    b. & c. The findings of these studies do not indicate that a minimum level of arousal is necessary for an emotional experience nor that applying a cognitive label must be simultaneous with arousal.

41. **c.** is the answer. (p. 401)

    a. & b. These are true of cultures that emphasize individuality rather than interdependence.

42. **b.** is the answer. The James-Lange theory proposes that the experienced emotion is an awareness of a prior body response. Your pulse races and so you feel nervous. (p. 413)

    a. According to the Cannon-Bard theory, your body's reaction would occur simultaneously with, rather than before, your experience of the emotion.

    c. The opponent-process theory states that each time an emotion occurs, an opposing emotion is triggered as well.

    d. The adaptation-level principle concerns our tendency to judge stimuli on the basis of recent experience.

43. **b.** is the answer. Expressions may amplify the associated emotions. (pp. 402–403)

    a. Laboratory studies have shown that facial expressions *intensify* emotions.

    c. Arousal of the sympathetic nervous system, such as occurs when one is afraid, slows digestive function.

    d. Increased body temperature accompanies anger but not fear.

44. **d.** is the answer. According to the two-factor theory, it is cognitive interpretation of the same general physiological arousal that distinguishes the two emotions. (pp. 414–415)

    a. According to the James-Lange theory, if the same physical arousal occurred in the two instances, the same emotions should result.

    b. The Cannon-Bard theory argues that conscious awareness of an emotion and body reaction occur at the same time.

    c. The oppoent-process theory, which states that every emotion triggers an opposing emotion, has no particular relevance to the example.

    e. Adaptation level concerns our tendency to judge things relative to our experiences.

45. **e.** is the answer. (pp. 396–397)

46. **b.** is the answer. Professor Simon's judgment of his office is affected by his recent experience: When that experience was of a smaller office, his new office seemed terrific; now, however, it is commonplace. (p. 410)

    a. Relative deprivation is the sense that one is better or worse off than those with whom one compares oneself.

    c. This is the theory that every emotion triggers an opposing emotion.

    d. This is the principle that there is an inverse relationship between the difficulty of a task and the optimum level of arousal.

47. **b.** is the answer. The parasympathetic division is involved in calming arousal. (p. 394)

    a. The sympathetic division is active during states of arousal and hence would *not* be active in the situation described.

    c. The skeletal division is involved in transmitting sensory information and controlling skeletal muscles; it is not involved in arousing and calming the body.

    d. This answer is too general, since the peripheral nervous system includes not only the parasympathetic division but also the sympathetic division and the skeletal division.

48. **c.** is the answer. (p. 408)

   a., b., & d. The James-Lange, Cannon-Bard, and two-factor theories of emotion do not address situations such as Rosalina's, in which conflicting emotions are experienced.

49. **c.** is the answer. (p. 398)

   a., b., & d. Direct stimulation of these brain areas will not trigger fear or rage.

50. **c.** is the answer. (video)

   a. These children are *more susceptible* to depression.

   b. These individuals tend to be optimistic.

   d. Those who habitually make *global*, *internal*, and *stable* explanations are at increased risk for chronic illness.

Key Terms

Textbook Terms

1. **Motivation** is a need or desire that energizes and directs behavior. (p. 363)

2. An **instinct** is a complex behavior that is rigid, patterned throughout a species, and unlearned. (p. 364)

3. **Drive-reduction theory** attempts to explain behavior as arising from a physiological need that creates an aroused tension state (drive) that motivates an organism to satisfy the need. (p. 364)

4. **Homeostasis** refers to the body's tendency to maintain a balanced or constant internal state. (p. 365)

5. **Incentives** are positive or negative environmental stimuli that motivate behavior. (p. 365)

6. Maslow's **hierarchy of needs** proposes that human motives may be ranked from the basic, physiological level through higher-level needs for safety, love, esteem, and self-actualization, and that until they are satisfied, the more basic needs are more compelling than the higher-level ones. (p. 366)

7. **Glucose**, or blood sugar, is the major source of energy for the body's tissues. Elevating the level of glucose in the body will reduce hunger. (p. 369)

8. **Set point** is an individual's regulated weight level, which is maintained by adjusting food intake and energy output. (p. 370)

9. **Metabolic rate** is the body's base rate of energy expenditure. (p. 370)

10. **Anorexia nervosa** is an eating disorder, most common in adolescent females, in which a person restricts food intake to become significantly underweight and yet still feels fat. (p. 371)

11. **Bulimia nervosa** is an eating disorder characterized by private "binge-purge" episodes of overeating followed by vomiting or laxative use. (p. 372)

12. The **sexual response cycle** described by Masters and Johnson consists of four stages of bodily reaction: excitement, plateau, orgasm, and resolution. (p. 375)

13. The **refractory period** is a resting period after orgasm, during which a male cannot be aroused to another orgasm. (p. 375)

14. **Estrogen** is a sex hormone secreted in greater amounts by females than by males. In mammals other than humans, estrogen levels peak during ovulation and trigger sexual receptivity. (p. 376)

15. A **sexual disorder** is a problem—such as impotence, premature ejaculation, and orgasmic disorder—that consistently impairs sexual arousal or functioning. (p. 378)

16. **Sexual orientation** refers to a person's enduring attraction to members of either the same or the opposite gender. (p. 379)

17. **Emotion** is a response of the whole organism involving three components: (1) physical arousal, (2) expressive behaviors, and (3) conscious experience. (p. 393)

18. **Catharsis** is emotional release; according to the catharsis hypothesis, by expressing our anger, we can reduce it. (p. 406)

19. The **feel-good, do-good phenomenon** is the tendency of people to be helpful when they are in a good mood. (p. 407)

20. **Subjective well-being** refers to a person's sense of satisfaction with his or her life. (p. 407)

21. The **adaptation-level phenomenon** refers to our tendency to judge things relative to our prior experience. (p. 410)

22. The principle of **relative deprivation** is the sense that we are worse off relative to those with whom we compare ourselves. (p. 411)

23. The **James-Lange theory** states that emotional experiences are based on an awareness of the body's responses to emotion-arousing stimuli: a stimulus triggers the body's responses, which in turn trigger the experienced emotion. (p. 413)

24. The **Cannon-Bard theory** states that the conscious, subjective experience of an emotion occurs at the same time as the body's physical reaction. (p. 413)

25. The **two-factor theory** of emotion proposes that emotions have two ingredients: physical arousal and a cognitive label. Thus, physical arousal is a necessary, but not a sufficient, component of emotional change. For an emotion to be experienced, arousal must be attributed to an emotional cause. (p. 414)

Program Terms

26. **Attributional style** is the characteristic way in which people account for events in their lives as either internal, unstable, and specific or external, stable, and global.

27. In the context of this material, **optimism** refers to the tendency to attribute failure to external, unstable, or temporary events and to attribute success to stable factors.

28. **Pessimism** is the tendency to attribute failure to stable or unchangeable internal factors and to attribute success to global external factors, such as luck.

PROGRAM 13

The Mind Awake and Asleep

TEXTBOOK ASSIGNMENT: Chapter 7: States of Consciousness, pp. 207–221

ORIENTATION

Programs 13 and 14 concern consciousness—our awareness of ourselves and our environment. Interest in consciousness as a subject for scientific inquiry has waxed and waned throughout the history of psychology. Although for much of the twentieth century the topic was shunned as a serious subject matter for psychology, contemporary psychologists are exploring many aspects of consciousness. Program 13 traces the history of the modern study of consciousness and discusses research on several everyday states, including focused attention, daydreaming, sleep, and dreaming.

NOTE: Answer guidelines for all Program 13 questions begin on page 247.

GOALS

After completing your study of the program and reading assignment, you should be prepared to:

1. Trace the significance of consciousness in the history of psychology.
2. Discuss the nature of attention, daydreams and fantasies, and the mind's unconscious processing of everyday information.
3. Discuss the nature of sleep, including its cyclical nature, the major sleep disorders, and the possible functions of dreams.

GUIDED STUDY

Textbook Assignment

The text chapter should be studied one section at a time. Before you read, preview each section by skimming it, noting headings and boldface items. Then read the appropriate section objectives from the following outline. Keep these objectives in mind and, as you read the chapter section, search for the information that will enable you to meet each objective. Once you have finished a section, write out answers for its objectives.

Waking Consciousness (pp. 207–210)

1. Discuss the nature of consciousness and its significance in the history of psychology. (program and text)

2. Discuss the different levels of information processing.

Sleep and Dreams (pp. 210–221)

3. Discuss the nature and potential functions of daydreams and fantasies.

4. Describe the cyclical nature of sleep.

5. Discuss possible functions of sleep and the effects of sleep deprivation.

6. Identify and describe the major sleep disorders.

7. Describe the normal content of dreams.

8. Discuss the possible functions of dreams as revealed in various theories.

Program Assignment

Read the following objectives before you watch Program 13. As you watch, be alert for information that will help you answer each objective. Taking notes during the program will help you to formulate your answers later. After the program, write answers to the objectives. If you have access to the program on videotape, you may replay portions to refresh your memory.

1. Discuss the nature and advantages of the mind's unconscious processing of information.

2. Differentiate the positions of structuralism, functionalism, and behaviorism regarding the study of consciousness.

3. Describe the nature of attention.

4. Explain Ernest Hartmann's views on the functions of sleep and discuss Freud's theory of dreams.

5. Explain the activation-synthesis theory of dreaming and identify its supporting evidence.

6. Explain the "middle ground" theory of dreaming described in the program.

7. Discuss Steven LaBerge's research on dreaming.

PROGRESS TEST

Circle your answers to the following questions and check them with the answers on page 250. If your answer is incorrect, read the explanation for why it is incorrect and then consult the appropriate pages of the text (in parentheses following the correct answer).

1. When our _____ is disrupted, we experience jet lag.
   a. daydreaming
   b. REM sleep
   c. circadian rhythm
   d. Stage 4 sleep
   e. Stage 1 sleep

2. Sleep spindles predominate during which stage of sleep?
   a. Stage 2
   b. Stage 3
   c. Stage 4
   d. REM sleep

3. During which stage of sleep does the body experience increased heart rate, rapid breathing, and genital arousal?
   a. Stage 2
   b. Stage 3
   c. Stage 4
   d. REM sleep

4. Consciousness includes which of the following?
   a. daydreaming
   b. sleeping
   c. dreaming
   d. all of the above

5. The part of the brain that serves as the "interior decorator" imposing order on experience is the:
   a. cerebral cortex.
   b. hypothalamus.
   c. medulla.
   d. corpus callosum.

6. Sleep deprivation typically leads to:
   a. disruption of muscular coordination.
   b. hallucinations and other abnormal conditions.
   c. misperceptions on monotonous tasks.
   d. all of the above.

7. One effect of sleeping pills is to:
   a. depress REM sleep.
   b. increase REM sleep.
   c. depress Stage 2 sleep.
   d. increase Stage 2 sleep.

8. Which of the following is *not* a theory of dreaming mentioned in the text?
   a. Dreams facilitate information processing.
   b. Dreaming stimulates the developing brain.
   c. Dreams result from random neural activity originating in the brainstem.
   d. Dreaming is an attempt to escape from social stimulation.

9. REM sleep occurs:
    a. in birds and mammals.
    b. only in primates.
    c. only in humans.
    d. throughout the animal kingdom.

10. The sleep-waking cycles of people isolated without clocks or daylight typically are _____ hours in duration.
    a. 23
    b. 24
    c. 25
    d. 26

11. Which of the following statements regarding REM sleep is true?
    a. Adults spend more time than infants in REM sleep.
    b. REM sleep deprivation results in a REM rebound.
    c. People deprived of REM sleep adapt easily.
    d. After a stressful experience, a person's REM sleep decreases.
    e. REM sleep periods become shorter as the night progresses.

12. Which of the following examples involves lower-level sensory processing that is automatic and unconscious?
    a. playing tennis
    b. estimating the distance and size of objects
    c. savoring a pleasant aroma
    d. reading a novel

13. At its beginning, psychology focused on the study of:
    a. observable behavior.
    b. consciousness.
    c. abnormal behavior.
    d. all of the above.

14. Functionalists such as William James regarded consciousness as:
    a. the mind's reflection on external behavior.
    b. the underlying structure of the human mind.
    c. unique to each individual and essential for adapting to his or her environment.
    d. a scientifically worthless subject.

15. A person whose EEG shows a high proportion of alpha waves is most likely:
    a. dreaming.
    b. in Stage 2 sleep.
    c. in Stage 3 sleep.
    d. in Stage 4 sleep.
    e. awake and relaxed.

16. Circadian rhythms are the:
    a. brain waves that occur during Stage 4 sleep.
    b. muscular tremors that occur during opiate withdrawal.
    c. regular body cycles that occur on a 24-hour schedule.
    d. brain waves that are indicative of Stage 2 sleep.

17. Which of the following is characteristic of REM sleep?
    a. genital arousal
    b. increased muscular tension
    c. night terrors
    d. slow, regular breathing
    e. alpha waves

18. Under the influence of John Watson, the focus of psychology shifted to the study of:
    a. observable behavior.
    b. consciousness.
    c. abnormal behavior.
    d. attention.

19. Which of the following is *not* characteristic of attention?
    a. It has a limited capacity.
    b. It is a selective filter.
    c. It is a state of focused awareness.
    d. It is an inner private reality unconnected to the world around us.

20. *Consciousness* is defined in the text as:
    a. mental life.
    b. selective attention to ongoing perceptions, thoughts, and feelings.
    c. information processing.
    d. a vague concept no longer useful to contemporary psychologists.
    e. our awareness of ourselves and our environment.

21. Which of the following is true?
    a. REM sleep tends to increase following intense learning periods.
    b. Non-REM sleep tends to increase following intense learning periods.
    c. REM-deprived people remember less presleep material than people deprived of Stage 1–4 sleep.
    d. Sleep control centers are located in the higher, association areas of the cortex, where memories are stored.

22. According to Seligman and Yellen, dreaming represents:
    a. the brain's efforts to integrate unrelated bursts of activity in the visual cortex with emotional tone provided by activity in the limbic system.
    b. a mechanism for coping with the stresses of daily life.
    c. a symbolic depiction of a person's unfulfilled wishes.
    d. an information-processing mechanism for converting the day's experiences into long-term memory.

23. A person who falls asleep in the midst of a heated argument probably suffers from:
    a. sleep apnea.
    b. narcolepsy.
    c. night terrors.
    d. insomnia.

24. The "hypnogogic state" refers to:
    a. the focused attention accompanying extreme alertness.
    b. the reveries of the onset of sleep.
    c. the thought processes associated with meditation.
    d. a drug-induced alteration of awareness.

25. In Donald Broadbent's experiment, subjects listened to different stories played into their left and right ears. When they were asked to pay attention to only one of the stories:
    a. they nevertheless remembered details from both stories.
    b. they remembered only the attended story.
    c. they were unable to remember either story.
    d. they integrated material from the unattended story into the attended story.

26. One positive function of daydreaming is that it:
    a. keeps our minds active when they would otherwise be understimulated.
    b. reduces stimulation.
    c. prevents sensory overload.
    d. allows us to deal subconsciously with threatening thoughts.

27. REM sleep is referred to as "paradoxical sleep" because:
    a. studies of people deprived of REM sleep indicate that REM sleep is unnecessary.
    b. the body's muscles remain relaxed while the brain and eyes are active.
    c. it is very easy to awaken a person from REM sleep.
    d. the body's muscles are very tense while the brain is in a nearly meditative state.
    e. erection during REM sleep indicates sexual arousal.

28. Jill dreams that her boyfriend pushes her into the path of an oncoming car. Her psychoanalyst suggests that the dream might symbolize her fear that her boyfriend is rushing her into sexual activity she is not yet ready for. The analyst is evidently attempting to interpret the _____ content of Jill's dream.
    a. manifest
    b. latent
    c. dissociated
    d. overt

29. Ernest Hartmann believes that the function of sleep is to:
    a. restore brain and body processes.
    b. make connections in the brain between the day's events and previous experiences.
    c. help relieve pain and stress-related illnesses.
    d. do both a. and b.
    e. do a., b., and c.

30. A lucid dream is one in which:
    a. you know you are dreaming.
    b. you believe you are dreaming but you are actually fully awake.
    c. you are able to perform a task that normally would require conscious attention.
    d. dream content reflects the day's events.

31. Barry has just spent four nights as a subject in a sleep study in which he was awakened each time he entered REM sleep. Now that the experiment is over, which of the following can be expected to occur?
    a. Barry will be extremely irritable until his body has made up the lost REM sleep.
    b. Barry will sleep so deeply for several nights that dreaming will be minimal.
    c. There will be an increase in sleep Stages 1–4.
    d. There will be an increase in Barry's REM sleep.

32. Which of the following statements concerning daydreaming is true?
    a. People prone to violence or drug use tend to have fewer vivid daydreams.
    b. Most daydreaming involves the familiar details of our everyday lives.
    c. Psychologists consider children's daydreams to be unhealthy.
    d. All the above are true.

33. As a child, Jane enjoyed intense make-believe play with dolls, stuffed animals, and imaginary companions. As an adult, she spends an unusually large amount of time fantasizing. She is sometimes uncertain whether an event was real or imagined. A psychologist would most likely describe Jane as:
    a. highly suggestible to hypnosis.
    b. a fantasy-prone personality.
    c. a daydreamer.
    d. a dissociator.

34. According to Freud, dreams are:
    a. a symbolic fulfillment of erotic wishes.
    b. the result of random neural activity in the brainstem.
    c. the brain's mechanism for self-stimulation.
    d. transparent representations of the individual's conflicts.

35. According to McCarley and Hobson's activation-synthesis theory of dreaming:
    a. electrical signals from the pons to the forebrain activate dreaming.
    b. dreams are activated by spontaneous activity of the cerebral cortex.
    c. dreams are the mind's way of dealing with stress.
    d. dreams are entirely psychological in origin.
    e. both c. and d. are true.

KEY TERMS

Using your own words, write a brief definition or explanation of each of the following terms.

Textbook Terms

1. consciousness

2. fantasy-prone personality

3. circadian rhythm

4. REM sleep

5. alpha waves

6. hallucinations

7. delta waves

8. insomnia

9. narcolepsy

10. sleep apnea

11. night terrors

12. manifest content

13. latent content

14. REM rebound

Program Terms

15. attention

16. structuralism

17. functionalism

18. hypnogogic state

19. activation-synthesis theory

20. lucid dream

ANSWERS

Guided Study

The following guidelines provide the main points that your answers should have touched upon.

Textbook Assignment

1. At its beginning, psychology focused on the description and explanation of states of consciousness. The difficulty of scientifically studying consciousness and the emergence of the school of behaviorism, however, caused psychology to shift to the study of overt behavior. By 1960, advances in neuroscience made it possible to relate brain activity to various mental states; as a result, mental concepts began to reenter psychology.

    Contemporary psychologists define consciousness as "our awareness of ourselves and our environment," and conduct research on attention, sleeping, dreaming, and altered states of consciousness induced by hypnosis and drugs.

2. Research reveals that information processing occurs at many levels, depending on the difficulty and familiarity of a task. Much information is processed without awareness. Less habitual tasks require conscious attention. Unlike the relatively slow, limited-capacity, serial processing of conscious information, subconscious information can be processed in parallel.

3. Daydreams help people prepare for future events by serving as mental rehearsals. For children, daydreaming is a form of imaginative play that fosters social and cognitive development. Daydreams may also substitute for impulsive behavior.

    Approximately 4 percent of people can be characterized as fantasy-prone. These individuals spend more than half their time fantasizing and may have trouble separating fantasy from reality.

4. The sleep-waking cycle is a circadian (24-hour) rhythm. The cycle of sleep is a 90- or 100-minute rhythm that consists of five distinct stages. During Stage 1 sleep, which lasts about 2 minutes, breathing rate slows, brain waves become slow and irregular, and people often experience hallucination-like and hypnogogic sensations. The approximately 20 minutes of Stage 2 sleep are characterized by bursts of brain-wave activity (sleep spindles). Starting in Stage 3 and increasingly in Stage 4, the sleeper's brain

emits large, slow delta waves, which last about 30 minutes. During Stage 4 sleep, it is difficult to awaken a sleeper. During REM sleep, brain waves, heart rate, and breathing become more rapid; genital arousal and rapid eye movements occur; and dreaming is common. Over the course of a night's sleep, REM sleep increases in duration, while Stages 3 and 4 become shorter.

5. Why people need sleep is not fully understood. Sleep may have evolved for two reasons. First, sleep kept our ancestors out of harm's way during the dangerous hours of darkness. Second, sleep helps restore body tissues, especially those of the brain. That sleep plays a role in the growth process is indicated by evidence that during deep sleep, the pituitary gland releases a growth hormone.

    The major effect of sleep deprivation is sleepiness. Other effects include impaired creativity and concentration, diminished immunity to disease, irritability, slight hand tremors, slowed performance, and occasional misperceptions on monotonous tasks. On short, highly motivating tasks, however, sleep deprivation has little effect.

6. Approximately 10 to 15 percent of adults suffer recurring problems in falling or staying asleep (insomnia). People with narcolepsy suffer overwhelming bouts of sleepiness and, in severe cases, collapse directly into a brief period of REM sleep. Those who suffer from sleep apnea intermittently stop breathing for a minute or so when they sleep. Unlike nightmares, which typically occur during early morning REM sleep, night terrors usually occur early in the night and during Stage 4 sleep; they are characterized by high arousal and an appearance of being terrified.

7. REM dreams are vivid, emotional, and bizarre. Many dreams, however, are rather ordinary and deal with daily life events. People commonly dream of failure; of being attacked, pursued, or rejected; or of experiencing misfortune. Sexual imagery in dreams is less common than is popularly believed. Women dream of males and females equally often, but 65 percent of men's dream characters are males. Occasionally, people experience "lucid dreams," in which they are sufficiently aware during a dream to wonder whether they are, in fact, dreaming and are able to test their state of consciousness.

8. Freud argued that dreams are a psychic safety valve that discharges threatening feelings. According to this view, a dream's manifest content is a symbolic version of its true underlying meaning (latent content), which consists of unacceptable drives and erotic wishes.

    According to the information-processing theory, dreams help with the processing and storage of daily experiences. In support of this theory is evidence that following stressful or intense learning periods, REM sleep increases.

    Another theory holds that dreams provide the brain with needed stimulation that promotes development of neural pathways. In support of this theory is evidence that infants spend more time in REM sleep than adults.

    Seligman and Yellen believe that dreams are the brain's attempt to integrate unrelated bursts of activity in the visual cortex, imposing meaning on meaningless stimuli. The emotional "tone" of dreams is provided by activity in the limbic system.

Program Assignment

1. Throughout the day, we experience systematic changes in our internal states of blood pressure, temperature, energy level, and consciousness.

These changes follow a 24-hour schedule, or circadian rhythm. In general, we are consciously aware of only a small portion of what is happening in and around us. What we perceive, know, and can do is not constrained by the narrow limits of our conscious awareness, however. Continual processing takes place at nonconscious levels. For example, most of the physiological "housekeeping" of our bodies occurs automatically. We don't have to think about functions such as breathing, blood flow, and digestion unless something goes wrong. Most lower-level processing of sensory input, such as estimating the distance and size of objects and recognizing patterns, is also nonconscious.

Learned skills that become routinized and automatic are carried out with minimal awareness. This frees our conscious mind to deal more with the new and less predictable.

As our consciousness works on this higher level, it reduces the continual bombardment of sensory stimulation to two categories: the relevant and noticed and the irrelevant and ignored. Without this filter we would be overwhelmed by sensory data.

2. Scientific interest in consciousness has waxed and waned. At the end of the nineteenth century, Wilhelm Wundt and Edward Titchener explored the conscious thoughts of subjects in the hopes of revealing the underlying structure of the mind. This brand of psychology was known as *structuralism*. On the other side of the debate were researchers such as William James, who believed that consciousness should be studied not in terms of its contents but its functions in helping us to adapt to our environment. He believed that consciousness was personal and unique, continuous, changing, and selective. This brand of psychology was known as *functionalism*. In the 1920s, behaviorists such as John Watson declared that consciousness was a scientifically worthless concept. Watson believed that only external behavior can be observed and studied. Not until the late 1950s was consciousness reintroduced by a new brand of cognitive psychologists.

3. Attention is the bridge across which information travels from the external world to the subjective internal world of consciousness. It is a state of focused awareness in which sensory signals are transformed into perceptions, thoughts, and experiences. Attention serves as the selective filter that excludes much of the available stimuli that bombard us in order to reduce confusion and prevent sensory overload.

In an ingenious experiment, Donald Broadbent demonstrated how attention works. Through stereo headphones, two different stories were presented to subjects' right and left ears. The subjects were instructed to pay attention to only one of the stories. When tested later, they were unable to remember anything of the story presented to the unattended ear. If the information in the unattended channel had special significance, however, the subjects did notice and remember it. This experiment demonstrated that attention has a limited capacity and selectively filters our experiences.

4. According to Ernest Hartmann (Tufts University), sleep has two restorative functions. One involves physical restoration of the entire body through protein synthesis. The other involves integrating new material from the day's activities with old material in memory.

In Freud's theory, dreams reveal the presence of deep secrets that the unconscious is trying to hide from conscious awareness. Freud believed that these hidden associations were represented symbolically in his patients' dreams and that many of their unconscious desires and fears were sexual in nature.

5. The activation-synthesis theory proposed by Robert McCarley and J. Alan Hobson (Harvard Medical School) maintains that dreams begin with spontaneous bursts of electrical impulses within the brainstem. According to this theory, every 90 minutes the pons of the brainstem automatically sends electrical impulses to the forebrain of the cortex (activation). The higher centers of the dreamer's brain then attempt to make sense of these spontaneous discharges by creating a story line (synthesis). These automatic bursts of activity are purely physiological in nature and have no more meaning than other basic body functions such as breathing or blood flow.

   Support for the theory lies in the fact that REM sleep is present throughout the entire mammal kingdom and in birds, and it's hard to imagine lower animals dreaming because of psychological processes. Another line of evidence that dreams are purely physiological processes comes from the fact that newborn humans, who are *un*likely to have complex psychological "needs" for dreaming, spend over half their sleep in REM; it is more likely that REM sleep serves to promote growth and development.

6. According to this theory, the only reality that the sleeping (but ever-active) brain has to model is its internal one. Our recent experiences, stored memories, concerns, and expectations can be activated by electrical discharges within the brain itself. Therefore, dreams are merely the interplay between the physiological triggering of brain waves and the psychological functioning of the imaginative and interpretive parts of the mind.

7. Steven LaBerge (Stanford University) has found a striking correspondence between dream content and physiological processes. When a person dreams that he or she is running, for example, the brain sees it as if the body actually is running. The same parts of the brain that are active when a person is actually running are activated during the dream. Fortunately, the brain sends impulses that inhibit the muscles and prevent the dreamer from actually acting out the dream.

   LaBerge also studies the phenomenon of lucid dreaming, in which a dreamer knows that he or she is dreaming. LaBerge has taught subjects to clench their fists and use specific eye movements when they are experiencing a lucid dream. He then triggers a flashing light that brings the dreamer to conscious awareness of the dream, allowing him or her to take conscious control of the dream and even alter its outcome. Changing the direction of dreams, says LaBerge, can have positive consequences on people, such as giving them greater waking confidence after facing fearful dreams. The idea of changing the direction of a dream remains highly controversial, however. Other psychologists believe that dreams should be allowed to run their course so that the dreamer can fully benefit from a dream's symbolism.

Progress Test

1. **c.** is the answer. Jet lag is experienced because, having traveled across time zones, we are awake at a time when our biological clock says, "Sleep!" This biological clock is the circadian rhythm. (p. 211)

2. **a.** is the answer. (p. 212)

   b. & c. Delta waves predominate during Stages 3 and 4. Stage 3 is the transition between Stages 2 and 4 and is associated with a pattern that has elements of both stages.

   d. Faster, nearly waking brain waves occur during REM sleep.

3. **d.** is the answer. (pp. 212–213)

a., b., & c. During non-REM Stages 1–4 heart rate and breathing are slow and regular and the genitals are not aroused.

4. **d.** is the answer. (video; p. 208)

5. **a.** is the answer. (video)

    b. A part of the limbic system, the hypothalamus regulates hunger, thirst, and body temperature. It also governs the endocrine system through the pituitary gland.

    c. Located in the brainstem, the medulla is involved in the regulation of breathing and heart rate.

    d. The corpus callosum is the thick band of nerve fibers that links the right and left cerebral hemispheres.

6. **c.** is the answer. Sleep deprivation can have serious consequences for monotonous tasks like long-distance driving, although short, highly motivated tasks are evidently unaffected. No significant physical, emotional, or cognitive effects have been found. (p. 214)

7. **a.** is the answer. Like alcohol, sleeping pills carry the undesirable consequence of reducing REM sleep and may make insomnia worse in the long run. (p. 217)

    b., c., & d. Sleeping pills do not produce these effects.

8. **d.** is the answer. (pp. 219–220)

    a., b., & c. Each of these describes a valid theory of dreaming that was mentioned in the text.

9. **a.** is the answer. (video)

10. **c.** is the answer. In the absence of these cues, the normal circadian (24-hour) rhythm shifts to a 25-hour cycle. (video; p. 211)

11. **b.** is the answer. Following REM deprivation, people temporarily increase their amount of REM sleep, in a phenomenon known as REM rebound. (p. 220)

    a. & e. Just the opposite is true: The amount of REM sleep is greatest in infancy, and the amount increases during the night.

    c. Deprived of REM sleep by repeated awakenings, people return more and more quickly to the REM stages after falling back to sleep. They by no means adapt easily to the deprivation.

    d. Just the opposite occurs: Following stressful experiences, REM sleep tends to increase.

12. **b.** is the answer. (video)

    a., c., & d. These are behaviors that require conscious processing either because of their complexity (a. and d.) or because the novelty of stimulation (c.) captures one's attention.

13. **b.** is the answer. (video; p. 207)

    a. The behaviorists' emphasis on observable behavior occurred much later in the history of psychology.

    c. Psychology has never been primarily concerned with abnormal behavior.

14. **c.** is the answer. (video)

    a. This does not express the position of any particular school of psychology.

    b. This expresses the position of structuralists such as Edward Titchener.

    d. This expresses the position of behaviorists such as John Watson.

15. **e.** is the answer. (p. 212)

   a. The brain waves of REM sleep (dream sleep) are more like those of nearly awake, Stage 1 sleepers.

   b. Stage 2 is characterized by sleep spindles.

   c. & d. Stages 3 and 4 are characterized by slow, rolling delta waves.

16. **c.** is the answer. (video; p. 210)

17. **a.** is the answer. (p. 213)

   b. During REM sleep, muscular tension is low.

   c. Night terrors are associated with Stage 4 sleep.

   d. During REM sleep, respiration is rapid and irregular.

   e. Alpha waves are characteristic of Stage 1 sleep.

18. **a.** is the answer. (video)

19. **d.** is the answer. On the contrary, attention often *focuses* awareness on the external world. (video)

20. **e.** is the answer. (video; p. 208)

21. **a.** is the answer. The fact that REM sleep tends to increase following intense learning periods has led to the theory that dreams may help sift, sort, and fix in memory the day's experiences. (p. 219)

   b. Non-REM sleep usually does *not* increase following intense learning periods.

   c. There is no evidence that REM-deprived people have poorer recall of presleep experiences than non-REM-deprived people.

   d. Sleep control centers are actually located in the lower centers of the brainstem, not in the association areas of the cortex.

22. **a.** is the answer. Seligman and Yellen believe that the brain's attempt to make sense of random neural activity is consistent with people's well-established tendencies to impose meaning on even meaningless stimuli. (p. 220)

   b. & c. These essentially Freudian explanations of the purpose of dreaming are based on the idea that a dream is a psychic safety valve that harmlessly discharges otherwise inexpressible feelings.

   d. This explanation of the function of dreaming is associated with the information-processing viewpoint, but not with Seligman and Yellen.

23. **b.** is the answer. Narcolepsy is the sleep disorder characterized by uncontrollable sleep attacks. (p. 217)

   a. Sleep apnea is characterized by the temporary cessation of breathing while asleep.

   c. Night terrors are characterized by high arousal and terrified behavior, occurring during Stage 4 sleep.

   d. Insomnia refers to chronic difficulty in falling or staying asleep.

24. **b.** is the answer. (video; p. 212)

25. **b.** is the answer. This finding demonstrates that attention has a limited capacity. (video)

26. **a.** is the answer. (video)

   b. & c. Daydreaming often occurs when external stimulation is minimal and, if anything, serves to *increase* the mind's stimulation.

d. Daydreaming is a conscious rather than unconscious phenomenon.

27. **b.** is the answer. Although the body is aroused internally, the messages of the activated motor cortex do not reach the muscles. (p. 213)

    a. Studies of REM-deprived subjects indicate just the opposite.

    c. It is difficult to awaken a person from REM sleep.

    d. Just the opposite occurs in REM sleep: The muscles are relaxed, yet the brain is aroused.

    e. Arousal is usually not caused by sexual dreams.

28. **b.** is the answer. The analyst is evidently trying to go beyond the events in the dream and understand the dream's hidden meaning, or the dream's latent content. (p. 218)

    a. The manifest content of a dream is its actual story line.

    c. Dissociation refers to a split in levels of consciousness.

    d. There is no such term. In any case, "overt" would be the same as "manifest" content.

29. **d.** is the answer. (video)

30. **a.** is the answer. (video; p. 218)

31. **d.** is the answer. Because of the phenomenon known as REM rebound, Barry, having been deprived of REM sleep, will now increase his REM sleep. (p. 220)

    a. Increased irritability is an effect of sleep deprivation in general, not of REM deprivation specifically.

    b. REM rebound will cause Barry to dream more than normal.

    c. The increase in REM sleep is necessarily accompanied by decreases in Stages 1–4 sleep.

32. **b.** is the answer. (p. 209)

33. **b.** is the answer. Although all people daydream, people with fantasy-prone personalities daydream far more and far more vividly. (p. 209)

    a. Jane may very well also be suggestible to hypnosis; fantasy-prone personalities tend to be. The stated characteristics, however, do not necessarily indicate that she is.

    c. The description indicates that Jane's behavior involves much more than simple daydreaming.

    d. There is no such personality as a "dissociator." Dissociation refers to a split in consciousness that allows some thoughts and behaviors to occur simultaneously with others.

34. **a.** is the answer. Freud saw dreams as psychic escape valves that discharge unacceptable feelings that are often related to erotic wishes. (video; p. 218)

    b. & c. These physiological theories of dreaming are not associated with Freud.

    d. According to Freud, dreams represent the individual's conflicts and wishes but in disguised, rather than transparent, form.

35. **a.** is the answer. (video)

Key Terms

Textbook Terms

1. The text defines **consciousness** as our awareness of ourselves and our environment. (p. 208)

2. The **fantasy-prone personality** is one who has a vivid imagination and spends an unusual amount of time fantasizing. (p. 209)

3. A **circadian rhythm** is any regular biological rhythm, such as body temperature and sleep-wakefulness, that follows a 24-hour cycle. (p. 210)

   Memory aid: In Latin, *circa* means "about" and *dies* means "day." A **circadian rhythm** is one that is about a day, or 24 hours, in duration.

4. **REM sleep** is the sleep stage in which the brain and eyes are active, the muscles are relaxed, and vivid dreaming occurs; also known as paradoxical sleep. (p. 211)

   Memory aid: **REM** is an acronym for rapid eye movement, the distinguishing feature of this sleep stage that led to its discovery.

5. **Alpha waves** are the relatively slow brain waves characteristic of an awake, relaxed state. (p. 212)

6. **Hallucinations** are false sensory experiences that occur without any sensory stimulus. (p. 212)

7. **Delta waves** are the larger, slow brain waves associated with deep sleep. (p. 212)

8. **Insomnia** is a sleep disorder in which the person regularly has difficulty in falling or staying asleep. (p. 216)

9. **Narcolepsy** is a sleep disorder in which the victim suffers sudden, uncontrollable sleep attacks, often characterized by entry directly into REM. (p. 217)

10. **Sleep apnea** is a sleep disorder in which the person ceases breathing while asleep, briefly arouses to gasp for air, falls back asleep, and repeats this cycle throughout the night. (p. 217)

    Example: One theory of the sudden infant death syndrome is that it is caused by **sleep apnea**.

11. A person suffering from **night terrors** experiences episodes of high arousal with apparent terror. Night terrors usually occur during Stage 4 sleep. (p. 217)

12. In Freud's theory of dreaming, the **manifest content** is the remembered story line. (p. 218)

13. In Freud's theory of dreaming, the **latent content** is the underlying but censored meaning of a dream. (p. 218)

    Memory aids for 12 and 13: *Manifest* means "clearly apparent, obvious"; *latent* means "hidden, concealed." A dream's **manifest content** is that which is obvious; its **latent content** remains hidden until its symbolism is interpreted.

14. The **REM rebound** is the tendency for REM sleep to increase following deprivation. (p. 220)

Program Terms

15. **Attention** is a state of focused awareness in which sensory signals are transformed into perceptions, thoughts, and experiences.

16. **Structuralism** is the school of psychology associated with Wilhelm Wundt, Edward Titchener, and other pioneers of the new discipline. These researchers explored the conscious thoughts of subjects in the hopes of revealing the underlying structure of the mind.

17. **Functionalism** is the school of psychology that emerged under the influence of William James. In contrast to structuralists, functionalists believed that consciousness should be studied not in terms of its contents, but in terms of its functional value in helping people adapt to their environments.

18. The **hypnogogic state** refers to the contents of consciousness during the reveries people experience at the onset of sleep.

19. The **activation-synthesis theory** maintains that dreams are triggered by spontaneous bursts of electrical impulses that originate within the brainstem and stimulate the forebrain of the cerebral cortex (activation). The higher centers of the dreamer's brain then attempt to make sense of these discharges by creating a story line (synthesis).

20. A **lucid dream** is one in which the dreamer knows that he or she is dreaming.

PROGRAM 14

The Mind Hidden and Divided

TEXTBOOK ASSIGNMENT: Chapter 7: States of Consciousness, pp. 221–241

ORIENTATION

Western civilization has traditionally held that the mind is a single entity, and that we have ready access to its contents. Program 14 challenges this view, presenting evidence that the brain is organized into many separate "minibrains," each of which is designed to perform a specific function, often outside conscious awareness. It also explores hypnosis, multiple personality disorder (now referred to as dissociative identity disorder), and the division of human consciousness into "two minds" when the two cerebral hemispheres are surgically separated.

The reading assignment examines the nature of drug-altered states and near-death experiences. It discusses whether hypnosis is a unique state of consciousness or merely a state of heightened suggestibility and investigates the psychological and social roots of drug use.

NOTE: Answer guidelines for all Program 14 questions begin on page 267.

GOALS

After completing your study of the program and reading assignment, you should be prepared to:

1. Identify several popular misconceptions about hypnosis and discuss whether hypnosis is an altered state of consciousness.

2. Identify the major psychoactive drugs, describe their physiological and psychological effects, and discuss the biological, psychological, and social roots of drug use.

3. Cite evidence that the brain is organized into separate "minibrains."

GUIDED STUDY

Textbook Assignment

The text chapter should be studied one section at a time. Before you read, preview each section by skimming it, noting headings and boldface items. Then read the appropriate section objectives from the following outline. Keep these objectives in mind and, as you read the chapter section, search for the information that will enable you to meet each objective. Once you have finished a section, write out answers for its objectives.

Hypnosis (pp. 221–228)

1. Define hypnosis and discuss several popular misconceptions about hypnosis.

2. Discuss the controversy over whether hypnosis is an altered state of consciousness.

Drugs and Consciousness (pp. 229–238)

3. Discuss the physiological and psychological effects common to all psychoactive drugs and state three common misconceptions about addiction.

4. Describe the physiological and psychological effects of depressants, stimulants, and hallucinogens.

5. Discuss the biological, psychological, and social roots of drug use.

Near-Death Experiences (pp. 238–240)

6. Describe the near-death experience and the controversy over the separability of mind and body.

Program Assignment

Read the following objectives before you watch Program 14. As you watch, be alert for information that will help you answer each objective. Taking notes during the program will help you to formulate your answers later. After the program, write answers to the objectives. If you have access to the program on videotape, you may replay portions to refresh your memory.

1. Discuss the results and significance of the surgery experiment that opens the program.

2. Explain the traditional, Western view of the nature of the mind and the alternative view of some contemporary psychologists.

3. State an underlying theme regarding the mind that is found in world literature and myth, and identify several ways in which consciousness can be altered.

4. Explain the meaning of dissociation, and profile the typical victim of the multiple personality (dissociative identity) disorder.

5. State Freud's views regarding repression and the origins of mental illness.

6. Describe the changes in consciousness that occur during hypnosis.

7. Explain how the normal brain receives information from the outside world and what happens when the corpus callosum is severed.

8. Discuss what research with split-brain patients reveals regarding normal brain functioning, and explain Michael Gazzaniga's use of the term *interpreter*.

PROGRESS TEST

Circle your answers to the following questions and check them with the answers on page 270. If your answer is incorrect, read the explanation for why it is incorrect and then consult the appropriate pages of the text (in parentheses following the correct answer).

1. Cocaine and crack produce a euphoric rush by:
   a. blocking the actions of serotonin.
   b. depressing neural activity in the brain.
   c. blocking the reabsorption of excess dopamine, norepinephrine, and serotonin.
   d. stimulating the brain's production of endorphins.
   e. preventing the body from producing endorphins.

2. Which of the following is classified as a depressant?
   a. amphetamines   d. alcohol
   b. LSD   e. PCP
   c. marijuana

3. The program describes an experiment in which patients were exposed to a positive or a negative message regarding their health during surgery. What effect did receiving a positive message have?
   a. None; the patients were unaware of the message.
   b. The patients developed unrealistic expectations regarding their recovery.
   c. The patients required fewer painkillers following surgery and were discharged earlier from the hospital.
   d. The length of time of the operation was reduced.

4. In Western culture, the traditional image of the mind is as a(n):
   a. largely unconscious entity.
   b. collection of separate, independent "minibrains."
   c. often irrational decision maker.
   d. rational entity, whose contents are readily accessible to consciousness.

5. The modern discovery of hypnosis is generally attributed to:
   a. Freud.
   b. Mesmer.
   c. Spanos.
   d. Hilgard.

6. Which of the following statements concerning hypnosis is true?
   a. People will do anything under hypnosis.
   b. Hypnosis is the same as sleeping.
   c. Hypnosis is not associated with a distinct physiological state.
   d. Hypnosis improves memory recall.

7. Psychoactive drugs affect behavior and perception through:
   a. the power of suggestion.
   b. the placebo effect.
   c. alteration of neural activity in the brain.
   d. psychological, not physiological, influences.

8. Consciousness-altering practices such as fasting, meditation, or the use of mind-altering drugs:
   a. are practiced by the vast major of societies around the world.
   b. are rarely found today.
   c. are more common in industrialized societies.
   d. have been directly linked to the prevalence of mental illness in a given society.

9. Which theorists believe that the mind and the body are separate entities?
   a. the behaviorists
   b. the monists
   c. the dualists
   d. the Freudians

10. Alcohol has the most profound effect on:
    a. the transfer of experiences to long-term memory.
    b. immediate memory.
    c. previously established long-term memories.
    d. all of the above.

11. Dr. Jekyll, of Jekyll and Hyde fame, was probably a victim of:
    a. major depression.
    b. a phobia.
    c. schizophrenia.
    d. dissociative identity disorder.

12. Symptoms of multiple personality (dissociative identity) disorder usually:
    a. are present at birth.
    b. appear by age 5 or 6.
    c. appear during adolescence.
    d. surface during middle adulthood.

13. Most victims of multiple personality (dissociative identity) disorder:
    a. first display their symptoms at midlife.
    b. had extremely overbearing parents.
    c. were only children.
    d. were severely abused as children.

14. A person who requires increasing amounts of a drug in order to feel its effect has developed:
    a. tolerance.
    b. physical dependence.
    c. psychological dependence.
    d. resistance.
    e. withdrawal symptoms.

15. Which of the following is *not* a stimulant?
    a. amphetamines
    b. caffeine
    c. nicotine
    d. alcohol

16. Hypnotic responsiveness is:
    a. the same in all people.
    b. generally greater in women than men.
    c. generally greater in men than women.
    d. greater when people are led to *expect* it.

17. According to the Freudian perspective, a student who frequently "slips" and calls her teacher "mom" *probably*:
    a. has some unresolved conflicts concerning her mother.
    b. is fixated in the oral stage of development.
    c. did not receive unconditional positive regard from her mother.
    d. can be classified as having a weak sense of personal control.

18. According to Freud, mental illness arises when:
    a. people repress unpleasant memories.
    b. ego defense mechanisms are gradually overwhelmed in their efforts to repress threatening thoughts.
    c. a person copes with his or her own feelings of inadequacy by using ego defense mechanisms.
    d. any of the above occur.

19. According to Hilgard, hypnosis is:
    a. no different from a state of heightened motivation.
    b. a hoax perpetrated by frauds.
    c. the same as dreaming.
    d. a dissociation between different levels of consciousness.
    e. a type of "animal magnetism."

20. Which of the following is a psychoactive drug?
    a. LSD
    b. sleeping pills
    c. caffeine
    d. All of the above are psychoactive drugs.

21. Drugs such as LSD, psilocybin, and mescaline are classified as:
    a. stimulants.
    b. depressants.
    c. hallucinogens.
    d. opiates.

22. If you stare straight ahead at an object, with only your right eye open, the sensory information is routed to:
    a. the right hemisphere only.
    b. the left hemisphere only.
    c. both hemispheres.
    d. either hemisphere, depending on the size of the object.

23. The nerve fibers that have been severed in split-brain patients form a structure called the:
    a. reticular formation.
    b. association area.
    c. corpus callosum.
    d. parietal lobe.

24. As a form of therapy for relieving problems such as headaches, hypnosis is:
    a. ineffective.
    b. no more effective than positive suggestions given without hypnosis.
    c. highly effective.
    d. more effective with adults than children.

25. Which of the following is usually the most powerful determinant of whether teenagers begin using drugs?
    a. family strength
    b. religiosity
    c. school adjustment
    d. peer influence

26. THC is the major active ingredient in:
    a. nicotine.
    b. LSD.
    c. marijuana.
    d. cocaine.
    e. amphetamine.

27. Those who believe that hypnosis is a social phenomenon argue that "hypnotized" individuals are:
    a. consciously faking their behavior.
    b. merely acting out a role.
    c. underachievers striving to please the hypnotist.
    d. all of the above.

28. A split-brain patient has a picture of a knife flashed to her left hemisphere and that of a fork to her right hemisphere. She will be able to identify the:
    a. fork using her left hand.
    b. knife using her left hand.
    c. knife using either hand.
    d. fork using either hand.

29. According to Michael Gazzaniga, the "interpreter" of the brain:
    a. is a function of the left cerebral hemisphere.
    b. derives from the individual's unique sense of self.
    c. integrates all of a person's thoughts and behaviors.
    d. is characterized by all of the above.

30. How a particular psychoactive drug affects a person depends on:
    a. the dosage and form in which the drug is taken.
    b. the user's expectations and personality.
    c. the situation in which the drug is taken.
    d. all of the above.

31. Which of the following was *not* suggested by the text as an important aspect of drug prevention and treatment programs?
    a. education about the long-term costs of a drug's temporary pleasures
    b. efforts to boost people's self-esteem and purpose in life
    c. attempts to modify peer associations
    d. "scare tactics" that frighten prepubescent children into avoiding drug experimentation

32. An attorney wants to know if the details and accuracy of an eyewitness's memory for a crime would be improved under hypnosis. Given the results of relevant research, what should you tell the attorney?
    a. Most hypnotically retrieved memories are either false or contaminated.
    b. Hypnotically retrieved memories are usually more accurate than conscious memories.
    c. Hypnotically retrieved memories are purely the product of the subject's imagination.
    d. Hypnosis only improves memory of anxiety-provoking childhood events.

33. Dan has recently begun using an addictive, euphoria-producing drug. Which of the following will probably occur if he repeatedly uses this drug?
    a. As tolerance to the drug develops, Dan will experience increasingly pleasurable "highs."
    b. The dosage needed to produce the desired effect will decrease.
    c. After each use, he will become more and more depressed.
    d. Dependence will become less of a problem.
    e. All of the above will probably occur.

34. Roberto is moderately intoxicated by alcohol. Which of the following changes in his behavior is likely to occur?
    a. If angered, he is more likely to become aggressive than when he is sober.
    b. He will be less self-conscious about his behavior.
    c. If sexually aroused, he will be less inhibited about engaging in sexual activity.
    d. The next day he may be unable to remember what happened while he was drinking.
    e. All of the above are likely.

35. The left hemisphere of the brain is superior at:
    a. solving perceptual problems.
    b. perceiving spatial relationships.
    c. pattern recognition.
    d. analytical reasoning.

36. Of the following individuals, who is likely to be the most hypnotically suggestible?
    a. Bill, a reality-oriented stockbroker
    b. Janice, a fantasy-prone actress
    c. Megan, a sixth-grader who has trouble focusing her attention on a task
    d. Darren, who has never been able to really "get involved" in movies or novels

37. Which of the following statements concerning alcoholism is *not* true?
    a. Adopted individuals are more susceptible to alcoholism if they had an alcoholic adoptive parent.
    b. Having an alcoholic identical twin puts one at increased risk of becoming alcoholic.
    c. Compared to children of nonalcoholics, children of alcoholics have a higher tolerance for multiple alcoholic drinks.
    d. Researchers have bred rats that prefer alcohol to water.

38. Research studies of the effectiveness of hypnosis as a form of therapy have demonstrated that:
    a. for problems of self-control, such as smoking, hypnosis is equally effective with subjects who can be deeply hypnotized and those who cannot.
    b. posthypnotic suggestions have helped alleviate headaches, asthma, warts, and certain skin disorders.
    c. positive suggestions given without hypnosis are often as effective as hypnosis as a form of therapy.
    d. all of the above are true.

39. Levar believes that once the body has died, the mind ceases to exist as well. Evidently, Levar is a(n):
    a. behaviorist.
    b. monist.
    c. dualist.
    d. atheist.
    e. mesmerist.

40. "A special form of dissociation in which a person's expectations strongly influence his or her mood, behavior, and perceptions" describes:
    a. meditation.
    b. daydreaming.
    c. hypnosis.
    d. multiple personality syndrome.

KEY TERMS

Using your own words, write a brief definition or explanation of each of the following terms.

Textbook Terms

1. hypnosis

2. posthypnotic amnesia

3. posthypnotic suggestion

4. dissociation

5. hidden observer

6. psychoactive drugs

7. tolerance

8. withdrawal

9. physical dependence

10. psychological dependence

11. depressants

12. stimulants

13. hallucinogens

14. barbiturates

15. opiates

16. amphetamines

17. LSD (lysergic acid diethylamide)

18. THC

19. near-death experience

20. dualism

21. monism

Program Terms

22. hypnotic analgesia

23. ego defense mechanism

24. repression

25. dissociation

26. corpus callosum

27. split-brain patient

ANSWERS

Guided Study

The following guidelines provide the main points that your answers should have touched upon.

Textbook Assignment

1. Hypnosis is a social interaction in which a hypnotist suggests to a subject that certain perceptions, feelings, thoughts, or behaviors will spontaneously occur. Approximately 20 percent of people are highly susceptible to hypnosis, although studies show that anyone can experience hypnotic responsiveness if led to expect it.
   Studies of hypnotic memory refreshment and age regression demonstrate that hypnosis does not boost memory. Age-regressed people merely act as they believe appropriate for a certain age.
   The belief that hypnosis can force people to act against their will, or perform acts that fully conscious people cannot, is also unsubstantiated.
   Posthypnotic suggestions have been used to help people alleviate headaches, asthma, warts, and stress-related skin disorders. But controlled studies demonstrate that giving patients positive suggestions without hypnosis is equally effective.
   Hypnosis can relieve pain, perhaps by allowing a person to dissociate the pain from conscious awareness or by focusing attention elsewhere. Several studies have shown that hypnosis relieves pain no better than relaxing and distracting people without hypnosis.

2. Most studies have found that hypnosis does not produce any unique physiological changes that would indicate it is an altered state of consciousness. Nor is the behavior of hypnotized people fundamentally different from that of fully conscious people. Therefore, hypnosis may be mainly a social phenomenon, with hypnotized subjects acting out the role of a "good hypnotic subject."
   The controversial divided-consciousness theory is based on Hilgard's idea that during hypnosis consciousness splits into a cooperating, suggestible component and a hidden observer that is passively aware of what is happening.

3. All psychoactive drugs can produce tolerance and both physical and psychological dependence. This dependence is made clear by the fact that when

a user stops taking a psychoactive drug, he or she experiences the undesirable side effects of withdrawal.

There are several misconceptions about addiction, including the myth that psychoactive drugs automatically cause addiction, that addictions cannot be overcome without therapy, and that the addiction-as-disease-needing-treatment model can be profitably extended to many other pleasure-seeking behaviors.

4. Depressants such as alcohol, barbiturates, and opiates calm activity in the sympathetic nervous system and slow down body functions. Behaviorally, alcohol intake promotes aggressive, sexual, or helpful urges that the user's normal restraints might otherwise inhibit. Alcohol also disrupts the processing of recent experiences into long-term memories, reduces self-awareness, and suppresses REM sleep. The barbiturate drugs have effects similar to those of alcohol. With repeated use of artificial opiates, the brain stops producing endorphins, which leads to the agony of withdrawal when the drug is withdrawn.

   The stimulants, which include caffeine, nicotine, amphetamines, and cocaine, speed up body functions. When stimulants wear off, there is a compensatory slowdown of behavior that includes symptoms of tiredness, headaches, irritability, and depression. Cocaine produces its effects by blocking the reabsorption of excess dopamine, norepinephrine, and serotonin.

   Hallucinogens such as marijuana, PCP, and LSD distort perceptions and evoke unpredictable psychological effects. Many hallucinogens produce their effects by blocking the actions of the neurotransmitter serotonin. Like alcohol, marijuana relaxes, disinhibits, and impairs memory and perceptual and motor skills. Marijuana may also depress male sex hormones and hasten the loss of brain cells.

5. Drug use among teenagers and adults declined during the 1980s, indicating a changing national attitude toward drugs. Beginning in the early 1990s, however, drug use has rebounded.

   That some people may be biologically vulnerable to drug use is indicated by evidence that heredity influences alcoholic tendencies. Males having an alcoholic identical twin, for example, or those who have a particular gene on chromosome 11, are at increased risk for problems.

   Several psychological factors may promote addiction, including feeling that one's life is meaningless, experiencing significant stress or failure, and depression.

   Especially for teenagers, social influences on drug use are strong. This is evident from differing rates of drug use across cultural groups. Peers influence attitudes about drugs, provide drugs, and establish the social context for their use. If an adolescent's friends use drugs, the odds are that he or she will, too.

6. Approximately 30 to 40 percent of people who have come close to death report some sort of near-death experience involving visions of tunnels, bright lights, out-of-body sensations, or replays of old memories. Dualists, who believe the mind can exist separate from the body, have glorified such experiences as evidence of life after death. Monists, who contend that the mind and body are inseparable, argue that near-death experiences are similar to the hallucinations people experience while using drugs or when their brains are deprived of oxygen. Monists believe that near-death experiences mean nothing more than that the brain has been traumatized.

Program Assignment

1. In this experiment, patients under anesthesia were given positive or negative messages about their condition during surgery. Although none of the patients reported any awareness of the messages, under hypnosis many did recall them. Moreover, those who received positive messages about their health felt better, needed smaller amounts of painkillers, and were discharged earlier than those who heard music or silence during their surgery. This finding suggests that the brain processes some information subconsciously, which can alter mood and even influence behavior and health.

2. The Western view has traditionally been that reason, free choice, and carefully weighed decisions guide behavior, and that we have ready access to the contents of the mind. This traditional view has been challenged by recent experiments suggesting that our brains are organized into many separate "minibrains," or cognitive modules, each of which is designed to perform a certain function. One function apparently is to block out unpleasant memories and experiences. To "know thyself" one therefore needs to explore both the unconscious and the subconscious.

3. Throughout history, people have been fascinated by the idea that their behavior can be taken over by hidden identities. This "Jekyll and Hyde" theme appears in literature and myths. Consciousness can undoubtedly be altered by psychoactive drugs called hallucinogens. These include LSD, psilocybin, mescaline, and marijuana. In addition, most of the world's societies practice some culturally patterned form of consciousness alteration, sometimes with the assistance of drugs, fasting, or meditation. Consciousness can also be altered by mental illness.

4. Psychologists use the term *dissociation* to refer to the functioning of consciousness at different levels without a complete transfer of information from one level to another. The most dramatic form of dissociation is multiple personality disorder, in which several distinct personalities develop in the same individual. F. W. Putnam notes that before age 12 victims of the disorder suffered severe repetitive and usually sadistic child abuse. The distinctive personalities serve to keep painful memories out of awareness. The multiple personalities exist in the unconscious and often are unaware of one another. (See also Chapter 15 of the text.)

5. According to Freud, our primal sexual desires, aggressive urges, and painful memories are exiled in the unconscious, kept there by the process he called *repression*. He saw feelings of acute anxiety as an alarm that warns a person when repressed feelings are about to break through into consciousness. In order to prevent this from occurring, new ego defense mechanisms are called upon to restrain the repressed feelings. Mental illness develops when these defense mechanisms are gradually overwhelmed, leaving the person with less and less energy to deal with reality.

6. During hypnosis, suggestible subjects can experience remarkable changes in perception, memory, emotions, and bodily function. Psychologists believe that hypnosis is a special form of dissociated consciousness in which the subject's expectations (in response to the hypnotist's suggestions) block other (sometimes conflicting) messages. Posthypnotic suggestions can direct waking behavior, altering memory and even the perception of pain.

7. In a person with an intact brain, information in the left or right visual field of both eyes projects directly to the opposite hemisphere of the brain and is quickly passed to the other hemisphere through the corpus callosum, the nerves that link the two cerebral hemispheres. In the split-brain patient,

however, a briefly flashed image on the subject's right, for example, will be perceived only in the left hemisphere. By flashing images in this way, researchers are able to send information to either the left or right hemisphere and thereby determine its capabilities.

8. Although the idea that parts of the mind can function separately is difficult for many to accept, support comes from studies of patients with severe epilepsy who have had their corpus callosum severed. In such studies, Michael Gazzaniga (Dartmouth College) has demonstrated that the right hemisphere is superior to the left at perceptual problems, pattern recognition, and spatial relationships; the left hemisphere is superior at language, analysis, and creating explanations.

   Gazzaniga's research also points to the left hemisphere as the site of the brain's "interpreter," a cognitive system that integrates all our thoughts and behaviors. The interpreter is believed to pull together all our experiences, stamping them with our unique identity and enabling our own unique sense of self.

Progress Test

1. **c.** is the answer. (p. 233)

   a. This answer describes the effect of amphetamines.

   b. Depressants such as alcohol have this effect. Cocaine and crack are classified as stimulants.

   d. None of the psychoactive drugs has this effect. Opiates, however, *suppress* the brain's production of endorphins.

   e. Use of opiates eventually does this.

2. **d.** is the answer. Alcohol, which slows body functions and neural activity, is a depressant. (p. 231)

   a. Amphetamines are stimulants.

   b., c., & e. LSD, marijuana, and PCP are hallucinogens.

3. **c.** is the answer. (video)

4. **d.** is the answer. (video)

5. **b.** is the answer. Hypnosis was originally referred to as "mesmerism." (pp. 221–222)

   a. In the area of consciousness, Freud is best known for his theory of dreaming.

   c. Spanos is best known for his contention that hypnosis is an extension of everyday social behavior.

   d. Hilgard is known for his theory of dissociation and the hidden observer in hypnosis.

6. **c.** is the answer. (p. 226)

   a. Hypnotized subjects usually perform only acts they might perform normally.

   b. The brain waves of hypnotized subjects are like those seen in relaxed, awake states, not like those associated with sleeping.

   d. Hypnosis typically *disrupts*, or contaminates, memory.

7. **c.** is the answer. Such drugs work primarily at synapses, altering neural transmission. (p. 231)

   a. What people believe will happen after taking a drug will likely have some effect on their individual reaction, but psychoactive drugs actually work by altering neural transmission.

b. Since a placebo is a substance without active properties, this answer is incorrect.

d. This answer is incorrect because the effects of psychoactive drugs on behavior, perception, and so forth have a physiological basis.

8. **a.** is the answer. (video)

9. **c.** is the answer. (p. 240)

   a. Behaviorists focus on observable behaviors and avoid concepts like the mind.

   b. Monists believe that the mind and body are one.

   d. Freudians focus on unconscious and conscious aspects of the mind and have little to say regarding the mind-body relationship.

10. **a.** is the answer. Alcohol disrupts the processing of experiences into long-term memory but has little effect on either immediate or previously established memories. (p. 231)

11. **d.** is the answer. In this dissociative disorder, the person exhibits two or more distinct personalities. (video; see also Chapter 15 in the text)

    a. In this mood disorder, a person exhibits passive, resigned, and self-defeating thoughts and behaviors for no discernible reason.

    b. In this anxietry disorder, a person exhibits a persistent, irrational fear and avoidance of a specific object or situation.

    c. Schizophrenia refers to a group of disorders whose symptoms may include disorganized thinking, inappropriate emotions and actions, and disturbed perceptions.

12. **c.** is the answer. (video)

13. **d.** is the answer. (video)

14. **a.** is the answer. (p. 229)

    b. Physical dependence may occur in the absence of tolerance. The hallmark of physical dependence is the presence of withdrawal symptoms when off the drug.

    c. Psychological dependence refers to a felt, or psychological, need to use a drug, for example, a drug that relieves stress.

    d. There is no such thing as drug "resistance."

    e. Withdrawal symptoms occur when the drug is no longer being taken.

15. **d.** is the answer. Alcohol is a depressant. (p. 231)

16. **d.** is the answer. (p. 222)

    a. Hypnotic responsiveness varies greatly from person to person.

    b. & c. There is no evidence of a gender difference in hypnotic responsiveness.

17. **a.** is the answer. Freud believed that dreams and such slips of the tongue reveal unconscious conflicts. (video)

    b. A person fixated in the oral stage might have a sarcastic personality; this child's slip of the tongue reveals nothing about her psychosexual development.

c. & d. Unconditional positive regard and personal control are not psychoanalytic concepts.

18. **b.** is the answer. (video)

19. **d.** is the answer. Hilgard believes that hypnosis reflects a dissociation, or split, in consciousness, as occurs normally, only to a much greater extent. (video; p. 227)

20. **d.** is the answer. All of these are psychoactive drugs. (pp. 231–234)

21. **c.** is the answer. These psychoactive drugs are noted for their consciousness-altering effects. (video; see p. 234)

22. **c.** is the answer. (video)

    a. & b. Although light reflected from an object to the subject's right or left visual field is transmitted initially only to the opposite hemisphere, an object directly in front of a person will be simultaneously represented in both hemispheres. Moreover, in both cases information is relayed between the two hemispheres via the corpus callosum.

    d. An object's size does not influence where it is represented in the brain.

23. **c.** is the answer. (video; see also Chapter 2 in the text)

24. **b.** is the answer. (p. 226)

    a. & c. Hypnosis *can* be helpful in treating these problems, but it is no more effective than other forms of therapy.

    d. Adults are not more responsive than children to hypnosis.

25. **d.** is the answer. If adolescents' friends use drugs, the odds are that they will, too. (p. 237)

    a., b., & c. These are also predictors of drug use but seem to operate mainly through their effects on peer association.

26. **c.** is the answer. (p. 234)

27. **b.** is the answer. (p. 227)

    a. & c. There is no evidence that hypnotically responsive individuals fake their behaviors or that they are underachievers.

28. **a.** is the answer. The left hand, controlled by the right hemisphere, would be able to identify the fork, the picture of which is flashed to the right hemisphere. (video; see also Chapter 2 in the text)

29. **d.** is the answer. (video)

30. **d.** is the answer. (p. 234)

31. **d.** is the answer. (p. 238)

32. **a.** is the answer. Although people recall more under hypnosis, they "recall" a lot of fiction along with fact and appear unable to distinguish between the two. (p. 223)

    b. Hypnotically refreshed memories are usually no more accurate than conscious memories.

    c. Although the hypnotized subject's imagination may influence the memories retrieved, some actual memory retrieval also occurs.

    d. Hypnotically retrieved memories don't normally focus on anxiety-provoking events.

33. **c.** is the answer. Continued use of a drug produces a tolerance, so, to experience the same "high," Dan will have to use larger and larger doses. As the doses become larger, the negative aftereffects, or withdrawal symptoms, become worse. (p. 229)

34. **e.** is the answer. Alcohol reduces self-consciousness and it loosens inhibitions, making people more likely to act on their feelings of anger or sexual arousal. It also disrupts the processing of experience into long-term memory. (pp. 241–242)

35. **d.** is the answer. (video; see also Chapter 2)

36. **b.** is the answer. Fantasy-prone people have essentially the characteristics associated with hypnotic suggestibility: rich fantasy lives, the ability to become imaginatively absorbed, etc. The fact that Janice is an actress also suggests she possesses such traits. (p. 222)

    a. Bill's reality orientation makes him an unlikely candidate for hypnosis.

    c. The hypnotically suggestible are generally able to focus on tasks or on imaginative activities.

    d. People who are hypnotically suggestible tend to become deeply engrossed in novels and movies.

37. **a.** is the answer. Adopted individuals are more susceptible to alcoholism if they had an alcoholic biological parent. (p. 237)

    b., c., & d. Each of these is true, which indicates that susceptibility to alcoholism is at least partially determined by heredity.

38. **d** is the answer. (pp. 224, 226)

39. **b.** is the answer. Monists such as Levar believe that the mind and body are inseparable. Thus, when the body dies, the mind ceases to exist. (p. 240)

    a. Behaviorists avoid references to the mind.

    c. Dualists believe that the mind can exist apart from the body.

    d. The text does not discuss the relationship between religious belief and near-death experiences.

    e. This refers to followers of Mesmer, who was responsible for the early popularity of hypnosis.

40. **c.** is the answer. (video)

Key Terms

Textbook Terms

1. **Hypnosis** is a social interaction in which one person (the hypnotist) suggests to another (the subject) that certain perceptions, feelings, thoughts, or behaviors will spontaneously occur. (p. 221)

2. **Posthypnotic amnesia** is the condition in which, in response to the hypnotist's suggestion, subjects are unable to recall what happened while they were under hypnosis. (p. 221)

3. A **posthypnotic suggestion** is a suggestion made during a hypnosis session that is to be carried out when the subject is no longer hypnotized. (p. 224)

4. **Dissociation** is a split between different levels of consciousness, allowing a person to divide attention between two or more thoughts. (p. 226)

5. According to Hilgard, the **hidden observer** is a part of a hypnotized person's consciousness that remains aware of happenings even under hypnosis. Hilgard believes the hidden observer is an example of dissociation. (p. 228)

6. **Psychoactive drugs**—which include stimulants, depressants, hallucinogens—are chemical substances that alter mood and perception. They work by affecting or mimicking the activity of neurotransmitters. (p. 229)

7. **Tolerance** is the diminishing of a psychoactive drug's effect that occurs with repeated use and the need for progressively larger doses in order to produce the same effect. (p. 229)

8. **Withdrawal** refers to the discomfort and distress that follow the discontinued use of addictive drugs. (p. 229)

9. **Physical dependence** is a physiological need for a drug that is indicated by the presence of withdrawal symptoms when the drug is not taken. (p. 229)

10. The psychological need to use a drug is referred to as **psychological dependence**. (p. 229)

11. **Depressants** are psychoactive drugs, such as alcohol, opiates, and barbiturates, that reduce neural activity and slow body functions. (p. 231)

12. **Stimulants** are psychoactive drugs, such as caffeine, nicotine, amphetamines, and cocaine, that excite neural activity and speed up body functions. (p. 231)

13. **Hallucinogens** are psychoactive drugs, such as LSD and marijuana, that distort perception and evoke sensory imagery in the absence of sensory input. (p. 231)

14. **Barbiturates** are depressants, sometimes used to induce sleep or reduce anxiety. (p. 232)

15. **Opiates** are depressants derived from the opium poppy, such as opium, morphine, and heroin; they reduce neural activity and relieve pain. Opiates are among the most strongly addictive of all psychoactive drugs. (p. 232)

16. **Amphetamines** are a type of stimulant and, as such, speed up body functions and neural activity. (p. 232)

17. **LSD (lysergic acid diethylamide)** is a powerful hallucinogen capable of producing vivid false perceptions and disorganization of thought processes. LSD produces its unpredictable effects partially because it blocks the action of the neurotransmitter serotonin. (p. 234)

18. The active ingredient in marijuana, **THC** is classified as a mild hallucinogen. (p. 234)

19. The **near-death experience** is an altered state of consciousness that has been reported by some people who have had a close brush with death. (p. 238)

20. **Dualism** is the philosophical belief that the mind and body are distinct entities—the mind nonphysical, the body physical. (p. 240)

    Example: Those who believe that **near-death experiences** are proof of immortality are expressing the **dualist** position that mind and body are separate entities.

21. **Monism** is the philosophical belief that the mind and body are different aspects of the same thing. (p. 240)

    Example: The belief that death is final and that no afterlife exists is a reflection of the **monist** position that mind and body are one.

Program Terms

22. **Hypnotic analgesia** is the reduced perception of painful stimuli a suggestible person may experience under hypnosis.

23. In Freud's theory, **ego defense mechanisms** are the mind's way of unconsciously protecting itself against anxiety.

24. **Repression** is the unconscious exclusion of painful impulses or memories from the conscious mind.

25. **Dissociation** is a split between different levels of consciousness.

26. The **corpus callosum** is the thick band of nerve fibers that links the right and left cerebral hemispheres.

27. The **split-brain patient** has had the major connections between the two cerebral hemispheres (the corpus callosum) severed, literally resulting in a split brain.

PROGRAM 15

The Self

TEXTBOOK ASSIGNMENT: Chapter 14: Personality, pp. 419–430 and 436–451

ORIENTATION

For much of the twentieth century, the concept of self (our personal awareness of identity) was considered too "fuzzy" a subject for scientific inquiry. Today, however, many psychologists are exploring how our self-concept influences our behavior and, conversely, how our behavior influences our sense of self. Program 15 traces the development of the self-concept from the wisdom of the ancient philosophers to the research of contemporary psychologists. It also addresses several related issues, including shyness, self-esteem, and the impact of prejudice on the self-concept of minority group members.

The reading assignment examines three of the four major perspectives on personality. The psychoanalytic theory emphasizes the unconscious and irrational aspects of personality. The humanistic theory draws attention to the concept of self and to human potential for human growth. The social-cognitive perspective focuses on the self in relation to the environment.

NOTE: Answer guidelines for all questions for Program 15 begin on page 289.

GOALS

After completing your study of the program and reading assignment, you should be prepared to:

1. Explain and evaluate Freud's theory of personality structure and development.

2. Explain and evaluate the humanistic perspective on personality, focusing on the basic ideas of Maslow and Rogers.

3. Discuss the impact of self-efficacy and self-presentation on one's behavior and sense of self.

4. Explain how shyness, self-handicapping, and prejudice undermine self-esteem.

GUIDED STUDY

Textbook Assignment

The text chapter should be studied one section at a time. Before you read, preview each section by skimming it, noting headings and boldface items. Then read the appropriate section objectives from the following outline. Keep these objectives in mind and, as you read the chapter section, search for the information that will enable you to meet each objective. Once you have finished a section, write out answers for its objectives.

The Psychoanalytic Perspective (pp. 420–430)

1. Describe how Freud's search for the psychological roots of nervous disorders led to his study of the unconscious and explain psychoanalysis.

2. Describe Freud's views of personality structure.

3. Outline and describe Freud's psychosexual stages of personality development.

4. Explain Freud's view of maladaptive behavior and describe how defense mechanisms operate.

5. Discuss the major ideas of the neo-Freudians and today's psychodynamic theorists.

6. Explain how projective tests are used to assess personality and describe research findings regarding their validity and reliability.

7. Evaluate the psychoanalytic perspective.

The Humanistic Perspective (pp. 436–444)

8. Describe the humanistic perspective on personality and discuss the basic ideas of Maslow and Rogers.

9. Describe recent research on the way people view themselves.

10. Discuss how culture affects one's sense of self, including research findings on stigmatized groups and differences between individualist and collectivist cultures.

11. Evaluate the humanistic perspective.

The Social-Cognitive Perspective (pp. 445–451)

12. Describe the social-cognitive perspective and define reciprocal determinism, giving three examples.

13. Discuss research findings on personal control.

14. Describe how social-cognitive researchers study behavior and evaluate this perspective on personality.

Program Assignment:

Read the following objectives before you watch Program 15. As you watch, be alert for information that will help you answer each objective. Taking notes during the program will help you to formulate your answers later. After the program, write answers to the objectives. If you have access to the program on videotape, you may replay portions to refresh your memory.

1. Define the concept of self, differentiating its three aspects and tracing its history during the twentieth century.

2. Discuss Carl Rogers's views regarding the self-concept and explain the role of the self in directing behavior.

3. Describe Bandura's theory of self-efficacy and cite evidence that one's sense of self-efficacy can influence performance.

4. Define the social self and explain how Ryan's "social status" influences our interactions with others.

5. Explain how strategic self-presentation elicits behavioral confirmation, using the behavior of a depressed person as an example.

6. Explain how shyness and self-handicapping can undermine self-esteem.

7. Explain how society can undermine the self-concept and inhibit creativity.

PROGRESS TEST

Circle your answers to the following questions and check them with the answers on page 294. If your answer is incorrect, read the explanation for why it is incorrect and then consult the appropriate pages of the text (in parentheses following the correct answer).

1. The text defines *personality* as:
    a. the set of personal attitudes that characterizes a person.
    b. an individual's characteristic pattern of thinking, feeling, and acting.
    c. a predictable set of responses to environmental stimuli.
    d. an unpredictable set of responses to environmental stimuli.

2. Which of the following is the correct order of the psychosexual stages proposed by Freud?
    a. oral; anal; phallic; latency; genital
    b. anal; oral; phallic; latency; genital
    c. oral; anal; genital; latency; phallic
    d. anal; oral; genital; latency; phallic
    e. oral; phallic; anal; genital; latency

3. Neo-Freudians such as Adler and Horney believed that:
   a. Freud placed too great an emphasis on the conscious mind.
   b. Freud placed too great an emphasis on sexual and aggressive instincts.
   c. the years of childhood were more important in the formation of personality than Freud had indicated.
   d. Freud's ideas about the id, ego, and superego as personality structures were incorrect.

4. Which of the following is *not* an aspect of the self according to William James?
   a. material self
   b. spiritual self
   c. social self
   d. cognitive self

5. Individuation refers to the process by which:
   a. a child gradually separates from his or her mother.
   b. individuals resist the pressure of groups.
   c. the id becomes differentiated from the ego.
   d. our views of ourselves are shaped by other people.

6. The humanistic perspective on personality:
   a. emphasizes the driving force of unconscious motivations in personality.
   b. emphasizes the growth potential of "healthy" individuals.
   c. emphasizes the importance of interaction with the environment in shaping personality.
   d. was the first to recognize the importance of the mind within.

7. According to Rogers, three conditions are necessary to promote growth in personality. These are:
   a. honesty, sincerity, and empathy.
   b. high self-esteem, honesty, and empathy.
   c. high self-esteem, genuineness, and acceptance.
   d. high self-esteem, acceptance, and honesty.
   e. genuineness, acceptance, and empathy.

8. During the twentieth century, who did the most to promote acceptance of the concept of self as valid subject matter for psychology?
   a. behaviorists such as B. F. Skinner
   b. Sigmund Freud
   c. Carl Rogers
   d. William James

9. Who offered a pessimistic view of personality, focusing on the individual as conflicted and impulse-driven?
   a. Carl Rogers
   b. Sigmund Freud
   c. William James
   d. Albert Bandura

10. Who offered an optimistic view of personality, claiming that each individual has an inner guiding force that moves the person toward positive actions, enhancement, and self-fulfillment?
    a. Carl Rogers
    b. Sigmund Freud
    c. William James
    d. Albert Bandura

11. Regarding the self-serving bias, humanistic psychologists have emphasized that self-affirming thinking:
    a. is generally maladaptive to the individual because it distorts reality by overinflating self-esteem.
    b. is generally adaptive to the individual because it maintains self-confidence and minimizes depression.
    c. tends to prevent the individual from viewing others with compassion and understanding.
    d. tends not to characterize people who have experienced unconditional positive regard.

12. Which of Freud's ideas would *not* be accepted by most contemporary psychologists?
    a. Development is essentially fixed in childhood.
    b. Sexuality is a potent drive in humans.
    c. The mind is an iceberg with consciousness being only the tip.
    d. Repression can be the cause of forgetting.

13. For humanistic psychologists, many of our attitudes and behaviors are ultimately shaped by whether our _____ is _____ or _____ .
    a. ego; strong; weak
    b. locus of control; internal; external
    c. personality structure; introverted; extraverted
    d. self-concept; positive; negative

14. Id is to ego as _____ is (are) to _____ .
    a. reality principle; pleasure principle
    b. pleasure principle; reality principle
    c. conscious forces; unconscious forces
    d. conscience; "personality executive"

15. To say that the self-concept is used as a schema means that:
    a. others react to us according to their expectations about who we are.
    b. we assume that others don't know how we feel or who we are.
    c. we use the self-concept to organize information about ourselves.
    d. we gauge our behavior with others based on our relative social status.

16. In one experiment, subjects were led to believe that successful performance on a task depended primarily on their innate ability. Compared to those who were told that success was based on acquirable knowledge, these subjects:
    a. tended to proceed more cautiously.
    b. set lower goals for themselves.
    c. experienced falling levels of confidence as they made mistakes.
    d. did all of the above.

17. While speaking to another person, Yolanda remains calm, uses complete sentences, and maintains eye contact. What does her behavior during this transaction signal?
    a. low status
    b. equal status
    c. high status
    d. It cannot be determined.

18. According to Freud's theory, personality arises in response to conflicts between:
    a. our unacceptable urges and our tendency to become self-actualized.
    b. the process of identification and the ego's defense mechanisms.
    c. the collective unconscious and our individual desires.
    d. our biological impulses and the social restraints against them.

19. Research has shown that individuals who are made to feel insecure are subsequently:
    a. more critical of others.
    b. less critical of others.
    c. more likely to display a self-serving bias.
    d. less likely to display a self-serving bias.

20. According to research on behavioral confirmation, how do most people react to someone who is depressed?
    a. excessively cheerful
    b. in a sympathetic way
    c. in a negative, rejecting manner
    d. no differently than they react to a cheerful person

21. Which of the following is *not* true concerning shyness?
    a. About 40 percent of adults in the United States claim to be shy.
    b. It is a form of social anxiety.
    c. It causes others to react negatively, reinforcing the shy person's self-doubts.
    d. It can be overcome through training in which a person learns to anticipate all the possible negative outcomes of social interactions.

22. Which of the following statements about self-esteem is *not* correct?
    a. People with low self-esteem tend to be negative about others.
    b. People with high self-esteem are less prone to drug addiction.
    c. People with low self-esteem tend to be nonconformists.
    d. People with high self-esteem suffer less from insomnia and ulcers.
    e. People with high self-esteem are more persistent at difficult tasks.

23. The Oedipus and Electra complexes have their roots in the:
    a. anal stage.
    b. oral stage.
    c. latency stage.
    d. phallic stage.
    e. genital stage.

24. Which of the following is a common criticism of the humanistic perspective?
    a. Its concepts are vague and subjective.
    b. The emphasis on the self encourages selfishness in individuals.
    c. It fails to appreciate the reality of evil in human behavior.
    d. All of the above are common criticisms.

25. Although for two weeks David knew of an important meeting, he put off preparing for it until the very last minute. When his supervisor chided him for his lack of preparation, David said he just didn't have enough time. David's procrastination is an example of:
    a. individuation.
    b. behavioral confirmation.
    c. self-handicapping.
    d. strategic self-presentation.

26. Which of the following was *not* mentioned in the text as a criticism of Freud's theory?
    a. The theory is sexist.
    b. It offers few testable hypotheses.
    c. There is no evidence of anything like an "unconscious."
    d. The theory ignores the fact that human development is lifelong.

27. According to Freud, _____ is the process by which children incorporate their parents' values into their _____ .
    a. reaction formation; superegos
    b. reaction formation; egos
    c. identification; superegos
    d. identification; egos

28. In promoting personality growth, the person-centered perspective emphasizes all but:
    a. empathy.
    b. acceptance.
    c. genuineness.
    d. altruism.

29. In Teresa Amabile's experiment, the artwork of 7- to 11-year-old girls was much more creative when:
    a. the girls knew it would be judged by others.
    b. a prize was offered for the most creative project.
    c. competition with others was emphasized.
    d. competition with others was deemphasized.

30. A psychoanalyst would characterize a person who is impulsive and self-indulgent as possessing a strong _____ and a weak _____ .
    a. id and ego; superego
    b. id; ego and superego
    c. ego; superego
    d. id; superego
    e. superego; ego

31. Jill has a biting, sarcastic manner. According to Freud, she is:
    a. projecting her anxiety onto others.
    b. fixated in the oral stage of development.
    c. fixated in the anal stage of development.
    d. displacing her anxiety onto others.

32. James attributes his failing grade in chemistry to an unfair final exam. His attitude exemplifies:
    a. internal locus of control.
    b. unconditional positive regard.
    c. the self-serving bias.
    d. reciprocal determinism.

33. According to Freud, a person who is overzealous in campaigning against pornography may be displaying:
    a. regression.
    b. displacement.
    c. rationalization.
    d. reaction formation.

34. According to Freud, the part of personality that is the unconscious repository of instinctual drives is the:
    a. id.
    b. ego.
    c. superego.
    d. collective unconscious.

35. Randy "lives for the moment," squandering his paycheck as soon as he receives it. According to Freud, Randy's behavior is dominated by the:
    a. id.
    b. ego.
    c. superego.
    d. self-serving bias.

36. Andrew's grandfather, who has lived a rich and productive life, is a spontaneous, loving, and self-accepting person. Maslow might say that he:
    a. has an internal locus of control.
    b. has a strong sense of personal control.
    c. has resolved all the conflicts of the psychosexual stages.
    d. is a self-actualizing person.

37. The school psychologist believes that having a positive self-concept is necessary before students can achieve their potential. Evidently, the school psychologist is working within the _____ perspective.
    a. psychoanalytic
    b. trait
    c. humanistic
    d. social-cognitive

38. Wanda wishes to instill in her children an accepting attitude toward other people. Maslow and Rogers would probably recommend that she:
    a. teach her children first to accept themselves.
    b. use discipline sparingly.
    c. be affectionate with her children only when they behave as she wishes.
    d. do all of the above.

39. Suzy bought a used, high-mileage automobile because it was all she could afford. Attempting to justify her purchase, she raves to her friends about the car's attractiveness, good acceleration, and stereo. According to Freud, Suzy is using the defense mechanism of:
    a. displacement.
    b. reaction formation.
    c. rationalization.
    d. projection.

40. According to Freud, the part of personality that most directly corresponds to the self is the:
    a. id.
    b. ego.
    c. superego.
    d. collective unconscious.

KEY TERMS

Using your own words, write a brief definition or explanation of each of the following terms.

Textbook Terms

1. personality

2. free association

3. psychoanalysis

4. unconscious

5. preconscious

6. id

7. ego

8. superego

9. psychosexual stages

10. Oedipus complex

11. identification

12. gender identity

13. fixation

14. defense mechanisms

15. repression

16. regression

17. reaction formation

18. projection

19. rationalization

20. displacement

21. collective unconscious

22. projective tests

23. Thematic Apperception Test (TAT)

24. Rorschach inkblot test

25. self-actualization

26. unconditional positive regard

27. self-concept

28. self-esteem

29. self-serving bias

30. individualism

31. collectivism

32. reciprocal determinism

33. personal control

34. external locus of control

35. internal locus of control

36. learned helplessness

Program Terms

37. individuation

38. behavioral confirmation

39. self-handicapping

40. self-efficacy

ANSWERS

Guided Study

The following guidelines provide the main points that your answers should have touched upon.

Textbook Assignment

1. Freud discovered that, under hypnosis, his patients were sometimes able to talk freely about their neurological symptoms, which led to their improvement. He later began using free association instead of hypnosis, believing that this technique triggered a chain of thoughts leading into a patient's unconscious, thereby retrieving and releasing painful unconscious memories.

    Psychoanalysis is based on Freud's belief that below our surface consciousness is a much larger, unconscious region that contains thoughts, feelings, wishes, and memories of which we are unaware. Although some of these thoughts are held in a preconscious area and can be retrieved at will into consciousness, some unacceptable thoughts and wishes are forcibly blocked, or repressed, from consciousness. These unconscious thoughts and urges often are expressed in troubling symptoms.

2. To Freud, personality is composed of three interacting, and often conflicting, systems: the id, ego, and superego. Operating on the pleasure principle, the unconscious id strives to satisfy basic drives to survive, reproduce, and aggress. Operating on the reality principle, the ego seeks to gratify the id's impulses in realistic and nondestructive ways. The superego, which represents the individual's internalization of the morals and values of parents and

culture, forces the ego to consider not only the real but also the ideal. Because the ego must intervene among the impulsive demands of the id, the restraining demands of the superego, and those of the external world, it is the personality "executive."

3. Freud believed that children pass through a series of psychosexual stages, during which the id's pleasure-seeking energies focus on particular erogenous zones. Between birth and 18 months (oral stage), pleasure centers on the mouth. Between 18 and 36 months (anal stage), pleasure focuses on bowel and bladder retention and elimination. Between 3 and 6 years (phallic stage), the pleasure zone shifts to the genitals and boys develop unconscious sexual desires for their mothers and the fear that their fathers will punish them (Oedipus complex). Children eventually cope with these threatening feelings by repressing them and identifying with their same-sex parent.

   Between 6 years of age and puberty (latency stage), sexual feelings are repressed and redirected. At puberty, sexual interests mature as youths begin to experience sexual feelings toward others (genital stage).

4. According to Freud, maladaptive adult behavior results from unresolved conflicts during earlier psychosexual stages. Such unresolved conflicts may cause the person's pleasure-seeking energies to become fixated in one psychosexual stage, leading to later problem behaviors or distinctive personality characteristics.

   Defense mechanisms are the ego's attempt to reduce or redirect anxiety by distorting reality. Examples of defense mechanisms include the banishing of thoughts from consciousness (repression), retreating to behavior characteristic of an earlier stage (regression), turning threatening impulses into their opposites (reaction formation) or attributing them to others (projection), self-justification of unacceptable actions (rationalization), and diverting sexual or aggressive impulses to a more acceptable object (displacement).

5. The neo-Freudians placed more emphasis than Freud on the role of the conscious mind in determining personality and less emphasis on sex and aggression as all-consuming motivations. Alfred Adler and Karen Horney emphasized the importance of social rather than sexual tensions in the formation of the child's personality. Horney also countered the male bias inherent in Freud's theory. Carl Jung expanded Freud's view of the unconscious into the idea of a collective unconscious, a common reservoir of thoughts derived from the experiences of our ancestors.

   Psychodynamic theorists downplay the importance of sex in personality formation. They do agree with Freud, however, that much of mental life is unconscious, that childhood shapes personality and attachment, and that we often struggle with inner conflicts.

6. Projective tests, such as the Thematic Apperception Test and the Rorschach inkblot test, ask people to describe or tell a story about an ambiguous stimulus that has no inherent meaning. In doing so, people presumably project their own interests and conflicts and provide a sort of psychological "x-ray" of their personalities. Despite their widespread use, projective tests are considered by most researchers to be lacking in validity and reliability. For example, there is no single accepted scoring system for interpreting the Rorschach, so two raters may not interpret a subject's responses similarly (although a new computer-aided scoring and interpretation tool is improving agreement among raters and enhancing validity). Furthermore, the test is not very successful at predicting future behavior or discriminating between groups.

7. Freud's idea that development is fixed in childhood has been contradicted by research showing that development is lifelong. It is also clear that children gain their gender identity earlier than Freud believed and become strongly feminine or masculine even without a same-sex parent present. Freud's theory of dreams, memory losses, and defense mechanisms as disguising unfulfilled or repressed urges also has been disputed, as has his idea about the natural superiority of men. Today's researchers contend that repression is actually quite rare and, contrary to Freud's views, occurs as a mental response to terrible trauma. In addition, Freud's theory has been criticized for offering after-the-fact explanations of behavior, yet failing to generate testable predictions of those behaviors. Freud's ideas concerning our limited access to all that goes on in the mind, the importance of sexuality, our attempts to defend ourselves against anxiety, and the tension between our biological impulses and our social well-being have endured, however.

8. The humanistic perspective emerged as a reaction against several other perspectives on personality. In contrast to Freud's study of the negative motives of "sick" people, the humanistic psychologists have focused on the strivings of "healthy" people. Unlike the trait theorists, they view people as whole persons, rather than as collections of individual traits.

    Abraham Maslow proposed that people are motivated by a hierarchy of needs and that if basic needs are fulfilled, people will strive to reach their highest potential (self-actualization). Carl Rogers agreed with much of Maslow's thinking, adding that people nurture others' actualizing tendencies by being genuine, accepting, and empathic. For both theorists a central feature of personality is a person's self-concept.

9. Research on the self documents the concept of possible selves, including people's visions of the self or selves they would like to become as motivating their behavior. Another finding is that people with high self-esteem have fewer physical problems, strive more at difficult tasks, and are happier than people with low self-esteem. One of the most firmly established findings is people's readiness to perceive themselves favorably through the self-serving bias. This bias is revealed in the willingness of people to accept responsibility for good deeds and successes more readily than for bad deeds and failures, and in the tendency of people to see themselves as better than average on nearly any desirable dimension.

10. Contrary to popular belief, and despite discrimination and lower social status, ethnic minorities, people with disabilities, and women do not suffer lower self-esteem.

    Individualist cultures nurture the development of personal goals and define identity in terms of individual attributes. Collectivist cultures give priority to the goals of their groups—often the family, clan, or work group. While individualists easily move in and out of social groups, collectivists have fewer but deeper, more stable attachments to their groups and friends. Collectivist cultures also place a premium on maintaining harmony and allowing others to save face. People in individualist cultures have greater personal freedom and more privacy. But compared to collectivists, individualists also tend to be lonelier, more likely to divorce, more homicidal, and more vulnerable to stress-related diseases.

11. The ideas of humanistic psychologists have influenced counseling, education, child-rearing, and management. Critics contend, however, that the concepts of humanistic psychology are vague, subjective, and so focused on the individual that they promote self-indulgence, selfishness, and an erosion of moral restraints. Furthermore, the humanistic psychologists have been

accused of being naively optimistic and unrealistic, and failing to appreciate the human capacity for evil.

12. The social-cognitive perspective applies principles of learning, cognition, and social behavior to personality and emphasizes the ways in which our personalities shape and are shaped by external events. Reciprocal determinism refers to the ways in which our personalities are influenced by the interaction of our situations, our thoughts and feelings, and our behaviors. There are many examples of reciprocal determinism. For one, different people choose different environments. For another, our personalities shape how we interpret and react to events. Finally, our personalities help create the situations to which we react.

13. Whether people see themselves as controlling, or being controlled by, their environments is an important aspect of their personalities. Research reveals that people who perceive an internal locus of control achieve more in school and are more independent, less depressed, better able to delay gratification, and better able to cope with various life stresses than people who perceive an external locus of control. Seligman found that animals and people who experience uncontrollable negative events may perceive a lack of control in their lives and develop the passive resignation of learned helplessness. One measure of how helpless or effective people feel is whether they generally are optimistic or pessimistic.

14. Social-cognitive researchers study personality by exploring the effect of differing situations on people's behavior patterns and attitudes. This perspective has increased our awareness of how social situations influence, and are influenced by, individuals. Critics contend, however, that the theory explains behavior after the fact and that it focuses so much on the situation that it ignores the importance of people's inner traits, unconscious motives, and emotions in the formation of personality.

Program Assignment

1. The "self" refers to the individual's conscious awareness of his or her own identity. In 1890, William James pioneered the scientific study of the self by differentiating three aspects of identity: the material self (our awareness of the physical world), the spiritual self (our awareness of ourselves as thinkers), and the social self (our awareness of the impression we make on others).

    For much of the twentieth century the concept of self was considered inappropriate for scientific study. The behaviorists thought it too "fuzzy," and Freud thought it less important than either the superego or the id in the formation of personality.

2. Carl Rogers led the humanistic movement, which was most responsible for psychology's renewed interest in the conscious self later in this century. In contrast to Freud's pessimistic view of a conflicted, impulse-driven individual, Rogers offered an optimistic view of psychological growth and health. He believed that the individual has an inner guiding force that moves the person toward positive actions, enhancement, and self-fulfillment.

    The self-concept, which is a central feature of humanistic psychology, refers to the individual's awareness of his or her continuing identity as a person; as such, it is our internal regulator of thoughts, feelings, and behavior. We organize information about ourselves in terms of schemas, or knowledge clusters, such as those related to masculinity or femininity or to weight. One schema, our self-schema, has a particularly powerful impact on behavior. If this image is good, we try to live up to this standard and we often succeed. If our self-image is bad, we fail more often and feel badly.

3. Albert Bandura's theory of self-efficacy is concerned with people's beliefs in their capabilities to exercise control over situations that affect their lives. People who have a high sense of efficacy tend to take on challenges, whereas those plagued by self-doubts tend to shy away from situations that they feel exceed their capabilities.

    In one experiment, some subjects were led to believe that successful performance on a task depended primarily on their innate ability. These subjects tended to proceed cautiously, setting lower goals for themselves and experiencing falling levels of confidence and self-efficacy when they met with failure. Other subjects were given the same task but told that successful performance depended on their effort. These subjects tended to be less frustrated by mistakes, seeing them as a necessary part of learning and profiting from them. They also experienced an increasing sense of self-efficacy, as measured by goal setting and confidence levels.

4. The social self refers to our perception of how others perceive us. "Status," which has to do with how we present ourselves to others, has several manipulable, nonverbal aspects, including eye contact, the fluidity of body movements, and characteristics of speech. The prototype for high status is a person who is calm, speaks in complete sentences without jerky movements, breathes deeply, and maintains eye contact. Status transactions are a form of interpersonal communication in which people establish their relative degrees of social status and power.

5. Strategic self-presentation refers to our efforts to present ourselves to others so that they see us the way we see ourselves. This process of self-presentation elicits what Mark Snyder calls *behavioral confirmation*. Other people react to us according to the context our behavior has created; we then see the way they respond to us, which confirms our original belief about the kind of person we really are. This explains why depressed people elicit negative reactions and are often treated as if they were inadequate, while extraverts tend to elicit positive responses.

6. Shy people anticipate all the possible negative consequences of interactions with others, then behave in ways that tend to elicit the very reactions they fear. A form of social anxiety, shy behavior typically results in negative evaluations from others, which further reinforce feelings of low self-esteem and self-doubt. Self-handicapping occurs when people try to explain away potential failures by blaming them on factors other than their lack of ability. This protection of their sense of competence takes many forms, including procrastination, forgetting of important assignments or events, escape behaviors such as the use of alcohol or drugs, and even neurotic behaviors such as avoiding phone calls.

7. Ethnic and racial prejudices of the majority culture can eat away at the self-concepts of minority group members. Prejudice is a kind of "psychological genocide" that works across generations. Its effects can be seen in the high rates of despair, alcoholism, drug abuse, and violence in urban ghettos.

    Researcher Teresa Amabile has found that social evaluation can undermine creativity. In one study, 7- to 11-year-old girls were less creative in their artwork when they expected it to be judged by others than when the situation was noncompetitive. Amabile has found that people will be most creative when they are motivated by their interest in and enjoyment of a task rather than by external pressures.

Progress Test

1. **b.** is the answer. Personality is defined as patterns of response—of thinking, feeling, and acting—that are relatively consistent across a variety of situations. (p. 419)

2. **a.** is the answer. (pp. 422–423)

3. **b.** is the answer. (p. 425)

    a. According to most neo-Freudians, Freud placed too great an emphasis on the *unconscious* mind.

    c. Freud placed great emphasis on early childhood, and the neo-Freudians basically agreed with him.

    d. The neo-Freudians accepted Freud's ideas about the basic personality structures.

4. **d.** is the answer. (video)

5. **a.** is the answer. (video)

6. **b.** is the answer. (video; p. 436)

    a. This is true of the psychoanalytic perspective.

    c. This is true of the social-cognitive perspective.

    d. This refers to William James's beliefs.

7. **e.** is the answer. (p. 437)

8. **c.** is the answer. (video)

    a. & b. The concept of self was largely *rejected* by psychoanalysts such as Freud, as well as by behaviorists such as Skinner.

    d. James set the stage for the concept of self, but during the nineteenth century.

9. **b.** is the answer. (video; pp. 420–421)

    a., c., & d. These theorists offered a more optimistic view of personality, focusing on the self-concept.

10. **a.** is the answer. (video; pp. 437–438)

    b. Freud had a pessimistic view of personality.

    c. James is noted for differentiating three aspects of the self: material, spiritual, and social.

    d. Bandura is noted for his research on self-efficacy.

11. **b.** is the answer. Humanistic psychologists emphasize that for the individual, self-affirming thinking is generally adaptive (therefore, not a.); such thinking maintains self-confidence, minimizes depression, and enables us to view others with compassion and understanding (therefore, not c.); unconditional positive regard tends to promote self-esteem and thus self-affirming thinking (therefore, not d.). (pp. 440–441)

12. **a.** is the answer. Developmental research indicates that development is lifelong. (p. 427)

    b., c., & d. To varying degrees, research has partially supported these Freudian ideas.

13. **d.** is the answer. (video; p. 438)

    a. & c. Personality structure, of which the ego is a part, is a concern of the psychoanalytic perspective.

b. Locus of control is a major focus of the social-cognitive perspective.

14. **b.** is the answer. In Freud's theory, the id operates according to the pleasure principle; the ego operates according to the reality principle. (p. 421–422)

    c. The id is presumed to be unconscious.

    d. The superego is, according to Freud, the equivalent of a conscience; the ego is the "personality executive."

15. **c.** is the answer. (video)

16. **d.** is the answer. (video)

17. **c.** is the answer. (video)

18. **d.** is the answer. (p. 421)

    a. Self-actualization is a concept of the humanistic perspective.

    b. Through identification, children reduce conflicting feelings as they incorporate their parents' values.

    c. Jung, rather than Freud, proposed the concept of the collective unconscious.

19. **a.** is the answer. Feelings of insecurity reduce self-esteem, and there is a tendency for those who feel negative about themselves to feel negative about others as well. (p. 439)

20. **c.** is the answer. This rejection often reinforces the depressed person's feelings of inadequacy. (video)

21. **d.** is the answer. On the contrary, shy people are noted for *dwelling* on all the possible negative outcomes of social interactions. (video)

22. **c.** is the answer. In actuality, people with *high* self-esteem are generally more independent of pressures to conform. (pp. 438–439)

23. **d.** is the answer. (pp. 422–423)

24. **d.** is the answer. (pp. 443–444)

25. **c.** is the answer. (video)

    a. This is the process by which a child establishes independence from his or her parents.

    b. This is the process by which our behavior creates a context in which others react to us in a manner that confirms our original belief about the kind of person we really are.

    d. This refers to our efforts to present ourselves to others so that they see us the way we see ourselves.

26. **c.** is the answer. Although many researchers think of the unconscious as information processing without awareness rather than as a reservoir of repressed information, they agree with Freud that we do indeed have limited access to all that goes on in our minds. (pp. 427–429)

27. **c.** is the answer. (p. 423)

    a. & b. Reaction formation is the defense mechanism by which people transform unacceptable impulses into their opposites.

    d. It is the superego, rather than the ego, that represents parental values.

28. **d.** is the answer. (p. 437)

29. **d.** is the answer. (video)

30. **d.** is the answer. Impulsiveness is the mark of a strong id; self-indulgence is the mark of a weak superego. Because the ego serves to mediate the demands of the id, the superego, and the outside world, its strength or

weakness is judged by its decision-making ability, not by the character of the decision—so the ego is not relevant to the question asked. (video; pp. 421–422)

31. **b.** is the answer. Sarcasm is said to be an attempt to deny the passive dependence characteristic of the oral stage. (p. 423)

    a. A person who is projecting attributes his or her own feelings to others.

    c. Such a person might be either messy and disorganized or highly controlled and compulsively neat.

    d. Displacement involves diverting aggressive or sexual impulses onto a more acceptable object than that which aroused them.

32. **c.** is the answer. (p. 440)

    a. A person with an internal locus of control would be likely to *accept* responsibility for a failing grade.

    b. Unconditional positive regard is an attitude of total acceptance directed toward others.

    d. Reciprocal determinism refers to the mutual influences among personality, environment, and behavior.

33. **d.** is the answer. The ego unconsciously makes unacceptable impulses look like their opposites. The person vehemently crusading against pornography would be moved by sexual desires he or she found unacceptable. (p. 424)

    a. Regression is retreating to an earlier, more infantile stage of development.

    b. Displacement refers to diverting aggressive or sexual impulses toward an object other than the one responsible for the impulses.

    c. To rationalize is to generate inaccurate, self-justifying explanations for our actions.

34. **a.** is the answer. (video; p. 421)

    b. The ego is the conscious "executive" of personality.

    c. The superego is the division of personality that contains the conscience.

    d. This is not an aspect of personality in Freud's theory.

35. **a.** is the answer. Operating according to the pleasure principle, the id's impulses, unless checked by the ego, might lead to such behavior. (p. 421)

    b. The ego is the rational part of the personality that mediates between the demands of the id, the superego, and reality. If the ego dominates, such pleasure-seeking behavior is unlikely.

    c. The superego is the conscience of personality; if it is dominant, such pleasure-seeking behavior is unlikely.

    d. The self-serving bias is the tendency of people to perceive themselves favorably; it is not part of Freud's theory.

36. **d.** is the answer. (p. 436)

    a. & b. These are concepts used by social-cognitive theorists rather than humanistic theorists such as Maslow.

    c. This reflects Freud's viewpoint.

37. **c.** is the answer. (p. 438)

    a., b., & d. The self-concept is not relevant to the psychoanalytic, trait, or social-cognitive perspectives.

38. **a.** is the answer. (p. 437)

    b. The text does not discuss the impact of discipline on personality.

c. This would constitute *conditional*, rather than unconditional, positive regard and would likely cause the children to be *less* accepting of themselves and others.

39. **c.** is the answer. Suzy is trying to justify her purchase by generating (inaccurate) explanations for her behavior. (p. 424)

   a. Displacement is the redirecting of impulses toward an object other than the one responsible for them.

   b. Reaction formation is the transformation of unacceptable impulses into their opposites.

   d. Projection is the attribution of one's own unacceptable thoughts and feelings to others.

40. **b.** is the answer. (video)

Key Terms

Textbook Terms

1. **Personality** is an individual's characteristic pattern of thinking, feeling, and acting. (p. 419)

2. **Free association** is the Freudian technique in which the person is encouraged to say whatever comes to mind as a means of exploring the unconscious. (p. 421)

3. In Freud's theory, **psychoanalysis** refers to the treatment of psychological disorders by seeking to expose and interpret the tensions within a patient's unconscious, using methods such as free association. (p. 421)

4. In Freud's theory, the **unconscious** is the repository of mostly unacceptable thoughts, wishes, feelings, and memories. According to contemporary psychologists, it is a level of information processing of which we are unaware. (p. 421)

5. In Freud's theory, the **preconscious** area is a region of the unconscious that contains material that is retrievable at will into conscious awareness. (p. 421)

   Example: The Freudian notion of a **preconscious** is similar to the concept of long-term memory: Material is accessible but not currently in our awareness.

6. In Freud's theory, the **id** is the unconscious division of personality, consisting of basic sexual and aggressive drives, that supplies psychic energy to personality. (p. 421)

7. In psychoanalytic theory, the **ego** is the conscious division of personality that attempts to mediate between the demands of the id, the superego, and reality. (p. 422)

8. In Freud's theory, the **superego** is the division of personality that contains the conscience and develops by incorporating the perceived moral standards of society. (p. 422)

9. Freud's **psychosexual stages** are developmental periods children pass through during which the id's pleasure-seeking energies are focused on different erogenous zones. (p. 422)

10. According to Freud, boys in the phallic stage develop a collection of feelings, known as the **Oedipus complex**, that center on sexual attraction to the mother and resentment of the father. Some psychologists believe girls have a parallel Electra complex. (p. 422)

11. In Freud's theory, **identification** is the process by which the child's superego develops and incorporates the parents' values. Freud saw identification as crucial, not only to resolution of the Oedipus complex but also to the development of gender identity. (p. 423)

12. **Gender identity** is a person's sense of being male or female. (p. 423)

13. In Freud's theory, **fixation** occurs when development becomes arrested, due to unresolved conflicts, in an immature psychosexual stage. (p. 423)

14. In Freud's theory, **defense mechanisms** are the ego's methods of unconsciously protecting itself against anxiety by distorting reality. (p. 423)

15. The basis of all defense mechanisms, **repression** is the unconscious exclusion of anxiety-arousing thoughts, feelings, and memories from the conscious mind. Repression is an example of motivated forgetting: One "forgets" what one really does not wish to remember. (p. 423)

16. **Regression** is the defense mechanism in which a person faced with anxiety reverts to a less mature pattern of behavior. (p. 423)

17. **Reaction formation** is the defense mechanism in which the ego converts unacceptable impulses into their opposites. (p. 424)

18. In psychoanalytic theory, **projection** is the unconscious attribution of one's own unacceptable feelings, attitudes, or desires to others. (p. 424)

    Memory aid: To project is to thrust outward. **Projection** is an example of thrusting one's own feelings outward to another person.

19. **Rationalization** is the defense mechanism in which one devises self-justifying but incorrect reasons for one's behavior. (p. 424)

20. **Displacement** is the defense mechanism in which a sexual or aggressive impulse is shifted to a more acceptable object than the one that originally aroused the impulse. (p. 424)

21. The **collective unconscious** is Jung's concept of an inherited unconscious shared by all people and deriving from our early ancestors' universal experiences. (p. 425)

22. **Projective tests**, such as the TAT and Rorschach, present ambiguous stimuli onto which people supposedly *project* their own inner feelings. (p. 426)

23. The **Thematic Apperception Test (TAT)** is a projective test that consists of ambiguous pictures about which people are asked to make up stories. (p. 426)

24. The **Rorschach inkblot test**, the most widely used projective test, consists of ten inkblots that people are asked to interpret. (p. 426)

25. In Maslow's theory, **self-actualization** describes the process of fulfilling one's potential and becoming spontaneous, loving, creative, and self-accepting. Self-actualization is at the very top of Maslow's need hierarchy and therefore becomes active only after the more basic physical and psychological needs have been met. (p. 436)

26. **Unconditional positive regard** is, according to Rogers, an attitude of total acceptance and one of the three conditions essential to a "growth-promoting" climate. (p. 437)

27. **Self-concept** refers to one's personal awareness of "who I am." In the humanistic perspective, the self-concept is a central feature of personality; life happiness is significantly affected by whether the self-concept is positive or negative. (p. 438)

28. In humanistic psychology, **self-esteem** refers to an individual's sense of self-worth. (p. 438)

29. The **self-serving bias** is the tendency to perceive oneself favorably. (p. 440)

30. **Individualism** is a cultural emphasis on personal goals over group goals, and defining one's identity in terms of personal attributes rather than group identifications. (p. 441)

31. **Collectivism** is a cultural emphasis on the goals of one's group, and defining one's identity accordingly. (p. 441)

32. According to the social-cognitive perspective, personality is shaped through **reciprocal determinism**, or the interaction between personality and environmental factors. (p. 445)

33. **Personal control** refers to a person's sense of controlling the environment. (p. 445)

34. **External locus of control** is the perception that one's fate is determined by forces not under personal control. (p. 446)

35. **Internal locus of control** is the perception that to a great extent one controls one's own destiny. (p. 446)

36. **Learned helplessness** is the passive resignation and perceived lack of control that a person or animal develops from repeated exposure to inescapable aversive events. (p. 446)

Program Terms

37. **Individuation** refers to the gradual emotional and cognitive separation of a child from its mother. Some psychologists believe that individuation is essential for developing a unique sense of self and a healthy personality.

38. **Behavioral confirmation** refers to the process by which we create a context in which others react to us in a manner that confirms our belief about the kind of person we really are.

39. **Self-handicapping** is the process by which we attempt to explain away potential failures by blaming them on something other than our lack of ability.

40. **Self-efficacy** refers to our belief in our capability to exercise control over situations that affect our lives.

PROGRAM 16

Testing and Intelligence

TEXTBOOK ASSIGNMENT: Chapter 11: Intelligence, pp. 333–361

ORIENTATION

Can tests really tell us how smart we are, how well adjusted we are, and what goes on in our subconscious minds? Or are they unfair barriers, narrowing our definitions of intelligence and mental health? These questions are the subject matter of an enduring controversy in psychology: How do we define and measure intelligence?

The program and reading assignment describe the historical origins of intelligence testing and discuss several important issues concerning its use. These include the methods by which intelligence tests are constructed and whether such tests are valid, reliable, and free of bias. Also discussed is research that attempts to assess the stability of intelligence, whether intelligence is a single general ability or several specific ones, and the extent of biological and environmental influences on intelligence.

NOTE: Answer guidelines for all Program 16 questions begin on page 312.

GOALS

After completing your study of the program and reading assignment, you should be prepared to:

1. Trace the origins of intelligence testing.

2. Discuss evidence regarding intelligence as a stable general mental ability and/or as many changing specific abilities.

3. Describe modern tests of mental abilities and identify the major principles of good test construction, noting how psychological assessment is sometimes misused.

4. Discuss evidence for both genetic and environmental influences on intelligence.

GUIDED STUDY

Textbook Assignment

The text chapter should be studied one section at a time. Before you read, preview each section by skimming it, noting headings and boldface items. Then read the appropriate section objectives from the following outline. Keep these objectives in mind and, as you read the chapter section, search for the information that will enable you to meet each objective. Once you have finished a section, write out answers for its objectives.

The Origins of Intelligence Testing (pp. 334–336)

1. Trace the origins of intelligence tests.

What Is Intelligence? (pp. 336–342)

2. Describe the nature of intelligence and discuss whether it is culturally defined or culture-free.

3. Describe the factor-analysis approach to understanding intelligence and discuss evidence regarding intelligence as a general mental ability and/or as many specific abilities.

4. Discuss neurological approaches to the measurement of intelligence.

Assessing Intelligence (pp. 342–347)

5. Distinguish between aptitude and achievement tests and describe modern tests of mental abilities.

6. Identify the major principles of good test construction and illustrate their application to intelligence tests.

The Dynamics of Intelligence (pp. 348–352)

7. Discuss the stability of intelligence test scores and the two extremes of intelligence.

8. Identify the factors associated with creativity.

Genetic and Environmental Influences on Intelligence (pp. 352–360)

9. Discuss evidence for both genetic and environmental influences on intelligence.

10. Describe group differences in intelligence test scores and show how they can be explained in terms of environmental factors.

11. Discuss whether intelligence tests are biased and/or discriminatory.

Program Assignment

Read the following objectives before you watch Program 16. As you watch, be alert for information that will help you answer each objective. Taking notes during the program will help you to formulate your answers later. After the program, write answers to the objectives. If you have access to the program on videotape, you may replay portions to refresh your memory.

1. Describe the field of psychological assessment, including its goals and basic methods.

2. Discuss Alfred Binet's impact on the field of psychological assessment.

3. Explain how Binet's goals for intelligence testing were revised under the influence of Lewis Terman and other American psychologists.

4. Identify several ways in which intelligence tests are misused.

5. State the views of Howard Gardner and Robert Sternberg regarding the nature of intelligence.

6. Explain the significance of the P300 brain wave in the measurement of intelligence.

PROGRESS TEST

Circle your answers to the following questions and check them with the answers on page 316. If your answer is incorrect, read the explanation for why it is incorrect and then consult the appropriate pages of the text (in parentheses following the correct answer).

1. A 6-year-old child has a mental age of 9. The child's IQ is:
   a. 96
   b. 100
   c. 125
   d. 150
   e. 166

2. Which of the following tests consists of eleven subtests and yields separate intelligence scores for verbal and performance categories?
   a. WAIS-R
   b. SAT
   c. ACT
   d. Stanford-Binet

3. Standardization refers to the process of:
   a. determining the accuracy with which a test measures what it is supposed to.
   b. defining meaningful scores relative to a representative pretested group.
   c. determining the consistency of test scores obtained by retesting people.
   d. measuring the success with which a test predicts the behavior it is designed to predict.

4. The test created by Alfred Binet was designed specifically to:
   a. measure inborn intelligence in adults.
   b. measure inborn intelligence in children.
   c. predict school performance in children.
   d. identify mentally retarded children so that they could be institutionalized.
   e. do all of the above.

5. Most psychologists believe that racial gaps in test scores:
   a. have been exaggerated when they are, in fact, insignificant.
   b. indicate that intelligence is in large measure inherited.
   c. are in large measure caused by environmental factors.
   d. are decreasing.

6. Down syndrome is normally caused by:
   a. an extra chromosome in the person's genetic makeup.
   b. a missing chromosome in the person's genetic makeup.
   c. malnutrition during the first months of life.
   d. prenatal exposure to an addictive drug.

7. Which of the following is *not* a requirement of a good test?
   a. reliability
   b. standardization
   c. reification
   d. validity
   e. criterion

8. If a test designed to indicate which applicants are likely to perform the best on the job fails to do so, the test has:
   a. low reliability.
   b. low content validity.
   c. low predictive validity.
   d. not been standardized.

9. The formula for the intelligence quotient was devised by:
   a. Galton.
   b. Gall.
   c. Binet.
   d. Terman.
   e. Stern.

10. Originally, IQ was defined as:
    a. mental age divided by chronological age and multiplied by 100.
    b. chronological age divided by mental age and multiplied by 100.
    c. mental age subtracted from chronological age and multiplied by 100.
    d. chronological age subtracted from mental age and multiplied by 100.

11. Weinberg and colleagues found that black children adopted and raised in the culture of the IQ tests had intelligence scores:
    a. comparable to those of the average white child.
    b. lower than those of white children.
    c. higher than those of white children.
    d. higher than those of black children in general but lower than those of adopted white children.

12. Which of the following statements is true?
    a. The predictive validity of intelligence tests is not as high as their reliability.
    b. The reliability of intelligence tests is not as high as their predictive validity.
    c. Modern intelligence tests have extremely high predictive validity and reliability.
    d. The predictive validity and reliability of most intelligence tests are very low.

13. Before about age _____ , intelligence tests generally do not predict future scores.
    a. 3
    b. 5
    c. 7
    d. 10
    e. 15

14. Sorting children into gifted and nongifted educational groups:
    a. presumes that giftedness is a single trait.
    b. does not result in higher academic achievement scores.
    c. promotes racial segregation and prejudice.
    d. sometimes creates self-fulfilling prophecies.
    e. has all of the above effects.

15. In terms of his viewpoint on the determinants of intelligence, Lewis Terman would probably have allied himself most closely with:
    a. Galton.
    b. Binet.
    c. Sternberg.
    d. Gardner.
    e. Wagner.

16. Jake takes the same test of mechanical reasoning on several different days and gets virtually identical scores. This suggests that the test has:
    a. high content validity.
    b. high reliability.
    c. high predictive validity.
    d. been standardized.
    e. all of the above qualities.

17. Which of the following best describes the relationship between creativity and intelligence?
    a. Creativity appears to depend on the ability to think imaginatively and has little if any relationship to intelligence.
    b. Creativity is best understood as a certain kind of intelligence.
    c. The more intelligent a person is, the greater his or her creativity.
    d. A certain level of intelligence is necessary but not sufficient for creativity.

18. Studies of 2- to 7-month-old babies show that babies who quickly become bored with a picture:
    a. often develop learning disabilities later on.
    b. score lower on infant intelligence tests.
    c. score higher on intelligence tests several years later.
    d. score very low on intelligence tests several years later.

19. According to the text and the program, what can be concluded from early intelligence testing in the United States.
    a. Most European immigrants were "feeble-minded."
    b. Army recruits of other than Western European heritage were intellectually deficient.
    c. The tests were biased against people who did not share the culture assumed by the test.
    d. Both a. and b. could be concluded.

20. If asked to guess the intelligence score of a stranger, your best guess would be:
    a. 75.
    b. 100.
    c. 125.
    d. "I don't know, intelligence scores vary too widely."

21. The existence of _____ reinforces the generally accepted notion that intelligence is a multidimensional quality.
    a. adaptive skills
    b. mental retardation
    c. general intelligence
    d. savant syndrome

22. Which of the following provides the strongest evidence of the role of heredity in determining intelligence?
    a. The IQ scores of identical twins raised separately are very similar.
    b. The intelligence scores of fraternal twins are more similar than those of ordinary siblings.
    c. The intelligence scores of identical twins raised together are more similar than those of identical twins raise apart.
    d. The intelligence scores of adopted children show relatively weak correlations with scores of adoptive as well as biological parents.

23. By creating a label such as "gifted," we begin to act as if all children are naturally divided into two categories, gifted and nongifted. This logical error is referred to as:
    a. rationalization.
    b. nominalizing.
    c. factor analysis.
    d. reification.
    e. heritability.

24. The goal of psychological assessment is to:
    a. find out how people differ in ability, behavior, and personality.
    b. diagnose mental problems.
    c. determine the origins of intelligence.
    d. determine the stability of intelligence.

25. What problem of earlier tests was David Wechsler's intelligence test designed to overcome?
    a. low reliability of scores
    b. low validity of scores
    c. cultural bias
    d. dependence on language

26. Current intelligence tests compute an individual's mental ability score as:
    a. the ratio of mental age to chronological age multiplied by 100.
    b. the ratio of chronological age to mental age multiplied by 100.
    c. the amount by which the test-taker's performance deviates from the average performance of others the same age.
    d. the ratio of the test-taker's verbal intelligence score to his or her nonverbal intelligence score.

27. When performing a task, the brains of highly skilled people:
    a. require less glucose energy.
    b. register simple stimuli more quickly.
    c. demonstrate a more complex brain-wave response to stimuli.
    d. do all of the above.

28. Gerardeen has superb social skills, manages conflicts well, and has great empathy for her friends and co-workers. Peter Salovey and John Mayer would probably say that Gerardeen possesses a high degree of:
    a. g.
    b. social intelligence.
    c. practical intelligence.
    d. emotional intelligence.

29. By what age does a child's performance on an intelligence test become stable?
    a. 2
    b. 4
    c. 6
    d. 7
    e. 12

30. The "P300 test" of intelligence is based on the assumption that intelligence involves:
    a. a single general ability.
    b. several specific abilities.
    c. rapid adaptation to interruption.
    d. low excitability.

31. Most experts view intelligence as a person's:
    a. ability to perform well on intelligence tests.
    b. innate mental capacity.
    c. capacity for goal-directed adaptive behavior.
    d. diverse skills acquired throughout life.

32. Of the following, who would probably be the most skeptical about the prospects for a "culture-free" test of intelligence?
   a. those who view intelligence as successful adaptation to the environment
   b. those who view intelligence as a single entity
   c. those who view intelligence as multifaceted
   d. those who view intelligence as largely innate

33. Tests of _____ measure what an individual can do now, whereas tests of _____ predict what an individual will be able to do later.
   a. aptitude; achievement
   b. achievement; aptitude
   c. reliability; validity
   d. validity; reliability

34. Sternberg's test of practical intelligence is based on:
   a. attributes of successful people in a specific profession.
   b. logic and mathematical reasoning.
   c. linguistic skills.
   d. creativity.

35. Which of the following statements most accurately reflects the text's position regarding the relative contribution of genes and environment in determining intelligence?
   a. Except in cases of a neglectful early environment, each individual's basic intelligence is largely the product of heredity.
   b. With the exception of those with genetic disorders such as Down syndrome, intelligence is primarily the product of environmental experiences.
   c. Both genes and life experiences significantly influence performance on intelligence tests.
   d. Because intelligence tests have such low predictive validity, the question cannot be addressed until psychologists agree on a more valid test of intelligence.

36. Vanessa is a very creative sculptress. We would expect that Vanessa also:
   a. has an exceptionally high intelligence score.
   b. is quite introverted.
   c. has a venturesome personality and is intrinsically motivated.
   d. lacks expertise in most other skills.
   e. is more successful than other sculptors.

37. Howard Gardner views intelligence as:
   a. composed of seven different dimensions.
   b. the ability to adapt to, change, or create a suitable environment.
   c. an inborn general ability.
   d. measurable in terms of brain waves.

38. A school psychologist found that 85 percent of those who scored above 115 on an aptitude test were "A" students and 75 percent of those who scored below 85 on the test were "D" students. The psychologist concluded that the test had high _____ validity because scores on it correlated highly with the _____ behavior.
   a. content; criterion
   b. predictive; criterion
   c. content; target
   d. predictive; target

39. If you compare the same trait in people of similar heredity who live in very different environments, heritability for that trait will be _____ ; heritability is most likely to be _____ among people of very different heredities who live in similar environments.
    a. low; high
    b. high; low
    c. environment; genetic
    d. genetic; environmental

40. Cultural bias in intelligence testing often leads to the undervaluing of which attribute(s)?
    a. verbal ability
    b. mathematical ability
    c. creativity
    d. common sense
    e. c. and d.

KEY TERMS

Using your own words, write a brief definition or explanation of each of the following terms.

Textbook Terms

1. intelligence test

2. mental age

3. Stanford-Binet

4. intelligence quotient (IQ)

5. intelligence

6. factor analysis

7. general intelligence (g factor)

8. savant syndrome

9. emotional intelligence

10. aptitude test

11. achievement test

12. Wechsler Adult Intelligence Scale (WAIS)

13. standardization

14. normal curve

15. reliability

16. validity

17. content validity

18. criterion

19. predictive validity

20. mental retardation

21. Down syndrome

22. creativity

23. heritability

Program Terms
24. psychometrics

25. cognitive test

26. personality test

27. projective test

28. norm

29. practical intelligence

30. P300 wave

ANSWERS

Guided Study

The following guidelines provide the main points that your answers should have touched upon.

Textbook Assignment

1. Sir Francis Galton was the first to attempt to measure individual mental abilities. Galton, who founded the eugenics movement, assumed that intelligence was inherited and attempted (without success) to equate intelligence with head size and later with reaction time, sensory acuity, muscular power, and body proportions. Modern intelligence testing began when Alfred Binet developed a test to predict children's future school performance. Binet's test was designed to compute a mental age for each child. Lewis Terman's revision of Binet's test, known as the Stanford-Binet, computed an IQ score as the ratio of mental age to chronological age. Modern intelligence tests no longer compute an intelligence quotient; instead, they produce a mental ability score based on the test-taker's performance relative to the average of others the same age.

2. Most experts view intelligence as a person's capacity for "goal-directed adaptive behavior" that reflects an ability to learn from experience, solve problems, and reason clearly. Psychologists who view intelligence as successful adaptation to the environment contend that what is considered highly intelligent behavior in one culture may not be in another. Others view intelligence as basic problem-solving abilities that are important in any culture.

3. Factor analysis is a statistical technique used to identify clusters of test items that measure a common ability, such as spatial or reasoning ability.
   Although psychologists agree that people have specific abilities, such as verbal or mathematical intelligence, they do not agree about the existence of an underlying general intelligence factor. People with savant syndrome, who score very low on intelligence tests but possess extraordinary specific abilities, provide support for the viewpoint that there are multiple intelligences, each independent of the others. Sternberg and Wagner, for example, distinguish among three intelligences—academic, practical, and creative—while Cantor and Kihlstrom distinguish between academic and social intelligence (including emotional intelligence) and Gardner among seven different intelligences.

4. Efforts to link brain structure and cognition continue. Recent studies using MRI and PET scans reveal modest correlations between brain size and IQ, and between ability on a specific task and neurological efficiency. Other researchers have found that people with high intelligence scores react faster than low-scoring people on tests that measure speed of processing simple information.

5. Aptitude tests, such as a college entrance exam, are intended to predict a person's ability to learn new skills. Achievement tests, such as a final exam in a college course, are intended to measure what already has been learned.
   The most widely used intelligence tests, the WAIS for adults and the

WISC for children, consist of a number of subtests and yield an overall intelligence score, as well as separate verbal and performance scores.

6. Good intelligence tests have been standardized and are reliable and valid. Standardization is the process of defining meaningful scores on the test relative to a pretested group. A random group of test results should form a normal distribution.

    Reliability is the extent to which a test yields consistent results. To check a test's reliability, people are tested twice using the same or a different form of the test. If the scores correlate, the test is reliable. The Stanford-Binet, WAIS, WISC, and American college aptitude tests all have high reliabilities of about +.9.

    Validity is the extent to which a test actually measures the behavior (content validity) it claims to, or predicts some criterion, such as future performance (predictive validity). The predictive validity of general aptitude tests is not as high as their reliability.

7. The stability of intelligence test scores increases with age. Infants who become quickly bored with a picture score higher on intelligence tests several years later. By age 3, children's performances on intelligence tests begin to predict their adolescent and adult scores. By late adolescence, aptitude scores are quite stable.

    Approximately 1 percent of the population have very low intelligence scores, experience difficulty adapting to the normal demands of living independently, and are labeled as mentally retarded. Severe mental retardation sometimes results from physical causes, such as Down syndrome.

    Approximately 3 to 5 percent of children are labeled "gifted." Contrary to popular myth, gifted children are not frequently maladjusted. The segregation of children into gifted and nongifted educational tracks remains controversial. Critics of ability tracking contend that it does not result in higher achievement scores, that it lowers all students' self-concepts, and that it promotes racial segregation and prejudice. Ability tracking also is based on the possibly erroneous notion that giftedness is a single trait rather than any one of many specific abilities.

8. Creativity is the ability to produce novel and valuable ideas. Although people with high intelligence scores do well on tests of creativity, beyond an intelligence score of about 120, the correlation between intelligence scores and creativity disappears.

    Studies suggest five components to creativity other than intelligence: expertise, imaginative thinking skills, a venturesome personality, intrinsic motivation, and a creative environment.

9. Both genes and environment influence intelligence. Studies of twins and adopted children point to the influence of heredity. For example, the most genetically similar people have the most similar intelligence scores, and adopted children's intelligence scores are more like their biological parents' scores than their adoptive parents' scores. It is estimated that the *heritability* of intelligence is about 50 to 70 percent; that is, 50 to 70 percent of the variation in intelligence within a *group* of people can be attributed to heredity.

    Other studies that compare children reared in neglectful environments with those who have been reared in enriched environments, or in different cultures, point to the impact of environmental experiences on intelligence scores. Findings regarding Head Start and other preschool programs indicate that high-quality programs can generate short-term cognitive gains and long-term positive effects.

10. On average, there *are* group differences in intelligence scores. For example, Asian students outperform North American students on math achievement and aptitude tests, females score higher than males in math computation, and white Americans tend to score higher than African-Americans on IQ tests.

    Although heredity contributes to individual differences in intelligence, it does not necessarily contribute to group differences. Most experts believe that the intelligence score gaps between groups are the result of differences between privileged and disadvantaged groups around the world, as well as cultural differences in educational enrichment.

11. In the sense that intelligence scores are sensitive to differences caused by cultural experience, aptitude tests are certainly biased. In terms of predictive validity, however, most experts agree that the major intelligence tests are not racially biased.

    Because intelligence tests are designed to distinguish different levels of aptitude, their purpose in this sense *is* to discriminate among individuals. In another sense, however, intelligence tests reduce discrimination by reducing the use of subjective criteria in school and job placement.

Program Assignment

1. The goal of psychological assessment is to find out how people differ in their abilities, behavior, and personalities. Using *psychometrics*, or mental testing, psychologists have devised tests that measure intelligence and learning in specific subject areas—for example, IQ tests, the SAT, and the ACT. Collectively known as cognitive tests, these tests measure various aspects of mental ability. Personality tests such as the MMPI attempt to measure the noncognitive parts of personality—your interests, values, and personality traits. By contrast, projective tests such as the Rorschach help clinical psychologists assess mental and emotional problems. With all tests, a person's responses are used to predict their future performance in some real life situation.

2. In 1905, Alfred Binet published the first workable intelligence test; devised to measure the intellectual performance of schoolchildren, the test was designed to enable teachers to objectively classify and separate retarded from normal children.

    The key to Binet's approach was to quantify a student's performance relative to the norm, or average score, for a given age. Binet's dream was that psychological assessment would replace subjective, biased evaluations with objective ones.

    Binet's tests had a great impact in the United States, where a vast public school system was emerging. They were used to quickly assess the abilities of the thousands of children who emigrated to this country, as well as soldiers recruited to serve during World War I. Assessment was seen as an inexpensive, democratic method for bringing order to chaos, a way to separate those who had the aptitude to benefit from education or military training from those who were deemed incompetent. With the growth of the testing movement, many began to believe that tests could be used to differentiate people in terms of socially important characteristics, such as leadership ability, and to believe that they showed intellectual differences according to race and ethnic background. Statistics were used to support bogus arguments that certain racial and ethnic groups were intellectually inferior.

3. In 1916, Lewis Terman adapted Binet's test for American schoolchildren. His test, called the Stanford-Binet, introduced the concept of the intelli-

gence quotient (IQ) and quickly became a standard instrument in clinical psychology, psychiatry, and educational counseling. More important, Terman and others came to believe (unlike Binet) that intelligence was an inner quality that had a large hereditary component. The implicit assumption was that IQ measures something essential and unchanging about human nature—our inherited intelligence. In the United States, psychological assessment has been championed as a democratic tool to eliminate arbitrary, biased evaluations of people based on such irrelevant criteria as race, sex, nationality, and appearance. Unfortunately, competency tests are subject to misuse, and assessment has become the single most controversial subfield of psychology.

4. One way in which tests are misused is to indicate that certain people are not capable of doing something when they really are. Tests often fail to take into account different ways in which people can do the same job. Many educators also worry about the problem of "teaching for tests," instead of for basic knowledge.

    There are many other ways in which psychological assessment is less than fully objective. A person's IQ score, for example, can become a label that creates a self-fulfilling prophecy regarding his or her ability. Test scores may also cause administrators to overlook actual job performance as a criterion for hiring. And the cultural biases inherent in many tests may place too much emphasis on certain attributes, such as verbal ability or social conformity, while undervaluing other important ones, such as creativity and common sense.

    The most serious misuse of tests is rooted in the mistaken belief that a test reveals basic unchanging qualities of mind or character. Psychologist W. Curtis Banks notes that many intelligence tests were standardized using homogeneous groups of white males, instead of groups consisting of equal proportions of various minorities. When norms from such tests are used to predict performance, minority group members are at a serious disadvantage.

5. Howard Gardner has challenged the idea of intelligence as a single, general ability. He believes that there are at least seven different kinds of "intelligences" and that each society or culture determines the relative importance of each. Gardner's seven intelligences include linguistic, logical-mathematical, musical, spatial, bodily-kinesthetic, interpersonal, and intrapersonal. Gardner's theory recognizes that people think differently, use different strategies for learning, and have different ways of mentally representing information.

    Robert Sternberg has introduced the notion of practical intelligence, which he defines as the ability to adapt to existing environments, to change an environment so as to make it more suitable to one's interests and abilities, and to select a new environment. With Richard Wagner, Sternberg has developed a test of practical intelligence, which measures attributes of people already successfully employed in a specific field.

6. Some neuroscientists propose to measure intelligence in a way that bypasses both mind and environment. The P300 is a brain wave that is evoked by a sudden stimulus that interrupts an ongoing cognitive task. The theory is that the "smarter" brains will have smaller P300 waves over time because they adjust more rapidly and absorb new inputs more readily. Whether these measures are valid, however, is as yet unknown.

Progress Test

1. **d.** is the answer. If we divide 9, the measured mental age, by 6, the chronological age, and multiply the result by 100, we obtain 150. (video; p. 335)

2. **a.** is the answer. (video; p. 343)

   b. & c. The SAT and ACT yield separate math and verbal scores, but not an overall intelligence score.

   d. The Stanford-Binet yields an overall IQ score only.

3. **b.** is the answer. (video; p. 344)

   a. This answer refers to a test's content validity.

   c. This answer refers to a test-retest reliability.

   d. This answer refers to predictive validity.

4. **c.** is the answer. French compulsory education laws brought more children into the school system and the government didn't want to rely on teachers' subjective judgments to determine which children would require special help. (video; p. 335)

   a. & b. Binet's test was intended for children, and Binet specifically rejected the idea that his test measured inborn intelligence, which is an abstract capacity that cannot be quantified.

   d. This was not a purpose of the test, which dealt with children in the school system.

5. **c.** is the answer. (pp. 356–357)

   a. On the contrary, many *group* differences are highly significant, even though they tell us nothing about specific *individuals*.

   b. Although heredity contributes to individual differences in intelligence, it does not necessarily contribute to group differences.

   d. The text does not present evidence that group differences are decreasing.

6. **a.** is the answer. (p. 349)

   b. Down syndrome is normally caused by an extra, rather than a missing, chromosome.

   c. & d. Down syndrome is a genetic disorder that is manifest during the earliest stages of prenatal development, well before malnutrition and exposure to drugs would produce their harmful effects on the developing fetus.

7. **c.** is the answer. Reification is a reasoning error, in which an abstract concept like IQ is regarded as though it were real. (pp. 344–350)

8. **c.** is the answer. Predictive validity is the extent to which tests predict wht they are intended to predict. (video; p. 345)

   a. Reliability is the consistency with which a test samples the particular behavior of interest.

   b. Content validity is the degree to which a test measures what it is designed to measure.

   d. Standardization is the process of defining meaningful test scores based on the performance of a representative group.

9. **e.** is the answer. (video; p. 335)

10. **a.** is the answer. (video; p. 335)

11. **a.** is the answer. Weinberg's study indicates that a privileged, middle-class upbringing results in the same range of intelligence scores, regardless of one's race. (p. 357)

12. **a.** is the answer. (p. 346)

    c. & d. Most modern tests have high reliabilities of about +.9; their validity scores are much lower.

13. **a.** is the answer. (p. 348)

14. **e.** is the answer. (pp. 350–351)

15. **a.** is the answer. Terman and Galton both believed that important traits, such as intelligence, are inherited. (video; p. 336)

    b., c., d., & e. Neither the program nor the text describes the viewpoints of Binet, Sternberg, Gardner, or Wagner concerning the determinants of intelligence.

16. **b.** is the answer. (video; p. 345)

17. **d.** is the answer. Up to an intelligence score of about 120, there is a positive correlation between intelligence and creativity. But beyond this point the correlation disappears, indicating that factors other than intelligence are also involved. (p. 351)

    a. The ability to think imaginatively and intelligence are *both* components of creativity.

    b. Creativity, the capacity to produce ideas that are novel and valuable, is related to and depends in part on intelligence but cannot be considered simply a kind of intelligence.

    c. Beyond an intelligence score of about 120 there is no correlation between intelligence scores and creativity.

18. **c.** is the answer. (p. 348)

19. **c.** is the answer. (video; p. 336)

20. **b.** is the answer. Modern intelligence tests are periodically restandardized so that the average remains near 100. (video; p. 335)

21. **d.** is the answer. That people with savant syndrome excel in one area but are intellectually retarded in others suggests that there are multiple intelligences. (p. 338)

    a. The ability to adapt defines the capacity we call intelligence.

    b. Mental retardation is an indicator of the range of human intelligence.

    c. A general intelligence factor was hypothesized by Spearman to underlie each specific factor of intelligent behavior, but its existence is controversial and remains to be proved.

22. **a.** is the answer. Identical twins who live apart have the same genetic makeup but different environments; if their scores are more similar than those of fraternal twins (with their somewhat different genetic makeups) raised together, this is evidence for the role of heredity. (p. 353)

    b. Since fraternal twins are no more genetically alike than ordinary siblings, this could not provide evidence for the role of heredity.

    c. That twins raised together have more similar scores than twins raised apart provides evidence for the role of the environment.

    d. As both sets of correlations are weak, little evidence is provided either for or against the role of heredity.

23. **d.** is the answer. Reification is the error of creating a concept and then assuming the created concept has a concrete reality. (pp. 337, 350)

    a. To rationalize is to develop self-satisfying explanations of one's behavior.

    b. The term *nominalizing* has no relevance to psychology.

c. Factor analysis is a statistical procedure that identifies clusters of related items, or factors, on a test.

e. Heritability is the proportion of variation among individuals in a trait that is attributable to genes.

24. **a.** is the answer. (video)

25. **d.** is the answer. (video; p. 343)

26. **c.** is the answer. (p. 335)

   a. This is William Stern's original formula for the intelligence quotient.

   b. & d. Neither of these formulas is used to compute the score on current intelligence tests.

27. **d.** is the answer. (video; p. 341)

28. **d.** is the answer. (p. 340)

   a. The concept of general intelligence pertains more to academic skills.

   b. Although emotional intelligence *is* a key component of social intelligence, Salovey and Mayer coined the newer term "emotional intelligence" to refer to skills such as Gerardeen's.

   c. Practical intelligence is that which is required for everyday tasks, not all of which involve emotions.

29. **d.** is the answer. Intelligence test performances begin to become predictive at about age 3 and become stable by about age 7. (p. 348)

30. **c.** is the answer. (video)

31. **c.** is the answer. (p. 337)

   a. Performance ability and intellectual ability are separate traits.

   b. This has been argued by some, but certainly not most, experts.

   d. Although many experts believe that there are multiple intelligences, this would not be the same thing as diverse acquired skills.

32. **a.** is the answer. In this view, what is intelligent in one environment may not be in another, and tests are necessarily making judgments about what's adaptive. (p. 337)

   b., c., & d. The issues of whether intelligence is innate and whether it is a single entity or multifaceted have relatively little bearing on the question of the potential for culture-free tests.

33. **b.** is the answer. (p. 342)

   c. & d. Reliability and validity are characteristics of good tests.

34. **a.** is the answer. (video)

35. **c.** is the answer. (p. 354)

   a. & b. Studies of twins, family members, and adopted children point to a significant hereditary contribution to intelligence scores. These same studies, plus others comparing children reared in neglectful or enriched environments, indicate that life experiences also significantly influence performance.

   d. Although the issue of how intelligence should be defined is controversial, intelligence tests generally have predictive validity, especially in the early years.

36. **c.** is the answer. (p. 351)

   a. Beyond an intelligence score of about 120, creativity and intelligence scores are not correlated.

b. & d. There is no evidence that creative people are more likely to be introverted or unskilled outside their particular area of creativity.

e. This may be true, but it cannot be assumed to be a result of creativity.

37. **a.** is the answer. (video; pp. 338–339)
38. **b.** is the answer. (p. 345)

    a., c., & d. Content validity is the degree to which a test measures what it claims to measure. Furthermore, *target behavior* is not a term used by intelligence researchers.

39. **a.** is the answer. If everyone has nearly the same heredity, then heritability—the variation in a trait attributed to heredity—must be low. If individuals within a group come from very similar environments, environmental differences cannot account for variation in a trait; heritability, therefore, must be high. (p. 354)

40. **e.** is the answer. (video)

Key Terms

Textbook Terms

1. **Intelligence tests** measure people's mental aptitudes and compare them to others' through numerical scores. (p. 333)

2. A concept introduced by Binet, **mental age** is the chronological age that most typically corresponds to a given level of performance. (p. 335)

3. The **Stanford-Binet** is Lewis Terman's widely used revision of Binet's original intelligence test. (p. 335)

4. The **intelligence quotient**, or **IQ**, was defined originally as the ratio of mental age to chronological age multiplied by 100. Contemporary tests of intelligence assign a score of 100 to the average performance for a given age and define other scores as deviations from this average. (p. 335)

5. Most experts define **intelligence** as the capacity for goal-directed adaptive behavior. (p. 337)

6. **Factor analysis** is a statistical procedure that identifies factors, or clusters of items, that seem to define a common ability. Using this procedure, psychologists have identified several clusters, including verbal intelligence, spatial ability, and reasoning ability factors. (p. 338)

7. **General intelligence**, or *g* factor, underlies each of the more specific intelligence clusters identified through factor analysis. (p. 338)

8. A person with **savant syndrome** has a very low intelligence score yet possesses one exceptional ability, for example, in music or drawing. (p. 338)

9. **Emotional intelligence** is the ability to perceive, express, understand, and regulate emotions. (p. 340)

10. **Aptitude tests** are designed to predict future performance. They measure your capacity to learn new information, rather than measuring what you already know. (p. 342)

11. **Achievement tests** measure a person's current knowledge. (p. 342)

12. The **Wechsler Adult Intelligence Scale (WAIS)** is the most widely used intelligence test. It is individually administered, contains 11 subtests, and yields separate verbal and performance intelligence scores, as well as an overall intelligence score. (p. 343)

13. **Standardization** is the process of defining meaningful scores on a test by pretesting a large, representative sample of people. (p. 344)

14. The **normal curve** is a bell-shaped curve that represents the distribution (frequency of occurrence) of many physical and psychological attributes. The curve is symmetrical, with most scores near the average and fewer near the extremes. (p. 344)

15. **Reliability** is the extent to which a test produces consistent results. (p. 345)

16. **Validity** is the degree to which a test measures or predicts what it is supposed to. (p. 345)

17. The **content validity** of a test is the extent to which it samples the behavior that is of interest. (p. 345)

18. A test's **criterion** is the behavior the test is designed to predict. (p. 345)

19. **Predictive validity** is the extent to which a test predicts the behavior it is designed to predict. (p. 345)

20. The two criteria that designate **mental retardation** are an IQ below 70 and difficulty adapting to the normal demands of independent living. (p. 349)

21. A common cause of severe retardation and associated physical disorders, **Down syndrome** is usually the result of an extra chromosome in the person's genetic makeup. (p. 349)

22. Most experts agree that **creativity** refers to an ability to generate novel and valuable ideas. People with high IQs may or may not be creative, which indicates that intelligence is only one component of creativity. (p. 351)

23. **Heritability** is the proportion of variation among individuals in a trait that is attributable to genetic factors. Current estimates place the heritability of intelligence at about 50 to 70 percent. (p. 354)

Program Terms

24. **Psychometrics** is the science of mental testing.

25. **Cognitive tests**, such as the Stanford-Binet and the Wechsler intelligence scales, are designed to measure various aspects of mental ability.

26. **Personality tests** such as the MMPI are designed to measure noncognitive aspects of personality such as a person's interests, values, and traits.

27. **Projective tests** such as the Rorschach help clinical psychologists assess mental and emotional problems.

28. In psychological assessment, a **norm** is the average score on a specific test that is made by a person of a given age.

29. According to Sternberg, **practical intelligence** is the ability to adapt to or change an existing environment, or to select a new environment more suitable to one's interests and abilities.

30. A brain wave that is triggered by sudden stimuli, the **P300 wave** is being studied as a possible index of intelligence. The theory is that the brain of a smarter person will have smaller P300 waves over time because it adjusts more rapidly to interruptions and absorbs new inputs more readily.

PROGRAM 17

Sex and Gender

TEXTBOOK ASSIGNMENT: None

ORIENTATION

Is gender genetically based or do we learn to be feminine or masculine? How important is gender to children? What sexual stereotypes does our culture create? These questions form the subject matter for Program 17. Although for most traits variation within any group is greater than that between groups, our identity as male or female exerts a strong influence on our self-concept and on our judgments of others.

NOTE: Answer guidelines for all Program 17 questions begin on page 326.

GOALS

After completing your study of the program and reading assignment, you should be prepared to:

1. Define sex, gender identity, gender-typing, and gender role, and discuss their origins.

2. Discuss sex differences in patterns of play, aggression, social dominance, and language.

3. Discuss how children actively participate in constructing their understanding of gender, and identify several of the positive and negative consequences of gender differences.

GUIDED STUDY

Program Assignment

Read the following objectives before you watch Program 17. As you watch, be alert for information that will help you answer each objective. Taking notes during the program will help you to formulate your answers later. After the program, write answers to the objectives. If you have access to the program on videotape, you may replay portions to refresh your memory.

1. Explain how innate biological differences are used to categorize people from birth.

2. Differentiate sex, gender, and gender role, and define the traditional male and female gender roles in the United States.

3. Explain Sandra Bem's views regarding gender roles and psychological androgyny.

4. Describe sex differences in patterns of play and in crying, and discuss the possible origins of these differences.

5. Explain how biological and psychological factors interact in promoting sex differences in physical health.

6. Explain how society promotes children's adherence to gender roles.

7. In the program, Professor Zimbardo states, "We tend to give girls roots and boys wings." What does he mean?

8. Discuss some of the positive and negative consequences of gender differences.

9. Explain Eleanor Maccoby's views on how children actively participate in shaping their own understanding of gender.

10. Discuss the relationship between gender stereotypes and innate sex differences, and explain how gender roles channel our behavior.

PROGRESS TEST

Circle your answers to the following questions and check them with the answers on page 328. If your answer is incorrect, read the explanation for why it is incorrect and then consult the appropriate pages of the text (in parentheses following the correct answer).

1. Which of the following statements concerning gender differences is true?
    a. In many traits, the sexes are alike.
    b. Most gender differences do not become obvious until adulthood.
    c. Gender differences peak in late adulthood.
    d. No consistent evidence has been found for a gender-based difference in any ability.

2. Compared to the other sex, you are less likely to be color-blind and generally more resistant to heart disease and lung cancer, but you are more vulnerable to depression. You are probably a:
    a. male.
    b. female.

3. The different ways in which parents describe their newborn sons and daughters is primarily a reflection of:
    a. differences in babies' temperaments.
    b. physical differences in newborns' size, weight, and strength.
    c. the parents' expectations regarding males and females.
    d. all of the above.

4. Gender refers to:
   a. innate physical differences between males and females.
   b. the psychological and social meanings attached to being male or female.
   c. traits shared by both males and females.
   d. the male or female identity assigned to a newborn by an obstetrician.

5. In the United States, the female gender role has been described as:
   a. aggressive, independent, dominant.
   b. attractive, creative, nurturing.
   c. ambitious, caring, dependent.
   d. gentle, emotional, dependent.

6. Which of the following sex differences has been linked to prenatal hormone stimulation?
   a. Boys play in smaller groups than girls do.
   b. Girls are less likely to prefer same-sex playmates than boys.
   c. Boys engage more often in rough-and-tumble play.
   d. Boys' play more often involves rehearsing appropriate behaviors.

7. Neuroscientist Michael Meaney states that sex differences in play exist because these behaviors "feel good." By this he means that the behaviors:
   a. stimulate different regions of the brain.
   b. trigger the release of different hormones.
   c. are socially rewarded by peers and adults.
   d. are typically gross, rather than fine, motor activities.

8. Compared to women, men are more likely to:
   a. smoke.
   b. drink alcohol.
   c. take risks.
   d. work in hazardous environments.
   e. do all of the above.

9. In terms of sex differences in susceptibility to heart disease, cirrhosis, and lung cancer:
   a. until middle age, men and women are at equal risk.
   b. beginning in late adulthood, men are at greater risk.
   c. throughout the life span, men are at greater risk.
   d. none of the above is true; susceptibility to these diseases depends primarily on innate individual differences.

10. A set of expected behaviors for males or females is called:
    a. gender assignment.   c. gender identity.
    b. gender.   d. gender role.

11. According to Sandra Bem, psychological androgyny:
    a. is more acceptable in women than in men.
    b. is more acceptable in men than in women.
    c. results in greater behavioral adaptiveness than rigid adherence to one or the other gender role.
    d. is an outmoded, sexist stereotype.

12. Sex differences in crying:
    a. develop over time as part of the socialization process.
    b. are caused by innate biological differences in males and females.
    c. are present at birth and fostered by differences in how parents treat sons and daughters.
    d. exist only in certain cultures of the world.

13. According to psychologist Jean Block, gender messages create different psychological environments for girls and boys that influence the way they think about themselves and the world around them. One such difference is that the context for girls tends to be:
    a. more structured, restricted, and supervised.
    b. more achievement oriented.
    c. less stimulating.
    d. less focused on play.
    e. both c. and d.

14. Compared to girls, boys' friendship circles tend to be:
    a. smaller.
    b. less fluid.
    c. smaller and more intimate.
    d. larger and less intimate.

15. By what age do children begin to prefer same-sex playmates?
    a. 1 year
    b. 2 years
    c. 3 years
    d. 4 years

16. According to Bem, parents who want to raise children who are less gender-typed should:
    a. make gender irrelevant to job assignments at home.
    b. completely reverse the traditional gender roles at home.
    c. avoid transmitting their social convictions to their children.
    d. encourage and reward strongly gender-typed behaviors.

17. According to Eleanor Maccoby, the preference for same-sex playmates first appears among _____ because they _____ .
    a. boys; prefer to play with those who have comparable gross motor skills
    b. boys; are more competitive than girls
    c. girls; prefer to play with those who have comparable fine motor skills
    d. girls; prefer play relations in which partners influence each other's behavior equally

KEY TERMS

Using your own words, write a brief definition or explanation of each of the following terms.

Program Terms

1. psychological androgyny

2. rough-and-tumble play

ANSWERS

Guided Study

The following guidelines provide the main points that your answers should have touched upon.

Program Assignment

1. Sex is the first, and perhaps the most basic, way in which we categorize people throughout their lives. This biological category is universal and essential for reproduction. We have very different perceptions of what the sexes are like, what they are capable of, what we expect of them, and even their value to society. Research reveals that as early as 24 hours after birth boys and girls are perceived differently. Girl babies are described as beautiful, delicate, and weak, while sons are seen as strong, coordinated, and alert. These descriptions emerge even when no actual differences in the weight, health, or strength of boy and girl babies exist.

2. Sex refers to the biologically based characteristics that distinguish males and females. Gender is the culturally defined category that includes all the psychological and social characteristics of being male or female. Learned rather than innate, gender encompasses our definitions of women and men in terms of the way they behave, the rules they follow, and the different gender roles they are encouraged and allowed to play.

    Gender roles are sets of traits based on socially prescribed expectations for the ideal male and female sexual types. The feminine gender role in the United States is gentle, emotional, and dependent; the masculine role is aggressive, independent, and dominant.

3. Although gender roles are often portrayed as mutually exclusive polar opposites, psychologist Sandra Bem argues that everyone has both masculine and feminine traits. Bem believes that this blend of traits, called *psychological androgyny*, results in greater behavioral adaptiveness than rigid adherence to one or the other gender role.

4. One of the most reliably found sex differences is that boys are more likely than girls to engage in rough-and-tumble play. This difference seems to be linked to sex hormones, although the amount and form of social play is also shaped by cultural learning experiences. Girls are more likely to engage in quieter social activities such as grooming, tending to infants, and discrete fine motor activities.

    Neuroscientist Michael Meaney of McGill University believes that these differences in social play evolved because the sex hormones of prenatal development stimulate different brain regions in males and females. Because of these brain differences, boys and girls find different forms of social play more rewarding.

    Some sex differences, such as crying, develop over time as part of the socialization process. Although both boy and girl babies cry, as they grow boys learn to suppress their crying, while girls learn that crying is acceptable and at times reinforced.

5. In all stages of the life cycle, men are at greater risk for genetically based diseases and physical handicaps, such as hemophilia and color blindness. Learned behaviors play an even larger part in sex differences in physical health. Men are more likely to smoke, drink alcohol, use weapons, take risks, and work in hazardous environments. As a result, they are more likely to die from heart disease, cirrhosis, lung cancer, emphysema, bronchitis, accidents, homicide, and suicide.

6. From the day they are born, children grow up in a world that is full of messages about gender. They are dressed differently, and they are given different toys to play with and different chores to do around the house. And, of course, they observe gender patterns in the behavior of parents and other adults. Furthermore, boys and girls are constantly rewarded for behaving in gender-appropriate ways and punished for gender-inappropriate responses. These social rewards and punishments are provided by parents, peers, and teachers.

7. According to psychologist Jean Block, gender messages create different psychological environments for girls and boys that influence the way they think about themselves and the world around them. A girl's environment tends to be more structured, restricted, and supervised, so that she is protected from experience. Furthermore, the embeddedness of girls in the family network and home insulates them to some extent from experience. Boys, who may also be more naturally curious than girls, are provided more opportunities to explore and to actively understand their world. They enter the world with the premise that they can innovate and have an impact on their environments.

    Boys also tend to have a more extensive network of friends, although these friendships are typically not as intimate as those formed by girls. For females, interpersonal relationships appear to be more salient and important.

8. Although boys are more likely to be given the freedom to take risks, to innovate, and to explore, as men they run the risk of forming an identity tied to success in a career rather than to feelings of personal satisfaction or a sense of belonging to a community or a tight-knit family.

    Although girls are more able to express their feelings and take the time to build a social support network, as women they are more likely to be the victims of societal constraints on intellectual development and career paths. Furthermore, their greater focus on feelings and moods makes women more susceptible to depression.

9. By age 2, both boys and girls begin to show a preference for same-sex playmates, playing more actively and comfortably than with those of the other sex. This voluntary segregation becomes more absolute after age 4, when children have a much firmer idea of their own and others' genders. Maccoby believes that children, rather than adults, are responsible for the tendency of children to congregate in same-sex groups. Even at a very young age they actively monitor one another and exert social pressure on those who fail to conform.

    Another reason for the separation of play groups by sex is that boys and girls use language differently. Boys are more demanding and commanding in their styles of persuasion. Girls are more likely to use language for social cohesion within the group. Consequently, boys find it easier to influence girls, rather than vice versa. At any age, friendships are more likely to last when both parties feel that they have an equal influence on each other's behavior. This may explain the tendency of girls to be the first to prefer same-sex play groups.

10. Researchers have never been able to link different sex roles to innate sex differences. In most ways, men and women are more similar than different. Furthermore, their differences are more a matter of degree than a difference in kind. For example, in physical competition, male and female abilities overlap when their training, nutrition, and expectations are comparable. The same is true for most jobs. Traditionally, however, many jobs have been defined so that only one sex is seen fit for the job in question.

It is important to recognize that how we think males and females differ influences our judgments more than how they actually do or don't differ. Gender represents an important way in which we make social categorizations about people. The gender stereotypes we form strongly influence our expectations, judgments, and behavior. We act according to these stereotypes because we think others expect it of us. We also tend to elicit from others the kind of stereotyped behavior we expect of them. Thus, gender stereotypes channel our behavior and narrow our range of experiences.

Progress Test

1. **a.** is the answer.
    b. Many gender differences appear much earlier than adulthood.
    c. Gender differences *decrease* during middle and late adulthood.
    d. Some abilities, such as spatial and mathematical ability, do show consistent gender differences.

2. **b.** is the answer.

3. **c.** is the answer.
    a. The program does not discuss this issue.
    b. On the contrary, parents describe sons and daughters differently even when there are no obvious physical differences.

4. **b.** is the answer. (video; p. 666)

5. **d.** is the answer. (video)
    a. This describes the male gender role in the United States.

6. **c.** is the answer. (video)
    a. In fact, boys tend to play in *larger* groups than girls.
    b. Both boys and girls prefer same-sex playmates.
    d. The play of both sexes often involves rehearsing adult behaviors.

7. **a.** is the answer. (video)

8. **e.** is the answer. (video)

9. **c.** is the answer. (video)

10. **d.** is the answer. (video; p. 677)
    a. In the past, when an infant's biological sex was ambiguous, physicians and parents chose the baby's gender. This was known as gender assignment. (Now tests can determine genetic sex.)
    b. Gender refers to the social category of male or female.
    c. Gender identity is an individual's sense of male or female.

11. **c.** is the answer. (video)

12. **a.** is the answer. (video)
    b., c., & d. The crying of boy and girl babies is indistinguishable at birth.

13. **a.** is the answer. (video)

14. **d.** is the answer. (video)

15. **b.** is the answer. (video)

16. **a.** is the answer. (video; p. 679)

b. Reversing the traditional gender roles would probably produce gender confusion or reverse gender-typing.

c. A parent wishing to raise less gender-typed children would probably want to transmit the conviction that gender differences are not crucial.

d. This strategy would probably result in an even more strongly gender-typed child.

17. **d.** is the answer. (video)

Key Terms

Program Terms

1. **Psychological androgyny** refers to the presence of both male and female qualities (as conventionally defined) in an individual. For example, an androgynous person might be both independent and nurturing.

2. **Rough-and-tumble play** is the very physical, often playfully aggressive pattern of play that boys engage in more often than girls.

PROGRAM *18*

Maturing and Aging

TEXTBOOK ASSIGNMENT: Chapter 4: Adolescence and Adulthood, pp. 127–145

ORIENTATION

A key assumption of modern developmental psychology is that development is lifelong. Program 18 and the accompanying reading assignment explore physical, cognitive, and social development during adulthood. Although the processes of biological aging are inevitable, lifestyle factors exert an important influence on the course of physical development during old age. The psychological aspects of aging are also influenced by a variety of factors, including expectations about aging, self-esteem, and sense of personal control.

A central theme of this material is that the elderly are not nearly as fragile as many believe. The program concludes with a discussion of age-related myths and stereotypes, including suggestions for eliminating them. The final section of the text reconsiders two major developmental issues: whether development is a continuous process or occurs in stages and whether it is characterized more by stability over time or by change.

NOTE: Answer guidelines for all Program 18 questions begin on page 339.

GOALS

After completing your study of the program and reading assignment, you should be prepared to:

1. Discuss the major physical and cognitive changes that occur in adulthood and old age.

2. Discuss the stage theories of development proposed by Erikson, Levinson, and Kübler-Ross, noting the strengths and weaknesses of each.

3. Describe several common myths about aging, noting their origins and suggestions for correcting them.

GUIDED STUDY

Textbook Assignment

The text chapter should be studied one section at a time. Before you read, preview each section by skimming it, noting headings and boldface items. Then read the appropriate section objectives from the following outline. Keep these objectives in mind and, as you read the chapter section, search for the information that will enable you to meet each objective. Once you have finished a section, write out answers for its objectives.

Adulthood (pp. 127–142)

1. Identify the major physical changes that occur in middle adulthood and later life.

2. Describe the major cognitive changes that occur in adulthood and old age.

3. Explain why stage theories of adult social development, such as that proposed by Levinson, are controversial.

4. Discuss the importance of family and career commitments in adult development, and describe the sense of well-being across the life-span.

5. Discuss the psychological reactions of those who have lost a loved one, and describe how the terminally ill cope with impending death.

Reflections on Life-Span Development (pp. 142–145)

6. State current views of psychologists on the issues of continuity versus stages and stability versus change in lifelong development.

Discovering Psychology

Program Assignment

Read the following objectives before you watch Program 18. As you watch, be alert for information that will help you answer each objective. Taking notes during the program will help you to formulate your answers later. After the program, write answers to the objectives. If you have access to the program on videotape, you may replay portions to refresh your memory.

1. Explain the concept of life-span development in psychology.

2. Outline the stages of adult development proposed by Erik Erikson.

3. Discuss Daniel Levinson's stage theory of development.

4. Discuss the nature and significance of Diana Woodruf-Pak's research on memory.

5. Discuss the physical and psychological aspects of aging, focusing on age-related myths and life-style factors that influence the consequences of aging.

6. Discuss the nature and incidence of senile dementia, and identify one reason for the persistence of negative stereotypes about aging.

7. Discuss Werner Schaie's findings regarding aging.

8. Explain why nursing homes often lead to rapid deterioration among the elderly and identify a three-step solution to the major social problems that confront the aged.

PROGRESS TEST

Circle your answers to the following questions and check them with the answers on page 343. If your answer is incorrect, read the explanation for why it is incorrect and then consult the appropriate pages of the text (in parentheses following the correct answer).

1. Which of the following stage theorists is associated with the idea that adult development proceeds through cycles of stability and change?
    a. Erikson
    b. Levinson
    c. Kohlberg
    d. Kübler-Ross
    e. Piaget

2. In Kübler-Ross's theory, which of the following is the correct sequence of stages?
    a. denial; anger; bargaining; depression; acceptance
    b. anger; denial; bargaining; depression; acceptance
    c. depression; anger; denial; bargaining; acceptance
    d. bargaining; anger; depression; denial; acceptance

3. A person's general ability to think abstractly is called _____ intelligence. This ability generally _____ with age.
    a. fluid; increases
    b. fluid; decreases
    c. crystallized; decreases
    d. crystallized; increases

4. According to Erikson, the central psychological challenges pertaining to adolescence, young adulthood, and middle age, respectively, are:
    a. identity formation; intimacy; generativity.
    b. intimacy; identity formation; generativity.
    c. generativity; intimacy; identity formation.
    d. intimacy; generativity; identity formation.

5. An elderly person who can look back on life with satisfaction and reminisce with a sense of completion has attained Erikson's stage of:
    a. generativity.
    b. intimacy.
    c. integrity.
    d. acceptance.

6. Which of the following cognitive abilities has been shown to decline during adulthood?
   a. ability to recall new information
   b. ability to recognize new information
   c. ability to learn meaningful new material
   d. ability to use judgment in dealing with daily life problems

7. Which of the following statements concerning the effects of aging is true?
   a. Aging almost inevitably leads to dementia if the individual lives long enough.
   b. Aging increases susceptibility to short-term ailments such as the flu.
   c. Significant increases in life satisfaction are associated with aging.
   d. The aging process can be significantly affected by the individual's activity patterns.

8. Of the following, which is a possible cause of dementia?
   a. stroke
   b. brain tumor
   c. alcoholism
   d. all of the above

9. Most contemporary developmental psychologists believe that:
   a. personality is essentially formed by the end of infancy.
   b. personality continues to be formed until adolescence.
   c. the shaping of personality continues during adolescence and well beyond.
   d. adolescent development has very little impact on adult personality.

10. *Psychological adolescing* refers to:
    a. developing to one's full psychological potential.
    b. age-related declines in cognitive ability.
    c. the cognitive changes that accompany senile dementia.
    d. the childish attitude of a person experiencing a midlife crisis.

11. According to Daniel Levinson, during which era of life do people face the hazard of feeling irrelevant?
    a. childhood
    b. early adulthood
    c. middle adulthood
    d. late adulthood

12. Longitudinal tests:
    a. compare people of different ages.
    b. study the same people at different times.
    c. usually involve a larger sample than do cross-sectional tests.
    d. usually involve a smaller sample than do cross-sectional tests.
    e. are less informative than cross-sectional tests.

13. The ending of menstruation is called:
    a. menarche.
    b. menopause.
    c. the midlife crisis.
    d. generativity.

14. Diana Woodruf-Pak's research on memory reveals that the eye-blink response of older rabbits and people:
    a. cannot be classically conditioned.
    b. takes longer to classically condition.
    c. takes less time to classically condition.
    d. shows no age-related changes in classical conditioning.

15. *Hospice* refers to:
    a. a group of terminally ill patients involved in educating the general public as to the needs of the dying.
    b. a group of physicians who believe that terminally ill patients should be allowed to die whenever they wish to.
    c. a research institution studying the causes of Alzheimer's disease.
    d. an organization that supports dying people and their families.

16. The cross-sectional method:
    a. compares people of different ages with one another.
    b. studies the same group of people at different times.
    c. tends to paint too favorable a picture of the effects of aging on intelligence.
    d. is a more appropriate method for studying intellectual change over the live span than the longitudinal method.

17. The *social clock* refers to:
    a. an individual or society's distribution of work and leisure time.
    b. adulthood responsibilities.
    c. typical ages for starting a career, marrying, etc.
    d. age-related changes in one's circle of friends.

18. What percentage of people over age 80 suffer from senile dementia?
    a. 5 percent
    b. 10 percent
    c. 20 percent
    d. 40 percent

19. *Ageism* refers to:
    a. age-related declines in physical and mental ability.
    b. society's negative stereotypes of the elderly.
    c. the childlike way in which the aged are treated in nursing homes.
    d. our tendency to overgeneralize from vivid examples of a phenomenon.

20. After menopause, most women:
    a. experience anxiety and a sense of worthlessness.
    b. lose interest in sex.
    c. secrete unusually high levels of estrogen.
    d. gain a lot of weight.
    e. feel a new sense of freedom.

21. After their grown children have left home, most couples experience:
    a. the distress of the "empty nest syndrome."
    b. increased strain in their marital relationship.
    c. both a. and b.
    d. greater happiness and enjoyment in their relationship.

22. Underlying Alzheimer's disease is a deterioration in neurons that produce:
    a. epinephrine.
    b. norepinephrine.
    c. serotonin.
    d. acetylcholine.
    e. dopamine.

23. A person's accumulation of stored information, called _____ intelligence, generally _____ with age.
    a. fluid; decreases
    b. fluid; increases
    c. crystallized; decreases
    d. crystallized; increases

24. Research by Werner Schaie demonstrates that those who cope best with the challenges of old age are people with:
    a. flexible attitudes.
    b. large incomes.
    c. deep religious faith.
    d. high IQs.

25. The psychological aspects of aging are influenced by:
    a. expectations about aging.
    b. self-esteem.
    c. a sense of personal control.
    d. the ability to live independently.
    e. all of the above.

26. In terms of incidence, susceptibility to short-term illnesses _____ with age and susceptibility to long-term ailments _____ with age.
    a. decreases; increases
    b. increases; decreases
    c. increases; increases
    d. decreases; decreases

27. One criticism of stage theories is that they fail to consider that development may be significantly affected by:
    a. variations in the social clock.
    b. each individual's experiences.
    c. each individual's historical and cultural setting.
    d. all of the above.

28. Compared with her teenage brother, 14-year-old Samantha is likely to play in groups that are:
    a. larger and less competitive.
    b. larger and more competitive.
    c. smaller and less competitive.
    d. smaller and more competitive.

29. The staff of nursing homes often treat the elderly in a childlike manner. What effect does this often have?
    a. It angers them and promotes their acting more independently.
    b. It comforts them, making their final years a happier time.
    c. It encourages dependence and childlike behavior.
    d. It encourages the elderly to develop a more narrow focus on what makes them happy.

30. Cross-sectional studies of intelligence are potentially misleading because:
    a. they are typically based on a very small and unrepresentative sample of people.
    b. retesting the same people over a period of years allows test performance to be influenced by practice.
    c. they compare people who are not only different in age, but of different eras, education levels, and affluence.
    d. of all the above reasons.

31. Which statement illustrates cognitive development during the course of adult life?
    a. Adults in their forties have better recognition memory than adults in their seventies.
    b. Recall and recognition memory both remain strong throughout life.
    c. Recognition memory decreases sharply at midlife.
    d. Recall memory remains strong until very late in life.
    e. Adults in their forties have better recall memory than adults in their seventies.

32. New research points to several factors that predict rapid deterioration among those in nursing homes. These include being:
    a. cheerful and cooperative.
    b. suspicious and aggressive.
    c. introverted.
    d. highly emotional.
    e. b. and c.

33. With regard to the psychological aspects of aging, which of the following is *not* true?
    a. The elderly are not as psychologically fragile as many believe.
    b. The elderly typically develop a more narrow focus on what makes them happy.
    c. Stress-related disorders are no more common among the elderly than among younger adults.
    d. The elderly are more susceptible to anxiety and depression.

34. Given the text discussion of life satisfaction patterns, which of the following people is likely to report the greatest life satisfaction?
    a. Billy, a 7-year-old second-grader
    b. Kathy, a 17-year-old high school senior
    c. Alan, a 30-year-old accountant
    d. Mildred, a 70-year-old retired teacher
    e. too little information to tell

35. Which of the following statements is consistent with the current thinking of developmental psychologists?
    a. Development occurs in a series of sharply defined stages.
    b. The first two years are the most crucial in determining the individual's personality.
    c. The consistency of personality in most people tends to increase over the life span.
    d. Social and emotional style are among the characteristics that show the least stability over the life span.

36. Research on personality development over the life span reveals that, all else being equal, an aggressive 8-year-old will probably become a(n) _____ 30-year-old.
    a. shy
    b. aggressive
    c. happy and well-adjusted
    d. aggressive or shy (There is no basis for such a prediction.)

37. In Levinson's theory, the early forties is a time of great struggle or even of feeling struck down by life. This has been referred to as:
    a. midlife crisis.
    b. identity crisis.
    c. menopause.
    d. generativity crisis.

38. After a series of unfulfilling relationships, 30-year-old Carlos tells a friend that he doesn't want to marry because he is afraid of losing his freedom and independence. Erikson would say that Carlos is having difficulty with the psychosocial task of:
    a. trust versus mistrust.
    b. autonomy versus doubt.
    c. intimacy versus isolation.
    d. identity versus role confusion.
    e. generativity versus stagnation.

39. Which of the following is *false*?
    a. Beginning in young adulthood there is a small, gradual loss of brain cells.
    b. Adults who remain mentally active retain more of their cognitive capacity in later years.
    c. The symptoms of Alzheimer's disease are merely an accelerated version of normal aging.
    d. As people age, the speed of their neural processes slows.

40. Society's negative stereotypes about aging persist in part because:
    a. there are few examples of happy, productive people among the aged.
    b. of the increasing prevalence of memory disorders such as senile dementia and Alzheimer's disease.
    c. the percentage of elderly people in the population is decreasing.
    d. dramatic negative images of the elderly are overrepresented in our memory.

KEY TERMS

Using your own words, write a brief definition or explanation of each of the following terms.

Textbook Terms

1. menopause

2. Alzheimer's disease

3. cross-sectional study

4. longitudinal study

5. crystallized intelligence

6. fluid intelligence

7. social clock

8. hospice

Program Terms

9. biological senescing

10. life-span development

11. psychological adolescing

12. selective optimization

13. senile dementia

ANSWERS

Guided Study

The following guidelines provide the main points that your answers should have touched upon.

Textbook Assignment

1. Muscular strength, reaction time, sensory keenness, and cardiac output all peak by the mid-twenties and begin to decline thereafter. Health and exercise habits are important factors in the rate of physical decline.
   For women, menopause is the foremost biological change related to aging. Despite popular belief, menopause usually does not create psychological problems for women. Men experience a gradual decline in sperm count, testosterone level, and speed of erection and ejaculation as they get older.

Decline in the functioning of the body's disease-fighting immune system makes the elderly more susceptible to life-threatening ailments such as cancer and pneumonia. Older people suffer short-term ailments, such as colds and the flu, less often, however.

Aging also slows neural processes and results in a small, gradual loss of brain cells. Some adults experience the mental erosion of dementia that results from a series of strokes, a brain tumor, or alcoholism. A small percentage of older adults suffer Alzheimer's disease, in which acetylcholine-producing neurons degenerate.

2. Individual variation in learning ability and memory throughout adulthood makes it difficult to generalize about age-related changes in cognition. Typically, however, the ability to recall (but not to recognize) new information, particularly material that is not meaningful to the individual, declines.

Longitudinal studies of intelligence have laid to rest the myth that intelligence sharply declines with age. Whether intelligent performance on a task increases or decreases with age depends largely on the task. Tests of accumulated knowledge reveal that crystallized intelligence increases up to old age. Tests measuring one's ability to reason abstractly reveal that fluid intelligence decreases with age. These differences help explain why people in different professions produce their most notable work at different ages.

3. Levinson suggested that adults progress through stages of stability alternating with times of upheaval and change. For example, the early forties were supposedly a time of emotional instability, when a "midlife transition," or crisis, was likely. Research has not found, however, that emotional distress of this kind peaks at any particular age.

Researchers are skeptical of stage theories of adult social development for several reasons. For one, the settings of the *social clock* prescribing "proper" ages for various life events vary from culture to culture and from era to era. Even more important than one's age in defining new life stages are life events such as marriage, parenthood, job changes, divorce, and retirement. Increasingly, events such as these are occurring at unpredictable ages.

4. According to Erikson, the tasks of forming close relationships (intimacy) and being productive and supporting future generations (generativity) dominate adulthood. Freud expressed the same viewpoint in saying that the healthy adult is one who can love and work.

Despite the rising divorce rate, most married Europeans and North Americans generally feel happier than those who are unmarried, separated, or divorced. Although having a child is for most people a happy event, as children begin to absorb time, money, and emotional energy, satisfaction with marriage often declines.

Despite the popular belief that the departure of adult children usually causes parents to feel great distress and a loss of purpose, research reveals that those whose nest has emptied generally report greater happiness and enjoyment of their marriage.

Studies of the relationship between happiness and having a career have compared employed and unemployed women. The results of these studies reveal that what matters is not which role(s) a woman occupies—as worker, wife, and/ or mother—but the quality of her experience in each. People of all ages report similar feelings of happiness and satisfaction with life. As people age, however, emotions typically become less intense.

5. The normal range of reactions to the loss of a loved one is much wider than most people suppose. Grief is especially severe when death comes before its expected time.

From her interviews with dying patients, Kübler-Ross proposed that the terminally ill pass through five stages: denial of death; anger; bargaining for more time; depression; and, finally, peaceful acceptance. Critics have questioned the generality of such stages, however, stressing that each person's experience is unique.

6. Although research casts doubt on the idea that life proceeds through neatly defined, age-linked stages of cognitive, moral, and social development, the concept of stage remains useful. Stage theories show the order in which abilities develop and help focus awareness on how people of one age think and act differently when they arrive at a later age.

   Recent research has revealed that there is a consistency to personality due to an underlying stability in basic social and emotional styles. Although the first 2 years of life provide a poor basis for predicting eventual traits, after age 30 dispositions become quite stable and attitudes much more predictable.

Program Assignment

1. Until recently, most developmental theorists focused primarily on early life, believing that after adolescence few important changes occurred. Beginning in the 1950s, however, research on aging has revealed otherwise. One of the most important things to emerge from this research was the idea of life-span development—the idea that many aspects of human nature continue to develop throughout the life cycle.

   Development is not the same as growth, however; it includes both biological senescing (growing old physically) and psychological adolescing (developing psychologically to one's full potential.)

2. Erik Erikson identified eight stages of psychosocial development, from birth to late adulthood, in which the individual is challenged by specific crises or developmental tasks. In each task, the individual must balance or integrate two opposite demands. Failure to do so may lead to isolation or feelings of unfulfillment.

   During early adulthood, the crisis of *intimacy versus isolation* focuses on our ability to make a full commitment to another person. This requires accepting responsibility and giving up some privacy and independence. Failure to resolve this crisis can lead to isolation and a lack of meaningful psychological connections with other people. Research reveals that anything that isolates people from sources of social support increases their risk for a number of physical and mental problems.

   During the thirties and forties, people struggle with the crisis of *generativity versus stagnation*. At this time, people usually move beyond the focus on self to wider commitments to family, work, and society. For those who haven't resolved the earlier crises of intimacy and identity, a midlife crisis may occur. People in such a crisis are self-indulgent; they want to give up their commitments for "one last fling," and opt for freedom at the expense of security and responsibility to others.

   The final crisis of *ego-integrity versus despair* comes at the end of the life course. A person who has successfully resolved the earlier crises of life enjoys a sense of wholeness and satisfaction with life. When the person has a sense of regret at having too many unfulfilled aspirations, this final stage may be accompanied by feelings of futility, despair, and anger.

3. Daniel Levinson of Yale University considers the life course of adults as consisting of a sequence of developmental stages or eras. The first era, childhood and adolescence, runs from birth until about age 20. The second, early adulthood, is from age 20 until the early 40s; during this time, people

establish a place in society, begin a career, and start a family. The era of middle adulthood runs from the early forties to the early sixties; during this stage, people assume the major responsibilities of their lives. During late adulthood, which runs from the early sixties to the early eighties, people begin to move out of the center stage of society. Although they no longer have major responsibilities and may enjoy life more, they run the risk of feeling that they are now irrelevant.

4. Diana Woodruf-Pak (University of California, Berkeley) is using classical conditioning to explore age-related memory changes in humans and rabbits. In her research, a tone is sounded just before subjects receive a puff of air to their eyes. Over successive trials, the subjects learn to avoid the air puff by blinking to the tone. She has found that older rabbits take two to three times longer to learn than younger rabbits. Starting as early as the forties, humans also take longer. Since the neural circuits underlying this form of learning are well known (from research by Richard Thompson, as you'll recall from Program 8), Woodruf-Pak's research may lead to surgical or pharmacological treatments that improve memory and learning in the elderly.

5. Although the processes of biological aging are inevitable, diet and exercise can retard the physical aspects of aging. The psychological aspects of aging are influenced by a variety of factors, including expectations, self-esteem, sense of personal control, and the ability to live independently.

    Research has shown that the elderly are not as psychologically fragile as many believe. They are not more susceptible to anxiety or depression and do not experience an increase in stress-related disorders, despite the stressful life events that accompany aging. The elderly are surprisingly hardy, given their physical changes, sources of stress, and society's negative attitudes toward aging. Through *selective optimization*, the elderly typically develop a more narrow focus on what makes them happy, for example, by limiting social contacts to those most important in their lives.

6. Dementia is a severe deterioration in mental abilities due to brain injury or disease. Senile dementia is a late life condition in which a gradual reduction in mental efficiency occurs due to biochemical and neuronal changes in the brain. Dementia can have devastating consequences, including loss of memory, learning and language abilities, orientation, and self-care. Only 5 percent of people over 65 and 20 percent of those over 80 suffer from dementia.

    Research questions why society's negative stereotypes about aging persist. It may be because of the availability heuristic. Dramatic or vivid media images of the elderly are overrepresented in our memory so that we get a falsely exaggerated picture despite the numerous examples of outstanding accomplishments and self-satisfaction among the elderly.

7. Werner Schaie (Pennsylvania State University) has found that age-related changes occur much more slowly than most people think. Cognitive abilities peak in the forties and fifties, and then follow a trajectory that depends on each individual's lifestyle. People who do well as they age are those who lead a healthy, active life, and have a flexible attitude that allows them to enjoy new experiences and take the changes that occur with aging as challenges rather than threats and defeats.

8. The physical and psychological care of nursing homes is often inadequate. There is a loss of privacy, individuality, and self-management. Sexuality is discouraged and family contacts often diminish because of the unpleasantness of the environment. The excessive medication and bed rest often accelerate physical and mental decline. Staff often treat the elderly as children

rather than as wise senior citizens. The more they are perceived this way, the more childlike and dependent they become.

New research points to several factors that predict rapid deterioration and death among those in nursing homes. Ironically, being cheerful, cooperative, and outward-reaching results in more rapid deterioration than being suspicious and aggressive.

Many of the problems of old age can be ameliorated by education, training, and environmental changes. The first step is to dispel myths about aging and change society's negative stereotypes about the elderly. The next is to redesign the environment and health care delivery systems to make them more accessible to the elderly. Third, early intervention by therapists to identify and help those experiencing difficulty is needed.

Progress Test

1. **b.** is the answer. (video; p. 136)

    a. Erikson was best known for his theory of psychosocial development over the life span.

    b. Piaget is known for his work on cognitive development in children.

    c. Kohlberg is known for his work on the development of moral reasoning.

    d. Kübler-Ross is known for her work on the emotional stages through which the terminally ill pass.

2. **a.** is the answer. (p. 141)

3. **b.** is the answer. (p. 135)

    a. Fluid intelligence tends to decrease with age.

    c. & d. Crystallized intelligence refers to the accumulation of facts and general knowledge that takes place during a person's life. Crystallized intelligence generally *increases* with age.

4. **a.** is the answer. (video)

5. **c.** is the answer. (video, p. 142)

    a. Generativity is associated with middle adulthood.

    b. Intimacy is associated with young adulthood.

    d. The term *acceptance* is not associated with Erikson's theory; rather, it is the final stage in Kübler-Ross's theory of emotions experienced by the terminally ill.

6. **a.** is the answer. (pp. 133–134)

    b., c., & d. These cognitive abilities remain essentially unchanged as the person ages.

7. **d.** is the answer. "Use it or lose it" seems to be the rule: Often, changes in activity patterns contribute significantly to problems regarded as being part of usual aging. (video; p. 132)

    a. Most elderly people do not develop dementia; even among the very old, the risk of dementia is only 40 percent.

    b. Although the elderly are more subject to long-term ailments than younger adults, they actually suffer fewer short-term ailments.

    c. There is no tendency for people of any particular age to report greater happiness or satisfaction with life.

8. **d.** is the answer. (p. 132)

9. **c.** is the answer. (video)

10. **a.** is the answer. (video)

11. **d.** is the answer. (video, p. 136)

12. **b.** is the answer. (p. 134)

   a. This answer describes cross-sectional research.

   c. & d. Sample size does not distinguish cross-sectional from longitudinal research.

   e. Just the opposite is true.

13. **b.** is the answer. (p. 128)

   a. Menarche refers to the onset of menstruation.

   c. When it does occur, the midlife crisis is a psychological, rather than biological, phenomenon.

   d. Generativity is Erikson's term for productivity during middle adulthood.

14. **b.** is the answer. (video)

15. **d.** is the answer. Hospice staff and volunteers work in special facilities and in people's homes to support the terminally ill. (p. 142)

16. **a.** is the answer. (p. 134)

   b. This answer describes the longitudinal research method.

   c. & d. Cross-sectional studies have tended to exaggerate the effects of aging on intellectual functioning; for this reason they may not be the most appropriate method for studying life-span development.

17. **c.** is the answer. Different societies and eras have somewhat different ideas about the age at which major life events should ideally occur. (p. 136)

18. **c.** is the answer. (video)

19. **b.** is the answer. (video)

20. **e.** is the answer. (p. 128)

   a. Most women do not experience anxiety and distress following menopause; moreover, the woman's experience will depend largely on her expectations and attitude.

   b. Sexual interest does not decline in postmenopausal women.

   c. Menopause is caused by a *reduction* in estrogen.

   d. This was not mentioned in the text.

21. **d.** is the answer. (p. 138)

   a., b., & c. Most couples do not feel a loss of purpose or marital strain following the departure of grown children.

22. **d.** is the answer. Significantly, drugs that block the activity of the neurotransmitter acetylcholine produce Alzheimer-like symptoms. (p. 132)

   a. & b. Epinephrine and norepinephrine are hormones produced by glands of the endocrine system.

   c. & e. Serotonin and dopamine are neurotransmitters, and hence produced by neurons, but they have not been implicated in Alzheimer's disease.

23. **d.** is the answer. (p. 135)

   a. & b. Fluid intelligence, which decreases with age, refers to the ability to reason abstractly.

   c. Crystallized intelligence increases with age.

24. **a.** is the answer. (video)

25. **e.** is the answer. (video)

26. **a.** is the answer. (p. 131)

27. **d.** is the answer. (pp. 136–137)

28. **c.** is the answer. (p. 123)

29. **c.** is the answer. (video)

30. **c.** is the answer. Because several variables (education, affluence, etc.) generally distinguish the various groups in a cross-sectional study, it is impossible to rule out that one or more of these, rather than aging, is the cause of the measured intellectual decrease. (p. 134)

    a. Small sample size and unrepresentativeness generally are not limitations of cross-sectional research.

    b. This refers to longitudinal research.

31. **e.** is the answer. (p. 133)

    a. & c. In tests of recognition memory, the performance of older persons shows little decline.

    b. & d. The ability to recall material, especially meaningless material, declines with age.

32. **a.** is the answer. (video)

33. **d.** is the answer. (video)

34. **e.** is the answer. Research has not uncovered a tendency for people of any particular age group to report greater feelings of satisfaction or well-being. (p. 140)

35. **c.** is the answer. Although some researchers emphasize consistency and others emphasize potential for change, they all agree that consistency increases over the life span. (pp. 143–144)

    a. One criticism of stage theories is that development does not occur in sharply defined stages.

    b. Research has shown that individuals' adult personalities cannot be predicted from their first two years.

    d. Social and emotional style are two of the most stable traits.

36. **b.** is the answer. Because basic social and emotional styles show an underlying stability, the most aggressive children typically become the most aggressive adults. (p. 144)

37. **a.** is the answer. (video; p. 136)

    b. In Erikson's theory, identity is the crisis of adolescence, not middle adulthood.

    c. Menopause usually comes about a decade later and refers specifically to the cessation of the menstrual cycle in women.

    d. In Erikson's theory, generativity refers to the impulse toward productivity and is the crisis of middle adulthood.

38. **c.** is the answer. Carlos's age and struggle to form a close relationship place him squarely in this stage. (p. 123)

    a. Trust versus mistrust is the psychosocial task of infancy.

    b. Autonomy versus doubt is the psychosocial task of toddlerhood.

d. Identity versus role confusion is the psychosocial task of adolescence.

   e. Generativity versus stagnation is the task of middle adulthood.

39. **c.** is the answer. The neural deterioration that accompanies Alzheimer's disease is an abnormality. (p. 132)

40. **d.** is the answer. This is the availability heuristic in operation. (video)

   a. In fact, there are many examples of happy, productive people among the aged.

   b. The incidence of these disorders is not increasing.

   c. The percentage of elderly people is *increasing*.

Key Terms

Textbook Terms

1. **Menopause** is the cessation of menstruation and typically occurs in the early fifties. It also refers to the biological and psychological changes experienced during a woman's years of declining ability to reproduce. (p. 128)

2. **Alzheimer's disease** is an irreversible brain disorder caused by deterioration of neurons that produce acetylcholine. It is characterized by a progressive loss of memory and general cognitive function. (p. 132)

3. In a **cross-sectional study**, people of different ages are compared with one another. (p. 134)

4. In a **longitudinal study**, the same people are tested and retested over a period of years. (p. 134)

5. **Crystallized intelligence** refers to those aspects of intellectual ability, such as vocabulary and general knowledge, that reflect accumulated learning. Crystallized intelligence tends to increase with age. (p. 135)

6. **Fluid intelligence** refers to a person's ability to reason speedily and abstractly. Fluid intelligence tends to decline with age. (p. 135)

7. The **social clock** refers to the culturally preferred timing of social events, such as leaving home, marrying, having children, and retiring. (p. 136)

8. A **hospice** is an organization that provides support for the terminally ill and for their families either in specialized facilities or in people's own homes. (p. 142)

Program Terms

9. **Biological senescing** refers to the physical changes that accompany aging.

10. **Life-span development** refers to the new perspective in psychology that significant changes in personality and development occur throughout the life cycle.

11. **Psychological adolescing** refers to the development of one's psychological potential that takes place even during old age.

12. **Selective optimization** is making the best of one's resources at each stage of life. For example, through selective optimization the elderly typically develop a more narrow focus on what makes them happy.

13. **Senile dementia** is a late life condition in which a gradual reduction in mental efficiency occurs due to biochemical and neuronal changes in the brain. It includes both biological senescing (growing old physically) and psychological adolescing (developing psychologically to one's full potential).

PROGRAMS *19 & 20*

The Power of the Situation
Constructing Social Reality

TEXTBOOK ASSIGNMENT: Chapter 18: Social Psychology, pp. 549–564; 571–578; 580–587

ORIENTATION

Programs 19 and 20 and Chapter 18 of the text explore the powerful influences of social situations on the behavior of individuals. Central to this topic are research studies on attitudes and actions, conformity, compliance, and group influence, as well as aggression, altruism, and attraction. The social principles that emerge help us to understand how individuals are influenced by advertising, political candidates, and the various groups to which they belong. Although social influences are powerful, it is important to remember the significant role of individuals in choosing and creating the social situations they are influenced by.

Although there is some terminology for you to learn in this unit, your primary task is to absorb the findings of the many research studies discussed. The chapter headings, which organize the findings, should prove especially useful to you here. In addition, you might, for each main topic (conformity, group influence, aggression, and so on), ask yourself the question, "What situational factors promote this phenomenon?" The research findings can then form the basis for your answers.

NOTE: Answer guidelines for all questions for Programs 19 and 20 begin on page 361.

GOALS

After completing your study of the program and reading assignment, you should be prepared to:

1. Discuss the origins and scope of social psychology.

2. Discuss the reciprocal influences among attitudes, cognitive control, and actions.

3. Discuss how the presence of others may produce conformity, social facilitation, social loafing, deindividuation, or groupthink.

4. Discuss the impact of biological and social factors in promoting aggression, altruism, and attraction toward others.

GUIDED STUDY

Textbook Assignment

The text chapter should be studied one section at a time. Before you read, preview each section by skimming it, noting headings and boldface items. Then

read the appropriate section objectives from the following outline. Keep these objectives in mind and, as you read the chapter section, search for the information that will enable you to meet each objective. Once you have finished a section, write out answers for its objectives.

Social Thinking (pp. 549–554)

1. Discuss attribution theory, focusing on the fundamental attribution error, and describe some possible effects of attribution.

2. Define *attitude* and identify the conditions under which attitudes predict behavior.

3. Describe how actions influence attitudes and explain how cognitive dissonance theory accounts for this phenomenon.

Social Influence (pp. 555–564)

4. Describe the results of Asch's experiments on conformity and distinguish between normative and informational social influence. (text and video)

5. Summarize the findings from Milgram's obedience studies. (text and video)

6. Discuss how the presence of others may produce social facilitation, social loafing, or deindividuation.

7. Describe group polarization, and show how it can be a source of groupthink.

8. Discuss how personal control and social control interact in guiding behavior and explain how a minority can influence the majority.

Social Relations (pp. 571–578; 580–587)

9. Describe the impact of biology, aversive events, and learning experiences on aggressive behavior.

10. Discuss the effects of television violence and pornographic films on viewers.

11. Describe and explain the bystander effect.

12. Discuss how social exchange theory, social norms, and evolutionary psychology variously explain altruism.

13. Identify the determinants of social attraction and distinguish between passionate and companionate love.

Program Assignment

Read the following objectives before you watch Programs 19 and 20. As you watch, be alert for information that will help you answer each objective. Taking notes during the programs will help you to formulate your answers later. After the programs, write answers to the objectives. If you have access to the programs on videotape, you may replay portions to refresh your memory.

Program 19

1. Describe the scope of social psychology, and discuss its origins.

2. Explain Kurt Lewin's findings regarding the effects of different leadership styles on group behavior.

3. Explain the nature and origins of the fundamental attribution error.

4. Discuss Philip Zimbardo's prison experiment, including ethical considerations regarding its conduct.

5. Describe two experiments in which social power was shown to have positive effects.

Program 20

6. Explain the concept of "cognitive control" and its role in creating an "us versus them" perception of the world.

7. Discuss the results and significance of Jane Elliot's classroom experiment.

8. Identify four factors that account for the self-fulfilling prophecy of the Pygmalion effect.

9. Explain the nature of the "jigsaw classroom."

10. Discuss six tactics used by salespeople, fund-raisers, and advertisers to influence people.

PROGRESS TEST

Circle your answers to the following questions and check them with the answers on page 365. If your answer is incorrect, read the explanation for why it is incorrect and then consult the appropriate pages of the text (in parentheses following the correct answer).

1. According to cognitive dissonance theory, dissonance is most likely to occur when:
   a. a person's behavior is not based on strongly held attitudes.
   b. two people have conflicting attitudes and find themselves in disagreement.
   c. an individual does something that is personally disagreeable.
   d. an individual is coerced into doing something that he or she does not want to do.

2. One reason that people comply with social pressure is to avoid rejection or gain approval. This is called:
   a. informational social influence.
   b. the fundamental attribution error.
   c. normative social influence.
   d. deindividuation.

3. The phenomenon in which individuals lose their identity and relinquish normal restraints when they are part of a group is called:
   a. groupthink.
   b. cognitive dissonance.
   c. empathy.
   d. deindividuation.

4. Social psychologists are primarily concerned with:
   a. evolutionary pressures on how people behave in groups.
   b. how human behavior is influenced by other people.
   c. cross-cultural differences in human behavior.
   b. the behavior of people in the workplace.

5. In Lewin's study, the boys were the most productive when the group leader adopted which style of leadership?
   a. autocratic
   b. laissez-faire
   c. democratic
   d. It depended on the size of the group.

6. Findings from cross-cultural studies of aggression suggest that aggression is:
   a. not a human instinct.
   b. just one instinct among many.
   c. instinctive but shaped by learning.
   d. the most important of the human instincts.

7. Research studies have indicated that the tendency of viewers to misperceive normal sexuality, devalue their partners, and trivialize rape is:
   a. increased by exposure to pornography.
   b. not changed after exposure to pornography.
   c. decreased in men by exposure to pornography.
   d. decreased in both men and women by exposure to pornography.

8. Increasing the number of people that are present during an emergency tends to:
   a. increase the likelihood that people will cooperate in rendering assistance.
   b. decrease the empathy that people feel for the victim.
   c. increase the role that social norms governing helping will play.
   d. decrease the likelihood that anyone will help.

9. In his study of obedience, Stanley Milgram found that the majority of subjects:
   a. refused to shock the learner even once.
   b. complied with the experiment until the "learner" first indicated pain.
   c. complied with the experiment until the "learner" began screaming in agony.
   d. complied with all the demands of the experiment.

10. The fundamental attribution error refers to the tendency of people to:
    a. focus on personal traits in explaining others' behavior.
    b. underestimate the effects of the situation on others' behavior.
    c. conform to the will of a group under most circumstances.
    d. do both a. and b.

11. Which of the following conclusions did Milgram draw from his studies of obedience?
    a. Even ordinary people, without any particular hostility, can become agents in a destructive process.
    b. Most people are able, under the proper circumstances, to suppress their natural aggressiveness.
    c. The need to be accepted by others is a powerful motivating force.
    d. All of the above conclusions were reached.

12. In one experiment, college men were physically aroused and then introduced to an attractive woman. Compared to men who had not been aroused, these men:
    a. reported more positive feelings toward the woman.
    b. reported more negative feelings toward the woman.
    c. were ambiguous about their feelings toward the woman.
    d. were more likely to feel that the woman was out of their league in terms of attractiveness.
    e. focused more on the woman's attractiveness and less on her intelligence and personality.

13. Regarding the influence of alcohol and testosterone on aggressive behavior, which of the following is true?
    a. Consumption of alcohol increases aggressive behavior; injections of testosterone reduce aggressive behavior.
    b. Consumption of alcohol reduces aggressive behavior; injections of testosterone increase aggressive behavior.

c. Consumption of alcohol and injections of testosterone both promote aggressive behavior.
d. Consumption of alcohol and injections of testosterone both reduce aggressive behavior.

14. The Stanford prison experiment demonstrated that:
    a. education is the single most important factor in predicting whether a person will conform to group pressure.
    b. a simple request for assistance often is all that is needed to mobilize empathy from a stranger.
    c. deep down, most people are basically kind-hearted.
    d. social roles, and the norms and expectations they create, have a powerful influence on our behavior.

15. In one experiment, researcher Tom Moriarty staged the theft of a radio in front of sunbathers on a beach. Onlookers intervened to prevent the robbery when:
    a. the "victim" simply asked them to watch her things.
    b. a large sign warned them that the beach was patrolled by police.
    c. the "thief" was of the opposite sex.
    d. they were in a good mood after "finding" some money on the beach.

16. Most people prefer mirror-image photographs of their faces. This is best explained by:
    a. the principle of equity.
    b. the principle of self-disclosure.
    c. the mere exposure effect.
    d. mirror-image perceptions.
    e. deindividuation.

17. Which of the following best expresses the social exchange theory of altruistic behavior?
    a. People help others because they have learned that it is right to help those who have helped them.
    b. People help others out of a sense of guilt or pity.
    c. People help others because they expect to benefit from doing so.
    d. People are most likely to extend help to those who are related to them.

18. When subjects in an experiment were told that a woman to whom they would be speaking had been instructed to act in a friendly or unfriendly way, most of them subsequently attributed her behavior to:
    a. the situation.
    b. the situation *and* her personal disposition.
    c. her personal disposition.
    d. their own skill or lack of skill in a social situation.

19. Which of the following most accurately states the effects of crowding on behavior?
    a. Crowding makes people irritable.
    b. Crowding sometimes intensifies people's reactions.
    c. Crowding promotes altruistic behavior.
    d. Crowding usually weakens the intensity of people's reactions.

20. In Ellen Langer's experiment, Air Force ROTC cadets who were treated like real pilots during a flight simulation:
   a. performed better on the same test of vision they had taken before the experiment began.
   b. obediently followed the experimenter's order to "bomb" a target.
   c. were less likely to follow orders than cadets who were treated less professionally.
   d. were more likely to re-enlist in the ROTC training program.

21. Psychologists refer to the power of people's beliefs to give different meanings to situations as:
   a. the Pygmalion effect.
   b. deindividuation.
   c. the fundamental attribution error.
   d. cognitive control.

22. Which of the following best summarizes the relative importance of personal control and social control of our behavior?
   a. Situational influences on behavior generally are much greater than personal influences.
   b. Situational influences on behavior generally are slightly greater than personal influences.
   c. Personal influences on behavior generally are much greater than situational influences.
   d. Situational influences and personal influences interact in determining our behavior.

23. Which of the following is important in promoting conformity in individuals?
   a. whether an individual's behavior will be observed by others in the group
   b. whether the individual is male or female
   c. the size of the room in which a group is meeting
   d. the age of the members in a group
   e. whether the individual is of a higher status than other group members

24. Which theory describes how we explain others' behavior as being due to internal dispositions or external situations?
   a. social exchange theory
   b. reward theory
   c. two-factor theory
   d. attribution theory

25. When Jane Elliot divided her students into brown-eyed and blue-eyed groups, what did she observe?
   a. Students with the lowest self-esteem were the most likely to go along with the experiment.
   b. Most students quickly saw the absurdity of equating intelligence with eye color.
   c. The blue-eyed children acted as if they were superior to the brown-eyed children.
   d. Children who were members of actual minority groups "got the message" more quickly than their majority classmates.

26. After waiting in line for an hour to buy concert tickets, Teresa is told that the concert is sold out. In her anger she pounds her fist on the ticket counter, frightening the clerk. Teresa's behavior is best explained by:
    a. evolutionary psychology.
    b. the reciprocity norm.
    c. social exchange theory.
    d. the frustration-aggression principle.

27. Before she gave a class presentation favoring gun control legislation, Wanda opposed it. Her present attitude favoring such legislation can best be explained by:
    a. attribution theory.
    b. cognitive dissonance theory.
    c. social exchange theory.
    d. evolutionary psychology.
    e. two-factor theory.

28. In the Rosenthal and Jacobsen experiment, the academic performance of some students improved over the course of the school year because:
    a. they were seated at the front of the class.
    b. the teachers were led to believe that these students were more capable and so treated them accordingly.
    c. the children were told that they were smarter than others in the class.
    d. being more attractive than their classmates, these children received more of the teacher's attention.

29. What is the central idea behind the "jigsaw classroom"?
    a. Children learn best when grouped with others according to ability.
    b. Children learn best when grouped with others of greater, and lesser, ability.
    c. Cooperation, not competition, fuels achievement.
    d. Prejudice is less likely to develop in multiracial classrooms.

30. Which of the following would most likely be subject to social facilitation?
    a. running quickly around a track
    b. proofreading a page for spelling errors
    c. typing a letter with accuracy
    d. playing a difficult piece on a musical instrument
    e. giving a speech

31. Jane and Sandy were best friends as freshmen. Jane joined a sorority; Sandy didn't. By the end of their senior year, they found that they had less in common with each other than with the other members of their respective circles of friends. Which of the following phenomena most likely explains their feelings?
    a. group polarization
    b. groupthink
    c. deindividuation
    d. social facilitation

32. José is the one student member on the college board of trustees. At the board's first meeting, José wants to disagree with the others on several issues but in each case decides to say nothing. Studies on conformity suggest all except one of the following are factors in José's not speaking up. Which one is *not* a factor?
    a. The board is a large group.
    b. The board is prestigious and most of its members are well known.
    c. The board members are already aware that José and the student body disagree with them on these issues.
    d. Because this is the first meeting José has attended, he feels insecure and not fully competent.

33. When Robert Cialdini cites the example of the Tupperware party, what principle of persuasion is he illustrating?
    a. scarcity
    b. reciprocity
    c. consensus
    d. liking

34. An army captain who gives a controversial order to destroy a village is concerned about whether the soldiers will comply. Which of the following would promote the greatest compliance?
    a. Orders are given immediately prior to the time fixed for the attack.
    b. A decision is made to launch the attack by air.
    c. Reinforcements are sent in to assist in the attack.
    d. When several soldiers balk at the orders, they are severely reprimanded in front of the others.

35. Maria recently heard a speech calling for a ban on aerosol sprays that endanger the earth's ozone layer. Maria's subsequent decision to stop using aerosol sprays is an example of:
    a. informational social influence.
    b. normative social influence.
    c. deindividuation.
    d. social facilitation.

36. Which of the following situations should produce the *greatest* cognitive dissonance?
    a. A soldier is forced to carry out orders he finds disagreeable.
    b. A student who loves animals has to dissect a cat in order to pass biology.
    c. As part of an experiment, a subject is directed to deliver electric shocks to another person.
    d. A student volunteers to debate an issue, taking the side he personally disagrees with.

37. According to the program, the behavior of people who followed Hitler in Nazi Germany, and of those who died at Jonestown, is best explained as a function of:
    a. immaturity and moral weakness.
    b. low self-esteem.
    c. the situation in which they found themselves.
    d. the power of a charismatic but laissez-faire leader.

38. In Solomon Asch's experiment, subjects were most likely to misjudge the length of the line segment when:
    a. the differences in the line segment choices were very small.
    b. they made their judgment in the presence of a group decision that was inaccurate but unanimous.
    c. the stimuli were presented very rapidly.
    d. the task was presented as an unimportant game, rather than as an actual test of perceptual ability.

39. Having read the chapter, which of the following is best borne out by research on attraction?
    a. Birds of a feather flock together.
    b. Opposites attract.
    c. Familiarity breeds contempt.
    d. Absence makes the heart grow fonder.

KEY TERMS

Using your own words, write a brief definition or explanation of each of the following terms.

Textbook Terms

1. social psychology

2. attribution theory

3. fundamental attribution error

4. attitudes

5. foot-in-the-door phenomenon

6. role

7. cognitive dissonance theory

8. conformity

9. normative social influence

10. norms

11. informational social influence

12. social facilitation

13. social loafing

14. deindividuation

15. group polarization

16. groupthink

17. aggression

18. frustration-aggression principle

19. mere exposure effect

20. passionate love

21. companionate love

22. equity

23. self-disclosure

24. altruism

25. bystander effect

26. social exchange theory

Program Terms
   Program 19
   27. autocratic leader

   28. laissez-faire leader

   Program 20
   29. cognitive control

   30. Pygmalion effect

ANSWERS

Guided Study

The following guidelines provide the main points that your answers should have touched upon.

Textbook Assignment

1. According to attribution theory, people explain others' behavior as being due either to their dispositions or to their situations. Because people have enduring personality traits, we tend to overestimate the influence of personality and underestimate the impact of situational influences, particularly when explaining others' behavior. This is called the *fundamental attribution error*. When explaining our own behavior, or when we take another's perspective, we are less likely to make this type of error. Our attributions, of course, have important practical consequences. For example, there are political implications to the question of whether people's behavior is attributed to social conditions or to their own choices, abilities, and shortcomings.

2. An attitude is a belief and feeling that predisposes our reactions to objects, people, and events. Our attitudes are most likely to guide our actions when outside influences on what we say and do are minimal, when the attitude is specifically relevant to the behavior, and when we are aware of our attitudes.

3. Studies of the foot-in-the-door phenomenon and role playing demonstrate that our actions can influence our attitudes. The foot-in-the-door phenomenon is the tendency for people who agree to a small request to comply later with a larger one. Similarly, people who play a role tend to adjust their attitudes to coincide with behavior enacted while playing the role. The theory of cognitive dissonance maintains that when our thoughts and behaviors don't coincide, we experience tension. To relieve this tension, we bring our attitudes into line with our actions.

4. Suggestibility studies conducted by Solomon Asch demonstrate that a unanimous group makes us unsure about our behavior or thinking, and so we are more likely to conform to the group standard, even if it is incorrect. Conformity is promoted when people feel incompetent or insecure, when they are in groups of three or more, when the group is unanimous and of high status and attractiveness, when no prior commitment has been made, when behavior will be observed, and when people have been socialized in a culture that encourages respect for social standards. We conform to gain social approval (normative social influence) or because the group provides valuable information (informational social influence).

5. Subjects in Milgram's experiments were ordered to teach a list of word pairs to another person by punishing the learner's wrong answers with electric shocks. Obedience was highest when the experimenter was nearby and was perceived as a legitimate authority supported by a prestigious institution, when the victim was depersonalized or at a distance, and when there was no role model for defiance.

6. Social facilitation occurs when tasks are simple or well-learned but not when they are difficult or unfamiliar. When observed by others, people become aroused. Arousal *facilitates* the most likely response—the correct one on an easy task, an incorrect one on a difficult task. Social loafing occurs when people who work anonymously as part of a group exert less effort than those individually accountable for performance. Deindividuation occurs when group participation makes individuals feel aroused, anonymous, and less self-conscious. The uninhibited and impulsive behavior of mobs may occur as a result of this phenomenon.

7. Group polarization refers to the enhancement of a group's prevailing tendencies that occurs when like-minded members discuss issues and attitudes. The unrealistic group decision making called groupthink occurs when the

desire for group harmony outweighs the desire for realistic thinking. It is fed by overconfidence, conformity, self-justification, and group polarization. Groupthink can be prevented when the leader welcomes dissenting opinions and invites criticism.

8. The power of the situation (social control) and of the individual (personal control) interact in two significant ways. First, when feeling pressured, people may react by doing the opposite. Second, people often choose or help create the situations that influence their behavior. Their expectations may cause them to act in ways that trigger the expected results. In this way, expectations may be self-fulfilling.

    The impact of a minority in swaying the majority opinion illustrates the power of personal control. Research reveals that a minority that unswervingly holds to its position is more likely to be successful in swaying the majority than a minority that waffles.

9. Biology influences aggression at three levels—the genetic, the neural, and the biochemical. Studies of human twins and selective breeding in animals reveal that genes influence aggression. Electrical stimulation and injuries to certain regions of the limbic system, such as the amygdala, suggest that animal and human brains have neural systems that control aggressive behavior (although no one spot in the brain actually controls aggression). Studies of animal aggression and violent criminals demonstrate that aggressive tendencies increase with blood levels of the hormone testosterone (although the reverse is also true).

    A variety of psychological factors influence aggression. The frustration-aggression principle indicates that pain, insults, excessive heat, and other aversive stimuli can evoke hostility. Learning also plays a role in aggression. Aggressive reactions are more likely in situations in which experience has taught the individual that aggression will be rewarded. Furthermore, children who observe aggressive models often imitate their behavior.

10. Correlational and experimental studies reveal a link between children's viewing of violent television programs and their later aggressiveness as teenagers and young adults. Experts maintain that the effects of viewing violent programs stem from a combination of factors, including arousal by the violent excitement, the strengthening of violence-related ideas, the erosion of inhibitions, and imitation.

    Research indicates that depictions of sexual violence portray women as enjoying being the victims of sexual aggression, and this perception increases the acceptance of coercion in sexual relationships. Repeated viewing of pornographic films can also lead viewers to trivialize rape and devalue their partners.

11. The bystander effect states that a bystander is less likely to give aid if other bystanders are present. Darley and Latané maintain that bystanders will help only if they notice the incident, interpret it as an emergency, and assume responsibility for helping. At each step in this decision-making process the presence of other bystanders makes it less likely a helping decision will be made. Further research reveals that bystanders are most likely to help when they have seen someone else being helpful, when they are not in a hurry, when the victim appears similar to them and deserving of assistance, when they are in a small town or rural area, when they feel guilty, when they are focused on others and not preoccupied, and when they are in a good mood.

12. The social exchange theory maintains that self-interest underlies all human interactions, including altruism, so that our constant goal is to maximize rewards and minimize costs. This theory helps explain why people often help those whose approval they seek or who can reciprocate favors in the future.

    People are also sensitive to social norms that promote helping. The reciprocity norm, for example, dictates that we should help those who have helped us. The social responsibility norm is the expectation that we should help those who need our help.

13. Studies of attraction indicate that proximity is the most powerful predictor of friendship, in part because being repeatedly exposed to any person or thing tends to increase our liking for it (mere exposure effect). Experiments also reveal that physical appearance is the most powerful factor in the first impression a person triggers. Although many aspects of attractiveness vary with place and time, some may be universal. Once relationships are formed, similarity of attitudes, beliefs, interests, and other characteristics increases attraction between people.

    Passionate love is an intense state of physical arousal triggered by another person, usually at the beginning of a relationship, that is cognitively labeled as love. Companionate love is the steadier, deeply felt attachment that emerges as love matures. Companionate love is fostered by feelings of equity between the partners in a relationship and the acceptability of self-disclosures.

Program 19 Assignment

1. Although most of psychology focuses on the individual, social psychology tries to understand human behavior within its broader social context. In the 1930s and 1940s, millions of ordinary people became victims of social-political structures in Europe that were powerful enough to exert control over them. Psychologists began to wonder how dictators could transform rational individuals into blindly obedient masses. Led by Kurt Lewin, a team of researchers in the United States began to study how leaders affect their followers and how groups change the behavior of individuals. Lewin hoped to demonstrate that it was possible to translate socially significant issues, like the power of leaders, into hypotheses that could be tested in controlled experiments. This was the beginning of modern social psychology.

2. In 1939, Lewin trained men to lead groups of boys using one of three styles of leadership: autocratic, laissez-faire, and democratic. (To be sure that the leader's style and not the boys' personality traits influenced behavior, Lewin had each group experience each style.) Under the autocratic (dictatorial) leader, the boys worked the hardest, but only when the leader was watching. Although the boys were more submissive to an autocratic leader, they also were more aggressive and hostile toward one another. When the group leader gave the boys total freedom without guidance (laissez-faire leadership), chaos ensued and little was accomplished. When the group was democratically run, the boys showed the highest levels of motivation and originality. The results demonstrated that leadership style and the social situation it created, rather than the personalities of group members, determined how the boys behaved.

3. In explaining the behavior of others, people typically focus on an individual's personality traits without sufficiently considering the impact of the situation. This dual tendency to attribute the causes of behavior to personal

factors while underestimating the effects of the situation is known as the *fundamental attribution error*. We all make this error, in part because our culture emphasizes individual accomplishments and in part because we have difficulty admitting how easily we ourselves can be manipulated by situational forces.

4. In Zimbardo's prison experiment, college students were randomly assigned to play the roles of either prisoners or prison guards. Uniforms, status symbols, rules, and rituals helped distinguish the two groups. The situation proved so powerful that the students quickly took on the personalities of passive zombie-like prisoners and dictatorial guards. Because a number of the prisoners developed extreme stress reactions during the experiment, what was planned as a 2-week experiment was called off after 6 days. This study demonstrates that everyone has the capacity for evil or good, depending on the situation.

    This experiment raised ethical questions about the treatment of research subjects because of concern for subjects' mental and emotional health. Today, ethics committees would probably not allow this experiment (or Milgram's earlier study).

5. Tom Moriarity staged the theft of an accomplice's unattended radio on a beach full of sunbathers. When the accomplice merely walked away from her blanket and possessions, no one intervened to prevent the theft. But when the "victim" first asked a neighboring sunbather to watch her things while she was away, bystander apathy was turned into action and the "stranger" intervened.

    In another experiment, Ellen Langer (Harvard University) demonstrated that treating people with greater professionalism can actually improve their performance. After taking a standard vision test, Air Force ROTC cadets were randomly assigned to one of two conditions. One group donned flight suits and took a training run in a fully operational flight simulator. During the training run, the cadets took the same vision test again. The second group of cadets, who were treated much more informally than the first, wore their street clothes and were tested under much less realistic flight conditions. Forty percent of the subjects in the first group improved their performance on the vision test. In contrast, none of the subjects in the second group improved his or her vision test score.

Program 20 Assignment

6. An important lesson of social psychology is that the situation matters not only in terms of its objective reality but also in terms of the way each person perceives, understands, and interprets it. Psychologists refer to this ability to create subjective realities as the *power of cognitive control*—the tendency of people's beliefs to give different meanings to situations, which then strongly influence social behavior. For example, a great deal of conflict among individuals and nations derives from the belief that "we" as reasonable people perceive the world accurately, while "they" are simply wrong.

7. The assumption of even minor differences between groups can trigger prejudice. A provocative demonstration of this occurred in Jane Elliot's third-grade classroom. She divided the class into two groups: "superior" blue-eyed children and "inferior" brown-eyed children. Elliot watched what had been "marvelous, cooperative children turn into nasty, vicious, discriminating third-graders in the space of 15 minutes." Those who were "inferior" began to feel and act as if they actually were inferior. Those who were "superior" acted and felt accordingly.

    Elliot's study demonstrates how easy it is to alter objective reality and substitute an arbitrary alternative conception of the world. No matter how superficial the differences between people may be, once those differences become indicators of superiority and inferiority, they become institutionalized, rules are made, norms are created, and expectations are created as to how people should behave.

8. Positive expectations can change a person's perceptions of a situation just as dramatically as negative expectations. Psychologists call this the Pygmalion effect. Robert Rosenthal (Harvard University) demonstrated this effect by showing how teacher expectations influence student performance. Rosenthal randomly labeled some students as academically superior and notified their teachers that these students had greater intellectual potential. One year later, these children actually did show intellectual gains, as measured by standard intelligence tests. Rosenthal identified four factors that mediate the power of these "self-fulfilling prophesies": climate, input, response opportunity, and feedback. Teachers create a warmer atmosphere, teach more material, allow more chances to respond, and give more differentiated feedback to children for whom they have higher expectations, as compared to children for whom they have lower expectations.

9. Elliot Aronson (University of California, Santa Cruz) and Alex Gonzales (Fresno State University) created the "jigsaw classroom" to test their theory that cooperation, not competition, increases achievement and instills self-respect. First, the class is divided into "expert groups," in which each student learns about a specific topic well enough to teach it to others. The class is then reconstituted into jigsaw groups comprised of members of the various expert groups. In the jigsaw group, each student teaches the others his or her part, and in the process everyone learns the entire lesson.

10. Nowhere is subjective reality more skillfully manipulated than in the field of advertising. Psychologist Robert Cialdini (Arizona State University) has divided the tactics used by salespeople, fund-raisers, and advertisers into six categories, each of which illustrates a principle of persuasion. The principle of *reciprocation* is that if someone first does us a favor, we are more likely to say "yes" when they ask for something in return. The principle of *scarcity* is based on our perception that things that are rare are more desirable. The principle of *authority* is based on the tendency of people to follow the recommendations of a person who is perceived as an authority on a subject or product. The principle of *commitment* is based on the fact that once a person has taken a position on an issue, he or she is more likely to consent to any request that is consistent with that commitment. The principle of *liking* capitalizes on the fact that people are more willing to be persuaded by people they know and like. Finally, the principle of *consensus* is that people are more willing to say yes to a request if they believe that others have also said yes.

Progress Test

1. **c.** is the answer. Cognitive dissonance is the tension we feel when we are aware of a discrepancy between our thoughts and actions, as would occur when we do something we find distasteful. (p. 557; see also Program 11)

    a. Dissonance requires strongly held attitudes, which must be perceived as not fitting behavior.

    b. Dissonance is a personal cognitive process.

    d. In such a situation the person is less likely to experience dissonance, since the action can be attributed to "having no choice."

2. **c.** is the answer. (p. 556)

   a. Informational social influence results from accepting the opinions of others about a situation one is unsure of.

   b. The fundamental attribution error is the tendency to underestimate situational influences on the behavior of others.

   d. Deindividuation is the loss of self-consciousness that sometimes occurs in individuals in groups.

3. **d.** is the answer. (p. 562)

   a. Groupthink refers to the mode of thinking that occurs when the desire for group harmony overrides realistic and critical thinking.

   b. Cognitive dissonance refers to the discomfort we feel when two thoughts (which include the knowledge of our *behavior*) are inconsistent.

   c. Empathy is feeling what another person feels.

4. **b.** is the answer. (video)

5. **c.** is the answer. (video)

6. **a.** is the answer. The very wide variations in aggressiveness from culture to culture indicate that aggression cannot be considered an instinct, or unlearned, universal characteristic of the species. (p. 571)

7. **a.** is the answer. (pp. 577–578)

8. **d.** is the answer. This phenomenon is known as the bystander effect. (p. 586)

   a. This answer is incorrect because individuals are less likely to render assistance at all if others are present.

   b. Although people are less likely to assume responsibility for helping, this does not mean that they are less empathic.

   c. This answer is incorrect because norms such as the social responsibility norm encourage helping others, yet people are less likely to help with others around.

9. **d.** is the answer. In Milgram's initial experiments, 63 percent of the subjects fully complied with the experiment. (video; pp. 557)

10. **d.** is the answer. (video; p. 549)

11. **a.** is the answer. (video; p. 559)

12. **a.** is the answer. This result supports the two-factor theory of emotion and passionate attraction, according to which arousal from any source can facilitate an emotion, depending on how we label the arousal. (p. 583–584)

13. **c.** is the answer. (p. 572)

14. **d.** is the answer. (video)

    a. The subjects in this experiment were all well-educated.

    b. & c. This study was not concerned with altruistic behavior.

15. **a.** is the answer. (video)

16. **c.** is the answer. The mere exposure effect refers to our tendency to like what we're used to, and we're used to seeing mirror images of ourselves. (p. 580)

    a. Equity refers to equality in giving and taking between the partners in a relationship.

     b. Self-disclosure is the sharing of intimate feelings with a partner in a loving relationship.

     d. Although people prefer mirror images of their faces, mirror-image perceptions are often held by parties in conflict. Each party views itself favorably and the other negatively.

     e. Deindividuation involves a loss of self-awareness.

17. **c.** is the answer. Social exchange theory says that our behaviors, including helping, constitute an exchange process, in which we aim to maximize benefits and minimize costs. (pp. 586–587)

    a. Helping for this reason would be based above all on the norm of social responsibility.

    b. According to social exchange theory, helping occurs when benefits are seen to outweigh costs. Alleviated guilt is a potential benefit, but many other costs and benefits would also be weighed.

    d. This reflects the theory of evolutionary psychology.

18. **c.** is the answer. In this example of the fundamental attribution error, even when given the situational explanation for the woman's behavior, students ignored it and attributed her behavior to her personal disposition. (p. 550)

19. **b.** is the answer. (p. 561)

    a. & c. Crowding may amplify irritability or altruistic tendencies that are already present. Crowding does not, however, produce these reactions as a general effect.

    d. In fact, just the opposite is true. Crowding often intensifies people's reactions.

20. **a.** is the answer. (video)

    b. & c. Langer's study was not concerned with obedience.

21. **d.** is the answer. (video)

    a. The Pygmalion effect is the effect of expectations on behavior.

    b. Deindividuation refers to the loss of self-awareness and self-restraint that sometimes occurs in group situations.

    c. This is our tendency to underestimate the impact of situations and to overestimate the impact of personal factors upon the behavior of others.

22. **d.** is the answer. The text emphasizes the ways in which personal and social controls interact in influencing behavior. It does not suggest that one factor is more influential than the other. (p. 564)

23. **a.** is the answer. As Solomon Asch's experiments demonstrated, individuals are more likely to conform when they are being observed by others in the group. The other factors were not discussed in the text and probably would not promote conformity. (p. 556)

24. **d.** is the answer. (p. 549)

25. **c.** is the answer. (video)

    a. Elliot's study did not measure the children's self-esteem.

    b. In fact, virtually all of the students quickly began acting as if eye color was equated with intelligence.

    d. None of the students "got the message" until afterward, when Elliot told them why she had introduced this myth.

26. d. is the answer. The frustration-aggression principle states that the blocking of an attempt to achieve some goal—in Teresa's case, buying concert tickets—creates anger and can generate aggression. (p. 573)

a. Evolutionary psychology maintains that aggressive behavior is a genetically based drive. Teresa's behavior clearly was a reaction to a specific situation.

b. The reciprocity norm—that we should return help to those who have helped us—would not engender Teresa's angry reaction.

c. Social exchange theory views behavior as an exchange process in which people try to maximize the benefits of their behavior by minimizing the costs. Teresa's behavior likely brought her few benefits while exacting some costs, including potential injury, embarrassment, and retaliation by the clerk.

27. b. is the answer. Dissonance theory focuses on what happens when our actions contradict our attitudes. (p. 554)

a. Attribution theory holds that we give causal explanations for the behavior of others, often by crediting either the situation or people's dispositions.

c. Social exchange theory maintains that social behaviors maximize benefits and minimize costs. It is not clear in this example whether Wanda perceives such costs and benefits.

d. & e. These are not theories of social influence.

28. b. is the answer. (video)

29. c. is the answer. (video)

30. a. is the answer. Social facilitation, or better performance in the presence of others, occurs for easy tasks but not for more difficult ones. For tasks such as proofreading, typing, playing a musical instrument, or giving a speech, the arousal resulting from the presence of others can lead to mistakes. (p. 561)

31. a. is the answer. Group polarization means that the tendencies within a group—and therefore the differences among groups—grow stronger over time. Thus, because the differences between the sorority and nonsorority students have increased, Jane and Sandy are likely to have little in common. (p. 562)

b. Groupthink is the tendency for realistic decision making to disintegrate when the desire for group harmony is strong.

c. Deindividuation is the loss of self-consciousness and restraint that sometimes occurs when one is part of a group.

d. Social facilitation refers to improved performance of a task in the presence of others.

32. c. is the answer. Prior commitment to an opposing view generally tends to work against conformity. In contrast, large group size, prestigiousness of a group, and an individual's feelings of incompetence and insecurity all strengthen the tendency to conform. (p. 556)

33. d. is the answer. Tupperware party hosts and hostesses typically invite friends and relatives, in the hopes that the bonds between them will lead to sales. (video)

34. b. is the answer. An air attack would depersonalize the villagers, leading to compliance from those who might not comply if they had to destroy the village at close range. The other factors should not promote compliance, which would, if anything, be reduced by the role models for defiance in d. (p. 558)

35. **a.** is the answer. As illustrated by Maria's decision to stop buying aerosol products, informational social influence occurs when people have genuinely been influenced by what they have learned from others. (p. 556)

    b. Had Maria's behavior been motivated by the desire to avoid rejection or to gain social approval (which we have no reason to suspect is the case), it would have been an example of normative social influence.

    c. Deindividuation refers to the sense of anonymity a person may feel as part of a group.

    d. Social facilitation is the improvement in performance of well-learned tasks that may result when one is observed by others.

36. **d.** is the answer. In this situation, the counter-attitudinal behavior is performed voluntarily and cannot be attributed to the demands of the situation. (p. 554)

    a., b., & c. In these situations, the counter-attitudinal behaviors should not arouse much dissonance, since they can be attributed to the demands of the situation.

37. **c.** is the answer. (video)

38. **b.** is the answer. (video; p. 556)

    a. The subjects conformed to the majority opinion even when the differences among the line segments were quite large.

    c. & d. These issues were not addressed in Asch's experiment.

39. **a.** is the answer. Friends and couples are much more likely than randomly paired people to be similar in views, interests, and a range of other factors. (p. 583)

    b. The opposite is true.

    c. The mere exposure effect demonstrates that familiarity tends to breed fondness.

    d. This is unlikely, given the positive effects of proximity and intimacy.

Key Terms

Textbook Assignment

1. **Social psychology** is the scientific study of how we think about, influence, and relate to one another. (p. 549)

2. **Attribution theory** deals with our causal explanations of behavior. We attribute behavior to the individual's disposition or to the situation. (p. 549)

3. The **fundamental attribution error** is our tendency to underestimate the impact of situations and to overestimate the impact of personal dispositions upon the behavior of others. (p. 549)

4. **Attitudes** are personal beliefs and feelings that may predispose a person to respond in particular ways to objects, people, and events. (p. 551)

5. The **foot-in-the-door phenomenon** is the tendency for people who agree to a small request to comply later with a larger request. (p. 552)

6. A **role** is a set of expectations about the behavior of someone in a particular social position. (p. 553)

7. **Cognitive dissonance theory** refers to the theory that we act to reduce the psychological discomfort we experience when our behavior conflicts with what we think and feel or, more generally, when two of our thoughts conflict. This is frequently accomplished by changing our attitude rather than our behavior. (p. 554)

   Memory aid: *Dissonance* means "lack of harmony." **Cognitive dissonance** occurs when two thoughts, or cognitions, are at variance with one another.

8. **Conformity** is the tendency to change one's thinking or behavior to coincide with a group standard. (p. 555)

9. **Normative social influence** refers to the pressure on individuals to conform in order to avoid rejection or gain social approval. (p. 556)

   Memory aid: *Normative* means "based on a norm, or pattern, regarded as typical for a specific group." **Normative social influence** is the pressure groups exert on the individual to behave in ways acceptable to the group standard.

10. **Norms** are understood social prescriptions, or rules, for accepted and expected behavior. (p. 556)

11. **Informational social influence** results when one goes along with a group when one is unsure or lacks information. (p. 556)

12. **Social facilitation** is the improvement in performance of simple or well-learned tasks that occurs when other people are present. (p. 561)

13. **Social loafing** is the tendency for individual effort to be diminished when one is part of a group working toward a common goal. (p. 562)

14. **Deindividuation** refers to the loss of self-awareness and self-restraint that sometimes occurs in group situations that foster arousal and anonymity. (p. 562)

    Memory aid: As a prefix, *de-* indicates reversal or undoing. To **deindividuate** is to undo one's individuality.

15. **Group polarization** refers to the enhancement of a group's prevailing tendencies through discussion, which often has the effect of accentuating the group's differences from other groups. (p. 562)

    Memory aid: To *polarize* is to "cause thinking to concentrate about two poles, or contrasting positions."

16. **Groupthink** refers to the unrealistic thought processes and decision making that occur within groups when the desire for group harmony becomes paramount. (p. 563)

    Example: The psychological tendencies of self-justification, conformity, and group polarization foster the development of the "team spirit" mentality known as **groupthink**.

17. **Aggression** is any physical or verbal behavior intended to hurt or destroy. (p. 571)

18. The **frustration-aggression principle** states that aggression is triggered when people become angry because their efforts to achieve a goal have been blocked. (p. 573)

19. The **mere exposure effect** refers to the fact that repeated exposure to an unfamiliar stimulus increases our liking of it. (p. 580)

20. **Passionate love** refers to an aroused state of intense positive absorption in another person, especially at the beginning of a relationship. (p. 583)

21. **Companionate love** refers to a deep, enduring, affectionate attachment. (p. 584)

22. **Equity** refers to the condition in which there is mutual giving and receiving between the partners in a relationship. (p. 585)

23. **Self-disclosure** refers to a person's sharing intimate feelings with another. (p. 585)

24. **Altruism** is unselfish regard for the welfare of others. (p. 585)

25. The **bystander effect** is the tendency of a person to be less likely to offer help to someone if there are other people present. (p. 586)

26. **Social exchange theory** states that our social behavior revolves around exchanges, in which we try to minimize our costs and maximize our benefits. (pp. 586–587)

Program 19 Terms

27. An **autocratic leader** is one who rules in a dictatorial fashion, without accepting input from members of the group.

28. A **laissez-faire leader** allows complete freedom among group members, providing no interference or guidance.

Program 20 Terms

29. **Cognitive control** refers to the power of people's beliefs to give different meanings to situations.

30. The **Pygmalion effect** refers to the power of expectations on behavior, creating a self-fulfilling prophecy that can have both positive and negative consequences on behavior.

PROGRAM 21

Psychopathology

TEXTBOOK ASSIGNMENT: Chapter 15: Psychological Disorders, pp. 453–485

ORIENTATION

Although there is no clear-cut line between normal and abnormal behavior, we can characterize as abnormal those behaviors that are atypical, disturbing, maladaptive, and unjustifiable. Program 21 and the reading assignment discuss the various types of anxiety, dissociative, mood, schizophrenia, and personality disorders, as classified by the *Diagnostic and Statistical Manual of Mental Disorders* (DSM-IV). The text also discusses the advantages and problems connected with the use of diagnostic labels. Although DSM-IV follows a medical model, in which disorders are viewed as illnesses, the program and text also discuss psychological factors in psychopathology. Thus, psychoanalytic theory, learning theory, social-cognitive theory, and other psychological perspectives are drawn on when relevant. The text assignment concludes with a discussion of the prevalence of the various disorders.

Your major task in this assignment is to learn about psychological disorders, their various subtypes and characteristics, and their possible causes.

NOTE: Answer guidelines for all Program 21 questions begin on page 383.

GOALS

After completing your study of the program and reading assignment, you should be prepared to:

1. Describe disordered behavior, and discuss the reasons for classification.

2. Discuss the advantages and disadvantages of diagnostic labels.

3. Discuss the different perspectives to the study of psychological disorders.

4. Identify the major categories of psychological disorders, and briefly describe the symptoms of their different forms.

GUIDED STUDY

Textbook Assignment

The text chapter should be studied one section at a time. Before you read, preview each section by skimming it, noting headings and boldface items. Then read the appropriate section objectives from the following outline. Keep these objectives in mind and, as you read the chapter section, search for the information that will enable you to meet each objective. Once you have finished a section, write out answers for its objectives.

Perspectives on Psychological Disorders (pp. 454–460)
1. List the criteria for judging whether behavior is disordered.

2. Explain and contrast two perspectives on psychological disorders.

3. Describe the system used to classify psychological disorders, and explain the reasons for its development.

4. Discuss the controversy surrounding the use of diagnostic labels.

Anxiety Disorders (pp. 460–465)
5. Describe the various anxiety disorders and discuss their possible causes.

Dissociative Disorders (pp. 465–467)
6. Describe the nature and possible causes of dissociative disorders.

Mood Disorders (pp. 468–475)

7. Describe the mood disorders and discuss the alternative explanations for their occurrence.

Schizophrenia (pp. 476–481)

8. Describe the symptoms of schizophrenia and discuss research on the causes of schizophrenia.

Personality Disorders (pp. 481–483)

9. Describe the nature and causes of personality disorders and the specific characteristics of the antisocial personality disorder.

Rates of Psychological Disorders (pp. 483–484)

10. Briefly discuss the prevalence of psychological disorders.

Program: Assignment

Read the following objectives before you watch Program 21. As you watch, be alert for information that will help you answer each objective. Taking notes during the program will help you to formulate your answers later. After the program, write answers to the objectives. If you have access to the program on videotape, you may replay portions to refresh your memory.

1. Differentiate *psychopathology* and *mental disorder*, and describe the process by which mental health professionals determine whether a person's behavior is abnormal.

2. Explain the differences among clinical psychologists, psychiatrists, and psychoanalysts, and identify several questions mental health professionals ask in determining whether a person suffers from a mental illness.

3. Identify four reasons that the classification of mental disorders is important.

4. Discuss the treatment of people with mental disorders over the course of history, and explain Thomas Szasz's viewpoint regarding mental illness.

5. Discuss the significance of David Rosenhan's mental illness "experiment."

6. Differentiate three models of the origins of mental illness.

7. Discuss Irving Gottesman and Fuller Torrey's research into the origins of schizophrenia.

8. Discuss the role of cultural factors in the prevalence of mental disorders, using Native Americans as an example.

PROGRESS TEST

Circle your answers to the following questions and check them with the answers on page 387. If your answer is incorrect, read the explanation for why it is incorrect and then consult the appropriate pages of the text (in parentheses following the correct answer).

1. Amnesia, fugue, and multiple personality are all examples of _____ disorders.
    a. anxiety
    b. mood
    c. dissociative
    d. personality

2. The criteria for classifying behavior as psychologically disordered:
    a. vary from culture to culture.
    b. vary from time to time.
    c. are characterized by both a. and b.
    d. have remained largely unchanged over the course of history.

3. Our early ancestors commonly attributed disordered behavior to:
    a. "bad blood."
    b. evil spirits.
    c. brain injury.
    d. laziness.

4. A major criterion in the diagnosis of a mental disorder is that a person's:
    a. behavior does not conform to social norms.
    b. ideas make others uncomfortable.
    c. functioning is clearly abnormal.
    d. behavior or mental state has been atypical for at least 6 months.

5. Evidence of environmental effects on psychological disorders is seen in the fact that certain disorders, such as _____ , are universal, while others, such as _____ , are culture-bound.
    a. schizophrenia; depression
    b. depression; schizophrenia
    c. antisocial personality; neurosis
    d. depression; anorexia nervosa

6. The diagnostic reliability of DSM-IV:
   a. is unknown.
   b. depends on the age of the patient.
   c. is very low.
   d. is relatively high.

7. Phobias and obsessive-compulsive behaviors are classified as:
   a. anxiety disorders.
   b. mood disorders.
   c. dissociative disorders.
   d. personality disorders.

8. Tyrone is a medical doctor who specializes in mental disorders. He would be classified as a:
   a. psychologist.
   b. psychiatrist.
   c. psychoanalyst.
   d. psychopathologist.

9. Many mental health workers today take an "interactionist" view. This means that they view disordered behaviors as:
   a. genetically triggered.
   b. organic diseases.
   c. arising from the interaction of biological and psychological factors.
   d. the product of learning.

10. The French reformer who insisted that madness was not demonic possession and who called for humane treatment of patients was:
    a. Nadel.
    b. Freud.
    c. Szasz.
    d. Spanos.
    e. Pinel.

11. According to the social-cognitive perspective, a person who experiences unexpected aversive events may develop helplessness and manifest a(n):
    a. obsessive-compulsive disorder.
    b. dissociative disorder.
    c. personality disorder.
    d. mood disorder.

12. Which of the following was presented in the text as evidence of biological influences on anxiety disorders?
    a. Identical twins often develop similar phobias.
    b. PET scans of persons with obsessive-compulsive disorder reveal unusually high activity in an area of the frontal lobes.
    c. Drugs that affect the neurotransmitter serotonin may control obsessive thoughts.
    d. All of the above were presented.
    e. None of the above were presented.

13. Which of the following is the most pervasive of the psychological disorders?
    a. depression
    b. schizophrenia
    c. hypochondriasis
    d. generalized anxiety disorder
    e. dissociative amnesia

14. According to psychoanalytic theory, memory of losses, especially in combination with internalized anger, is likely to result in:
    a. learned helplessness.
    b. the self-serving bias.

c. weak ego-defense mechanisms.
d. depression.

15. Hearing voices would be a(n) _____ ; believing that you are Napoleon would be a(n) _____ .
    a. obsession; compulsion
    b. compulsion; obsession
    c. delusion; hallucination
    d. hallucination; delusion

16. The fact that disorders such as schizophrenia are universal and influenced by heredity, whereas other disorders such as anorexia nervosa are culture-bound, provides evidence for the _____ model of psychological disorders.
    a. medical
    b. bio-psycho-social
    c. social-cultural
    d. psychoanalytic

17. Psychoanalytic theorists believe phobic symptoms represent the person's attempt to deal with:
    a. childhood conflicts that have been repressed.
    b. disorganized thought processes.
    c. hormonal imbalances.
    d. unpleasant responsibilities.

18. When schizophrenia is slow to develop, called _____ schizophrenia, recovery is _____ .
    a. reactive; unlikely
    b. process; likely
    c. process; unlikely
    d. reactive; likely

19. The text suggests that the disorganized thoughts of people with schizophrenia may be attributed to a breakdown in:
    a. selective attention.
    b. memory storage.
    c. motivation.
    d. memory retrieval.
    e. memory encoding.

20. While mountain climbing Jack saw his best friend killed by an avalanche. Jack himself was found months later, hundreds of miles away. On questioning, he claimed to be another person and, indeed, appeared to have no knowledge about any aspect of his former life. Most likely, Jack was suffering from:
    a. a dissociative fugue.
    b. dissociative schizophrenia.
    c. dissociative identity disorder.
    d. dissociative amnesia.

21. Bob has never been able to keep a job. He's been in and out of jail for charges such as theft, sexual assault, and spouse abuse. Bob would most likely be diagnosed as having:
    a. a dissociative identity disorder.
    b. major depressive disorder.
    c. schizophrenia.
    d. antisocial personality disorder.

22. Which of the following is *not* a symptom of schizophrenia?
    a. inappropriate emotions
    b. disturbed perceptions
    c. panic attacks
    d. disorganized thinking

23. Among the following, which is generally accepted as a possible cause of schizophrenia?
    a. an excess of endorphins in the brain
    b. being a twin
    c. extensive learned helplessness
    d. a genetic predisposition

24. Julia's psychologist believes that Julia's fear of heights can be traced to a conditioned fear she developed after falling from a ladder. This explanation reflects a _____ perspective.
    a. medical
    b. psychoanalytic
    c. social-cognitive
    d. learning

25. Jason is so preoccupied with staying clean that he showers as many as ten times each day. Jason would be diagnosed as suffering from:
    a. a dissociative disorder.
    b. generalized anxiety disorder.
    c. a personality disorder.
    d. obsessive-compulsive disorder.

26. (Close-Up) Although she escaped from her war-torn country two years ago, Zheina still has haunting memories and nightmares. Because she is also severely depressed, her therapist diagnoses her condition as:
    a. dissociative identity disorder.
    b. bipolar disorder.
    c. schizophrenia.
    d. post-traumatic stress disorder.

27. Joe has an intense, irrational fear of snakes. He is suffering from:
    a. generalized anxiety disorder.
    b. obsessive-compulsive disorder.
    c. a phobia.
    d. a mood disorder.
    e. bipolar disorder.

28. Sharon is continually tense, jittery, and apprehensive for no specific reason. She would probably be diagnosed as suffering from:
    a. a phobia.
    b. major depressive disorder.
    c. obsessive-compulsive disorder.
    d. generalized anxiety disorder.

29. Irene occasionally experiences unpredictable episodes of intense dread accompanied by chest pains and a sensation of smothering. Since her symptoms have no apparent cause, they would probably be classified as indicative of:
    a. schizophrenia.
    b. dissociative fugue.
    c. post-traumatic stress disorder.
    d. panic attack.

30. Dr. Jekyll, whose second personality was Dr. Hyde, had a(n) _____ disorder.
    a. anxiety
    b. dissociative
    c. mood
    d. personality

31. On Monday, Matt felt optimistic, energetic, and on top of the world. On Tuesday, he felt hopeless and lethargic, and thought that the future looked very grim. Matt would most likely be diagnosed as having:
    a. bipolar disorder.
    b. major depressive disorder.
    c. schizophrenia.
    d. a dissociative disorder.

32. Claiming that she heard a voice commanding her to warn other people that eating is harmful, Sandy attempts to convince others in a restaurant not to eat. The psychiatrist to whom she is referred finds that Sandy's thinking and speech are often fragmented and incoherent. In addition, Sandy has an unreasonable fear that someone is "out to get her" and consequently trusts no one. Her condition is most indicative of:
    a. schizophrenia.
    b. generalized anxiety disorder.
    c. a phobia.
    d. obsessive-compulsive disorder.
    e. a personality disorder.

33. Connie's therapist has suggested that her depression stems from unresolved anger toward her parents. Evidently, Connie's therapist is working within the _____ perspective.
    a. learning
    b. social-cognitive
    c. biological
    d. psychoanalytic

34. Ken's therapist suggested that his depression is a result of his self-defeating thoughts and negative assumptions about himself, his situation, and his future. Evidently, Ken's therapist is working within the _____ perspective.
    a. learning
    b. social-cognitive
    c. biological
    d. psychoanalytic

35. Alicia's doctor, who believes that Alicia's depression has a biochemical cause, prescribes a drug that:
    a. reduces norepinephrine.
    b. increases norepinephrine.
    c. reduces serotonin.
    d. increases acetylcholine.

36. What happened to David Rosenhan and his colleagues when they pretended to hear voices at a mental hospital and then later behaved normally?
    a. The staff quickly saw through their deception.
    b. They were admitted to the hospital and diagnosed as having schizophrenia.
    c. No one detected their sanity, even when they behaved normally in the hospital.
    d. both b. and c. occurred.

37. Wayne's doctor attempts to help Wayne by prescribing a drug that blocks receptors for dopamine. Wayne has apparently been diagnosed with:
    a. a mood disorder.
    b. an anxiety disorder.
    c. a dissociative disorder.
    d. schizophrenia.

38. In many movies, soap operas, and novels, the hero or heroine, who is under great stress, experiences a sudden loss of memory without leaving home or establishing a new identity. This is an example of:
    a. a dissociative disorder.
    b. dissociative fugue.
    c. dissociative amnesia.
    d. an anxiety disorder.

39. Janet, whose class presentation is entitled "Current Views on the Causes of Schizophrenia," concludes her talk with the statement:
    a. "Schizophrenia is caused by intolerable stress."
    b. "Schizophrenia is inherited."
    c. "Genes may predispose some people to react to particular experiences by developing schizophrenia."
    d. "As of this date, schizophrenia is completely unpredictable and its causes are unknown."

40. Irving Gottesman and Fuller Torrey have discovered that if the brain of an identical twin with schizophrenia is compared to the brain of his or her normal twin, the former has:
    a. larger ventricles.
    b. smaller frontal lobes.
    c. no corpus callosum.
    d. no detectable differences.

KEY TERMS

Using your own words, write a brief definition or explanation of each of the following terms.

Textbook Terms

1. psychological disorder

2. medical model

3. bio-psycho-social perspective

4. DSM-IV

5. neurotic disorders

6. psychotic disorders

7. anxiety disorders

8. generalized anxiety disorder

9. phobia

10. obsessive-compulsive disorder

11. panic disorder

12. dissociative disorders

13. dissociative amnesia

14. dissociative fugue

15. dissociative identity disorder

16. mood disorders

17. major depressive disorder

18. mania

19. bipolar disorder

20. schizophrenia

21. delusions

22. hallucinations

23. personality disorders

24. antisocial personality disorder

Program Terms

25. psychopathology

26. mental disorder

27. SPECT analysis

ANSWERS

Guided Study

The following guidelines provide the main points that your answers should have touched upon.

Textbook Assignment

1. In order to be classified as psychologically disordered, behavior must be atypical, disturbing to others, maladaptive, and unjustifiable.

2. According to the medical perspective, psychological disorders are sicknesses that can be diagnosed on the basis of their symptoms and cured through

therapy. Psychologists who work from the bio-psycho-social perspective assume that biological, sociocultural, and psychological factors combine and interact to produce psychological disorders.

3. DSM-IV groups some 230 psychological disorders into 17 major categories. Diagnostic classification is intended to describe a disorder, predict its future course, imply its appropriate treatment, and stimulate research into its causes.

4. Most clinicians believe that diagnostic labels help in describing, treating, and researching the causes of psychological disorders. Critics contend that these labels are arbitrary value judgments that create preconceptions that can bias our perceptions and interpretations. Labels can also affect people's self-images and stigmatize them in others' eyes. Finally, labels can change reality.

5. There are three types of anxiety disorder: generalized anxiety disorder, in which a person feels inexplicably tense and apprehensive; phobia, in which a person has an irrational fear of a specific object or situation; and obsessive-compulsive disorder, in which a person is troubled by repetitive thoughts or actions. An extreme form of generalized anxiety disorder is the panic disorder.

    Freud viewed an anxiety disorder as a manifestation of repressed impulses, ideas, and feelings that influence the sufferer's actions and emotions. Learning theorists link anxiety disorders with classical conditioning of fear, which may arise from stimulus generalization. Phobic and compulsive behaviors reduce anxiety by allowing the person to avoid or escape the feared situation. According to this perspective, fear may also be learned through observational learning. Biologically oriented researchers see these disorders as evolutionary adaptations or as genetic predispositions to particular fears and high anxiety. The anxiety of persons with obsessive-compulsive disorder, for example, is measurable as unusually high activity in a particular region of the frontal lobes.

6. In dissociative disorders, a person experiences a sudden loss of memory (dissociative amnesia) or change in identity (dissociative fugue) in response to extreme stress. Even more mysterious is dissociative identity disorder, in which people have two or more distinct personalities; however, some skeptics believe that such persons are merely enacting a role for strategic reasons.

    Psychoanalysts view the symptoms of these disorders as defenses against anxiety. Learning theorists see them as behaviors reinforced by anxiety reduction. Some theorists see dissociative behaviors as states that serve as protective escape responses to traumatic childhood experiences.

7. There are two principal mood disorders: major depressive disorder and the bipolar disorder. Major depressive disorder, the "common cold" of psychological disorders, occurs when signs of depression last 2 weeks or more without any discernible cause. Alternating between depressive episodes and the hyperactive, wildly optimistic state of mania is characteristic of bipolar disorder.

    According to the psychoanalytic perspective, depression occurs when significant losses evoke feelings associated with losses experienced in childhood and when unresolved anger is directed inward against the self.

    According to the biological perspective, mood disorders involve genetic predispositions and biochemical imbalances in which norepinephrine is overabundant during mania and scarce during depression. A second neurotransmitter, serotonin, is also scarce during depression. The brains of depressed people also tend to be less active and even have somewhat smaller frontal lobes.

According to the social-cognitive perspective, depression is a vicious cycle in which stressful experiences trigger self-focused negative thinking and a self-blaming style of explaining events that hamper the way the person thinks and acts. This negative thinking and self-blaming style leads to further negative experiences.

8. Schizophrenia is a cluster of disorders in which there is a split from reality that shows itself in disorganized and delusional thinking, disturbed perceptions, and inappropriate emotions and actions. *Positive symptoms* of schizophrenia include disorganized or deluded thinking and speech as well as inappropriate emotions. *Negative symptoms* include toneless voices, expressionless faces, or mute and rigid bodies. Schizophrenia may develop gradually (chronic, or process, schizophrenia), in which case recovery is doubtful, or rapidly (acute, or reactive, schizophrenia) in response to stress, in which case recovery is much more likely.

    Some schizophrenia patients have an excess of brain receptors for dopamine. Others have abnormally low brain activity in the frontal lobes or enlarged fluid-filled areas and a corresponding shrinkage of cerebral tissue. Evidence suggests that the brain abnormalities of schizophrenia might be caused by a problem during prenatal development, such as a midpregnancy viral infection. In addition, studies of identical twins and adopted children reveal a strong genetic link to schizophrenia. Genes may predispose some people to react to particular experiences by developing a form of schizophrenia. Psychological causes of schizophrenia are difficult to pinpoint due to the variety of forms of the disorder.

9. Personality disorders are inflexible and enduring behavior patterns, such as attention-getting emotionality or exaggerated self-importance, that impair a person's social functioning. Those with the antisocial personality disorder display a lack of conscience at an early age, as they begin to lie, steal, fight, or evidence unrestrained sexual behavior. As adults their antisocial behavior may manifest itself in an inability to hold down a job, in marital and parental irresponsibility, or in criminal behavior. Twin and adoption studies suggest that some individuals may possess a genetic vulnerability to the antisocial personality disorder, but the manifestation of the disorder also depends on environmental factors.

10. Research reveals that approximately 32 percent of American adults have experienced a psychological disorder at some time in their lives and that 20 percent have an active disorder. Those who experience a psychological disorder usually do so by early adulthood. Some disorders, such as the antisocial personality disorder and phobias, often appear earlier, during childhood.

Program Assignment

1. Psychopathology is the study of mental disorders. A mental disorder is defined as a clinically significant behavioral or psychological syndrome that is typically associated with a painful condition or impairment in one or more important areas of functioning. About 1 in every 5 Americans suffer from some form of recently diagnosed mental disorder.

    In order to be diagnosed as suffering from a mental disorder, a person's functioning has to be clearly abnormal. This judgment is made by observing behavior directly, analyzing scores on diagnostic tests, or evaluating reports by the person or by people who know him or her.

2. Mental health professionals include clinical psychologists, who have Ph.D.'s in psychology; psychiatrists, who are also medical doctors; and psychoanalysts, who specialize in using Freudian techniques in their therapy. In diagnosing mental disorders, mental health professionals ask several questions: Is the person suffering, acting in ways that work against personal well-being, or creating discomfort in others who feel threatened or distressed by his or her behavior? Other criteria come into play for more serious disorders such as schizophrenia: Does the person act or talk irrationally? Does he or she behave unpredictably from situation to situation? Is his or her appearance or behavior unconventional?

3. The classification of mental illnesses is important for several reasons: First, it helps mental health professionals plan an appropriate treatment. Second are legal reasons: The courts may use psychiatric diagnosis to decide whether a person is competent to stand trial or manage an estate. Third, classification helps researchers study different aspects of psychopathology and evaluate various forms of treatment. Fourth are economic reasons: Classification is necessary before insurance companies and health care plans will provide payments for treatment.

4. Until relatively recently, the mentally disordered were perceived as animals to be tortured, chained, or treated as criminals. In the eighteenth century, Phillipe Pinel, a French physician, suggested that mental problems should be viewed as sicknesses. Although the treatment of people with mental disorders has improved since the time of Pinel, psychiatrist Thomas Szasz argues that mental illness is a myth used even today as an excuse to punish people whose behavior merely violates social norms. For example, the medicalization of deviance was used by the former Soviet Union to justify the punishment of political prisoners. It was also used to justify the treatment of slaves in the United States.

5. Psychologist David Rosenhan (Stanford University) questioned whether the characteristics that lead to diagnoses of abnormality reside in people themselves or in the environmental contexts in which they are observed. Rosenhan and seven other sane people presented themselves for admission to various mental hospitals, complaining of hearing voices. Although they behaved normally once admitted, all were diagnosed as suffering from paranoid schizophrenia—a deception that was never discovered. Rosenhan's study demonstrates that virtually anyone can be diagnosed as mentally ill in the right situation.

6. The biological model considers schizophrenia, for example, a disease that impairs the chemistry or functioning of the brain. The psychological approach assumes that schizophrenia is caused by psychosocial factors, such as traumatic personal experiences. Most researchers take an interactionist perspective, seeing mental disorders as complex interactions of biological and psychological factors. According to this viewpoint, genetic predispositions may alter hormones and the functioning of the brain, but psychosocial stresses determine whether a mental disorder will actually surface.

7. Irving Gottesman (University of Virginia) and Fuller Torrey (National Institute of Mental Health) are studying pairs of identical twins in which one has the disease and the other does not. Torrey's view is that the disorder is caused by biological disease, genetics, brain tissue damage, or hormonal imbalance. Using magnetic resonance imaging (MRI), Gottesman and Torrey have found that the brain of a schizophrenia patient typically has larger ventricles (fluid-filled spaces in the brain) than the normal brain. Their research has convinced them that although genes are important in the

vast majority of cases of schizophrenia, heredity alone does not cause the disorder. Other psychological or biological factors, such as a severe viral infection, being involved in an accident, or being exposed to a drug such as LSD or PCP, may push the person over a threshold for the disorder.

8. Some researchers are exploring cultural factors in the origins of mental disorders. Teresa La Framboise (Stanford University), for example, believes that conflicts between Native American values and those that predominate in the culture around them are partly responsible for the prevalence of mental disorders among Native Americans.

Progress Test

1. **c.** is the answer. In each of these disorders a person's conscious awareness becomes dissociated, or separated, from painful memories, thoughts, and feelings. (pp. 465–466)

2. **c.** is the answer. (pp. 454–455)

3. **b.** is the answer. (video; p. 455)

4. **c.** is the answer. (video)

5. **d.** is the answer. Although depression is universal, anorexia nervosa and bulimia are rare outside of Western culture. (p. 456)

    a. & b. Schizophrenia and depression are both universal.

    c. The text mentions only schizophrenia and depression as universal disorders. Furthermore, neurosis is no longer utilized as a category of diagnosis.

6. **d.** is the answer. (p. 458)

    b. The text does not mention DSM-IV's reliability in terms of a person's age.

7. **a.** is the answer. (p. 460)

    b. The mood disorders include major depressive disorder and bipolar disorder.

    c. The dissociative disorders include dissociative amnesia, dissociative fugue, and dissociative identity disorder.

    d. The personality disorders include the antisocial and histrionic personalities.

8. **b.** is the answer. (video; see also p. 502)

    a. & c. Psychologists and psychoanalysts typically have Ph.D.'s rather than M.D.'s.

    d. This is not a term used by mental health professionals.

9. **c.** is the answer. (video)

10. **e.** is the answer. (video; p. 455)

11. **d.** is the answer. Learned helplessness may lead to self-defeating beliefs, which in turn are linked with depression, a mood disorder. (p. 472)

12. **d.** is the answer. (p. 464)

13. **a.** is the answer. (video; p. 468)

14. **d.** is the answer. A loss may evoke feelings of anger associated with an earlier loss. Such anger is unacceptable to the superego and is turned against the self. This internalized anger results in depression. (p. 471)

a. Learned helplessness would be an explanation offered by the social-cognitive perspective.

b. The self-serving bias is not discussed in terms of its relationship to depression.

c. This is the psychoanalytic explanation of anxiety.

15. **d.** is the answer. Hallucinations are false sensory experiences; delusions are false beliefs. (pp. 476–477)

    a. & b. Obsessions are repetitive and unwanted thoughts. Compulsions are repetitive behaviors.

16. **b.** is the answer. The fact that some disorders are universal and at least partly genetic in origin implicates biological factors in their origin. The fact that other disorders appear only in certain parts of the world implicates sociocultural and psychological factors in their origin. (p. 476)

17. **a.** is the answer. (video)

18. **c.** is the answer. (p. 477)

19. **a.** is the answer. Schizophrenia sufferers are easily distracted by irrelevant stimuli, evidently because of a breakdown in the capacity for selective attention. (p. 476)

20. **a.** is the answer. A dissociative fugue involves totally fleeing one's identity and home. (p. 465)

    b. There is no such disorder.

    c. In dissociative identity disorder, two or more personalities exist simultaneously, which is not the case in the example.

    d. Dissociative amnesia is generally a selective forgetting; it does not involve physical flight or total loss of identity.

21. **d.** is the answer. Repeated wrongdoing and aggressive behavior are part of the pattern associated with the antisocial personality disorder, which may also include marital problems and an inability to keep a job. (p. 481)

    a. Although dissociative identity disorder may involve an aggressive personality, there is nothing in the example to indicate a dissociation.

    b. Nothing in the question indicates that Bob is passive and resigned and having the self-defeating thoughts characteristic of depression.

    c. Bob's behavior does not include the disorganized thinking and disturbed perceptions typical of schizophrenia.

22. **c.** is the answer. Panic attacks are characteristic of certain anxiety disorders, not of schizophrenia. (video; pp. 476–477)

23. **d.** is the answer. Risk for schizophrenia increases for individuals who are related to a schizophrenia victim, and the greater the genetic relatedness, the greater the risk. (video; p. 478)

    a. Schizophrenia victims have an overabundance of the neurotransmitter dopamine, not endorphins.

    b. Being a twin is, in itself, irrelevant to developing schizophrenia.

    c. Although learned helplessnes has been suggested by social-cognitive theorists as a cause of self-defeating depressive behaviors, it has not been suggested as a cause of schizophrenia.

24. **d.** is the answer. In the learning perspective, a phobia, such as Julia's, is seen as a conditioned fear. (pp. 463–464)

a. Because the fear is focused on a specific stimulus, the medical model does not easily account for the phobic disorder. In any event, it would presumably offer an internal, biological explanation.

b. The psychoanalytic view of phobias would be that they represent incompletely repressed anxieties that are displaced onto the feared object.

c. The social-cognitive perspective would emphasize a person's conscious, cognitive processes, not reflexive conditioned responses.

25. **d.** is the answer. Jason is obsessed with cleanliness; as a result, he has developed a compulsion to shower. (pp. 462–463)

    a. Dissociative disorders involve a separation of conscious awareness from previous memories and thoughts.

    b. Generalized anxiety disorder does not have a specific focus.

    c. This disorder is characterized by maladaptive character traits.

26. **d.** is the answer. (p. 461)

    a. There is no evidence that Zheina has *lost* either her memory or her identity, as would occur in dissociative disorders.

    b. Although she has symptoms of depression, Zheina does not show signs of mania, which occurs in bipolar disorder.

    c. Zheina shows no signs of disorganized thinking or disturbed perceptions.

27. **c.** is the answer. An intense fear of a specific object is a phobia. (video; p. 462)

    a. His fear is focused on a specific object, not generalized.

    b. In this disorder a person is troubled by repetitive thoughts and actions.

    d. & e. Conditioned fears form the basis for anxiety rather than mood disorders.

28. **d.** is the answer. (video; pp. 460)

    a. In phobias, anxiety is focused on a specific object.

    b. Major depressive disorder does not include these symptoms.

    c. The obsessive-compulsive disorder (text) is characterized by repetitive and unwanted thoughts and/or actions.

29. **d.** is the answer. (video; p. 462)

    a. Baseless physical symptoms rarely play a role in schizophrenia.

    b. There is no indication that she has lost her identity.

    c. There is no indication that she has suffered a trauma.

30. **b.** is the answer. (pp. 465)

31. **a.** is the answer. Matt's alternating states of the hopelessness and lethargy of depression and the energetic, optimistic state of mania are characteristic of bipolar disorder. (video; p. 468)

    b. Although he was depressed on Tuesday, Matt's manic state on Monday indicates that he is not suffering from major depressive disorder.

    c. Matt was alternately euphoric and depressed, not detached from reality.

    d. That Matt has not lost his memory or changed his identity indicates that he is not suffering from a dissociative disorder.

32. **a.** is the answer. Because Sandy experiences hallucinations (hearing voices), delusions (fearing someone is "out to get her"), and incoherence, she would most likely be diagnosed as suffering from schizophrenia. (video; pp. 476–477)

b., c., d., & e. Neither anxiety disorders nor personality disorders are characterized by disorganized thoughts and perceptions.

33. **d.** is the answer. Freud believed that the anger once felt toward parents was internalized and would produce depression. (p. 471)

a. & b. The learning and social-cognitive perspectives focus on environmental experiences, conditioning, and self-defeating attitudes in explaining depression.

c. The biological perspective focuses on genetic predispositions and biochemical imbalances in explaining depression.

34. **b.** is the answer. (pp. 472–474)

35. **b.** is the answer. Norepinephrine, which increases arousal and boosts mood, is scarce during depression. Drugs that relieve depression tend to increase norepinephrine. (p. 471)

c. *Increasing* serotonin, which is sometimes scarce during depression, might relieve depression.

d. This neurotransmitter is involved in motor responses but has not been linked to psychological disorders.

36. **d.** is the answer. (video; p. 459)

37. **d.** is the answer. Schizophrenia patients sometimes have an excess of receptors for dopamine. Drugs that block these receptors can therefore reduce symptoms of schizophrenia. (p. 478)

a., b., & c. Dopamine receptors have not been implicated in these psychological disorders.

38. **c.** is the answer. Amnesia, which is a dissociative disorder, involves a sudden memory loss brought on by extreme stress. (p. 465)

a. Dissociative disorder is the *broad* category including amnesia, so this answer is not specific enough.

b. Fugue is a dissociative disorder in which flight from one's home and identity accompanies amnesia.

d. Anxiety disorders are not marked by memory loss.

39. **c.** is the answer. (pp. 478–479)

40. **a.** is the answer. (video)

Key Terms

Textbook Terms

1. In order to be classified as a **psychological disorder**, behavior must be atypical, disturbing, maladaptive, and unjustifiable. (p. 454)

2. The **medical model** holds that psychological disorders are illnesses that can be diagnosed, treated, and cured, using traditional methods of medicine and psychiatry. (p. 455)

3. The **bio-psycho-social perspective** assumes that *bio*logical, *psycho*logical, and *socio*cultural factors combine and interact to produce psychological disorders. (p. 456)

4. **DSM-IV** is a short name for the American Psychiatric Association's *Diagnostic and Statistical Manual of Mental Disorders* (*Fourth Edition*), which provides a widely used system of classifying psychological disorders. (p. 458)

5. **Neurotic disorders** is a former term for psychological disorders that, while distressing, still allow a person to think normally and function socially. The term is used mainly in contrast to *psychotic disorders*. (p. 458)

6. **Psychotic disorders** is a former term for psychological disorders that are severely debilitating and involve bizarre thoughts and behavior, and a break from reality. (p. 458)

7. **Anxiety disorders** involve distressing, persistent anxiety or maladaptive behaviors that reduce anxiety. (p. 460)

8. In **generalized anxiety disorder**, the person is continually tense, apprehensive, and in a state of autonomic nervous system arousal for no apparent reason. (p. 460)

9. A **phobia** is an anxiety disorder in which a person has a persistent, irrational fear and avoids a specific object or situation. (p. 460)

10. The **obsessive-compulsive disorder** is an anxiety disorder in which the person experiences uncontrollable and repetitive thoughts (obsessions) and actions (compulsions). (p. 460)

11. A **panic disorder** is an episode of intense dread accompanied by chest pain, dizziness, or choking. It is essentially an escalation of the anxiety associated with generalized anxiety disorder. (p. 462)

12. **Dissociative disorders** involve a separation of conscious awareness from one's previous memories, thoughts, and feelings. (p. 465)

    Memory aid: *To dissociate* is to separate or pull apart. In the **dissociative disorders** a person becomes dissociated from his or her memories and identity.

13. **Dissociative amnesia** is a selective loss of memory. Amnesia may be caused by illness or head injuries, but dissociative amnesia is usually precipitated by extreme stress. (p. 465)

14. **Dissociative fugue** is a dissociative disorder in which forgetting occurs and the person physically runs away from home and identity. (p. 465)

    Memory aid: **Fugue** and *fugitive* both derive from the same Latin root, meaning "to flee."

15. **Dissociative identity disorder** is a dissociative disorder in which a person exhibits two or more distinct and alternating personalities. (p. 466)

16. **Mood disorders** are characterized by emotional extremes. (p. 468)

17. **Major depressive disorder** is the mood disorder that occurs when a person exhibits the lethargy, feelings of worthlessness, or loss of interest in family, friends, and activities characteristic of depression for more than a 2-week period and for no discernible reason. Because of its relative frequency, depression has been called the "common cold" of psychological disorders. (p. 468)

18. **Mania** is the wildly optimistic, euphoric, hyperactive state that alternates with depression in bipolar disorder. (p. 468)

19. **Bipolar disorder** is the mood disorder in which a person alternates between depression and the euphoria of a manic state. (p. 468)

    Memory aid: *Bipolar* means having two poles, that is, two opposite qualities. In **bipolar disorder,** the opposing states are mania and depression.

20. **Schizophrenia** refers to the group of severe psychotic disorders whose symptoms may include disorganized and delusional thinking, inappropriate emotions and actions, and disturbed perceptions. (p. 476)

21. **Delusions** are false beliefs that often are symptoms of psychotic disorders. (p. 476)

22. **Hallucinations** are false sensory experiences that often are symptoms of schizophrenia. (p. 477)

23. **Personality disorders** are characterized by inflexible and enduring maladaptive character traits that impair social functioning. (p. 481)

24. The **antisocial personality disorder** is a personality disorder in which the person is aggressive, ruthless, and shows no sign of a conscience that would inhibit wrongdoing. (p. 481)

Program Terms

25. **Psychopathology** is the study of mental disorders.

26. A **mental disorder** is defined as a clinically significant behavioral or psychological syndrome that is typically associated with a painful condition or impairment in one or more important areas of functioning.

27. **SPECT analysis** is a diagnostic technique that measures blood flow in the brain while the subject performs some cognitive task.

PROGRAM 22

Psychotherapy

TEXTBOOK ASSIGNMENT: Chapter 16: Therapy, pp. 487–513

ORIENTATION

The program and reading assignment discuss the major psychotherapies and biomedical therapies for maladaptive behaviors. All of these psychotherapies derive from the psychological perspectives discussed earlier, namely, the psychoanalytic, humanistic, behavioral, and cognitive perspectives. The chapter groups the therapies by perspective but also emphasizes the common threads that run through them. In evaluating the therapies, the chapter points out that, although people who are untreated often improve, those receiving psychotherapy tend to improve somewhat more, regardless of the type of therapy they receive.

The biomedical therapies discussed are drug therapies; electroconvulsive therapy; and psychosurgery, which is seldom used. By far the most important of the biomedical therapies, drug therapies are being used in the treatment of psychotic, anxiety, and mood disorders.

Because the origins of problems often lie beyond the individual, the chapter and program conclude with approaches that aim at preventing psychological disorders by focusing on the family or on the larger social environment as possible contributors to psychological disorders.

NOTE: Answer guidelines for all Program 22 questions begin on page 404.

GOALS

After completing your study of the program and reading assignment, you should be able to:

1. Describe the major approaches to psychotherapy.

2. Identify and describe the drug therapies, and discuss the controversy over other biomedical therapies.

3. Discuss the current attempts to prevent psychological disorders by changing the social environment.

GUIDED STUDY

Textbook Assignment

The text chapter should be studied one section at a time. Before you read, preview each section by skimming it, noting headings and boldface items. Then read the appropriate section objectives from the following outline. Keep these objectives in mind and, as you read the chapter section, search for the information that will enable you to meet each objective. Once you have finished a section, write out answers for its objectives.

The Psychological Therapies (pp. 488–501)

1. Briefly explain the current approach to therapy.

2. Discuss the aims and methods of psychoanalysis and explain the critics' concerns with this form of therapy.

3. Identify the basic themes of humanistic therapies and describe Rogers's person-centered approach.

4. Describe Perls's Gestalt therapy.

5. Identify the basic assumptions of behavior therapy and discuss the classical conditioning therapies.

6. Describe the premise behind operant conditioning techniques and explain the critics' concerns with these techniques.

7. Identify the basic assumptions of the cognitive therapies and describe group therapy.

Evaluating Psychotherapies (pp. 501–507)

8. Discuss the findings regarding the effectiveness of psychotherapy.

9. Discuss the commonalities among the psychotherapies.

10. Discuss the role of culture and values in psychotherapy.

The Biomedical Therapies (pp. 507–512)

11. Identify the common forms of drug therapy.

12. Describe the use of electroconvulsive therapy and psychosurgery in the treatment of psychological disorders.

Preventing Psychological Disorders (pp. 512–513)

13. Explain the rationale and goals of preventive mental health programs.

Program Assignment

Read the following objectives before you watch Program 22. As you watch, be alert for information that will help you answer each objective. Taking notes during the program will help you to formulate your answers later. After the program, write answers to the objectives. If you have access to the program on videotape, you may replay portions to refresh your memory.

1. Identify the various professional mental health care providers, and describe the two basic categories of therapy.

2. Identify the various professionals who provide biomedical therapy, and discuss the controversy over the prefrontal lobotomy and electroconvulsive therapy.

3. Discuss drug therapy, including its history, advantages, and disadvantages.

4. Discuss what likely will be the "next great revolution" in biomedical therapy, citing research that pertains to the understanding of chronic depression.

5. Identify the major ingredients of psychodynamic therapy, and discuss how this category of therapy has changed in recent years.

6. Describe a new direction in mental health care today.

PROGRESS TEST

Circle your answers to the following questions and check them with the answers on page 408. If your answer is incorrect, read the explanation for why it is incorrect and then consult the appropriate pages of the text (in parentheses following the correct answer).

1. The effectiveness of psychotherapy has been assessed both through clients' perspectives and through controlled research studies. What have such assessments found?
   a. Clients' perceptions and controlled studies alike strongly affirm the effectiveness of psychotherapy.
   b. Whereas clients' perceptions strongly affirm the effectiveness of psychotherapy, studies point to more modest results.
   c. Whereas studies strongly affirm the effectiveness of psychotherapy, many clients feel dissatisfied with their progress.
   d. Clients' perceptions and controlled studies alike paint a very mixed picture of the effectiveness of psychotherapy.

2. An eclectic psychotherapist is one who:
   a. takes a nondirective approach in helping clients solve their problems.
   b. views psychological disorders as usually stemming from one cause, such as a biological abnormality.
   c. uses one particular technique, such as psychoanalysis or behavior modification, in treating disorders.
   d. uses a variety of techniques, depending on the client and the problem.

3. The technique of systematic desensitization is based on the premise that maladaptive symptoms are:
   a. a reflection of irrational thinking.
   b. conditioned responses.
   c. expressions of unfulfilled wishes.
   d. all of the above.

4. The two main therapeutic approaches to treating mental disorders are:
   a. the biomedical and the psychological.
   b. the Freudian and the biomedical.
   c. behavior modification and psychoanalysis.
   d. rational-emotive therapy and psychoanalysis.

5. According to Hans Strupp, how have psychodynamic therapies changed in recent years?
   a. Less emphasis is placed on early childhood experiences.
   b. The patient-therapist relationship is no longer emphasized.
   c. More emphasis is placed on treating symptoms rather than their underlying causes.
   d. Shorter courses of treatment are often used.

6. A person can derive benefits from psychotherapy simply by believing in it. This illustrates the importance of:
   a. spontaneous remission.
   b. the placebo effect.
   c. the transference effect.
   d. interpretation.

7. Before 1950, the main mental health providers were:
   a. psychologists.
   b. paraprofessionals.
   c. psychiatrists.
   d. the clergy.
   e. social workers.

8. The techniques of counterconditioning are based on principles of:
   a. observational learning.
   b. classical conditioning.
   c. operant conditioning.
   d. behavior modification.

9. Electroconvulsive therapy is most useful in the treatment of:
   a. schizophrenia.
   b. depression.
   c. personality disorders.
   d. anxiety disorders.
   e. bipolar disorder.

10. Which biomedical therapy is *most* likely to be practiced today?
    a. psychosurgery
    b. electroconvulsive therapy
    c. drug therapy
    d. counterconditioning
    e. aversive conditioning

11. A psychotherapist who believes that the best way to treat psychological disorders is to prevent them from developing would be *most* likely to view disordered behavior as:
    a. maladaptive thoughts and actions.
    b. expressions of unconscious conflicts.
    c. conditioned responses.
    d. an understandable response to stressful social conditions.

12. Which of the following is *not a* common criticism of behavior therapy?
    a. Clients may not develop intrinsic motivation for their new behaviors.
    b. Behavior control is unethical.
    c. Although one symptom may be eliminated, another may replace it unless the underlying problem is treated.
    d. All of the above are criticisms of behavior therapy.

13. The following are some of the conclusions drawn in the text regarding the effectiveness of psychotherapy. For which of these conclusions did the Massachusetts study of predelinquent boys provide evidence?
    a. Clients' perceptions of the effectiveness of therapy usually are very accurate.
    b. Clients' perceptions of the effectiveness of therapy differ somewhat from the objective findings.
    c. Individuals who receive treatment do somewhat better than individuals who do not.
    d. Overall, no one type of therapy is a "winner," but certain therapies are more suited to certain problems.

14. Which type of psychotherapy emphasizes the individual's inherent potential for self-fulfillment?
    a. behavior therapy
    b. psychoanalysis
    c. humanistic therapy
    d. biomedical therapy

15. Principles of operant conditioning underlie the techniques of:
    a. counterconditioning.
    b. systematic desensitization.
    c. rational-emotive therapy.
    d. aversive conditioning.
    e. the token economy.

16. Which type of therapy focuses on eliminating irrational thinking?
    a. Gestalt therapy
    b. person-centered therapy
    c. rational-emotive therapy
    d. behavior therapy

17. The most widely prescribed drugs in biomedical therapy are the:
    a. antianxiety drugs.
    b. antipsychotic drugs.
    c. antidepressant drugs.
    d. amphetamines.

18. Which form of therapy is *most* likely to be successful in treating depression?
    a. behavior therapy
    b. psychoanalysis
    c. cognitive therapy
    d. humanistic therapy

19. A meta-analysis of research studies comparing the effectiveness of professional therapists with paraprofessionals found that:
    a. the professionals were much more effective than the paraprofessionals.
    b. the paraprofessionals were much more effective than the professionals.
    c. except in treating depression, the paraprofessionals were about as effective as the professionals.
    d. the paraprofessionals were about as effective as the professionals.

20. Among the common ingredients of the psychotherapies is:
    a. the offer of a therapeutic relationship.
    b. the expectation among clients that the therapy will prove helpful.
    c. the chance to develop a fresh perspective on oneself and the world.
    d. all of the above.

21. Which of the following is the drug most commonly used to treat bipolar disorder?
    a. Valium
    b. chlorpromazine
    c. Librium
    d. lithium

22. The prefrontal lobotomy procedure is not widely used today because:
    a. it produces a lethargic, immature personality.
    b. it is irreversible.
    c. calming drugs became available in the 1950s.
    d. of all of the above reasons.

23. One reason that aversive conditioning may only be temporarily effective is that:
    a. for ethical reasons, therapists cannot use sufficiently intense unconditioned stimuli to sustain classical conditioning.
    b. patients are often unable to become sufficiently relaxed for conditioning to take place.
    c. patients know that outside the therapist's office they can engage in the undesirable behavior without fear of aversive consequences.
    d. most conditioned responses are elicited by many nonspecific stimuli, and it is impossible to countercondition them all.

24. During a session with his psychoanalyst, Jamal hesitates while describing a highly embarrassing thought. In the psychoanalytic framework, this is an example of:
    a. transference.
    b. insight.
    c. mental repression.
    d. resistance.

25. During psychoanalysis, Jane has developed strong feelings of hatred for her therapist. The analyst interprets Jane's behavior in terms of a _____ of her feelings toward her father.
    a. projection
    b. resistance
    c. regression
    d. transference

26. Given that Jim's therapist attempts to help him by offering genuineness, acceptance, and empathy, she is probably practicing:
    a. psychoanalysis.
    b. behavior therapy.
    c. Gestalt therapy.
    d. cognitive therapy.
    e. person-centered therapy.

27. After Darnel dropped a pass in an important football game, he became depressed and vowed to quit the team because of his athletic incompetence. The campus psychologist challenged his illogical reasoning and pointed out that Darnel's "incompetence" had earned him an athletic scholarship. The psychologist's response was most typical of a _____ therapist.
    a. Gestalt
    b. psychoanalytic
    c. person-centered
    d. rational-emotive

28. To help Sam quit smoking, his therapist blew a blast of smoke into Sam's face each time Sam inhaled. Which technique is the therapist using?
    a. rational-emotive therapy
    b. behavior modification
    c. systematic desensitization
    d. aversive conditioning

29. In an experiment testing the effects of a new antipsychotic drug, neither Dr. Cunningham nor her patients know whether the patients are in the experimental or the control group. This is an example of the _____ technique.
    a. meta-analysis
    b. within-subjects
    c. double-blind
    d. single-blind

30. Brad is seeking a psychotherapist who will help him get in touch with himself by bringing unconscious feelings into awareness and focusing on his present problems. Brad should probably choose a _____ therapist.
    a. psychoanalytic
    b. Gestalt
    c. humanistic
    d. behavioral

31. A relative wants to know which type of therapy works best. You should tell your relative that:
    a. psychotherapy does not work.
    b. behavior therapy is the most effective.
    c. cognitive therapy is the most effective.
    d. group therapy is best for his problem.
    e. no one type of therapy is consistently the most successful.

32. Seth enters therapy to talk about some issues that have been upsetting him. The therapist prescribes some medication to help him. The therapist is most likely a:
    a. psychologist.
    b. psychiatrist.
    c. psychiatric social worker.
    d. clinical social worker.

33. Ben is a cognitive behavior therapist. Compared to Rachel, who is a behavior therapist, Ben is more likely to:
    a. base his therapy on principles of operant conditioning.
    b. base his therapy on principles of classical conditioning.
    c. address clients' attitudes as well as behaviors.
    d. focus on clients' unconscious urges.

34. In order to help him overcome his fear of flying, Duane's therapist has him construct a hierarchy of anxiety-triggering stimuli and then learn to associate each with a state of deep relaxation. Duane's therapist is using the technique called:
    a. systematic desensitization.
    b. aversive conditioning.
    c. shaping.
    d. free association.
    e. rational-emotive therapy.

35. A patient in a hospital receives poker chips for making her bed, being punctual at meal times, and maintaining her physical appearance. The poker chips can be exchanged for privileges, such as television viewing, snacks, and magazines. This is an example of the _____ therapy technique called _____ .
    a. Gestalt; systematic desensitization
    b. behavior; the token economy
    c. cognitive; the token economy
    d. humanistic; systematic desensitization

36. Linda's doctor prescribes medication that blocks the activity of dopamine in her nervous system. Evidently, Linda is being treated with an _____ drug.
    a. antipsychotic
    b. antianxiety
    c. antidepressant
    d. anticonvulsive

37. Which type(s) of psychotherapy would be most likely to use the interpretation of dreams as a technique for bringing unconscious feelings into awareness?
    a. psychoanalysis
    b. Gestalt therapy
    c. cognitive therapy
    d. all of the above
    e. a. and b.

38. Abraham's doctor prescribes medication that increases the availability of norepinephrine in his nervous system. Evidently, Abraham is being treated with an _____ drug.
    a. antipsychotic
    b. antianxiety
    c. antidepressant
    d. anticonvulsive

39. Of the following therapists, who would be most likely to interpret a person's psychological problems in terms of repressed impulses?
    a. a behavior therapist
    b. a cognitive therapist
    c. a humanistic therapist
    d. a psychoanalyst

40. Rollo May was a _____ therapist who was one of the founders of _____ therapy.
    a. behavior; desensitization
    b. psychoanalytic; insight
    c. humanistic; person-centered
    d. cognitive; rational-emotive

KEY TERMS

Using your own words, write a brief definition or explanation of each of the following terms.

Textbook Terms

1. psychotherapy

2. eclectic approach

3. psychoanalysis

4. resistance

5. interpretation

6. transference

7. person-centered therapy

8. active listening

9. Gestalt therapy

10. behavior therapy

11. counterconditioning

12. systematic desensitization

13. aversive conditioning

14. token economy

15. cognitive therapy

16. rational-emotive therapy

17. family therapy

18. meta-analysis

19. psychopharmacology

20. lithium

21. electroconvulsive therapy (ECT)

22. psychosurgery

23. lobotomy

Program Terms

24. free association

25. biological biasing

26. genetic counseling

ANSWERS

Guided Study

The following guidelines provide the main points that your answers should have touched upon.

Textbook Assignment

1. Psychotherapy is the planned treatment of mental and emotional problems based on an emotionally charged, confiding interaction between a socially sanctioned healer and a sufferer. The various types of psychotherapy derive from psychology's major personality theories: psychoanalytic, humanistic, behavioral, and cognitive. Half of all contemporary psychotherapists take an eclectic approach, using a blend of therapies tailored to meet their clients' particular problems.

2. Psychoanalysis assumes that psychological problems are caused by repressed unconscious impulses and conflicts that develop during childhood, and so its goal is to bring these feelings into conscious awareness and help the person work through them.
    Psychoanalysts may ask their patients to report everything that comes to mind (free association). Blocks in the flow of retrieval (resistance) are believed to indicate the repression of sensitive material. The analyst's interpretations of resistances aim to provide the patient with insight into their underlying meaning. Psychoanalysts interpret dreams for their latent content and the transference of feelings from early relationships in order to expose repressed feelings.

Psychoanalysis has been criticized for offering interpretations that are impossible to prove or disprove and for being a lengthy and expensive process that only the relatively well-off can afford.

3. Humanistic therapists aim to boost self-fulfillment by helping people grow in self-awareness and self-acceptance. Unlike psychoanalysis, humanistic therapies focus on conscious thoughts as they occur in the present. Carl Rogers's nondirective person-centered therapy, which is based on the assumption that most people have within themselves the resources for growth, aims to provide an environment in which therapists exhibit genuineness, acceptance, and empathy. Humanistic therapists often use *active listening* to provide a psychological mirror that helps clients see themselves more clearly.

4. Perls's Gestalt therapy combines the psychoanalytic emphasis on bringing unconscious feelings into awareness with the humanistic emphasis on taking responsibility for oneself in the present. By using role-playing and other techniques, Gestalt therapists encourage clients to become more aware and expressive of their feelings.

5. Behavior therapy applies learning principles to eliminate unwanted behavior. Counterconditioning describes classical conditioning procedures that condition new responses to stimuli that trigger unwanted behaviors. One type of counterconditioning, systematic desensitization, is used to treat phobias, for example, by conditioning people to associate a pleasant, relaxed state with gradually increasing anxiety-provoking stimuli. Aversive conditioning is a type of counterconditioning that associates unwanted behavior (such as drinking alcohol) with unpleasant feelings (such as nausea).

6. Operant conditioning procedures are used to treat specific behavioral problems by reinforcing desired behaviors and withholding reinforcement for undesired behaviors. In institutional settings, for example, a token economy is employed to shape desired behaviors. With this procedure, patients earn tokens for exhibiting desired behavior, then exchange the accumulated tokens for various privileges.

    Critics note that because "behavior modification" depends on extrinsic rewards, the appropriate behaviors may disappear when the person leaves the conditioning environment. Second, critics question whether it is ethical for a therapist to exercise so much control over a person's behavior.

7. The cognitive therapies assume that our thinking influences our feelings and that maladaptive thinking patterns can be replaced with new, more constructive ones. Rational-emotive therapy is a confrontational cognitive therapy that challenges people's illogical, self-defeating attitudes and actions. Cognitive therapy for depression helps people to discover and reform their habitually negative patterns of thinking. Cognitive behavior therapy expands upon standard cognitive therapy to include helping people to practice their newly learned positive approach in everyday settings.

    Group therapies provide a social context which allows people to discover that others have similar problems and to try out new ways of behaving. Self-help and support groups are examples of the group approach to psychotherapy. Another is family therapy, which treats individuals within their family system.

8. The effectiveness of psychotherapy depends on how it is measured. Although clients' testimonials and clinicians' perceptions strongly affirm the effectiveness of psychotherapy, controlled research studies, such as those originated by Hans Eysenck, report a similar improvement rate among treated and untreated people. More recent research using meta-analysis—

combining the results of many different studies—reveals that psychotherapy is somewhat effective and that it is cost-effective compared with the greater costs of physician care for underlying psychological ailments. The same research revealed that although no particular type of therapy proved consistently superior, certain therapies work best with certain disorders. Behavioral conditioning therapies, for example, work best with specific behavior problems. With depression, the cognitive therapies prove most successful.

9. First, because they enable people to believe that things can and will get better, psychotherapies provide hope for demoralized people. This placebo effect explains why all sorts of treatments may produce cures. Second, therapy offers people a plausible explanation of problems and alternative ways of responding. Third, therapy establishes an empathic, trusting, caring relationship between client and therapist.

10. All therapists have their own values, which may differ radically, as illustrated by Albert Ellis's and Allen Bergin's widely divergent views. Because these values influence their therapy, they should be divulged to patients. Value differences may become particularly significant when a therapist from one culture meets a client from another.

11. Discoveries in psychopharmacology revolutionized the treatment of disordered people and greatly reduced the need for psychosurgery or hospitalization. Antipsychotic drugs such as Thorazine and Clozaril are used to reduce positive and negative symptoms of schizophrenia, respectively. These drugs work by blocking receptor sites for the neurotransmitter dopamine. Antianxiety drugs, such as Valium and Librium, reduce tension and anxiety by depressing central nervous system activity. Antidepressant drugs elevate mood by increasing the availability of the neurotransmitters norepinephrine and serotonin; fluoxetine (Prozac) blocks the reabsorption and removal of serotonin from synapses. The drug lithium is used to stabilize the manic-depressive mood swings of the bipolar disorder.

12. Electroconvulsive therapy (ECT), which is used by psychiatrists to treat severe depression, produces marked improvement in at least 80 percent of patients without discernible brain damage. ECT may work by increasing the release of norepinephrine or by inducing seizures that calm neural centers in which overactivity produces depression.

    Because its effects are irreversible, psychosurgery, which removes or destroys brain tissue to change behavior, is the most drastic biomedical intervention. The best-known form, the lobotomy, was developed by Moniz in the 1930s to calm emotional and violent patients. During the 1950s, with advances in psychopharmacology, psychosurgery was largely abandoned.

13. Psychotherapists who view psychological disorders as responses to a disturbed and stressful society contend that the best approach is to prevent problems from developing by treating not only the person but also the person's social context. Accordingly, programs that help alleviate poverty, discrimination, constant criticism, unemployment, sexism, and other demoralizing situations that undermine people's sense of competence, personal control, and self-esteem are thought to be effective in reducing people's risk of psychological disorders.

Program Assignment

1. Professional treatment for mental illness is available from a wide range of health specialists, including clinical psychologists, psychiatrists, psychoanalysts, psychological counselors, and psychiatrically trained social workers.

Because mental problems vary greatly in kind and severity, there are almost as many varieties of therapies as their are mental disorders—over 250.

Therapies can be divided into two major groups: the biomedical and psychological approaches. Biomedical therapy is based on the premise that certain mental disorders are diseases and that treatment must be biologically based to reverse or irradicate them. Psychological therapy can be divided into four major groups: psychodynamic (psychoanalytic), behavioral, cognitive, and humanist.

2. Biomedical therapists include psychiatrists, neurobiologists, and others who specialize in identifying specific disease states that are assumed to underlie mental disorders.

   Psychosurgical procedures are the most radical treatments of the biomedical approach. The prefrontal lobotomy—cutting the nerve fibers that connect the brain's frontal lobes with the thalamus—is the best known of these and was typically performed on an agitated schizophrenia patient or someone with extreme compulsions and intense anxiety. The operation eliminated these symptoms by, in effect, disconnecting the individual from his or her past traumas and anxieties about the future. But the operation resulted in emotional flatness, childlike emotions, and the loss of the ability to remember clearly and to plan ahead. Because the cure was often worse than the illness, its use is now restricted to the most extreme cases where no other treatment has helped.

   Electroconvulsive therapy is less dramatic in its effect and continues to be used as an antidepressant, but it does cause memory loss in some patients. (Guided Study text item 12 describes these procedures in more detail.)

3. The real revolution in biomedical therapy began in the mid-1950s, with the advent of tranquilizing drugs. Chlorpromazine was the first miracle drug that worked on many of the symptoms found in schizophrenia patients, including delusions, hallucinations, social withdrawal, and agitation. Lithium is used for bipolar disorder. In addition to controlling symptoms of mental disorders, drug therapies make it possible to conduct psychotherapy with patients who previously could not be reached. The danger with drug therapy is that overworked hospital staff may merely tranquilize patients and leave it at that, or that individuals may overmedicate themselves to cope with everyday life. For example, the nation's most popular tranquilizer, Valium, is also addictive and is taken daily by more than 8 million Americans, many of whom have given up trying to deal with the sources of their stress.

4. If chemotherapy was the last great revolution in biomedical therapy, genetics may be the next one. Evidence that some disorders are inherited has already led to genetic counseling, in which at-risk families are counseled about the probability of passing on defective genes. Chronic schizophrenia, some kinds of mental retardation, and depression are all disorders to which genetic factors contribute.

   Research involving the Amish community has identified the gene on chromosome 11 which when defective contributes to one type of depression. This is an example of biological biasing, in which people who are genetically primed for a disorder are more likely to get it than members of the general population, but *only* if they are also under prolonged psychological stress.

5. According to Hans Strupp (Vanderbilt University), the major ingredients of psychodynamic therapy are (1) a patient who can work in therapy, (2) a therapist who can work with this patient, (3) a relationship between the two

that makes it possible for them to work together over time, and (4) motivation on the part of the patient to improve.

Because it typically takes a year or more, traditional psychoanalysis is very expensive and reaches only a fraction of people who need psychotherapy. Consequently, over the years psychoanalysts have modified some of Freud's techniques. For example, the bulk of therapists today practice an intermediate form of therapy, which takes much less time.

6. A new direction in mental health care is preventing mental illness before it occurs. To this end many practitioners are adopting a public health model in which the source of the problem is seen as residing in the individual's social and physical environment.

For a new breed of specialists, called health psychologists, finding ways of changing the physical and social environment can be the key in helping prevent or minimize mental illness.

Progress Test

1. **b.** is the answer. Clients' testimonials regarding psychotherapy are generally very positive. The research, in contrast, seems to show that therapy is only *somewhat* effective. (pp. 501, 503–504)

2. **d.** is the answer. Today, half of all psychotherapists describe themselves as eclectic—as using a blend of therapies. (p. 488)

   a. An eclectic therapist may use a nondirective approach with certain behaviors; however, a more directive approach might be chosen for other clients and problems.

   b. In fact, just the opposite is true. Eclectic therapists generally view disorders as stemming from many influences.

   c. Eclectic therapists, in contrast to this example, use a combination of treatments.

3. **b.** is the answer. (p. 493)

   a. This reflects a cognitive perspective.

   c. This reflects a psychoanalytic perspective.

4. **a.** is the answer. (video; p. 487)

   b. Freudian therapy, more generally known as psychoanalysis, is but one variety of psychological therapy.

   c. & d. Each of these would be classified as a psychological therapy.

5. **d.** is the answer. (video)

6. **b.** is the answer. (p. 505)

   a. Spontaneous remission refers to improvement without any treatment.

   c. Transference is the psychoanalytic phenomenon in which a client transfers feelings from other relationships onto his or her analyst.

   d. Interpretation is the psychoanalytic procedure through which the analyst helps the client become aware of resistances and understand their meaning.

7. **c.** is the answer. (p. 501)

8. **b.** is the answer. Counterconditioning techniques involve taking an established CS, which triggers an undesirable CR, and pairing it with a new UCS in order to condition a new, and more adaptive, CR. (p. 493)

   a. As indicated by the name, counterconditioning techniques are a form of conditioning; they do not involve learning by observation.

   c. & d. The principles of operant conditioning are the basis of behavior modification, which, in contrast to counterconditioning techniques, involves use of reinforcement.

9. **b.** is the answer. Although no one is sure how ECT works, one possible explanation is that it increases release of norepinephrine, the neurotransmitter that elevates mood. (video; p. 510)

10. **c.** is the answer. (video; p. 507)

   a. The fact that its effects are irreversible makes psychosurgery a drastic procedure, and with advances in psychopharmacology, psychosurgery was largely abandoned.

   b. ECT is still widely used as a treatment of major depression, but in general it is not used as frequently as drug therapy.

   d. & e. Counterconditioning and aversive conditioning are not biomedical therapies.

11. **d.** is the answer. (video; p. 512)

   a. This would be the perspective of a cognitive behavior therapist.

   b. This would be the perspective of a psychoanalyst or Gestalt therapist.

   c. This would be the perspective of a behavior therapist.

12. **d.** is the answer. (p. 496)

13. **b.** is the answer. Although many of the treated men offered glowing reports of the effectiveness of their therapy, these testimonials did not accurately reflect the results. (p. 503)

   a. In fact, as this study showed, clients' perceptions of the effectiveness of psychotherapy are often very positive but inaccurate.

   c. On some measures, the treated men exhibited slightly *more* problems than the untreated men.

   d. This study did not compare the effectiveness of different forms of psychotherapy.

14. **c.** is the answer. (video; p. 490)

   a. Behavior therapy focuses on behavior, not self-awareness.

   b. Psychoanalysis focuses on bringing repressed feelings into awareness.

   d. Biomedical therapy focuses on physical treatment through drugs, ECT, or psychosurgery.

15. **e.** is the answer. (video; p. 495)

   a., b., & d. These techniques are based on classical conditioning.

   c. This is a type of cognitive therapy.

16. **c.** is the answer. (video; p. 496–497)

   a. Gestalt therapy, which was discussed in the text, aims to help people become more aware of and able to express their present-day feelings.

   b. In this humanistic therapy, the therapist facilitates the client's growth by offering a genuine, accepting, and empathic environment.

   d. Behavior therapy concentrates on modifying the actual symptoms of psychological problems.

17. **a.** is the answer. Antianxiety drugs are among the most heavily prescribed of all drugs. (p. 509)

18. **c.** is the answer. (p. 505)

a. Behavior therapy is most likely to be successful in treating specific behavior problems, such as phobias.

b. & d. The text does not single out particular disorders for which these therapies tend to be most effective.

19. **d.** is the answer. Even when dealing with seriously depressed adults, the paraprofessionals were as effective as the professionals. (p. 506)

20. **d.** is the answer. (pp. 505–506)

21. **d.** is the answer. Lithium works as a mood stabilizer. (video; p. 510)

    a. & c. Valium and Librium are antianxiety drugs.

    b. Chlorpromazine is an antipsychotic drug.

22. **d.** is the answer. (video; pp. 511–512)

23. **c.** is the answer. Although aversive conditioning may work in the short run, the person's ability to discriminate between the situation in which the aversive conditioning occurs and other situations can limit the treatment's effectiveness. (p. 495)

    a., b., & d. These were not offered in the textbook as limitations of the effectiveness of aversive conditioning.

24. **d.** is the answer. Resistances are blocks in the flow of free association that hint at underlying anxiety. (video; p. 489)

    a. In transference, a patient attributes feelings from other relationships to his or her analyst.

    b. The goal of psychoanalysis is for patients to gain insight into their feelings.

    c. Although such hesitation may well involve material that has been repressed, the hesitation itself is a resistance.

25. **d.** is the answer. In transference, the patient develops toward the therapist feelings that were experienced in important early relationships but were repressed. (p. 489)

    a. Projection is a defense mechanism in which a person imputes his or her own feelings to someone else.

    b. Resistances are blocks in the flow of free association that indicate repressed material.

    c. Regression is a defense mechanism in which a person retreats to an earlier form of behavior.

26. **e.** is the answer. According to Rogers's person-centered therapy, the therapist must exhibit genuineness, acceptance, and empathy if the client is to move toward self-fulfillment. (p. 490)

    a. Psychoanalysts are much more directive in providing interpretations of clients' problems than are humanistic therapists.

    b. Behavior therapists focus on modifying the behavioral symptoms of psychological problems.

    c. Like psychoanalysts, Gestalt psychologists emphasize bringing unconscious conflicts into conscious awareness.

    d. Cognitive therapists teach people to think and act in new, more adaptive ways.

27. **d.** is the answer. Because the psychologist is challenging Darnel's illogical, self-defeating attitude, this response is most typical of rational-emotive therapy. (video; pp. 496–497)

a. Gestalt therapists combine the psychoanalytic emphasis on bringing unconscious feelings to awareness with the humanistic emphasis on getting in touch with oneself.

b. Psychoanalysts focus on helping patients gain insight into previously repressed feelings.

c. Person-centered therapists attempt to facilitate clients' growth by offering a genuine, accepting, and empathic environment.

28. d. is the answer. Aversive conditioning is the classical conditioning technique in which a positive response is replaced by a negative response. (In this example, the UCS is the hot blast of smoke, the CS is the taste of the cigarette as it is inhaled, and the intended CR is aversion to cigarettes.) (p. 494)

    a. Rational-emotive therapy is a confrontational cognitive therapy.

    b. Behavior modification applies the principles of operant conditioning and thus, in contrast to the example, uses reinforcement.

    c. Systematic desensitization is used to help people overcome specific anxieties.

29. c. is the answer. (p. 508)

    a. This is a statistical technique used to combine the results of many different research studies.

    b. In this design, which is not mentioned in the text, there is only a single research group.

    d. This answer would be correct if the experimenter but not the subjects knew which condition was in effect.

30. b. is the answer. Gestalt therapists combine the psychoanalytic emphasis on bringing unconscious feelings into awareness with the humanistic emphasis on getting in touch with oneself. (p. 492)

    a. Psychoanalysts place more emphasis on understanding past feelings than on self-awareness of current problems.

    c. & d. These therapies make no reference to unconscious processes.

31. e. is the answer. (p. 505)

    a. Psychotherapy has proven "somewhat effective" and more cost-effective than physician care for psychological disorders.

    b. & c. Behavior and cognitive therapies are effective in treating specific behavior problems and depression, respectively, but not necessarily in treating other problems.

    d. The text does not specify which problems are best treated with group therapy.

32. b. is the answer. Psychiatrists are physicians who specialize in treating psychological disorders. As doctors they can prescribe medications. (video; p. 502)

    a., c., & d. These professionals cannot prescribe drugs.

33. c. is the answer. (video; p. 499)

    a. & b. Behavior therapists make extensive use of techniques based on both operant and classical conditioning.

    d. Neither behavior therapists nor cognitive behavior therapists focus on clients' unconscious urges.

34. a. is the answer. (p. 493)

b. Aversive conditioning associates unpleasant states with unwanted behaviors.

c. Shaping is an operant conditioning technique in which successive approximations of a desired behavior are reinforced.

d. Free association is a psychoanalytic technique in which a patient says whatever comes to mind.

e. Rational-emotive therapy is a confrontational cognitive therapy.

35. **b.** is the answer. (p. 495)

36. **a.** is the answer. (p. 508)

37. **e.** is the answer. Both psychoanalysis and Gestalt therapy seek insight into a patient's unconscious feelings. The analysis of dreams, slips of the tongue, and resistances are believed to be a window into these feelings. (video; pp. 489, 492)

    c. Cognitive therapists avoid reference to unconscious feelings and would therefore be uninterested in interpreting dreams.

38. **c.** is the answer. (p. 509)

39. **d.** is the answer. A key aim of psychoanalysis is to unearth and understand repressed impulses. (video; p. 489)

    a., b., & c. Behavior and cognitive therapists avoid concepts such as "repression" and "unconscious"; behavior and humanistic therapists focus on the present rather than the past.

40. **c.** is the answer. (video)

    a. The program did not mention a particular therapist in this area.

    b. There is no such thing as insight therapy.

    d. This answer would be a correct description of Albert Ellis.

Key Terms

Textbook Terms

1. **Psychotherapy** is an emotionally charged, confiding interaction between a trained therapist and someone who suffers from psychological difficulties. (p. 488)

2. With an **eclectic approach**, therapists are not locked into one form of psychotherapy but draw on whatever combination seems best suited to a client's needs. (p. 488)

3. **Psychoanalysis**, the therapy developed by Freud, attempts to give clients self-insight by bringing into awareness and interpreting previously repressed feelings. (p. 488)

   Example: The tools of the **psychoanalyst** include free association, the analysis of dreams and transferences, and the interpretation of repressed impulses.

4. **Resistance** is the psychoanalytic term for the blocking from consciousness of anxiety-provoking memories. Hesitation during free association may reflect resistance. (p. 489)

5. **Interpretation** is the psychoanalytic term for the analyst's helping the client to understand resistances and other aspects of behavior, so that the client may gain deeper insights. (p. 489)

6. **Transference** is the psychoanalytic term for a patient's redirecting to the analyst emotions from other relationships. (p. 489)

7. **Person-centered therapy** is a humanistic therapy developed by Rogers, in which growth and self-awareness are facilitated in an environment that offers genuineness, acceptance, and empathy. (p. 490)

8. **Active listening** is a nondirective technique of person-centered therapy, in which the listener echoes, restates, clarifies, but does not interpret, clients' remarks. (p. 491)

9. **Gestalt therapy** is a humanistic therapy developed by Perls that combines the humanistic emphases with those of psychoanalysis in an effort to help people become more aware of and responsible for their feelings in the present. (p. 492)

10. **Behavior therapy** is therapy that applies principles of operant or classical conditioning to the elimination of problem behaviors. (p. 492)

11. **Counterconditioning** is a category of behavior therapy in which new responses are classically conditioned to stimuli that elicit unwanted behaviors. (p. 493)

12. **Systematic desensitization** is a type of counterconditioning in which a state of relaxation is classically conditioned to a hierarchy of gradually increasing anxiety-provoking stimuli. (p. 493)

    Memory aid: This is a form of counterconditioning in which sensitive, anxiety-triggering stimuli are ***des*ensitized** in a progressive, or **systematic**, fashion.

13. **Aversive conditioning** is a form of counterconditioning in which an unpleasant state becomes associated with an unwanted behavior. (p. 494)

14. A **token economy** is an operant conditioning procedure in which desirable behaviors are promoted in people by rewarding them with tokens, or secondary reinforcers, which can be exchanged for privileges or treats. For the most part, token economies are used in hospitals, schools, and other institutional settings. (p. 495)

15. **Cognitive therapy** focuses on teaching people new and more adaptive ways of thinking and acting. The therapy is based on the idea that our feelings and responses to events are strongly influenced by our thinking, or cognition. (p. 496)

16. **Rational-emotive therapy** is a confrontational cognitive therapy that maintains that irrational thinking is the cause of many psychological problems. (pp. 496–497)

17. **Family therapy** views problem behavior as partially engendered by the client's family system and environment. Therapy therefore focuses on relationships and problems among the various members of the family. (p. 500)

18. **Meta-analysis** is a procedure for statistically combining the results of many different research studies. (pp. 503–504)

19. **Psychopharmacology** is the study of the effects of drugs on mind and behavior. (p. 508)

    Memory aid: Pharmacology is the science of the uses and effects of drugs. ***Psycho*pharmacology** is the science that studies the psychological effects of drugs.

20. **Lithium** is an antidepressant drug that is commonly used to stabilize the manic-depressive mood swings of the bipolar disorder. (p. 510)

21. In **electroconvulsive therapy (ECT)**, a biomedical therapy often used to treat major depressive disorder, electric shock is passed through the brain. ECT may work by increasing the availability of norepinephrine, the neurotransmitter that elevates mood. (p. 510)

22. **Psychosurgery** is a biomedical therapy that attempts to change behavior by removing or destroying brain tissue. Since drug therapy became widely available in the 1950s, psychosurgery has been infrequently used. (p. 511)

23. Once used to control violent patients, the **lobotomy** is a form of psychosurgery in which the nerves linking the emotion centers of the brain to the frontal lobes are severed. (p. 511)

Program Terms

24. **Free association** is a psychoanalytic technique in which a person says everything that comes to mind.

25. **Biological biasing** refers to a genetic predisposition that, when accompanied by exposure to prolonged or extreme stress, increases an individual's risk of developing a certain mental disorder.

26. **Genetic counseling** is counseling that advises a prospective parent about the probability of passing on defective genes to his or her children.

PROGRAM 23

Health, Mind, and Behavior

TEXTBOOK ASSIGNMENT: Chapter 17: Stress and Health, pp. 515–547

ORIENTATION

Behavioral factors play a major role in maintaining health and causing illness. The effort to understand this role more fully has led to the emergence of the interdisciplinary field of behavioral medicine and its subfield of health psychology. Health psychologists seek to answer questions such as: How do our perceptions of a situation determine the stress we feel? How do our emotions and personality influence our risk of disease? How can psychology contribute to the prevention of illness?

Program 23 introduces the "systems theory" perspective: Illness is assumed to result, not from a single cause, but from the interactions of various systems. Both the program and reading assignment address major issues in health psychology, the most significant of which is stress—its nature, its effects on the body, and ways in which it can be managed. The chapter also looks at the mechanisms by which stress contributes to heart disease, infectious diseases, and cancer. The chapter concludes by examining several factors that affect health, including smoking, nutrition, and obesity, and by looking at behaviors that promote good health.

NOTE: Answer guidelines for all Program 23 questions begin on page 425.

GOALS

After completing your study of the program and reading assignment, you should be prepared to:

1. Describe the field of health psychology, its origins and scope, and how its focus differs from that of the traditional medical model of health and illness.

2. Discuss the various ways in which health psychologists are studying stress, and describe the effects of stress on the body, individual differences in vulnerability and coping strategies, and stress-related diseases.

3. Discuss the various factors that affect health, including smoking, nutrition, and obesity.

GUIDED STUDY

Textbook Assignment

The text chapter should be studied one section at a time. Before you read, preview each section by skimming it, noting headings and boldface items. Then read the appropriate section objectives from the following outline. Keep these objectives in mind and, as you read the chapter section, search for the information that will enable you to meet each objective. Once you have finished a section, write out answers for its objectives.

1. Identify the major concerns of behavioral medicine and health psychology.

Stress and Illness (pp. 516–529)

2. Define *stress* and describe the body's response to stress.

3. Discuss research findings on the health consequences of stressful life events, as well as the factors that influence our vulnerability to stress.

4. Discuss the role of stress in coronary heart disease and contrast Type A and Type B personalities.

5. Describe how the immune system defends the body and discuss the effect of stress on the immune system.

Promoting Health (pp. 529–547)

6. Identify and discuss different strategies for coping with stress.

7. Describe the relationship between health and social support.

8. Explain why people smoke and discuss ways of preventing and reducing this health hazard.

9. Discuss the relationship between nutrition and physical well-being.

10. Discuss the factors that contribute to obesity.

11. Explain whether genes play no role, some role, or an exclusive role in causing obesity.

Program Assignment

Read the following objectives before you watch Program 23. As you watch, be alert for information that will help you answer each objective. Taking notes during the program will help you to formulate your answers later. After the program, write answers to the objectives. If you have access to the program on videotape, you may replay portions to refresh your memory.

1. Contrast the traditional biomedical model of illness with the new "systems theory" of health psychology.

2. Identify four ways in which psychology and medical problems interact.

3. Discuss research linking psychological factors to age-related declines in health.

4. Explain the biofeedback procedure.

5. Differentiate *stress* and *stressor*; identify several common sources of stress.

6. Outline the various stages of the general adaptation syndrome.

7. Explain how Selye's understanding of the effects of stress has been modified by more recent research.

8. Explain why the primary causes of death at the turn of the century are no longer the primary causes of death today.

9. Discuss the role of health psychology in controlling the AIDS epidemic and treating AIDS patients.

PROGRESS TEST

Circle your answers to the following questions and check them with the answers on page 429. If your answer is incorrect, read the explanation for why it is incorrect and then consult the appropriate pages of the text (in parentheses following the correct answer).

1. Behavioral and medical knowledge about factors influencing health form the basis of the field of:
    a. health psychology.
    b. holistic medicine.
    c. behavioral medicine.
    d. osteopathic medicine.

2. The stress hormones epinephrine and norepinephrine are released by the _____ gland in response to stimulation by the _____ branch of the nervous system.
    a. pituitary; sympathetic
    b. pituitary; parasympathetic
    c. adrenal; sympathetic
    d. adrenal; parasympathetic

3. The leading cause of death in North America is:
    a. lung cancer.
    b. AIDS.
    c. coronary heart disease.
    d. alcohol-related accidents.
    e. accidents.

4. During which stage of the general adaptation syndrome is a person especially vulnerable to disease?
    a. alarm reaction
    b. stage of resistance
    c. stage of exhaustion
    d. stage of adaptation

5. Stress has been demonstrated to place a person at increased risk of:
    a. cancer.
    b. tuberculosis.
    c. bacterial infections.
    d. viral infections.
    e. all of the above.

6. Researchers Friedman and Rosenman refer to individuals who are very time-conscious, super motivated, verbally aggressive, and easily angered as:
    a. ulcer-prone personalities.
    b. cancer-prone personalities.
    c. Type A.
    d. Type B.

7. One effect of the hormones epinephrine, norepinephrine, and cortisol is to:
    a. lower the level of cholesterol in the blood.
    b. promote the buildup of plaques on the artery walls.
    c. divert blood away from the muscles of the body.
    d. reduce stress.
    e. decrease the amount of fat stored in the body.

8. Genuine illnesses that are caused by stress are called _____ illnesses.
   a. psychophysiological
   b. hypochondriacal
   c. psychogenic
   d. psychotropic

9. Stress is defined as:
   a. unpleasant or aversive events that cannot be controlled.
   b. situations that threaten health.
   c. the whole process by which we perceive and respond to challenging or threatening events.
   d. anything that decreases immune responses.

10. The field of health psychology is concerned with:
    a. the prevention of illness.
    b. the promotion of health.
    c. the treatment of illness.
    d. all of the above.

11. In order, the sequence of stages in the general adaptation syndrome is:
    a. alarm reaction, stage of resistance, stage of exhaustion.
    b. stage of resistance, alarm reaction, stage of exhaustion.
    c. stage of exhaustion, stage of resistance, alarm reaction.
    d. alarm reaction, stage of exhaustion, stage of resistance.

12. In one experiment, both "executive" rats and "subordinate" rats received identical electric shocks, the only difference being whether the shocks could be:
    a. predicted.
    b. weakened.
    c. shortened.
    d. controlled.

13. Research on genetic influences on obesity reveals that:
    a. the body weight of adoptees correlates with that of their biological parents.
    b. the body weight of adoptees correlates with that of their adoptive parents.
    c. identical twins usually have very different body weights.
    d. the body weights of identical twin women are more similar than those of identical twin men.
    e. none of the above is true.

14. "Burnout" refers to the:
    a. physical, emotional, and mental exhaustion brought on by persistent job-related stress.
    b. formation of plaques in the coronary arteries.
    c. tendency to respond to stress with anger.
    d. suppression of immune responses.

15. According to the text, one-half of all deaths from the 10 leading causes of death in the United States can be attributed to:
    a. stress.
    b. obesity.
    c. nutrition.
    d. behavior.

16. Which of the following statements regarding Type A and B persons is true?
    a. Even when relaxed, Type A persons have higher blood pressure than Type B persons.
    b. When stressed, Type A persons show greater output of epinephrine, norepinephrine, and cortisol than Type B persons.

c. Type B persons tend to suppress anger more than Type A persons.
d. Type A persons tend to sleep more than Type B persons.
e. Type A persons tend to drink fewer caffeinated drinks than Type B persons.

17. In response to uncontrollable shock, levels of stress hormones _____ and immune responses are _____ .
    a. decrease; suppressed
    b. increase; suppressed
    c. decrease; increased
    d. increase; increased

18. The disease- and infection-fighting cells of the immune system are:
    a. B lymphocytes.
    b. T lymphocytes.
    c. both a. and b.
    d. antigens.

19. One effect of stress on the body is to:
    a. suppress the immune system.
    b. facilitate the immune system response.
    c. increase disease resistance.
    d. increase the proliferation of B and T lymphocytes.

20. During biofeedback training:
    a. a subject is given sensory feedback for a subtle body response.
    b. biological functions may come under conscious control.
    c. the accompanying relaxation is much the same as that produced by other, simpler methods of relaxation.
    d. all of the above occur.

21. Allergic reactions and arthritis are caused by:
    a. an overreactive immune system.
    b. an underreactive immune system.
    c. the presence of B lymphocytes.
    d. the presence of T lymphocytes.

22. The component of Type A behavior that is the most predictive of coronary disease is:
    a. time urgency.
    b. competitiveness.
    c. high motivation.
    d. impatience.
    e. anger.

23. Which of the following was offered in the text as a reason people continue to smoke?
    a. Social pressure from peers is strong.
    b. Cigarettes serve as powerful negative reinforcers.
    c. Regular use of nicotine impairs the brain's ability to produce neurotransmitters such as serotonin.
    d. Most adults who smoke don't really want to quit.

24. The tendency to overeat when food is plentiful:
    a. is a recent phenomenon that is associated with the luxury of having ample food.
    b. emerged in our prehistoric ancestors as an adaptive response to alternating periods of feast and famine.
    c. is greater in developed than in developing societies.
    d. is stronger in women than in men.

25. Connie complains to the campus psychologist that she has too much stress in her life. The psychologist tells her that the level of stress people experience depends primarily on:
    a. how many activities they are trying to "juggle."
    b. how they appraise the events of life.
    c. their physical hardiness.
    d. how predictable stressful events are.

26. When would you expect that your immune responses would be *weakest*?
    a. during summer vacation
    b. during exam weeks
    c. just after receiving good news
    d. Immune activity would probably remain constant during these times.

27. Which of the following is *not* necessarily a reason that obese people have trouble losing weight?
    a. Fat tissue has a lower metabolic rate than lean tissue.
    b. Once a person has lost weight, it takes fewer calories to maintain his or her current weight.
    c. The tendency toward obesity may be genetically based.
    d. Obese people tend to lack willpower

28. After an initial rapid weight loss, a person on a diet loses weight much more slowly. This slowdown occurs because:
    a. most of the initial weight loss is simply water.
    b. when a person diets, metabolism decreases.
    c. people begin to "cheat" on their diets.
    d. insulin levels tend to increase with reduced food intake.

29. According to the text, which of the following is true concerning smoking treatment programs?
    a. Most are effective in the long run.
    b. Hypnosis is more effective than behavior modification.
    c. Treatment programs are more effective with women than with men.
    d. Most participants eventually resume smoking.

30. Which of the following would be the *best* piece of advice to offer a person who is trying to minimize the adverse effects of stress on his or her health?
    a. "Avoid challenging situations that may prove stressful."
    b. "Learn to play as hard as you work."
    c. "Maintain a sense of control and a positive approach to life."
    d. "Keep your emotional responses in check by keeping your feelings to yourself."

31. Ricardo has an important psychology exam in the afternoon. In an effort to improve his concentration and alertness, he orders a lunch that is high in _____ and low in _____ .
    a. carbohydrates; protein
    b. carbohydrates; fat
    c. protein; carbohydrates
    d. protein; fat

32. (Close-Up) Which of the following would be the *worst* piece of advice to offer to someone trying to lose weight?
    a. "In order to treat yourself to one 'normal' meal each day, eat very little until the evening meal."
    b. "Reduce your consumption of saturated fats."
    c. "Boost your metabolism by exercising regularly."

d. "Without increasing total caloric intake, increase the relative proportion of carbohydrates in your diet."

33. Dr. Williams, a health psychologist who conducts smoking cessation clinics, explains to his clients that smoking is best understood as an interaction of psychological, biological, and social influences. Evidently, Dr. Williams is working from a _____ approach.
    a. holistic
    b. behavioral
    c. general adaptation syndrome
    d. psychophysiological

34. Each semester, Bob does not start studying until just before midterms. Then he is forced to work around the clock until after final exams, which makes him sick, probably because he is in the _____ phase of the _____ .
    a. alarm; post-traumatic stress syndrome
    b. resistance; general adaptation syndrome
    c. exhaustion; general adaptation syndrome
    d. depletion; post-traumatic stress syndrome

35. Karen and Kyumi are taking the same course with different instructors. Karen's instructor schedules quizzes every Friday, while Kyumi's instructor gives the same number of quizzes on an unpredictable schedule. Assuming that their instructors are equally difficult, which student is probably under more stress?
    a. Karen
    b. Kyumi
    c. There should be no difference in their levels of stress.
    d. It is impossible to predict stress levels in this situation.

36. Philip's physician prescribes a stress management program to help Philip control his ulcer. The physician has apparently diagnosed Philip's condition as a _____ illness, rather than a physical disorder.
    a. psychogenic
    b. hypochondriac
    c. psychophysiological
    d. biofeedback

37. In Rodin and Langer's research with nursing home patients, what variable was found to correlate with well-being and longevity?
    a. exercise
    b. personal control
    c. gender
    d. social support

38. Camelia is worried that her 12-year-old son might begin smoking because many of his classmates do. According to the text, Camelia can most effectively help her son not begin smoking by:
    a. telling him about the dangers of smoking.
    b. telling him that if he begins smoking she will withhold his allowance.
    c. using role-playing to teach him refusal techniques to counteract peer pressure to smoke.
    d. insisting that he not associate with anyone who smokes.

39. You have just transferred to a new campus and find yourself in a potentially stressful environment. According to the text, which of the following would help you cope with the stress?
    a. believing that you have some control over your environment
    b. being able to predict when stressful events will occur

c. feeling optimistic that you will eventually adjust to your new surroundings
d. All of the above would help.

40. In what way is the Navajo concept of *hozho* (harmony) consistent with the current approach to health?
    a. Both represent holistic approaches to health and well-being.
    b. Both equate health solely with physical well-being.
    c. Both place the blame for illness on the high levels of stress in society today.
    d. They are both relatively new ideas.

KEY TERMS

Using your own words, write a brief definition or explanation of each of the following terms.

Textbook Terms

1. behavioral medicine

2. health psychology

3. stress

4. general adaptation syndrome (GAS)

5. burnout

6. coronary heart disease

7. Type A

8. Type B

9. psychophysiological illness

10. lymphocytes

11. aerobic exercise

12. biofeedback

Program Terms

13. holistic approach

14. psychogenic

15. cognitive appraisal

ANSWERS

Guided Study

The following guidelines provide the main points that your answers should have touched upon.

Textbook Assignment

1. Because half the mortality from the 10 leading causes of death can be traced to people's behavior, the interdisciplinary field of behavioral medicine emerged with the goal of identifying and modifying these behavioral

sources of illness. Health psychology's major concerns include the following: how our emotions and responses to stress influence our risk of disease, how people decide they are sick and whether they will seek and follow treatment, what attitudes and behaviors help prevent illness and promote health and well-being, and how we can reduce or control stress.

2. Stress is the whole process by which we appraise and respond to events that threaten or challenge us. Stress triggers an outpouring of epinephrine, norepinephrine, and cortisol from nerve endings in the adrenal glands of the sympathetic nervous system. These stress hormones increase heart rate and respiration, divert blood to skeletal muscles, and release fat from the body's stores to prepare the body for "fight or flight." Hans Selye saw the body's reaction to stress as having three phases (general adaptation syndrome): the alarm reaction, in which the body's resources are mobilized; resistance, in which stress hormones flow freely to help cope with the stressor; and exhaustion, when reserves are depleted and illness is more likely.

3. Some studies have shown that stressful events, such as catastrophes, are closely followed by an increase in psychological disorders and even deaths. The level of stress we experience depends on how we appraise such events. Catastrophes, significant life changes, and daily hassles are especially stressful when they are appraised as uncontrollable and negative, and when we have a pessimistic outlook. A perceived loss of control, for example, triggers an outpouring of stress hormones. In such circumstances, the mental, physical, and emotional exhaustion of burnout can occur and vulnerability to disease may increase.

4. Friedman and Rosenman discovered that stress triggers a variety of physical changes, such as increased cholesterol and blood-clotting speed, that may promote coronary heart disease. According to their designation, Type A people are competitive, hard-driving, impatient, verbally aggressive, and easily angered, and thus more prone to coronary disease. The most significant factor is the tendency toward the negative emotions of anger and depression. In contrast, Type B people are more relaxed and easygoing.

5. The immune system includes two types of white blood cells (lymphocytes) that defend the body by destroying foreign substances. The B lymphocytes form in the bone marrow and release antibodies that combat bacterial infections. The T lymphocytes form in the thymus and other lymphatic tissue and attack cancer cells, viruses, and foreign substances. Another immune agent, the macrophage, identifies and ingests harmful invaders.

    Stress lowers the body's resistance to disease by suppressing the disease-fighting lymphocytes of the immune system. This may explain the link between stress and cancer. Animal research has shown that when the immune system is weakened by stress, tumor cells develop sooner and grow larger. Research has also shown that immune suppression can be classically conditioned. Conversely, studies of cancer patients demonstrate that reducing stress and creating a hopeful, relaxed state may improve chances of survival.

6. Stress management includes aerobic exercise, biofeedback, relaxation, and social support. Aerobic exercise can reduce stress, depression, and anxiety. Research has also shown that those who exercise regularly tend to live longer and suffer from fewer illnesses than those who don't. Exercise may produce its benefits by increasing the production of mood-boosting neurotransmitters, by strengthening the heart, and by lowering both blood pressure and the blood pressure reaction to stress.

Biofeedback systems allow people to monitor their subtle physiological responses and enjoy a calm, tranquil experience. Simple relaxation produces the same effects, however, including lowered blood pressure and strengthened immune defenses.

7. People with strong social support systems eat better, exercise more, smoke and drink less, and have more opportunities to confide painful feelings. Research shows that such people report fewer illnesses and are less likely to die prematurely than people who lack close supportive relationships.

8. Smoking usually begins during early adolescence among those who earn low grades, who feel less in control of their futures, and whose friends, parents, and siblings are smokers. Because adolescent smokers tend to be perceived by other teenagers as socially adept, self-conscious adolescents may begin to emulate these models in order to receive the social rewards of peer acceptance. People continue smoking because they develop dependence and tolerance, experience withdrawal symptoms when nicotine is not present, and because smoking serves as a reinforcer that terminates the aversive states that accompany nicotine withdrawal. Nicotine also triggers the release of epinephrine, norepinephrine, and other neurotransmitters, which boost alertness and calm anxiety.

    Smoking prevention programs that "inoculate" adolescents against peer pressure to smoke by teaching refusal skills have proven effective in reducing the rate of smoking. Programs for adults—counseling, drug treatments, hypnosis, and aversive conditioning, for example—are less effective because all but one-fifth of the participants eventually return to smoking.

9. High-carbohydrate foods increase the amount of the amino acid tryptophan reaching the brain, which raises the level of the relaxation-promoting neurotransmitter serotonin. Low-carbohydrate, high-protein foods improve alertness and concentration.

10. Obesity is a threat to both physical and psychological well-being. The number of fat cells in our bodies is determined by genetic predisposition, early eating patterns, and adult overeating. Fat cells may shrink in size with dieting, but they will never decrease in number. Because fat tissue has a low metabolic rate, it takes less food energy to maintain, and it is therefore difficult for dieters to lose weight. Because obese persons probably have a higher-than-average set-point weight, when they diet their hunger increases and metabolism decreases, making it even more difficult for them to lose weight.

11. Adoption and twin studies both provide evidence for a genetic influence on body weight. Recent animal studies reveal that obese mice may have a defective gene for producing the fat-signaling protein leptin. When obese mice are treated with leptin, they eat less, become more active, and lose weight. In obese humans, leptin receptors are insensitive to leptin. In spite of these studies, genes cannot explain the fact that obesity is much more common in lower-class than in upper-class women, more common among Americans than Europeans, and more common today than at the beginning of the century.

Program Assignment

1. Traditional Western thinking holds that the body is influenced solely by biological and physical events. Today, however, research is forcing a rethinking of the relationship between the activities of the mind and those of the body. There is now substantial evidence that the mind influences our susceptibility and resistance to disease. The biomedical model is being

joined by a bio-psycho-social model, which involves treating not just the body but the whole person in his or her social context. Each individual is seen as a human system in which mental and physical processes interact and affect each other. This holistic approach has been used by other cultures for centuries. Native Americans, for example, have traditionally placed great importance on the harmony between mind and body. In the Navajo world, illness is seen as the result of disharmony.

2. Psychology and medical problems interact as follows:
   a. Some organic malfunctioning or tissue damage may be psychogenic, that is, caused by an individual's state of anxiety, tension, or depression. For example, peptic ulcers, hypertension, allergies, and skin disorders can all be caused by tension.
   b. There may be no apparent organic basis; for example, headaches, exhaustion, and muscular weakness are symptoms of underlying sources of tension and personal problems. Once the problems are resolved, the symptoms often disappear.
   c. Psychological factors can also work indirectly by weakening or strengthening our resistance to disease.
   d. Psychological factors help cause unhealthful behaviors, which contribute to illness. In fact, half of all deaths in the United States are attributed to unhealthful behaviors such as smoking.

3. Judith Rodin (Yale University) and Ellen Langer (Harvard University) have shown that age-related declines in functioning are neither inevitable nor the same for every person. These researchers found that residents of nursing homes who were given a greater sense of personal control over their daily lives experienced better health, and lived longer, than those who were treated in ways that fostered greater dependence. Rodin and Langer believe that neural and endocrine connections between the brain and the immune system mediate the role of psychological factors in health.

4. In the biofeedback procedure, a subject learns to indirectly control some aspect of involuntary physiological functioning, such as heart rate, skin temperature, blood pressure, or muscle tension. A device such as a blood pressure monitor is connected to the subject, who is told to concentrate on raising or lowering the bodily response in question. As pioneer researcher Neal Miller (Rockefeller University) discovered many years ago with animals, many people quickly learn to use biofeedback to manage chronic pain and to lower their blood pressure. (See also pp. 530–532.)

5. *Stress* is defined as the pattern of responses an organism makes to events that disturb its equilibrium, tax its ability to cope, or exceed its ability to cope. These disturbing events are known as *stressors*. Stressors may be part of the physical environment, such as noise, disease, natural disasters, or overcrowding. Or they can come from the social environment—for example, unemployment, crime, family troubles, or loss of a loved one. Life's little hassles can also be stressful. Stress isn't just a matter of external events; we can also be a major source of stress to ourselves, by being overly competitive and aggressive, prone to anxiety, easily angered, or overly self-critical, rigid, or demanding. One of the most significant sources of stress is change. Virtually any event that represents a change from the ordinary can be a stressor. This includes not only negative events such as illness or loss of a loved one, but also positive events such as marriage or sudden business success.

6. The earliest research on stress was conducted by Hans Selye, who studied stressors that threaten physical functioning in animals. Selye discovered a general reaction to stress that was not tied to the particular nature of the stressor. He called this reaction the *general adaptation syndrome* and characterized it as having three stages. First, an alarm reaction stimulates the adrenal glands and pituitary to secrete hormones that mobilize the body's defenses. If the stressor continues, the stage of resistance is reached. In this stage, hormonal secretions are activated to counteract the effects of the stressor, but the body's reaction to other stressors is weakened. With continued exposure to a chronic stressful situation, all resistance breaks down, culminating in the stage of exhaustion. Prolonged exposure to stress can bring exhaustion, disease, and even premature death. (See also pp. 517–518.)

7. Although Selye's work helped explain the origins of many disorders that had baffled physicians, it overlooked the psychological meaning that a particular stressor has to the individual. The way in which an event is subjectively perceived and interpreted is often more important than the objective nature of the event itself. One person's stress is another's exciting challenge. We evaluate not only how serious a stressful event is, but also whether we have the resources to cope with it and what strategies we should use to deal with it. This kind of personal evaluation of stress has been called *cognitive appraisal*.

8. In 1900, the primary causes of death were infectious diseases such as smallpox, influenza, pneumonia, and tuberculosis. A mid-century revolution in public health brought these diseases under control. Today, in large part because of lifestyle factors, such as smoking and drinking too much, and failure to cope effectively with stress, the major causes of death are heart disease, cancer, cirrhosis of the liver, accidents, and suicide. Our psyches are making our bodies more vulnerable than they have to be and the mind-body connection is becoming increasingly deadly.

9. Health psychologist Thomas Coates is studying AIDS from a psychosocial perspective. He has called for a broader look at AIDS that combines medical and psychological research to improve our understanding of the disease. Although caused by a virus, the AIDS epidemic is primarily a behavioral problem. In order to stop the epidemic, we need a fuller understanding of the kinds of activities people engage in and the motivations for their behavior, and we need to find ways of changing those activities to prevent further spread of the disease. For example, from his interviews with at-risk groups, Coates has discovered that a major obstacle to condom usage (and, therefore, the elimination of AIDS) is the use of drugs and alcohol while having sex. In order to change such risky behavior, Coates believes there must be several targets of intervention, including educating people through media advertising that is based on sound psychology, motivating changes in their lifestyles, and even changing community norms. Furthermore, in treating AIDS patients, the psychologist needs to have almost as prominent a role as the physician. Psychologists can help AIDS patients in several ways, including increasing their quality of life and helping them to maintain a positive outlook and good health habits.

Progress Test

1. **c.** is the answer. (video; p. 515)

    a. Health psychology is a subfield within behavioral medicine.

b. Holistic medicine is an older term that refers to medical practitioners who take more of an interdisciplinary approach to treating disorders.

   d. Osteopathy is a medical therapy that emphasizes manipulative techniques for correcting physical problems.

2. **c.** is the answer. (p. 517)

   a., b., & d. The pituitary does not produce stress hormones, nor is the parasympathetic division involved in arousal.

3. **c.** is the answer. Coronary heart disease is followed by (all) cancer, stroke, and accidents (of whatever source). AIDS has not yet become one of the four leading causes of death in North America among the general population. (p. 515)

4. **c.** is the answer. (video; pp. 518)

   a. & b. During these stages, the body's defense mechanisms are at peak function.

   d. This is not a stage of the GAS.

5. **e.** is the answer. Because stress depresses the immune system, stressed individuals are prone to all of these conditions. (video; pp. 523–524)

6. **c.** is the answer. (p. 522)

   a. & b. Researchers have not identified such personality types.

   d. Individuals who are more easygoing are labeled Type B.

7. **b.** is the answer. These stress hormones accelerate the buildup of plaques, or masses formed by cholesterol deposits, on the artery walls. This likely occurs because during arousal blood is diverted from internal organs such as the liver, which removes cholesterol from the blood, to the muscles of the body. These hormones comprise a part of the body's response to stress; they do not reduce stress. (p. 522)

8. **a.** is the answer. (p. 523)

   b. Hypochondriacs think something is wrong with them, but nothing physical can be detected.

   c. *Psychogenic* means "originating in the mind." One's reaction to stress is partially psychological, but this term is not used to refer to stress-related illness.

   d. There is no such term.

9. **c.** is the answer. (video; pp. 516–517)

   a., b., & d. Whether an event is stressful or not depends on how it is appraised.

10. **d.** is the answer. (video; p. 515)

11. **a.** is the answer. (video; p. 518)

12. **d.** is the answer. (p. 520)

13. **a.** is the answer. (p. 542)

14. **a.** is the answer. (p. 520)

    b. This defines atherosclerosis.

    c. This defines the Type A personality.

15. **d.** is the answer. Behaviors that contribute to the leading causes of mortality include smoking, excessive alcohol consumption, maladaptive responses to stress, nonadherence to doctors' instructions, insufficient exercise, use of illicit drugs, and poor nutrition. (video)

16. **b.** is the answer. The greater reactivity of Type A people includes much higher levels of stress hormones in stress situations. (p. 522)

    a. Under relaxed situations, there is no difference in blood pressure.

    c. Anger, expressed and suppressed, is more characteristic of Type A people.

    d. & e. Type A persons tend to sleep less and drink more caffeinated drinks.

17. **b.** is the answer. Both human and animal studies indicate that uncontrollable negative events trigger an outpouring of stress hormones and a drop in immune responses. (pp. 520–521)

18. **c.** is the answer. B lymphocytes fight bacterial infections; T lymphocytes attack cancer cells, viruses, and foreign substances. (video; p. 523)

    d. Antigens are substances that cause the production of antibodies when they are introduced into the body.

19. **a.** is the answer. A variety of studies have shown that stress depresses the immune system, increasing the risk and potential severity of many diseases. (video; pp. 523–524)

20. **d.** is the answer. In biofeedback training, subjects are given sensory feedback about autonomic responses. Although biofeedback may promote relaxation, its benefits may be no greater than those produced by simpler, and less expensive, methods. (video; p. 531)

21. **a.** is the answer. (p. 523)

    b. An *under*reactive immune system would make an individual more susceptible to infectious diseases or the proliferation of cancer cells.

    c. & d. Lymphocytes are the disease- and infection-fighting white blood cells of the immune system.

22. **e.** is the answer. The crucial characteristic of Type A behavior seems to be a tendency to react with negative emotions, especially anger; other aspects of Type A behavior appear not to predict heart disease, and some appear to be helpful to the individual. (p. 522)

23. **b.** is the answer. By alleviating the aversive physiological state of nicotine withdrawal, cigarettes act as negative reinforcers. (p. 537)

    a. This is one explanation of why adolescents start smoking.

    c. There is no evidence that this occurs.

    d. Most smokers would like to quit smoking.

24. **b.** is the answer. (p. 540)

    c. If anything, just the opposite is true.

    d. Men and women do not differ in their tendency to overeat.

25. **b.** is the answer. (video)

    a., c., & d. Each of these is a factor in coping with stress, but it is how an event is *perceived* that determines whether it is stressful.

26. **b.** is the answer. Stressful situations, such as exam weeks, decrease immune responses. (video; p. 524)

27. **d.** is the answer. Most researchers today discount the idea that people are obese because they lack willpower. (p. 541)

28. **b.** is the answer. Following the initial weight loss, metabolism drops as the body attempts to defend its set-point weight. This drop in metabolism means that eating an amount that once produced a loss in weight may now actually result in weight gain. (p. 542)

29. **d.** is the answer. No particular treatment seemed to stand out in terms of effectiveness. All but one-fifth of the people who quit smoking in such programs eventually return to the habit. (p. 538)

30. **c.** is the answer. (video; pp. 520–521)

    a. This is not realistic.

    b. & d. These might actually *increase* the health consequences of potential stressors.

31. **c.** is the answer. High-protein foods seem to improve alertness, whereas high-carbohydrate foods seem to promote relaxation. (p. 539)

32. **a.** is the answer. Dieting, including fasting, lowers the body's metabolic rate and reduces the amount of food energy needed to maintain body weight. (p. 545)

    b., c., & d. Each of these strategies would be a good piece of advice to a dieter.

33. **a.** is the answer. (video)

    b. The behavioral approach would emphasize only learned factors in smoking.

    c. The general adaptation syndrome is a sequence of bodily responses to stress.

    d. Psychophysiological illnesses are illnesses not caused by any known physical disorder.

34. **c.** is the answer. According to Selye's general adaptation syndrome, diseases are most likely to occur in this final stage. (p. 518)

    a. & b. Resistance to disease is greater during the alarm and resistance phases, since the body's mobilized resources are not yet depleted.

    d. There is no such thing as the "depletion phase." Moreover, the post-traumatic stress syndrome refers to the haunting nightmares and anxiety of those who have suffered extreme stress, such as that associated with combat.

35. **b.** is the answer. Unpredictable events are more stressful than predictable events. (p. 520)

36. **c.** is the answer. (p. 523)

    a. The text does not discuss any such thing as a "psychogenic" illness.

    b. Hypochondriasis is the misinterpreting of normal physical sensations as symptoms of a disease.

    d. Biofeedback is a system for recording information regarding a subtle physiological state, such as blood pressure.

37. **b.** is the answer. (video)

38. **c.** is the answer. (p. 538)

39. **d.** is the answer. (pp. 520–521)

40. **a.** is the answer. (video)

b. On the contrary, both emphasize the interaction of mind and body in determining health.

   c. Both consider environmental stress to be only one of many factors in illness.

   d. The Navajo concept of *hozho* is very old.

Key Terms

Textbook Terms

1. **Behavioral medicine** is the interdisciplinary field that applies behavioral and medical knowledge to the treatment of disease and the promotion of health. (p. 515)

2. **Health psychology** is a subfield of psychology that studies how health and illness are influenced by emotions, stress, personality, life-style, and other psychological factors. (p. 515)

3. **Stress** refers to the process by which people perceive and react to stressors, or to events they perceive as threatening or challenging. (pp. 516–517)

4. The **general adaptation syndrome (GAS)** is the three-stage sequence of bodily reaction to stress outlined by Hans Selye. (p. 518)

5. **Burnout** refers to a state of physical, mental, and emotional exhaustion brought on by unrelenting job-related stress. (p. 520)

6. The leading cause of death in the United States today, **coronary heart disease** results from the clogging of the coronary arteries and the subsequent reduction in blood and oxygen supply to the heart muscle. (p. 521)

7. **Type A** personality is Friedman and Rosenman's term for the coronary-prone behavior pattern of competitive, hard-driving, impatient, verbally aggressive, and anger-prone people. (p. 522)

8. **Type B** personality is Friedman and Rosenman's term for the coronary-resistant behavior pattern of easygoing people. (p. 522)

9. A **psychophysiological illness** is any genuine illness such as hypertension and headaches that is apparently linked to stress rather than caused by a physical disorder. (p. 523)

   Memory aid: Psycho- refers to mind; physio- refers to body; a **psychophysiological illness** is a mind-body disorder.

10. **Lymphocytes** are the two types of white blood cells of the immune system that fight bacterial infections (B lymphocytes) and viruses, cancer cells, and foreign substances in the body (T lymphocytes). (p. 523)

11. **Aerobic exercise** is any sustained activity such as running, swimming, or cycling that promotes heart and lung fitness and may help alleviate depression and anxiety. (p. 529)

12. **Biofeedback** refers to a system for electronically recording, amplifying, and feeding back information regarding a subtle physiological state. (p. 531)

    Memory aid: A **biofeedback** device, such as a brain-wave trainer, provides auditory or visual feedback about biological responses.

Program Terms

13. According to the **holistic approach** to health, each individual is seen as a human system in which physical, mental, and environmental factors interact and affect each other.

14. **Psychogenic** refers to organic malfunction or tissue damage that is caused by anxiety, tension, or depression.

15. **Cognitive appraisal** refers to the way in which an event is subjectively perceived and interpreted.

PROGRAM 24

In Space, Toward Peace

TEXTBOOK ASSIGNMENT: Chapter 18: Social Psychology, pp. 564–571; 578–580; 587–589

ORIENTATION

In the preceding programs, we have seen how psychologists study human behavior and advance the knowledge base of their field. Psychologists also put their knowledge to work to solve practical, or applied, problems. As an example, Program 24 explores how psychologists are working to improve the quality of life for astronauts during extended space travel. The program also introduces peace psychology, which brings together psychologists, sociologists, political scientists, and many others concerned with promoting peace among nations. Research in this new field ranges from studies of arms negotiations and crisis management to how people respond emotionally to the possibility of nuclear war.

Chapter 18 of the text explores the influence of culture and gender roles on behavior. Although for most traits variation within any group is greater than that between groups, our identity as an individual, male or female, and as a member of various ethnic and racial groups exerts a strong influence on our self-concept and judgments about others.

The chapter also discusses how people respond to diversity: by rejecting it, developing prejudice, and provoking conflict; or by accepting it and promoting cooperation, communication, and conciliation among groups. The social, cognitive, and, in some cases, biological roots of these responses are explored, as are steps that might be taken to further constructive social relations. The chapter concludes with a discussion of situations that engender conflict, along with techniques that have been shown to promote conflict resolution.

NOTE: Answer guidelines for all Program 24 questions begin on page 443.

GOALS

After completing your study of the program and reading assignment, you should be prepared to:

1. Discuss ways in which psychologists are working to improve the quality of life in space and to promote peace among nations.
2. Discuss the influence of culture on social judgment and behavior.
3. Discuss the psychological roots of prejudice and conflict.

Discovering Psychology

GUIDED STUDY

Textbook Assignment

The text chapter should be studied one section at a time. Before you read, preview each section by skimming it, noting headings and boldface items. Then read the appropriate section objectives from the following outline. Keep these objectives in mind and, as you read the chapter section, search for the information that will enable you to meet each objective. Once you have finished a section, write out answers for its objectives.

Cultural Influences (pp. 564–566)

1. Discuss the influence of culture and gender roles on behavior.

Social Relations (pp. 567–571)

2. Describe the roles of social inequalities, ingroup bias, and scapegoating in prejudice.

3. Discuss the cognitive roots of prejudice.

4. Identify factors that fuel conflict and discuss effective ways of resolving such conflict.

Program Assignment

Read the following objectives before you watch Program 24. As you watch, be alert for information that will help you answer each objective. Taking notes during the program will help you to formulate your answers later. After the program, write answers to the objectives. If you have access to the program on videotape, you may replay portions to refresh your memory.

1. Describe several physical and psychological problems associated with extended space travel.

2. Give several examples of how psychological knowledge is being used to improve the quality of life for space travelers.

3. Identify several obstacles to negotiations between individuals and nations, focusing on factors that contribute to the international arms race.

4. Identify several psychological insights into aggressive behavior against individuals and other societies.

5. Explain the focus of peace psychologists such as John Mack.

PROGRESS TEST

Circle your answers to the following questions and check them with the answers on page 446. If your answer is incorrect, read the explanation for why it is incorrect and then consult the appropriate pages of the text or portion of the program.

1. Regarding cultural differences in personal space, which of the following is true?
   a. Arabs prefer less personal space than do Latin Americans.
   b. North Americans prefer more personal space than do Scandinavians.
   c. The British prefer less personal space than do the French.
   d. Latin Americans prefer less personal space than do North Americans.

2. Why is there more concern about psychological factors in space travel today than in the past?
   a. Because of greater international pressure today to be "first in space," it is imperative that NASA explore all aspects of space travel.
   b. The reduction in the military budget of the United States has made more money available for this type of research.
   c. Longer flights and more diversified crews have made space flight more stressful.
   d. Astronauts today are better informed of the importance of such factors.

3. An important factor in the motion sickness experienced by astronauts is the:
   a. rate of acceleration of the spacecraft.
   b. confined space astronauts work in.
   c. conflict between sensory information experienced by the eye and the ear.
   d. restricted diet astronauts are fed.

4. During extended space flight, astronauts often experience:
   a. a loss of bone density.
   b. paranoid feelings.
   c. lowered visual acuity.
   d. hearing loss.

5. *Cocooning* refers to the tendency of some astronauts and crews working in confined spaces to:
   a. develop claustrophobic feelings during and after spaceflight.
   b. become hostile toward others.
   c. develop irrational phobias during spaceflight.
   d. withdraw from social contacts to avoid hostile interactions with others.

6. Social traps are situations in which:
   a. conflicting parties realize that they have shared goals, the attainment of which requires their mutual cooperation.
   b. conflicting parties have similar, and generally negative, views of one another.
   c. conflicting parties each pursue their self-interest and become caught in mutually destructive behavior.
   d. two conflicting groups meet face-to-face in an effort to resolve their differences.

7. The belief that those who suffer deserve their fate is expressed in the:
   a. just-world phenomenon.
   b. phenomenon of ingroup bias.
   c. fundamental attribution error.
   d. mirror-image perception principle.

8. Which of the following was *not* mentioned in the text's discussion of the roots of prejudice?
   a. people's tendency to overestimate the similarity of people within groups
   b. people's tendency to assume that exceptional, or especially memorable, individuals are unlike the majority of members of a group
   c. people's tendency to assume that the world is just and that people get what they deserve
   d. people's tendency to discriminate against those they view as "outsiders"

9. Astronauts experience jet lag when:
   a. their circadian rhythms become out of sync with shipboard time.
   b. they return to the slower-paced environment of Earth.

c. the monotony of space travel causes excessive sleepiness.
d. stress hormone levels increase during spaceflight.

10. Pat Cowlings teaches astronauts how to voluntarily control symptoms such as heart rate, blood flow, and temperature changes in order to counteract feelings of:
    a. irritability.
    b. anxiety.
    c. motion sickness.
    d. claustrophobia.

11. The purpose of the virtual interactive environment workstation is to:
    a. reduce the physical stress on astronauts' muscles by designing efficient work environments.
    b. provide a simulated recreation environment for space travelers.
    c. improve astronauts' interpersonal communications skills.
    d. provide various perceptual tasks that help maintain astronauts' perceptual acuity while in space.

12. Regarding cultural diversity, which of the following is *not* true?
    a. Culture influences emotional expressiveness.
    b. Culture influences personal space.
    c. Culture does not have a strong influence on how strictly social roles are defined.
    d. All cultures evolve their own norms.

13. In space, voice pitch is:
    a. higher than it is on Earth.
    b. lower than it is on Earth.
    c. less important in intelligible communication than loudness.
    d. more variable than it is on Earth.

14. In zero-gravity environments, body fluids tend to concentrate in the astronauts' faces. Scientists are concerned about this because:
    a. of the possible damage to facial nerves.
    b. dehydration of other crucial body organs may result.
    c. facial expressions are distorted, possibly resulting in miscommunication among crew members.
    d. the bloated appearance of astronauts in space makes them more susceptible to eating disorders.

15. People with power and status may become prejudiced because:
    a. they tend to justify the social inequalities between themselves and others.
    b. those with less status and power tend to resent them.
    c. those with less status and power appear less capable.
    d. they feel proud and are boastful of their achievements.

16. Given the tendency of people to categorize information, which of the following stereotypes would Juan, a 65-year-old political liberal and fitness enthusiast, be most likely to have?
    a. "People who exercise regularly are very extraverted."
    b. "All political liberals are advocates of a reduced defense budget."
    c. "Young people today have no sense of responsibility."
    d. "Older people are lazy."

17. The biggest problem psychologists face in helping astronauts on extended missions is helping them:
    a. deal with the terrible sense of isolation and confinement.
    b. maintain their sense of self-esteem.
    c. avoid conflicts with other crew members.
    d. return to Earth in good mental health.

18. You believe that all overweight people are friendly, jolly, and cuddly. This is an example of:
    a. a stereotype.
    b. prejudice.
    c. discrimination.
    d. all of the above.

19. Which of the following best describes how GRIT works?
    a. The fact that two sides in a conflict have great respect for the other's strengths prevents further escalation of the problem.
    b. The two sides engage in a series of reciprocated conciliatory acts.
    c. The two sides agree to have their differences settled by a neutral, third-party mediator.
    d. The two sides engage in cooperation in those areas in which shared goals are possible.

20. How do Russian mission control specialists monitor cosmonauts' stress levels?
    a. through regular blood samples
    b. by measuring their in-flight job performance
    c. by monitoring speech characteristics
    d. through all of the above techniques

21. The walls of one astronaut's cabin are painted in a lighter color at the top than at the bottom. The purpose of this is to:
    a. provide a visual cue for spatial orientation.
    b. create a "warmer" aesthetic environment.
    c. brighten the cabin so that less intense lighting is necessary.
    d. create the appearance of a more spacious cabin.

22. Which of the following strategies would be *most* likely to foster positive feelings between two conflicting groups?
    a. Take steps to reduce the likelihood of social traps.
    b. Separate the groups so that tensions diminish.
    c. Have one representative from each group visit the other and field questions.
    d. Increase the amount of contact between the two conflicting groups.
    e. Have the groups work on a superordinate goal.

23. Ever since their cabin lost the camp softball competition, the campers have become increasingly hostile toward one camper in their cabin, blaming her for every problem in the cabin. This behavior is best explained in terms of:
    a. the ingroup bias.
    b. prejudice.
    c. the scapegoat theory.
    d. the reciprocity norm.
    e. mirror-image perceptions.

24. Research by Scott Plous exploring the attitudes of American and Soviet leaders demonstrates that:
    a. although both sides insisted they preferred disarmament, each was suspicious of the other's intentions.
    b. each side believed the other was negotiating unfairly.

c. each side believed the other was trustworthy.
d. cultural differences in negotiation styles were a major roadblock to reaching any settlement.

25. Students at State University are convinced that their school is better than any other; this most directly illustrates:
    a. an ingroup bias.
    b. prejudice and discrimination.
    c. the scapegoat effect.
    d. the just-world phenomenon.
    e. mirror-image perceptions.

26. George's discriminatory behavior toward minorities often provokes anger in its victims, which only serves to increase George's prejudice. George's behavior is an example of the:
    a. blame-the-victim dynamic.
    b. self-fulfilling prophecy.
    c. just-world phenomenon.
    d. scapegoat phenomenon.

27. The "zero-sum situation" is one in which:
    a. each side in a negotiation perceives that their gain is their enemy's loss.
    b. both parties in a negotiation share the same goals.
    c. neither party in a negotiation is trustworthy.
    d. differences between the goals of two negotiating parties prevent any settlement from being reached.

28. Mr. and Mrs. Samuels are constantly fighting, and each perceives the other as hard-headed and insensitive. Their conflict is being fueled by:
    a. self-disclosure.
    b. stereotypes.
    c. a social trap.
    d. mirror-image perceptions.

29. According to the program, the reason for portraying an enemy as a demon, liar, or monster is to:
    a. dehumanize them so that aggression against them is more acceptable.
    b. make them more fearful.
    c. make them seem easier to defeat in battle.
    d. do all of the above.

KEY TERMS

Using your own words, write a brief definition or explanation of each of the following terms.

Textbook Terms

1. culture

2. personal space

3. gender role

4. prejudice

5. stereotype

6. ingroup bias

7. scapegoat theory

8. just-world phenomenon

9. conflict

10. social trap

11. superordinate goals

12. GRIT

Program Terms

13. jet lag

14. peace psychology

15. "cocooning"

ANSWERS

Guided Study

The following guidelines provide the main points that your answers should have touched upon.

Textbook Assignment

1. We live in a global multicultural village and need to understand how our cultures and gender roles influence us. A culture is the enduring traditions, behaviors, ideas, and attitudes shared by a large group of people and passed from one generation to the next. All cultural groups evolve their own norms for acceptable and expected behavior. Because of differing norms, personal space, expressiveness, and pace of life, for example, misunderstandings are commonplace.

    Gender roles vary over time as well as across cultures. In nomadic societies, there is little division of labor by gender. In agricultural societies, men roam freely and women tend the homes. In industrialized societies, gender roles vary—in North America, men are doctors and dentists; in Russia, women are usually the doctors. In the United States, gender roles have shifted, with a large increase in women's employment.

2. Prejudice is an unjustifiable and usually negative attitude toward a group. People who have money, power, and prestige may become prejudiced toward those less fortunate in order to rationalize social inequalities. The reactions provoked in victims of discrimination may further increase prejudice. The tendencies to favor one's own group (ingroup bias) and to blame victims for their plight may also lead to prejudice. According to the scapegoat theory of prejudice, when people are frustrated or angry, blaming another individual or group may provide an outlet for their anger.

3. Stereotyped beliefs emerge as a result of our tendency to cognitively simplify the world. One way to do this is by categorizing people into groups and then overestimating the similarity of people within groups other than our own. Group stereotypes are also influenced by vivid but exceptional cases involving individuals from other groups, because they are more readily available to memory. Another cognitive root of prejudice is the just-world phenomenon, or the idea that good is rewarded and evil is punished, so those who are successful are good and those who suffer are bad. Hindsight bias also fosters prejudice, as people blame victims after the fact for "getting what they deserved."

4. Conflict is a seeming incompatibility of actions, goals, or ideas among individuals, groups, or nations. Conflict is fostered by social traps in which conflicting parties get caught up in mutually destructive behavior by pursuing their own self-interests. Another factor that fuels conflict is the tendency for those in conflict to form diabolical images of each other (mirror-image perceptions). The psychological roots of distorted perceptions include the self-serving bias, the fundamental attribution error, stereotyping, group polarization, and groupthink.

    Conflict resolution is most likely in situations characterized by cooperation, communication, and conciliation. Studies by Sherif and others demonstrate that cooperation between groups in the pursuit of superordinate goals is more effective than mere contact between conflicting groups in reducing differences. Communication between conflicting groups can be facilitated by a third-party mediator when conflicts are so intense that civil discussion between the groups is not possible. When cooperation and communication are impossible between conflicting groups, Osgood's "Graduated and Reciprocated Initiatives in Tension-Reduction" (GRIT) may help reduce hostilities. GRIT promotes trust and cooperation between groups by having each group initiate one or more small, conciliatory acts.

Program Assignment

1. Psychologists are studying several physical changes that occur during long-term space flight. One is motion sickness that is caused by sensory conflict between what the eye sees and the body equilibrium mechanisms of the inner ear feel. Another is changes in bone density. During an 80-day skylab flight, for example, astronauts lost approximately 5 percent of their bone mass.

    A variety of stressors in space could cause psychological and stress-related medical problems—for example, anxiety, boredom, loneliness, fatigue, depression, nausea, and irritability. Another is social withdrawal, or what Yvonne Clearwater (NASA–AMES) calls "cocooning," in which crew members live together without relating to one another. For example, a recent 7-month study of a small work crew in Antarctica found that crew members spent an average of 60 percent of their waking time alone, perhaps in an effort to reduce the possibility of conflict with other crew members.

    Another biobehavioral problem psychologists are studying is jet lag in space. Circling the earth many times a day can disrupt astronauts biological clocks. When their internal circadian rhythms are out of sync with shipboard time, astronauts often become disoriented and suffer from sleep disorders.

2. Research on biobehavioral reactions, group dynamics, personal adjustment, and communications is now being applied to the selection, training, and psychological care of astronauts. For example, Pat Cowlings (NASA–AMES) teaches astronauts how to overcome motion sickness in space by using psychological techniques. In the laboratory, she uses rotating rooms and linear accelerators to actually make trainees sick. Once each individual's specific symptoms are apparent, Cowlings teaches that astronaut how to voluntarily control symptoms such as heart rate, bloodflow, sweating, and temperature changes. This work has shown that astronauts gain enough control to either completely eliminate or diminish motion-sickness symptoms.

    The virtual interactive environment work station (VIEWS), developed by Scott Fisher, consists of a display unit that projects 360° computer-generated images. Using VIEWS, astronauts who have been in a confined environment for a period of time can be perceptually transported to a synthesized environment that simulates a beach or some other soothing recreational environment.

    Psychologists are also working on techniques for overcoming the distortions of voice, facial expression, and movement that accompany zero-gravity environments. In space, voice pitch is higher than on Earth, and shouting is often necessary to be heard. Facial expressions are masked by the puffiness that comes in zero gravity, when body fluids float up to the face. With more diversified crews on board, astronauts face potential crew problems caused by conflicts in status, language styles, and the culturally specific meaning of nonverbal gestures. Psychologists who specialize in small-group communication can help crew members learn how to bridge their differences and solve social problems that might result from such conflicts.

The biggest problem psychologists face is helping astronauts on extended missions deal with the terrible sense of isolation and confinement. Mission control specialists (especially in Russia) sometimes use voice-stress analysis of speech patterns to monitor crews. When crew tension is too high, they may beam up soothing music, alter the work routine, or have relatives communicate with crew members.

Psychologists are also studying ways of designing crew quarters and workstations to reduce the stresses of working and living in space. Among the variables they are exploring are the shape, size, and location of windows; the color and brightness of walls; and the selection of photographs to alleviate boredom and offer a link back to earth.

3. Scott Plous explored the attitudes of American and Soviet leaders during the Cold War. Although both sides insisted they preferred disarmament, each was suspicious of the other's intentions and believed that what the other side really wanted was not disarmament but an arms advantage. To have stopped the arms race, both sides would have had to become aware that they shared identical views of each other.

    Max Bazerman notes that the biggest mistake people make when negotiating is to think only about what they want, ignoring the feelings of the other party to the negotiation. As a result they waste time proposing settlements that the other side will consider unacceptable.

    At the international level, most crisis situations result because of decision biases by one or both sides. The U.S.-Soviet situation was often viewed as a zero-sum situation, where what one side gained the other side had to lose. By breaking out of this mentality, negotiators were beginning to produce results that would have benefited both sides.

4. Psychologists have gained insights into aggression by using controlled experiments, simulations, and interviews with people on the front lines. One of the most reliable findings is that it is easier to wage war on people once they've been dehumanized. If you perceive other people as evil, inferior creatures, then it is possible for even well-intentioned, ordinary people to hurt and kill. In one study, college students chose to give increasingly higher levels of shock to strangers who were described to them in dehumanized terms, compared to others who were described in neutral or humanized terms.

    No matter what the society, there's a striking similarity in the way enemies are portrayed. They are portrayed as monsters, demons, or vermin to be eradicated.

5. Peace psychology is an interdisciplinary approach to the prevention of international conflicts. John Mack (Director, Center of Psychological Studies in the Nuclear Age) studies the obstacles to conflict resolution. One is the existence of *ideological enmity*. The norm is to blame the other side, to create an enemy, and then to mobilize your people against it. Each society has a vested interest that prevents it from negotiating in any way other than that which best serves its own point of view. Consequently, each side finds it difficult to grasp the fact that it is as threatening to the other side as it is to them. Mack's group is studying how to break down these images of other nations and to create conditions that can defuse hostility.

Progress Test

1. **d.** is the answer. (p. 565)

2. **c.** is the answer. (video)

    a. If anything, the pressure to be "first in space" is less today than in the past.

    b. & d. Although these both may be true, NASA's concern about psychological factors in space is much more pragmatic.

3. **c.** is the answer. (video)

4. **a.** is the answer. (video)

5. **d.** is the answer. (video)

6. **c.** is the answer. Social traps foster conflict in that two parties, by pursuing their self-interests, create a result that neither group wants. (p. 578)

    a. As Sherif's studies demonstrated, the possession of shared, or superordinate, goals tends to reduce conflict between groups.

    b. This is an example of mirror-image perceptions, which, along with social traps, foster conflict.

    d. Face-to-face confrontations between conflicting parties generally do not reduce conflict, nor are they social traps.

7. **a.** is the answer. (p. 571)

    b. Ingroup bias is the tendency of people to favor their own group.

    c. The fundamental attribution error is the tendency of people to underestimate situational influences when observing the behavior of other people.

    d. Mirror-image perception refers to the tendency of conflicting parties to form similar, diabolical images of each other.

8. **b.** is the answer. In fact, people tend to overgeneralize from vivid cases, rather than assume that they are unusual. (pp. 569–571)

    a., c., & d. Each of these is an example of a cognitive (a. & c.) or a social (d.) root of prejudice.

9. **a.** is the answer. (video)

10. **c.** is the answer. (video)

11. **b.** is the answer. (video)

12. **c.** is the answer. Culture *does* have a strong influence on how rigidly social roles are defined. (pp. 565–566)

13. **a.** is the answer. (video)

14. **c.** is the answer. (video)

15. **a.** is the answer. Such justifications arise as a way to preserve inequalities. The just-world phenomenon presumes that people get what they deserve. According to this view, someone who has less must deserve less. (p. 571)

16. **c.** is the answer. People tend to overestimate the similarity of people within groups other than their own. Thus, Juan is not likely to form stereotypes of fitness enthusiasts (a.), political liberals (b.), or older adults (d.), because these are groups to which he belongs. (p. 570)

17. **a.** is the answer. (video)

18. **a.** is the answer. (p. 567)

b. & c. Prejudice and discrimination involve unjustifiable and negative attitudes and behaviors directed at another group.

19. **b.** is the answer. (p. 588)

    a. GRIT is a technique for reducing conflict through a series of conciliatory gestures, not for maintaining the status quo.

    c. & d. These measures may help reduce conflict but they are not aspects of GRIT.

20. **c.** is the answer. (video)

21. **a.** is the answer. (video)

22. **e.** is the answer. Sherif found that hostility between two groups could be dispelled by giving the groups superordinate, or shared, goals. (p. 587)

    a. Reducing the likelihood of social traps might reduce mutually destructive behavior, but it would not lead to positive feelings between the groups.

    b. Such segregation would likely increase ingroup bias and group polarization, resulting in further group conflict.

    c. This might help, or it might increase hostilities; it would not be as helpful a strategy as communication through an outside mediator or, as in e., cooperation toward a superordinate goal.

    d. Contact by itself is not likely to reduce conflict.

23. **c.** is the answer. According to the scapegoat theory, when things go wrong, people look for someone on whom to take out their anger and frustration. (p. 569)

    a. In this example the campers are venting their frustration on a member of their own cabin group (although this is not always the case with scapegoats).

    b. Prejudice refers to an unjustifiable and usually negative attitude toward another group.

    d. The reciprocity norm, which refers to our tendency to help those who have helped us, was not discussed as a root of prejudice.

    e. Mirror-image perceptions are reciprocal; here the hostility flowed in only one direction.

24. **a.** is the answer. (video)

    b. & c. In fact, just the opposite was true.

    d. If anything, the program suggests that the roadblock was caused by the *similar*, self-serving styles of negotiating parties.

25. **a.** is the answer. (p. 569)

    b. Prejudices are unjustifiable and usually negative attitudes toward other groups. They may result from an ingroup bias, but they are probably not the reason students favor their own university.

    c. Scapegoats are individuals or groups toward which prejudice is directed as an outlet for the anger of frustrated individuals or groups.

    d. The just-world phenomenon is the tendency for people to believe others "get what they deserve."

    e. Mirror-image perception refers to the tendency of conflicting parties to form similar, diabolical images of each other.

26. **b.** is the answer. By eliciting reactions in others that fuel his prejudice, George is fulfilling his expectation, or "prophecy," regarding members of a particular minority. (p. 564)

27. **a.** is the answer. If "I lose when you win," the net effect (in terms of hypothetical "points") is no change, or "zero-sum." (video; p. 579)

28. **d.** is the answer. The couple's similar, and presumably distorted, feelings toward each other fuel their conflict. (p. 579)

    a. Self-disclosure, or the sharing of intimate feelings, fosters love.

    b. Stereotypes are overgeneralized ideas about groups.

    c. Social traps are situations in which conflicting parties engage in mutually destructive behavior while pursuing their own self-interests.

29. **a.** is the answer. (video)

Key Terms

Textbook Terms

1. A **culture** is the enduring behaviors, ideas, attitudes, and traditions shared by a large group of people and transmitted from one generation to the next. (p. 564)

2. **Personal space** refers to the buffer zone, or mobile territory, that people like to maintain around their bodies. (p. 565)

3. A **gender role** is a culturally prescribed set of behaviors for males and females. (p. 566)

4. **Prejudice** is an unjustifiable and usually negative attitude toward a group and its members. (p. 567)

5. A **stereotype** is a generalized (often overgeneralized) belief about a group of people. (p. 567)

6. The **ingroup bias** is the tendency to favor one's own group. (p. 569)

7. The **scapegoat theory** proposes that prejudice provides an outlet for anger by finding someone to blame. (p. 569)

8. The **just-world phenomenon** is a manifestation of the commonly held belief that good is rewarded and evil is punished. The logic is indisputable: "If I am rewarded, I must be good." (p. 571)

9. **Conflict** is a perceived incompatibility of actions, goals, or ideas between individuals or groups. (p. 578)

10. A **social trap** is a situation in which conflicting parties become caught up in mutually harmful behavior as they pursue their perceived best interests. (p. 578)

11. **Superordinate goals** are mutual goals that require the cooperation of individuals or groups otherwise in conflict. (p. 587)

12. **GRIT** (Graduated and Reciprocated Initiatives in Tension-Reduction) is a strategy of conflict resolution based on the defusing effect that conciliatory gestures can have on parties in conflict. (p. 588)

Program Terms

13. **Jet lag** is a biobehavioral problem in which a person feels disoriented when his or her internal circadian rhythms are disrupted.

14. **Peace psychology** is an interdisciplinary field devoted to the prevention of war and the maintenance of peace.

15. **"Cocooning"** is the tendency of some astronauts to withdraw from social contacts during space flight to avoid hostile interactions with others.

PROGRAMS *25 & 26*

A Union of Opposites
New Directions

TEXTBOOK ASSIGNMENT: None

ORIENTATION

Psychological knowledge has opened up new realms of possibility for understanding how we function and why we think, feel, and act as we do. Psychologists are trained to constantly challenge their assumptions and to look at the familiar in creative ways.

The theme of Program 25 is that psychological knowledge may be organized in terms of opposites that complement each other, such as genes and the environment, the physical brain and the ephemeral mind, conditioned responses and behavioral freedom, the infant and the elder, the power and fallibility of the mind, and the individual and the group member. By way of illustrating each of these pairs of complementary opposites, Professor Zimbardo reviews many of the psychological principles, research studies, and theories that were the subject matter of the preceding programs.

Program 26 presents the views of leading psychologists regarding the future of psychology. Although contemporary psychologists share many of the same goals as their predecessors, they hold a variety of opinions regarding new directions for psychology and the extent to which it will help to alleviate individual and global problems.

NOTE: Answer guidelines for all questions for Programs 25 and 26 begin on page 454.

GOALS

After completing your study of the program, you should be prepared to:

1. Identify the major psychological insights into human nature that formed the basis for the *Discovering Psychology* series.

2. Discuss several new directions experts predict for the field of psychology.

GUIDED STUDY

Program Assignment

Read the following objectives before you watch Programs 25 and 26. As you watch, be alert for information that will help you answer each objective. Taking notes during the programs will help you to formulate your answers later. After the programs, write answers to the objectives. If you have access to the programs on videotape, you may replay portions to refresh your memory. (There is no text assignment for these programs. However, in reviewing the course, you may find it useful to review the program orientations and guided study answers for each of the programs assigned by your instructor.)

Program 25
1. Explain the nature-nurture issue in psychology, and give examples of research findings that illustrate both sides of the debate.

2. Discuss the relationship between the brain and the mind, citing examples of their reciprocal influences.

3. Discuss the importance of conditioned responses and behavioral freedom in human behavior.

4. Discuss whether infancy and adulthood truly represent psychological "opposites."

5. Contrast the cognitive power and fallibility of the mind.

6. Discuss the interplay of our opposite roles as individuals and as conforming members of groups.

Program 26

7. Contrast the views of psychologists who predict a trend toward greater specialization in psychology with those who see greater unification of the discipline in the future.

8. Contrast the views of B. F. Skinner and Teresa Amabile regarding the role of cognitive processes and emotions in psychology's future.

9. Cite the views of leading psychologists regarding the role of technology in psychology's future.

10. Discuss the views of psychologists regarding the future of intelligence and personality testing.

11. Discuss the views of psychologists regarding psychology's future contributions to improving the physical and mental health of individuals.

12. Contrast the views of B. F. Skinner and Philip Zimbardo regarding psychology's future contributions toward promoting human welfare.

PROGRESS TEST

Circle your answers to the following questions and check them with the answers on page 457. If your answer is incorrect, read the explanation for why it is incorrect and then consult the appropriate pages of the text (in parentheses following the correct answer).

1. Human and animal research on shyness has shown that shyness is largely the result of:
   a. a genetic predisposition.
   b. stressful experiences early in life.
   c. style of parenting.
   d. all of the above.

2. Research on the effects of a mother's touch on baby rats has shown that:
   a. the effects of maternal touch are short-lived.
   b. the need for touch is brain-based.
   c. excessive touch retards development.
   d. touch is only important in the development of premature infants.

3. Which of the following best expresses the relative importance of nature and nurture in development?
   a. For most aspects of behavior and mental functioning, nature is more important than nurture.
   b. For most aspects of behavior and mental functioning, nurture is more important than nature.
   c. For most aspects of behavior and mental functioning, what we are given by nature can be modified by nurture.
   d. It is impossible to generalize about the relative importance of nature and nurture.

4. Hypnosis demonstrates that:
   a. the mind can alter the functioning of the brain.
   b. the brain can alter the functioning of the mind.
   c. nearly everyone is susceptible to the power of suggestion.
   d. the brain and mind are separate entities.

5. Through the power of advertising, products often become associated with pleasurable stimuli. This phenomenon is an example of:
   a. reasoning by representativeness.
   b. operant conditioning.
   c. classical conditioning.
   d. neurometrics.

6. Operant conditioning demonstrates that:
   a. behavior is controlled by its immediate consequences on the environment.
   b. virtually any two perceivable stimuli can become associated.
   c. conditioned responses account for only a small fraction of human behavior.
   d. most human behavior is rigidly determined.

7. Which of the following most accurately expresses the relative importance of conditioning and free will in human behavior?
   a. Most of our behaviors are the product of classical conditioning.
   b. Most of our behaviors are the product of operant conditioning.
   c. The concept of "free will" has no place in the modern science of psychology.

d. Although most of what we do, think, or feel is the outcome of years of exposure to operant and classical conditioning, this doesn't mean that we are slaves to conditioning.

8. How has recent research in life-span development changed the way psychologists view infants?
   a. We now know that very little of human functioning is genetically predisposed.
   b. We now realize how vulnerable infants are to psychological disorders.
   c. We now have a much greater appreciation for their cognitive competence.
   d. We now understand that, for most abilities, gender differences in development are much greater than was once believed.

9. Regarding the cognitive ability of older adults, research has shown that:
   a. the elderly show relatively little cognitive decline in many abilities.
   b. the elderly often develop new cognitive insights that can be described as "wisdom."
   c. those who remain physically and mentally active tend to fare best in later life.
   d. all of the above are true.

10. Reasoning by representativeness demonstrates:
    a. the awesome scope of human information processing.
    b. that we shouldn't always trust our reasoning and intuition.
    c. that people do not form negative stereotypes as readily as was once believed.
    d. the power of the social situation to influence our behavior.

11. Compared to those in collectivist cultures, people in individualist cultures:
    a. are more likely to feel a sense of personal pride when success occurs.
    b. feel personally responsible when failure occurs.
    c. feel alienated from others.
    d. are more likely to experience all of the above.

12. Who of the following psychologists deplored the cognitive movement in psychology?
    a. Teresa Amabile   c. B. F. Skinner
    b. Howard Gardner   d. Philip Zimbardo

13. Experts on psychological testing predict that future testing will become more concerned with:
    a. developing "generic" standardized tests of personality and intelligence that can be used with all groups of people.
    b. the study of individual patterns and styles of thinking and learning.
    c. predicting mental health rather than illness.
    d. predicting vocational rather than academic success.

14. Martin Seligman predicts that psychology is shifting to a new model that emphasizes:
    a. early experiences in personality formation.
    b. unconscious processes in mental illness.
    c. the importance of the conditioning process in mental illness.
    d. mental health rather than mental illness.

15. Philip Zimbardo believes that the "new psychology":
    a. must view the individual as part of a complex interacting social network.
    b. will focus less on cognitive processes.

c. will become a subfield of the new interdisciplinary field of cognitive neuroscience.
d. will, unfortunately, have little power to prevent global problems such as pollution, overpopulation, and war.

ANSWERS

Guided Study

The following guidelines provide the main points that your answers should have touched upon.

Program Assignment

Program 25

1. The most basic pair of opposites in psychology is nature (genetic endowment) and nurture (experience). This issue focuses on the question of whether our personality and behavior patterns primarily reflect the unfolding of a set of genetic blueprints, or are primarily the product of the changing influences of family, friends, and society. As we have seen throughout the series, we are products of both nature and nurture working together. The influence of genes, for example, is made clear by research on shyness, which is largely determined by heredity. Animal research demonstrates that individuals with this characteristic begin to display it within the first weeks of life. The basis for shyness in monkeys is very similar, if not identical, to the basis for shyness in humans.

    Other research illustrates that without certain kinds of experience, nature will not take its course. Research with premature babies, for example, showed that those who were massaged daily gained more weight, and were more alert and active, than premature babies who were not massaged. Furthermore, animal research has shown that a parent's nurturing touch influences normal growth and development by altering the brain's chemistry.

    In most aspects of human functioning, what we are given by nature can be modified by nurture—by our cultural and personal experiences, environmental forces, learning, and opportunity. Understanding how nature and nurture interact to shape human behavior is one of psychology's most important challenges.

2. Neuroscientists have discovered that there is no split between brain and mind; rather, there is a continual interplay between our consciousness and the complex activities of nerve cells, synaptic connections, and biochemicals in the brain. The mind emerges from the activities of the brain. For example, psychologists have identified chemical changes in the brain that are linked to learning and memory, which are key functions of the mind. Animal and human research has also demonstrated that the brain can be coaxed into either forgetting an experience, or remembering it better, by stimulating some of the brain's neurotransmitters.

    Hypnosis demonstrates that the mind can also alter the brain's functioning. Through the sheer power of words, the brain can be made to ignore painful stimuli and misperceive everyday sensory events, such as the odor of perfume.

3. Conditioned responses illustrate the ways in which external influences shape our actions. Through classical conditioning, we learn associations between sensory events until we are able to respond to a neutral event as if it were a positive or negative one. Operant conditioning demonstrates that

behavior is also controlled by its immediate consequences on the environment.

Despite the automatic nature of conditioned responses, people remain free to make choices that reshape the situations in which the environment exerts its influence. Although most of what we do, think, or feel is the outcome of years of exposure to operant and classical conditioning, this doesn't mean that we are slaves to conditioning, because learning also enables us to profit from experience, thus freeing us from the constraints of tradition, environmental demands, and biological imperatives.

4. Research has shown that each stage of the life cycle has unexpected strengths and weaknesses. At one time it was assumed that the major stages of life represented a set of opposites: the power and vitality we possess as adults, in contrast to the helplessness of babies and the elderly. The newborn, however, is far from helpless. By 3 months, for example, babies begin to understand sophisticated concepts, such as object permanence. Furthermore, psychologists have found that the elderly generally experience less cognitive decline than was once believed. Those who remain physically and mentally active, and are healthy, can continue to function effectively and derive much satisfaction from life.

5. Psychological research has made clear the awesome capability of the mind to process information, giving us a new appreciation of the range and power of human intelligence. At the same time, the ways in which we process information (which ordinarily work remarkably well) can lead us to make bad decisions, to behave foolishly, and to hold irrational beliefs. As Amos Tversky and Daniel Kahneman note, human intuition is often wrong. Reasoning by representativeness is an example of this fallibility, in which we judge the likelihood of things in terms of how well they represent particular stereotypes about people and events. Our tendency to rely on mental shortcuts such as representativeness demonstrates that we should not blindly trust our intuition.

6. Western cultures emphasize individuality, independence, and self-reliance. Although this emphasis can bring a great sense of personal pride when success occurs, when failure occurs, the individual shoulders all the blame. In other cultures, the functional unit is the group or community, and praise and blame are shared by all.

Life in groups connects us with others, so that comfort, affection, and social support are readily available. On the negative side, however, when a group's values are warped, the results can be catastrophic.

All of us function both as individuals and as social units. The dark side is that as individuals we may become isolated; as group members we may become passive and conformist, or controlling and authoritarian. One of the goals of social psychologists is to study the delicate interplay between these two roles and the balance of human needs and social forces.

Program 26

7. Howard Gardner is representative of the field's movement toward specialization. Although pioneering psychologist William James believed that all the different aspects of human behavior and thought would eventually come together, Gardner predicts that psychology as a unified discipline does not have much of a future. He believes that some areas of research will branch off into specialized fields, while others will merge with disciplines such as sociology and anthropology. Those aspects of psychology that have to do with thinking will become part of cognitive science. Those that pertain

to the physical brain will become part of the field of neuroscience. The core of psychology—the study of personality—will become more closely aligned with literary studies of human nature, whether revealed through individuals in psychotherapy or characters in books.

A different point of view is expressed by psycholinguist Jean Berko Gleason, who speculates that psychology will become less fractionated. She believes that psychologists must study the whole person as a complex system, rather than as a collection of separate components, such as language, sex roles, and personality. Similarly, Steven Suomi sees fewer barriers between specific disciplines in the future and a greater integration of separate areas of interest.

Richard Thompson anticipates an increased emphasis on the study of the brain and the combination of what earlier were separate disciplines into the broad field of neuroscience, which explores both the biology of the brain and its adaptive behavior.

Psycholinguist Dan Slobin believes that in the future no one model of human nature will dominate the field and that there will be increased cross-fertilization of ideas among specialties.

8. B. F. Skinner is alarmed that psychology may be turning away from the influence of behaviorism. He deplores the growth of cognitive psychology, which he sees as of no use in explaining human behavior.

Teresa Amabile, who favors a more inward-looking approach to psychology, believes that psychologists will develop many new methods of studying the mind as psychology becomes more oriented toward human emotion.

9. Technologies such as the computer have provided psychologists with new tools for studying behavior. Richard Thompson foresees an increasing overlap of brain science, computer science, and artificial intelligence. E. Roy John sees new uses for the science of neurometrics, the advanced electrical measurement and imaging of neural functioning. For example, the imaging techniques that originally were developed for evaluating psychopathology are now being used to study thinking. This capability will cast new light on brain theories about almost any psychological phenomenon. Jean Berko Gleason notes that the computer has provided access to enormous data banks that have revolutionized how research is conducted.

10. Testing expert William Curtis Banks believes that psychology should assess the individual in narrower contexts. According to this view, if we attempt to understand cognition or personality as a generic phenomenon, we end up not understanding anybody. In the years ahead, he foresees the traditional study of basic psychological processes being supplanted by the study of individual patterns and styles of thinking and learning.

Howard Gardner foresees psychologists becoming more involved with educators in assessing individual learning styles. He also predicts a shift from standardized testing to assessment of learning in its context.

11. Health psychologist Judith Rodin predicts new insights into how the environment influences physiology. David Rosenhan predicts that the influence of personality and social context on biology and health will also become better understood. Martin Seligman believes that in the future psychologists will move away from a focus on illness and therapy toward a focus on health and prevention. Because of the impact of Freud, in which abnormality was the model of the human being, psychology once focused on giving therapy to troubled people. Seligman believes that psychology has nearly reached the limit on what it can contribute in this area. He foresees a future

focus on normality and health, in which psychologists study healthy individuals and ask how each individual's potential can be fulfilled. The tool for this will not be therapy, but prevention. Similarly, E. Roy John believes that neurometrics may one day be able to predict the onset of disease before it actually occurs, thereby allowing some form of preventive intervention.

12. B. F. Skinner is pessimistic about the ability of psychology to prevent disasters, such as global pollution, overpopulation, and nuclear holocaust. He is no longer sure that an increasing knowledge of human behavior will help to solve our problems.

    Philip Zimbardo is more optimistic that psychology can contribute to the reduction and prevention of even the most perplexing problems. But he stresses that the new psychology must not be confined to the traditional focus on individual actions and mental processes. It will have to view the individual as part of a complex interacting network that includes the social group, national institutions, and cultural values, along with historical, environmental, and political realities.

Progress Test

Unlike other answer sections, this section contains no references to the text or the videos; all answers apply to Program 25.

1. **a.** is the answer.

2. **b.** is the answer.
   a. In fact, the effects of maternal touch remained apparent even several months later.
   c. Maternal touch *promotes* development; furthermore, the program does not suggest that an animal can receive too much tactile stimulation.
   d. Although the study focused on premature rats, the implication of its findings is that touch is important to the healthy development of all newborns.

3. **c.** is the answer.

4. **a.** is the answer. The power of hypnosis to alter a person's sensitivity to painful stimuli, for example, illustrates the power of suggestion—clearly a function of the mind.
   b. Although this is true, it is not demonstrated by hypnosis.
   c. This is not true.
   d. The relationship between the brain and the mind continues to be a subject of debate.

5. **c.** is the answer.
   a. Reasoning by representativeness is a mental shortcut in which we judge the likelihood of an event in terms of our stereotypes regarding that event.
   b. Operant conditioning refers to the impact of the immediate consequences of a response on the likelihood of the response recurring in the future.
   d. Neurometrics is the science of brain imaging.

6. **a.** is the answer.
   b. This describes classical conditioning.
   c. In fact, many aspects of human functioning are influenced by conditioning.

d. Because learning enables us to profit from experience, it actually has the effect of freeing us from the constraints of tradition, environmental demands, and biological imperatives.

7. **d.** is the answer.

8. **c.** is the answer.

9. **d.** is the answer.

10. **b.** is the answer. This is so because representativeness leads to logical errors in reasoning.

11. **d.** is the answer.

12. **c.** is the answer.

   a., b., & d. In one way or another, each of these researchers is involved in work demonstrating the importance of cognitive processes in human functioning.

13. **b.** is the answer.

14. **d.** is the answer.

   a. & b. These describe Freudian psychology, which, according to Seligman, is the very model that psychology is moving *away* from.

   c. This describes the behaviorist position, which has waned in popularity in recent years.

15. **a.** is the answer.